Jean-Paul Sartre — Philosophy in the World

Ronald Aronson

NLB

Jean-Paul Sartre — Philosophy in the World

Parts of this book were published in
earlier versions in *Science and Society*,
Telos, and *Western Marxism — a Critical
Reader* (Verso 1978).

The author wishes to acknowledge
assistance from the National
Endowment for the Humanities.

**British Library
Cataloguing in Publication Data**

Aronson, Ronald
  Jean-Paul Sartre, philosophy in the world.
  1. Sartre, Jean-Paul
  I. Title
  194   B2430.S34

ISBN 0-86091-001-6
ISBN 0-86091-032-6 Pbk

NLB and Verso Editions, 7 Carlisle Street, London W1

Manufactured in the United States of America

Contents

Preface

One of the greatest thinkers of our century? In his last years Sartre rejected even the question as coming from the oppressive world of the 'star system'. His own analyses of seriality showed how the elevation of the few implies the alienation of the many; and his politics of the 1970s, directed against any and all elites, called for and tried to initiate a transformation of the social relations that make elites possible.

Yet to appreciate his achievement fully, it remains important to try to measure Sartre's real stature. Like the other major thinkers of his time, Sartre gave himself over without reservation to the invention of a theme — a theme pursued with immense energy, elaborated with originality and yet in an unceasingly self-critical spirit, a compelling and coherent vision of the world.

The main theme of Freud's life and work was the unconscious, Einstein's was relativity, Lenin's the socialist revolution. Jean-Paul Sartre's entire life and work were focused on *human freedom*. At the outset, he affirmed against all opposition that this freedom was absolute, the source of ourselves and all our attitudes towards the world. Then, as a fledgling political activist, he discovered ways in which contemporary social reality, above all the reality of class society, severely limited human freedom. At the same time he first encountered and criticized orthodox Marxism for denying human freedom while claiming to struggle towards it, and laboured to develop more adequate ways of accounting for human activity. Later, in the service of an enriched and concretized revision of his early theme of freedom, he came to accept Marxism as the essential truth — freedom, no longer our original curse and condition as individuals, was now to be achieved in collective struggle. He deepened his insistence on humans as the source of all things human, and created a remarkable series of works exploring how we make ourselves and our world and yet lose power over them. Sartre's revisions of Marx, then Freud, were decisive, as were the ways in which he tried to integrate them into each other. He sought to grasp the individual as the source of the society and its alienations, then the society as the source of individuals and their alienations.

As the margin of freedom narrowed in Sartre's argument, his sensitivity to its contours and his commitment to struggle for it only grew, as did his own direct participation in such struggles. Nearing the end of his career, Sartre both depicted Gustave Flaubert as a totally conditioned person and showed the latter absorbing these conditions into himself and re-exteriorizing them as his own self-creation. More deeply committed than ever to the struggle for a free society, Sartre, as he worked to complete his Flaubert, took the most radical turn of his political life, plunging into an unthinking activism.

Unlike Lenin, Freud or Einstein, however, Sartre did not dramatically change our world or our ordinary ways of thinking about it. His quality as a thinker must therefore be experienced directly. There are few Sartreans today: one must read Sartre himself. And even then, as the commentaries on Sartre amply demonstrate, serious misapprehensions are possible. My own history is probably not unrepresentative.

The stages I have passed through in comprehending Sartre reflect, although with a considerable time-lag, the development of his own thought. Before beginning this project, I had encountered Sartre as most American college students still do, as the high priest of existentialism. When for example, I read *Huis Clos* in a French class in the late 1950s, I had no inkling that this gloomy playwright had most recently written three plays of hope and struggle, *Le Diable et le bon Dieu, Kean,* and *Nekrassov. La Nausée, L'Etre et le Néant* and the short stories of *Le Mur* were the best-known of his works in America, and what they conveyed to me had little appeal in 1957: an argument for freedom alongside repeated demonstrations of the futility of our acts and the absurdity of the world. To a young American looking for commitment and a clear picture of experience, that Sartre was of no help. And of course I had no idea that the warmed-over Sartre accessible to someone of little intellectual and political sophistication was light-years from the concerns of Sartre himself at that time. I encountered him again only a few years later in the form of his 1946 lecture, *L'Existentialisme est un humanisme,* but was no more attracted or enlightened. His arguments for freedom made no significant impression on a young teacher and novice writer who was now moving towards political commitment and graduate school. Searching for direction in 1961, I recall only being struck by Sartre's discussion of how someone seeking answers chooses his adviser according to the direction he himself wants to take. But which path was I to take? For Sartre to insist that I was free told me nothing about what mattered most to me. He at any rate would not be my chosen adviser.

Only after I had found my own direction did I encounter Sartre again, and begin the project which led to this book. Marxism — specifically the philosophically-anchored Marxism that I learned from Herbert Marcuse — had given me intellectual bearings. Personally and politically I identified closely with the Free Speech and Civil Rights movements, becoming active myself early in 1965. At the same time, I began to search for a dissertation topic. Through studying Kant and Hegel at Brandeis University, and reading Marcuse, I had come to see art as presenting the vision of a world whose contradictions had been overcome. Because it was in some sense unreal, art could aesthetically resolve the problems of the real world. Because of its unique reconciling and integrating power, art became an important force *in* the world. I decided that my dissertation would explore this 'secret' of aesthetics and, after several months of study, discovered it in Sartre.

Why Sartre, and not William Morris, for example, or John Dewey — important thinkers who, like him, emphasized art's unique integrative traits, regarded it as a force *in* the world and saw it as foreshadowing an integrative socialist society? First, more than either Dewey or Morris, Sartre belonged to the tradition of the great rationalist thinkers whom I had studied under Marcuse: Plato, Aristotle, Kant, Hegel, Marx and Husserl. Second, I had by now discovered the post-war stage of Sartre's career, as reflected in his theory of engaged literature. In *Qu'est-ce que la littérature?*, the gloomy Sartre was becoming optimistic, the theoretician of inevitable human conflict was writing of solidarity, the individualist becoming socialist. Above all he was becoming politically active. His transformation fascinated me, as well as the question of whether it could be successfully completed, because I myself was in the midst of just such a transformation. I had written a novel, had been strongly influenced by the beat writers, and had myself now been drawn into political activism.

For several reasons, then, I undertook a dissertation entitled 'Art and Freedom in the Philosophy of Jean-Paul Sartre'. In it I wrestled with his early ideas on freedom, and within my Marxist framework tried to make room for what seemed irrefutable in his argument. But beyond this, Sartre touched me little. I studied him but he was not my teacher. I carefully traced the insoluble problems posed by his early thought and their temporary and unreal resolution in his discussion of art, his rethinking of the conflicts after the Second World War, and the resultant activist conception of literature. I acknowledged that in his own way Sartre recapitulated the development from Hegel to Marx. But rather than follow the main lines of that process into the 1950s to evaluate him as a mature political playwright, essayist and philosopher, I chose to focus on the years of his conversion. While gesturing towards the later political essays, and especially *Critique de la raison dialectique*, the final section of the dissertation was a detailed analysis of *Qu'est-ce que la littérature?*. Undertaken in 1968, my close reading of Sartre had a major limitation: it stopped at 1948.

When I returned to Sartre, two years later, one of my major purposes was to bring my study up to date. Why should I have done this, especially after I had decided that Sartre was not important for either my thinking or my politics? Beyond establishing my academic credentials for what I already sensed would be a struggle for survival in my job at Wayne State University, I returned to Sartre because I must have dimly glimpsed that his problems were also my own. As an aspiring writer, lower-middle-class intellectual, and patient in psychotherapy, I had not found the passage to Marxism and political activism an easy one. It demanded a shift from personal preoccupations to social commitment and from methodic doubt to a point of view which confidently claimed to answer the key questions. The passage was made yet more troubled by my difficulty in operating effectively as an activist-intellectual in the increasingly hysterical state of the Movement in 1970, a non-working-class movement which Marxism was unable either to account for or to guide.

After throwing myself into the Kent State-Cambodia upheaval in Detroit in May of 1970, I withdrew to the British Museum in London to work on Sartre. I returned to Sartre in order to find my bearings at a difficult time. Had *he* successfully made the passage to political thought and action? How had *he* functioned as a political intellectual? How did *he* come to grips with the glaring inadequacies of a Marxism whose fundamental truth he had nevertheless accepted? And how had *he* managed to function in a movement whose specific forms repelled him so?

I now set out to study Sartre's plays, some of his political essays, the *Critique*, and, as it appeared in 1971 and 1972, his biography of Gustave Flaubert. In conversations with a friend and student of mine, Bob Bailey, and with the help of a grant from the National Endowment for the Humanities, the project began to find its present shape: a critical study of Sartre's development organized around the key terms and tensions of his thought. As it became clear that the central problems of Sartre's development were rooted in his inability to overcome his original terms, I returned to his early encounter with Husserl and Heidegger. There I showed him defining his basic stance towards reality, described the terms at the core of his thought and their interaction with each other.

This work laid the basis for a critical evaluation of Sartre's later development. My persistent question was, did Sartre move decisively beyond his individualist, dualist and aestheticist starting point? Helped by several illuminating discussions with my colleague, comrade and friend, Ernst Benjamin, I began to see how even Sartre's Marxist thought had been undermined by his continued dependence on his orignal premises.

This was the main underpinning of my project between 1970 and 1973. There were two others. As a New Left intellectual, I found great difficulty in justifying my writing and Sartre's — in a world in which the war in Vietnam was taking place. I questioned my intellectual work constantly as to its political value, and I had also become firmly anti-elitist and oriented towards the experiential. I was determined that my readers think *with* me, not merely observe my results; that they too encounter and wrestle with the dynamic of Sartre's thought. In this sense, the work was conceived less as an essay about Sartre than a presentation *of* Sartre — from my point of view, to be sure, but an effort less to bring readers to agree with my argument than to present the actual itinerary and deep structure of Sartre's own thought. This is one reason why I am still less concerned, for example, to cite the vast secondary literature than to present Sartre himself; the other is that so few writers have struggled successfully to grasp and present his thought.

This goal of presenting Sartre himself, which I have tried to preserve as fully as possible through subsequent revisions, initially became intertwined with, and was confused by, another: my emphasis on the author's subjectivity. I was convinced that my own immediate reactions to Sartre would provide the keys to understanding him, and so the book was filled with such personal responses as excurses on the relevance of appealing to Kant, with reflections on my personal encounter with Sartre, complaints about the length of his books, letters I had written to him and conversation I had had about him. Useful from time to time as a writer's tactic, this approach began to affect the work itself. Like Sartre's study of Flaubert, my study of Sartre began to lose the distinction between the process of intellectual investigation and its socially communicable results.

One reason why such distinctions eluded me was that so much of this work seemed to be a race against time. I rushed to complete the book because I was now being considered for tenure — an avowed Marxist, a movement activist, a socially committed young faculty member who was supporting new programmes for workers, women and minorities.

In June 1973, I mailed off what I hoped was the completed manuscript, but within a few months it was read and severely criticized by my close friend and colleague, Steve Golin of Bloomfield College. He suggested that, when cutting out the distracting personal material, I should give greater attention to reporting Sartre's strengths. This led me to a new stage of comprehension. Freed of my earlier ambivalence about undertaking such a theoretical project in the first place, I cut nearly one-half of the manuscript. I was able for the first time to relax my combative stance and openly acknowledge the positive side of Sartre's career. I now began to appreciate how far Sartre had gone in grappling with the issue that so preoccupied me: what is the political role of the writer? Indeed, Sartre's efforts to answer this question began to emerge as the focus of my book.

Completed in the fall of 1974, this draft still judged Sartre too harshly, as if there were a 'true' Marxism apparent to all which he had obstinately ignored. A discouraged activist, I had begun to take refuge in a rather abstract and orthodox Marxist stance as a result of the Movement's disintegration — so much so that I strongly criticized in Sartre the very politics which had been the decisive shaping force in my own life. Still caught up in the insecurities of my career, I was no doubt hoping to make my mark by proving Sartre wrong. But as I completed this revised manuscript in Fall 1974, I knew quite well that I had not yet come to terms with a conversation I had a few years earlier with Doreen and Girard Horst (André Gorz). I could not reconcile Gorz's powerful optimism as a political thinker with the negativism I found at the heart of Sartre's thought. Similarly, I only dimly saw how central Sartre had been for R.D. Laing's brilliant analyses of schizophrenia as an intentional stance towards reality. It troubled me that thinkers whom I had so respected had found in Sartre much more than I had done.

Three events brought me to my present appreciation of the importance and value of Sartre's thought. First, I had become a tenured professor in late 1974. With my job secure now, I was free of any need to make my mark at Sartre's expense, and thus to see him so negatively. Having survived personally through what I experienced as an extreme situation, I was able to step back and appreciate Sartre's great triumph of the 1950s. Surviving and indeed growing in political and intellectual power during the Cold War, Sartre actually deepened his commitment to socialism at a time when one-time comrades were caving in under the strain. On his own and in the worst of times Sartre became one of a handful of intellectuals — Deutscher, Mandel and Marcuse come to mind — who laboured against the mainstream to revive Marxism as a living tool for the analysis of contemporary events.

Second, I soon returned to political activity. Since 1970 I had remained an activist teacher and had participated in several study groups. But for a political intellectual direct involvement in organized activity is quite a different — and in my view necessary — step. I became one of the organizers of the Detroit chapter of the New American Movement, a small national organization which sought to contribute to building an American socialist movement. No longer subject to the intense pressure of the 1960s and able now to regard Marxism with a critical eye, I became aware how problematic was the relation between theory and practice, the intellectual and action. My experiences with NAM led me to admire Sartre's indefatigable efforts to find appropriate ways to intervene politically, and equipped me to evaluate him as someone engaged in a project akin to my own.

Most important, however, upon agreeing to have New Left Books publish this study, I gained the invaluable editorial guidance of Perry Anderson, whose criticism led me to see that the revised version of my study was both not Marxist enough and too Marxist at the same time, lacking social and historical grounding and somewhat doctrinaire in many of its judgments. Or, to recast the point in terms of my own discipline and training, the study was not yet a fully developed contribution to the history of ideas. Since my apprenticeship at Brandeis University under Herbert Marcuse and Peter Diamandopolous, it has slowly taken shape as a kind of study distinct from but including and integrating philosophy, biography and political history. I had first tried to understand the basic terms of Sartre's philosophy as they developed, then seen them articulated and explored in his non-philosophical writings, and later identified the faults that had inhibited his development. Now I took a decisive further step, and began to incorporate the world of biographical, intellectual and political experience within which these faults had — perhaps inevitably — become constant traits of Sartre's work.

It was, after all, an historical individual who had written the works that I had studied so closely. Certain ideas were available to him, not others; he experienced certain social relations and historical events, not others; and his was a very particular life and no other. By looking more closely at their source, I came to understand Sartre's limitations with greater sympathy and, at the same time, became better able to appreciate his towering strengths.

The tone of Marxist certainty, the suggestion that Sartre could be measured against a codified truth, was abandoned now. No longer judging his plays as an activist socialist theatre — as if we had available for comparison other fully developed and unambiguous examples of such a project — I began to appreciate their problematic in its own terms. I began to see that it was in the plays, above all, that Sartre explored the theme of effective political action and, most acutely, the issue of doing evil in order to do good. Understanding the difficulties and complexities of Sartre's efforts to become a critical fellow-traveller in the 1950s — understanding indeed, the inherent

impossibility of such a stance — enabled me for the first time to appreciate the courage and striking originality of his studies of French
history, Hungary under the Red Army, and revolutionary Cuba.
Acknowledging that no body of thought, be it bourgeois sociology or
Marxism, had fully grasped the links between individual and society,
I became far more sympathetic to Sartre's monumental attempt to do
so, even when the attempt was thwarted by his peculiarly individualist social theory. As Sartre himself wrote in 1957, the Marxism
he encountered as he became politicized had stopped developing, had
become a set of doctrines and categories rather than a living body of
thought capable of illuminating the most significant human questions. Sartre's self-appointed task as thinker was not to appropriate
already existing and adequate tools, but to forge the necessary tools
himself.

It would be illegitimate in every respect to stand outside Sartre's
project and pronounce upon it as if from a superior position. One
must appreciate, if not actually share, his goals and preoccupations in
order truly to assess his accomplishments and his limitations. That is
to say, an adequate critique of Sartre must be an immanent critique,
one which tries to identify his purposes and to trace his own success
and failure in advancing them.

What were Sartre's goals? They changed at each stage of his career,
but he remained committed throughout to human freedom. How do
we make ourselves and our world, and how can we abolish the hells
that humans create for themselves and each other? With these questions in the forefront, Sartre tried to grasp human beings and human
history as a whole, to understand the results of human action on the
world and how humans are shaped by their world. Further he sought
to transform thought and writing, originally his means of withdrawal,
into effective political tools in the struggle for a humane world.

The student of Sartre will immediately respond that I have
distorted or disregarded this or that major purpose. As I complete this
study, I am convinced that I have grasped 'the' Sartre, but I am also
only too aware of how partial and limited it is, how much I have had
to omit, how many other books can, and must, be written on Jean-
Paul Sartre. If I am satisfied that I am conveying Sartre as he should
be conveyed, I am also aware that no study of a great thinker,
however perceptive and subtle, can substitute for the richness and
complexity of his works themselves, or should put an end to creative

study of them. I expect and welcome dispute, correction and revision.

I have been working on Sartre from 1966 to 1980. I have taken this study through my life, and sometimes on my travels. Work on it spanned my career from graduate student to tenured associate professor. I have already named a number of people who helped directly in its development towards its final form; certain others must also be mentioned, whose encouragement and support kept me going. This happily long list includes Phyllis Aronson, Ted Braude, Vicky Yelletz, Fred Lessing, Kent Baumkel, Larry Stettner, and Saul Wellman. If the main weakness I find in Sartre is that his peculiar individualism is blind to the social links at the heart of all human life, the main experience I have had in writing this book is how much it has depended on other people. I dedicate this book to all those, named and unnamed, who have become part of it and made it possible, and above all to the memory of Jean-Paul Sartre.

Wayne State University, Detroit
June 1980

One

Revealing the World, Leaving the World

1

Starting Points

The opening page of Jean-Paul Sartre's first published book, *L'Imagination,* may surprise anyone who knows him through his work of the past thirty years. A dialogue about blank pages, a review of theoreticians of the imagination — considering the values and commitments of the engaged intellectual whose apartment was bombed twice during the struggle over Algerian independence in the early sixties, these paragraphs, published amidst the political crises of 1936, seem arid and remote. Indeed, all of Sartre's early writings share this unworldly quality. Their purpose was to offer new approaches to apparently timeless problems, chiefly those concerning the nature of consciousness, the imagination, and reality. The first part of this study will examine these writings, in order to identify the inner impulses and tensions of Sartre's thought, and the problems created by his initial stance toward reality, and finally, to establish a measure by which to gauge the real distance of his later ideas from his original starting point.

Absorbed in academic and personal questions, Sartre's early writings seemed to come from a secure and peaceful world untouched by the social upheaval of the Popular Front, the rise of fascism, and the struggle over Spain. To be sure, *La Nausée* criticized the self-satisfaction of the bourgeoisie, but in the course of a moral and psychological exploration of its attitudes of dishonesty and hypocrisy. And if the short story 'L'Enfance d'un chef' portrayed a fascist in the making, it was without interest in the social issues involved. These and other literary works of Sartre's early period brilliantly explored much that was negative and sordid in bourgeois life, but with no apparent consciousness of a specific historically constituted social world. This reclusion was still more marked in his philosophical work. Thrilled to discover the writings of Husserl and Heidegger, the young *professeur* went to Berlin, and, seemingly indifferent to the human disaster taking place around him in the academic year 1933-34, immersed himself in phenomenology. He affirmed the new path to reality that the work of Husserl and Heidegger had opened up, at a time when the former, now in his last years, was suffering humiliation at the hands of the Nazis, while the latter, the first National Socialist rector of the University of Freiburg, was celebrating their victory. If we recall this now, it is not to criticize Sartre for somehow 'avoiding' reality — his courage and commitment in the face of historical crisis are by now a matter of unimpeachable record. It is rather to register the contrast between his earlier and later work and so to pose a crucial question. What was it in the substance and organization of his intellectual concerns or in his background that held Sartre at this remove from 'reality', in the turbulent years before the Second World War?

In order to answer this question it will be necessary to examine the internal structure and development of Sartre's thought, to see how this 'distance' is established in the concepts themselves. This attempt, which will occupy most of my book, is naturally concerned with ideas and not with their author. But the person who affirmed and remained bound by the series of propositions which we shall study, developed his ideas in a specific historical and intellectual context, under the weight of a specific personal and social experience. Certain ideas were available to aid his thinking, and others not; he lived in a certain world of experience and no other. As a thinker, he *interiorized* these tools and this experience, and *re-exteriorized* them in the structure of ideas we shall study. It is important, then, at each stage of our analysis, to ground our understanding of Sartre in this reality and, in the first place, to inquire into his personal, historical, and intellectual points of departure.

Starting Points: The Writer Faces the 1930s

Who was this young teacher who wrote the impressive and original series of works from *L'Imagination* and *La Nausée* to *L'Etre et le Néant*? In his own mind, he was above all a writer. Meeting Sartre in 1929, Simone de Beauvoir was struck by 'the calm and yet almost frenzied passion with which he was preparing for the books he was going to write'.[1] She herself intended to write; 'but he lived in order to

---

1. *Mémoires d'une jeune fille rangée*, Paris 1958, p.339; trans. James Kirkup, *Memories of a Dutiful Daughter*, Cleveland 1959, p.361. In all subsequent footnotes, the French edition will be cited first, followed by the English.

write'. What exactly he would write about was not of primary importance. To be sure, Sartre was 'interested in everything and never took anything for granted'.[2] 'In the notebooks he showed me, in his conversations and even in his university writings he persistently put forward a system of ideas whose originality and coherence astounded his friends.'[3] But alongside his developing philosophical project lay another commitment: the work of art or literature was, in his view, 'an absolute end in itself; and it was even — though he never said so, I was sure he believed this — the be-all and end-all of the entire universe.'[4]

This sense of the real world held at a distance is conveyed very clearly in *La Force de l'âge*, de Beauvoir's account of their shared life in the 1930s. Sartre has corroborated the essential truth of these memoirs on a number of occasions, in *Qu'est-ce que la littérature?*[5] and in his description, in the first volume of *Les Chemins de la liberté*, of Mathieu's refusal to commit himself either personally or politically during the summer of 1938.[6] Again and again, Simone de Beauvoir describes important political events and comments that she and Sartre 'remained spectators',[7] that literature was always the most important thing to him, that however indignantly they might denounce capitalism, they 'were not actively *for* anything'[8] that 'by and large the world about us was a mere backdrop against which our private lives were played out.'[9] Indeed, for much of *La Force de l'âge* one has the sense of her leafing through old newspapers at a library twenty years later to remind herself of the important public events that 'touched us scarcely at all.'[10] It is striking to read now about these two apolitical tourists: revolted, on an Italian vacation, by the Black Shirts but returning three years later just the same; wandering through Germany under Hitler; having a Spanish vacation heightened by the rising revolutionary fervour. Back at home they watched — but did not

2. Ibid., p.339; p.360.
3. Ibid., p.341, p.363.
4. Ibid., p.340, p.362.
5. See the final chapter, 'Situation de l'écrivain en 1947' ('Situation of the Writer in 1947'), *Qu'est-ce que la littérature?*, (QL),Paris 1948; trans. Bernard Frechtman, *What is literature?*, (WL), New York 1949.
6. *L'Age de raison*, Paris 1945; trans. Eric Sutton, *The Age of Reason*, New York, 1947.
7. *La Force de l'âge*, Paris 1960, p.224; trans. Peter Green, *The Prime of Life*, Cleveland 1962, p.175.
8. Ibid., p.147; p.116.
9. Ibid., p. 55; p.46.
10. Ibid., p.55; p.45.

march in — the gigantic Popular Front demonstration of half a million people on July 14, 1935. They supported — but did not vote in — the Popular Front electoral victory of May 1936.

Passive and apolitical as they were, their hearts were clearly with the Left. Insofar as they had a political outlook they were in general agreement with the Communist Party (PCF). They detested the bourgeoisie and longed for its overthrow. They 'regarded the working classes as pursuing one of the most exemplary forms of human activity',[11] and were filled with joy at the great working-class victory embodied in the Matignon Agreements. They despised the Socialist Party 'firstly on the grounds that it was infiltrated by the bourgeoisie and secondly because we were temperamentally opposed to the idea of reform: society, we felt, could change only as a result of sudden cataclysmic upheaval on a global scale.'[12] Extremist by temperament, both Sartre and de Beauvoir fervently wished for this upheaval that others would bring about. Yet, although they hoped for socialism, they feared it as well. Once the Popular Front had won office in 1936 they refused even to be spectators at the July 14 demonstration, finding 'conformity irritating, even when it changed the colour of its coat'.[13] While they hated capitalism and respected the proletariat, they believed above all in individual freedom; freedom to be oppositionists on principle, freedom to formulate the goals of their work and lives. 'We should not, we decided, feel at all at ease in a socialist world. In every society the artist or writer remains an outsider, and one which proclaimed with such dogmatic fervour its intention of " integrating " him struck us as being the most unfavourable environment he could have.'[14]

Such a society would be unfavourable, above all, to their stubborn bohemianism. Sartre's goal was to avoid all the conventional encumbrances of marriage, family, household, property and profession. This lifelong relationship with de Beauvoir was based rather on a distinctive combination of mutual respect, intimacy and freedom. Only once, when she was assigned to teach at Marseilles while Sartre was in Le Havre, did he relax this principle and suggest marriage. De Beauvoir's reflections on their attitude towards marriage are deeply

11. Ibid., p.118; p.94.
12. Ibid., p.34.; p.30.
13. Ibid., p.212; p.273.
14. Ibid., p.37; p.32.

revealing of their peculiar radical bohemianism. 'Hitherto we had not even considered the possibility of submitting ourselves to the common customs and observances of our society, and in consequence the notion of getting married had simply not crossed our minds. It offended our principles. There were many points over which we hesitated, but our anarchism was as deep-dyed and aggressive as that of the old libertarians, and stirred us, as it had done them, to withstand any encroachment by society on our private affairs. We were against institutionalism, which seemed incompatible with freedom, and likewise opposed to the bourgeoisie, from whom such a concept stemmed. We found it normal to behave in accordance with our convictions, and took the unmarried state for granted . . . '.[15] For a moment, they questioned this particular conviction, only to conclude that their independent development was more important than their common ties. De Beauvoir went off to Marseilles for the academic year 1931-32 and Sartre remained in Le Havre. They lived separately, spending weekends, vacations and summers together, until the autumn of 1937, when they both settled in Paris. But even then they did not set up a common household: they lived in separate apartments on different floors of the same building.

Anarchist, bohemian, rebel — such terms describe Sartre in the 1930s. He managed without great inner conflict to combine a vague, passive sympathy for the PCF with an individualist intellectual radicalism. It was not until later, when the fate of the Spanish Republic and the march towards war became manifest, that his stance began to change. Thus in the early and middle 1930s, he remained in contact with former schoolfriends like Raymond Aron, a Socialist, and Paul Nizan, a Communist. Indeed in 1931 Nizan, already a Communist and writing a critique of bourgeois philosophy, approvingly introduced a part of Sartre's *Légende de la verité* in a review he helped to edit, *Bifur*, writing this description of its author in the Note on Contributors: 'Young philosopher. Is at work on a volume of destructive philosophy.'[16]

The Pressure of Events

If these 'anarchists' kept aloof from historical reality, it was not in a

15. Ibid., p.81; p.66.
16. Ibid., p.84; p.68.

complacent spirit. 'For instance, we sketched out our conversation in the Café Victor as Dos Passos might have handled it: "The manager smiled in a satisfied way, and they both felt furious. Sartre drew at his pipe, and said that perhaps it was not enough merely to sympathize with the revolution. The Beaver pointed out that he had his own work to do. They ordered two large beers, and said how hard it was to sort out what you owed other people from what you owed yourself. Finally they declared that if they had been dock workers they would have undoubtedly joined the Communist Party, but in their present position all they could be expected to do was always side with the proletariat." Two *petits bourgeois* invoking their unwritten work as an excuse for avoiding political commitment: that was the truth, and indeed we had no intention of forgetting it.'[17]

In these ironies and intimations of bad conscience, another aspect of their situation was revealed: the increasingly powerful pressure of events. Politics was a more and more demanding presence in the 1930s. Fascism, the Spanish Civil War, the Popular Front, were facts that Sartre and de Beauvoir tried repeatedly to ignore, each time with less conviction. By 1939, *La Force de l'âge* shows, politics had penetrated to the centre of their lives, as a daily concern. In 1938, Sartre had decided to write the multi-volume novel in which he reflected on the vicissitudes of personal existence in the face of historical events. By the next year it had its title, *Les Chemins de la liberté*. In the first volume, *L'Age de raison,* the Spanish Civil War hangs in the air everywhere as Mathieu, a philosophy teacher, struggles to sustain a 'freedom' that increasingly comes to mean evasion of everything real.

Sartre's reflections on commitment — the heart of the trilogy — clearly indicate that he was himself moving towards the decision to become engaged. Why did Mathieu not go to Spain? Why did he not marry Marcelle and allow her to have his child? There is a carefully constructed unreality in Mathieu and his ponderings, in his inability to act and *be* in any authentic way, in his refusal to grow up. *La Force de l'âge* makes abundantly clear that Mathieu was a vehicle for exploring an essential side of themselves, people who 'were like elves', 'pursuing a dream' of absolute freedom until the world caught up with them.[18] Sartre contrasts Mathieu with, among others, Brunet,

17. Ibid.,pp.143-144; pp.113-114.
18. Ibid., pp.371-72; p.288.

Mathieu's childhood friend become Communist militant. An encounter between Brunet and Mathieu suggests the kind of pressure he himself may have felt in the face of Nizan's commitment. Brunet, cloaked in the false seriousness of the true believer, is at least *real* to Mathieu. ' "Everything you touch looks real. Since you have been in my room, it seems to me an actual room, and it revolts me." He added abruptly, "You are a man." '[19] In the early and mid-1930s, what had interested Sartre most in the newspapers were crime and trial reports, he and de Beauvoir often sympathizing with criminals as rebels against society. By the Munich crisis in the late summer of 1938, Sartre could no longer take a vacation without keeping up with events. By the end of September he was reading 'every edition of the daily papers'.[20] Both Sartre's and de Beauvoir's testimonies record how history forced itself upon them, how their stylish distance from events became impossible as Spain fell and war drew nearer — how, by September 1939, their literary posture had collapsed altogether.

Starting Points: Personal

Fundamentally estranged from historical reality, but slowly drawn towards it — this is one description of Sartre's stance in the 1930s. But the path to 'reality' lay across a great divide; and his thought — and life — were to be permanently marked by the peculiar nature of that divide and the means he chose to cross it.

At the most personal level, where did he begin? What does it mean that he 'was really seeking "salvation" in literature' in his twenties?[21] His autobiography, *Les Mots,* published in 1963, explores his childhood and its meaning for him: his initial choice of writing over living, his early immersion in a world of books, his almost total isolation from other children until the age of ten, the remoteness of his family from everyday concerns.

One has the sense, from the beginning, of a cloistered existence, a protected family life. This was due in part to his father's death, which sent his mother back, with her infant son, to live with her parents. And it was also due to the fact that the family of Charles Schweizer, professor of German and author of textbooks, lived comfortably, neither oppressed by material circumstances nor in a position to con-

---

19. *L'Age de raison,* pp.125-26; *The Age of Reason,* p.153.
20. *La Force de l'âge,* p.345; *The Prime of Life,* p.268.
21. *Mémoires,* p.341; *Memoirs,* p.362.

trol them. They were *petits bourgeois,* as Sartre never tired of pointing out, and certain basic traits of this existence were to stay with him always.

He never worried, it seems, about getting a living and never valued wealth. Already at the Ecole Normale Supérieure he 'couldn't reconcile himself to the idea of having a profession, colleagues, superiors, of having to observe and impose rules . . . .'[22] Of course, he had inherited a small legacy from his paternal grandmother that helped him to adjust comfortably from being a student to his new life as a professor. And during the worst years of the depression he never worried about a job: he had a secure position in the secondary school system. He and his companion were always free — and adventurous enough — to travel during their long summers: to Greece, North Africa and England, among many other places. After the war, on the strength of his royalties, Sartre left teaching altogether; and his poignant interview with Michel Contat, thirty years later, shows a man still untouched by material cares and ambitions.[23] Raised in a family of academic *petits bourgeois* whose unworldliness was a token of its lack of material worries, Sartre himself continued in the same class and with the same peculiar freedoms: large amounts of free time, a secure if not opulent living, the opportunity to travel widely, and protection from the worst shocks of economic fortune.

In *Les Mots* Sartre ponders at length the internal meaning of his specific family situation. And in doing so, remarkably, he uncovers many of the major themes of his later writing. Later I shall discuss how *Les Mots* expressed, and allows us to make sense of, the time of disillusionment in which it was written. For the present, three themes are particularly important.

The first was Sartre's recognition that his entire career had been marked by a fundamental unreality: his commitment to writing over living, his withdrawal from the world, his illusion about saving himself through writing: 'I never tilled the soil or hunted for nests. I did not gather herbs or throw stones at birds. But books were my birds and my nests, my household pets, my barn and my countryside. The library was the world in a mirror . . . .'[24] The boy rejected

22. Ibid., p.342; p.361.

23. See 'Autoportrait à soixante-dix ans,' *Situations,* X, Paris 1976; trans. Paul Auster and Lydia Davis, 'Self-Portrait at Seventy,' *Life/Situations: Essays Written and Spoken,* New York 1977.

24. *Les Mots,* (M), Paris 1964, p.37; trans. Bernard Frechtman, *The Words,* (w), New York 1964, p.49.

living in order to transform himself into 'twenty-five volumes, eighteen thousand pages of text, three hundred engravings, including a portrait of the author.'[25] Life was not about living, but about drawing up a balance sheet. 'Out of cowardice and with a good little boy's timidity, I had backed away from the risks of a free and open existence, an existence without a providential guarantee.'[26]

The little boy, adored by all but (he now realized) genuinely seen by none, living cut off from other children in his grandfather's study, first admired the rich, supple volumes, then picked them up and taught himself to read, then acted them out — and, finally, became a writer himself. *Les Mots* explores that fundamental choice to live in books rather than in reality. Feeling his own 'nothingness', his own 'contingency' — to use the terms of the later philosopher and novelist — the man's sole concern had been to 'save' himself — 'nothing in my hands, nothing up my sleeve — by work and faith.'[27] Writing in 1963, he saw that 'the eagerness to write involves the refusal to live'.[28]

Second, *Les Mots* showed Sartre to be awakening from his illusions. Struggling against unreality, the writer of 1963 had for the last ten years or so 'been a man who's been waking up, cured of a long, bittersweet madness, and who can't get over the fact, a man who can't think of his old ways without laughing and who doesn't know what to do with himself.'[29] But, paradoxically, we will see Sartre 'waking up' and 'discovering reality' at almost every stage of his career. His discovery of Husserl in the mid-1930s conveyed such a sense, as did *Les Mouches* in 1943 and, more explicitly, *Qu'est-ce que la littérature?* in 1947. And again, in the early 1950s, just before he began *Les Mots*, *Le Diable et le bon Dieu* showed Sartre undergoing an awakening from his past idealism. It was as if he was obliged repeatedly to discover reality, repeatedly to overcome the boy's decision to write in order to become unreal.

Les Mots seemed to terminate this series of 'awakenings', because — and this is the third consideration — it confirmed how limited and partial any resulting changes must be. It was as if Sartre had become aware of a fundamental and irreversible choice: 'one gets rid of a neurosis, one doesn't get cured of one's self.'[30] He might be disillu-

25. Ibid., p.161; p.194.
26. Ibid., pp.164-65; p.198.
27. Ibid., p.212; p.255.
28. Ibid., p.159; p.191.
29. Ibid., p.211; p.253.
30. Ibid., p.211; p.254.

sioned, but he could not really change. Writing as salvation, personal unreality, a sense of himself as embodied in books — these were the very substance of his character, he now concluded. The deepest and most abiding of needs had been at stake in his self-creation as writer. A choice to become unreal, disillusionment about that choice, and the awareness of its deep roots in his character: these themes will aid our exploration of Sartre's work. He lived as part of his very character a contradiction, an inner divide. To cross that self-created divide was no simple matter of personal evolution: the turn to the world involved a profound self-transformation — the bridging of a distance that was spontaneously reproduced in his own, equally profoundly determined activity.

What is the use of all this testimony in a study devoted primarily to the structure of Sartre's thought, its themes and their tensions? His concepts can and must be evaluated in their own right, in terms of their adequacy to the reality in question. But his historical and biographical circumstances help us to situate them. His strengths and limitations as thinker express, among other things, a certain life experience. Only the most abstract — and fundamentally misconceived — critique could demand of him more than his own internal and external realities made possible. I have attempted to outline Sartre's personal limits — the strengths that they encompassed, and the objectives that lay beyond them. We shall see how they conditioned his thought.

Starting Points: Intellectual

What were Sartre's intellectual starting points? His earliest writings include a number of texts published in student journals in the 1920s, a statement drawn up in 1928 for a survey of student attitudes, a speech he gave at the *lycée* in Le Havre in 1931; and there are also his later reflections on these years. Here is a part of his report on student attitudes, published early in 1929 in *Les Nouvelles littéraires*: 'it is a paradox of the human mind that Man, whose business it is to create the necessary conditions, cannot raise himself above a certain level of existence, like those fortune-tellers who can tell other people's future, but not their own. This is why, at the root of humanity, as at the root of nature, I can see only sadness and boredom. It's not that Man does not think of himself as a *being*. On the contrary, he devotes all his energies to becoming one. Whence derive our ideas of Good and Evil, ideas of men working to improve Man. But these concepts are useless. Useless, too, is the determinism which oddly enough attempts to create a synthesis of existence and being. We are as free as you like, but helpless . . . For the rest, the will to power, action and life are only useless ideologies. There is no such thing as the will to power. Everything is too weak: all things carry the seeds of their own death. Above all, adventure — by which I mean that blind belief in adventitious and yet inevitable concatenations of circumstances and events — is a delusion. In this sense, the "adventurer" is an inconsequential determinist who imagines he is enjoying complete freedom of action.'[31] This cheerless and pompous statement reveals the young Sartre as a confirmed iconoclast, unflinchingly self-confident at twenty-three about tackling philosophy's largest issues. Here too, some of his best-known themes were already apparent: our freedom, the futility of all our efforts, and our attempts to hide from our condition. Other well-known themes of his maturity appeared elsewhere in his student writings: his fascination with the perverse and disgusting, his preoccupation with individual isolation and personal freedom, his theory of contingency and critique of abstract and timeless truth.

His intellectual independence manifested itself very early. Of Sartre at seventeen, a philosophy teacher reported: 'Excellent student: mind already lively, good at discussing questions, but needs to depend a little less on himself.'[32] This weakness, rooted no doubt in a childhood spent among books, was to become the young man's greatest strength as he approached all writers, every field, every issue with supreme self-confidence. So strong was his spirit of contestation and of innovation that, as he remarked many years later, 'I have

31. *Mémoires*, pp.341-42; *Memoirs*, pp.363-64

32. This is quoted in the exhaustive and indispensable 'Bibliographical Life' of Sartre by Michel Contat and Michel Rybalka. *The Writings of Jean-Paul Sartre* Evanston 1974 (CRW) vol. I, p.5. In this model work, Contat and Rybalka have set Sartre scholarship on a solid footing by listing, describing, and commenting on virtually everything Sartre has written or spoken publicly in his entire lifetime. Equally useful, they quote at length, sometimes in full, from texts or statements that are no longer obtainable. Translated by Richard C. McCleary, the English version has been revised and updated since the original appearance of *Les Ecrits de Sartre: Chronologie, bibliographie commentée*, Paris 1970. References are to Volume I unless otherwise noted. Henceforth un-noted references to the details of Sartre's life will be mostly drawn from Contat and Rybalka or from Simone de Beauvoir's four volumes of memoirs.

never accepted anything without contesting it in some way.'[33]

Simone de Beauvoir and he devoured each year's new books, regularly read the vanguard literary journal *La Nouvelle revue française*, and became partisans of cinema, which Sartre regarded as a new art form.[34] His writings, as he was clear from the beginning, would be *new*: as literature, as psychology, as philosophy.

The young man's self-confidence extended to his attitude towards his professors. Looking back in 1969, Sartre dismissed the lectures of the *cours magistral* at the Sorbonne as having seemed 'idiotic', 'because the teachers who gave it had nothing to tell us.'[35] Writing his first major philosophical work, *L'Etre et le Néant*, he made only cursory reference to the most respected philosophy professors at the schools he had attended — Brunschvicg, Lalande and Alain. The young Sartre had been touched by France's most illustrious contemporary philosopher, Henri Bergson, while preparing to sit the entrance examination for the Ecole Normale Supérieure. Reading *Time and Free Will*, he was so struck by its concreteness and by its discussion of our consciousness of duration that he decided to study philosophy. But in his study of theories of imagination, based on a thesis written in 1926, Sartre was no longer impressed by Bergson's vitalism and commitment to spontaneity. Bergson was not radical enough, he now judged; he failed to examine his own premises and ultimately fell victim to associationism. 'One must begin all over again.'[36] In *L'Etre et le Néant* Bergson was mentioned several times, but usually on relatively minor points and then in dismissive tones.

Still Sartre needed, and sought outside himself, lenses through which to focus and clarify his ideas. Originally oriented towards literature, he was influenced by Proust and Valéry. But — in spite of

33. *Sartre: Un filme realisé par Alexandre Astruc et Michel Contat*, screenplay, Paris 1977, p.43; trans. Richard Seaver, *Sartre by Himself: A Film Directed by Alexandre Astruc and Michel Contat*, New York 1978 (I have used my own translations). This film and its screenplay are the only sequel to *Les Mots* that we are likely to see. *Sartre* presents an occasionally informative and penetrating sketch of its subject's life and work.

34. *La Force de l'âge*, p.53; *The Prime of Life*, p.44. See also 'Motion Picture Art' in CRW, Vol. II: *Selected Prose*, pp.53-59.

35. 'Itinerary of a Thought', *New Left Review* 58 (November-December 1969), p.64. One of the best of Sartre's interviews, this was later published in *Le Nouvel Observateur*, 26 janvier 1970, and as a chapter of *Situations*, IX, Paris 1972.

36. *L'Imagination*, (I), Paris 1936, p.57; trans. Forrest Williams, *Imagination: A Psychological Critique*, (IPC), Ann Arbor 1962, p.51.

the poor marks he received for merely summarizing Bergson's ideas — he decided to make a vocation of philosophy. And for this he needed theoretical guides to assist him in developing the main lines of his own outlook.

One of these was virtually immanent in the French educational system: Descartes. Insofar as Sartre found an intellectual starting point in his formal studies — one which his encounter with Bergson would confirm — it was Descartes. 'Any study of human reality must begin with the *cogito*,' he declared, in *L'Etre et le Néant.*[37] To be sure, Sartre reformulated 'I think, therefore I am' to reveal two distinct states of consciousness, but even as he corrected Descartes and built on his legacy, he accepted that inner sense of self-certainty as his absolute intellectual starting point. He began with *consciousness,* aware of itself, consulting itself, questioning itself, proving its own existence to itself. Indeed, his argument for freedom, a crucial theme in his work, based itself on the Cartesian discussion of doubt.

However, Descartes was only a starting point. Sartre developed his characteristic themes with the *cogito* as his point of departure, but in a direction sharply opposed to his professors who drew their inspiration from Descartes. If he began from the *cogito,* he refused, nevertheless, to dissolve all reality into consciousness, as he judged idealists like Brunschvicg to have done. In this dual commitment, both to the *cogito* and to the independent reality of the external world, we can discern the 'anarchist' who sympathized with the PCF and the writer who felt the pressure of history. His early theoretical goal was 'at bottom to provide a philosophical foundation for realism . . . In other words, how to give man both his autonomy and his reality among real objects, avoiding idealism without lapsing into mechanistic materialism.'[38] Where else might Sartre look for help in this project?

Neither Psychoanalysis nor Marxism

'Two disciplines might have clarified our thinking,' Simone de Beauvoir commented, reflecting on the period immediately after she and Sartre had passed their examinations for the *agrégation* at the Ecole Normale Supérieure: 'those of Marxism or psychoanalysis.'[39]

37. *L'Etre et le Néant: Essai d'ontologie phénoménologique* (EN), Paris 1943, p.127; trans. Hazel Barnes, *Being and Nothingness (*BN), New York 1956, p.84.
38. 'Itinerary of a Thought': p.46.
39. *La Force de l'âge,* pp.24-25; *The Prime of Life,* p.22.

Psychoanalysis was beginning to be known in France, and they had both read Freud's *Interpretation of Dreams* and *Psychopathology of Everyday Life*. But their reading was of 'the letter rather than the spirit'. Why was this? Sartre's retrospective judgment was that his hostility to Freud stemmed from his very 'French', Cartesian discomfort with the idea of the unconscious. 'You must never forget the weight of Cartesian rationalism in France. When you have just taken the *bachot* at the age of seventeen with the "I think, therefore I am" of Descartes as your set text, and you open *The Psychopathology of Everyday Life,* and you read the famous episode of Signorelli with its substitutions, combinations and displacements, implying that Freud was simultaneously thinking of a patient who had committed suicide and of certain Turkish mores, and so on — when you read all that, your breath is simply taken away.'[40] As for Marxism, both Sartre and de Beauvoir later reflected that it was their 'conditioning as young *petits bourgeois* intellectuals' that kept them at a distance.[41] There is no doubt that Sartre was not a likely candidate for conversion to Marxism in the 1930s, either politically or intellectually. His established commitments, to the *cogito* and to writing as a personal goal, were not such as to render Marxism's social analysis and emphasis on labour any more accessible or sympathetic than Freud's unconscious. Yet the summary self-description of *'petit-bourgeois* intellectual'* seems both dogmatic and historically misguided. It assumes a ready-made, intellectually vital Marxism which their class background alone kept them from encountering. But no such Marxism existed in France in the 1920s and early 1930s.

Had Charles Schweitzer not chosen France in 1871, his grandson would have been raised and schooled in a wholly different political-intellectual situation. Theodor Adorno, for example, was only two years older than Sartre, but was raised in Germany, not France. The son of a well-to-do assimilated Jewish wine merchant and a once-successful singer of German and French parents, his itinerary contrasts strikingly with that of the Alsatian professor's grandson. A student of Alban Berg, Adorno was also steeped in avant-garde literature and seemed committed to cultural elitism from an early age. By background, interests and temperament, he was in many

---

40. 'Itinerary of a Thought', p.46.
41. *La Force de l'âge,* p.25; *The Prime of Life,* p.22. Compare 'Itinerary of a Thought', p.46.

respects far less likely than Sartre to gravitate towards Marxism. But by 1928, after his return from Vienna, Adorno was involved with members of the avowedly Marxist Institute for Social Research, of which, eventually he became one of the most brilliant representatives.[42] Why was it that Adorno found his way to Marxism a full twenty years before Sartre?

The relative political tranquillity of France in the 1920s was certainly a factor. The victors of the Great War returned to a state of normality characterized by political stability and economic growth; the vanquished saw a series of revolutionary and counter-revolutionary waves, political assassinations, and attacks on the feeble political system itself by both Left and Right. But another decisive difference was the absence of anything even remotely like the Marxist Institute affiliated to the University of Frankfurt. Sartre himself later lamented that his university training had rendered Marxism unintelligible: educated 'without the Hegelian tradition, without Marxist teachers, without any planned program of study, without the instruments of thought, our generation, like the preceding ones and like that which followed, was wholly ignorant of historical materialism.'[43] The roots of this difference lay in the extent to which, in Germany, Marxism had both permeated political life and acquired intellectual legitimacy. Both wings of the massive German workers' movement professed an adherence to Marxism that reached back into the previous century. Moreover, not only Marx and Engels, but nearly all the non-Russian members of the next two generations of outstanding Marxist thinkers, had written in German.[44] In Austria and Germany, indeed, Marxism had penetrated the university, imposing itself as an inescapable point of reference in intellectual life.

In France, by contrast, Marxism had far less political and intellectual influence. Tenacious radical intellectual and political traditions pre-dating Marxism had inhibited its diffusion — Jacobin republicanism, Proudhonism, Blanquism, and anarcho-syndicalism were the central native currents of nineteenth-century class struggles, and the

---

42. See Martin Jay, *The Dialectical Imagination: A History of the Frankfurt School and the Institute for Social Research 1923-1950*, Boston 1973, pp. 20-24.

43. *Question de méthode*, *Critique de la raison dialectique* (QM, CRD), Paris 1960, p.22; trans. Hazel E. Barnes, *Search for a Method* (SM), New York 1963, p.17.

44. See the excellent overview sketched by Perry Anderson, *Considerations on Western Marxism*, London 1976, pp.5-13.

main legacy of those of the early twentieth, preventing France from developing a movement linked with Marxism until after the Bolshevik Revolution had cast its powerful spell over the working classes of Western Europe.[45]

Thus it was not until 1928, the very year of Adorno's return from Vienna, that a group of Sartre's contemporaries and friends in the orbit of the PCF — including Paul Nizan, Georges Politzer, and Henri Lefebvre — formed the first circle of young French intellectuals to criticize bourgeois philosophy from the Left and to propagate Marxism. But naturally, they could not simply summon a sophisticated and intellectually capable Marxism to their aid. Nizan's *Les Chiens de garde,* most certainly read by Sartre, reflected the severe philosophical limitations of the group. In it, Nizan sharply criticized his professors and their philosophical contemporaries for evading real-life issues and serving the interests of the bourgeoisie; but he made no philosophical attack on their doctrines. His polemic appeared as a spirited but narrow Marxist rejection of philosophy itself, hardly a philosophically adequate rejoinder to the 'official' thinkers.[46]

The difficulty was, for Sartre as well as his schoolmates, that the only Marxist theory available in France in the 1920s came via the Soviet Union — quite unlike Germany, which had an autonomous tradition. In the late twenties and thirties, more than ever before or since, the victory and consolidation of the Russian Revolution made Marxism the property of the official Communist movement, leaving few other rights of way to Marx's fertile thought. Marxism had already begun to be reduced to a doctrine to be instrumentalized by Soviet state ideologists and their PCF counterparts.[47] And if the dogmas of dialectical materialism were now spreading outwards from Moscow on the tide of Soviet hegemony over the national Communist parties, Marx's early philosophical works were not yet available in France. The temporary result of this conjuncture was a narrowing of the intellectual horizon of Marxism.

This apparent philosophical impasse was perhaps the main determinant of Sartre's aloofness from Marxism. Petit bourgeois or not, he could only have been challenged, not to say won, by a philosophically

45. Ibid., pp.34-40.
46. Paul Nizan, *Les Chiens de garde,* Paris 1960; trans. Paul Fittingorf, *The Watchdogs: Philosophers of the Established Order,* New York 1971.
47. Anderson, pp.13-21.

more developed Marxism — one which had available to it the legacy of Marx's response to Hegel and Marxism's relationship to philosophy, which would have been able to reflect both the role of creativity in human experience and the alienation of that creativity by class society. And indeed, when, thirty years later, such a Marxism began to take shape in France, one of its creators was Jean-Paul Sartre. But to the young Sartre, Marxism meant an impressive political and economic analysis tied to a movement with which he sympathized, but justified by a philosophy that he found ridiculous.[48]

Discovering Phenomenology

Where then was he to find guidance? There was one powerful contemporary school of philosophy that held promise for a young writer drawn towards yet distant from the political world, an aspiring philosopher and novelist pondering questions about the very nature of reality — one current of philosophy which seemed both to root itself in the individual and to reach towards the real world; as radical and self-confident as Sartre, leaving no presupposition unquestioned, and conceptually accessible to a product of the French school system; which left its proponents free to be philosophers and writers and did not call on them to become political activists. Sartre did not encounter it until the spring of 1933: 'Raymond Aron was spending a year at the French Institute in Berlin and studying Husserl simultaneously with preparing an historical thesis. When he came to Paris he spoke of Husserl to Sartre. We spent an evening together at the Bec de Gaz in the Rue Montparnasse. We ordered the specialty of the house, apricot cocktails; Aron said, pointing to his glass: "You see, my dear fellow, if you are a phenomenologist, you can talk about this cocktail and make philosophy out of it!" Sartre turned pale with emotion at this. Here was just the thing he had been longing to achieve for years — to describe objects just as he saw and touched them, and extract philosophy from the process. Aron convinced him that phenomenology exactly fitted in with his special preoccupations: bypassing the antithesis of idealism and realism, affirming

48. *La Transcendence de l'ego: Esquisse d'une description phénoménologigue* (TE). Paris 1965; trans. Forrest Williams and Robert Kirkpatrick, *The Transcendence of the Ego: An Existentialist Theory of Consciousness* (TEC), New York 1957, p.105. (It was perhaps for this reason that Sartre never publicly discussed his friend's *Les Chiens de garde*. Nizan's argument there moved on a technical plane far below his own.)

simultaneously both the supremacy of reason and the reality of the visible world as it appears to our senses. On the Boulevard Saint-Michel Sartre purchased Lévinas's book on Husserl, and was so eager to inform himself on the subject that he leafed through the volume as he walked along, without even having cut the pages.'[49]

The only two philosophers mentioned more often than Descartes in *L'Etre et le Néant* are Husserl and Heidegger. In the academic year 1933-34 Sartre, following Aron, studied their thought in Berlin. Returning home, he worked out his main ideas under the influence of the two philosophers, moving from the complex beginnings we have traced along paths provided by phenomenology. In the next five chapters we shall examine and evaluate the thought that now emerged.

49. *La Force de l'âge*, pp.141-2; *The Prime of Life*, p.112

Imagining Versus Perceiving

Sartre's analysis of imagination leads us towards the core of his thought. Imagination is a constant term in his conceptual scheme — to escape into it, his constant temptation. Moreover, Sartre's view of the real world is inseparable from his view of the imaginary. They are described in opposing and dialectically connected terms, and appear as such in almost every major early work: in *L'Imagination* and in the story *La Chambre*, in *L'Esquisse d'une théorie des émotions* and in *La Nausée*. My intention here is to examine Sartre's early analysis of imagination: to determine precisely what it argues, to show how his general world-view insinuates itself into his discussion, and so to illuminate the intellectual perspectives of *L'Etre et le Néant* and, later, of his encounter with Marxism and calls for an engaged literature.

Unexamined Presuppositions

L'Imagination (1936) and *L'Imaginaire* (1939) are more concrete in analysis, and more restricted in scope, than Sartre's best-known philosophical works — *L'Etre et le Néant* or the *Critique de la raison dialectique*. Written under the direct impact of phenomenology, their common topic is the imagination. What is the typical experience of imagining? Before the observing subject lies a sheet of paper. It is *there*, it *waits*; one need only look to see it. Then the subject looks away, at the wall, and *imagines* the vanished object. It now appears again, but not *in fact*, not as an object. This time it is seen as an image, an image which is immediately known not to be the real sheet of paper.

Any theory that seeks to explain the process of imagining must stay close to this experience, describing it faithfully. Yet, according to Sartre, writers on the imagination had not done this: 'all have built *a priori* their theories of the image. And when finally they took to consulting experience, it was too late. Instead of allowing themselves to be guided by experience, they have forced experience to answer yes or no to leading questions.'[1]

Among those so indicted were Descartes, Leibniz, Hume, Bergson, Taine and Spaier. All began with the naive assumption that the mind, where it encountered the external world, was one object among others. Images, which were 'in' the mind, were the perceptual residues of objects outside it. The image was supposed to have the same traits as the actual object itself: it was a thing-image, regarded as obeying the same laws, and as entering experience in the same way. Perception was passive, obedient to the mechanical laws of association and so too was imagination. In inquiring whether he perceived or dreamt, Descartes set out the problem for the next three centuries: the image was treated as a thing in the brain, left there by the physical effect of an external object. Imagination became a type of perception, distinguishable from ordinary perception of objects only afterwards. Followed out consistently, as it was by Hume, this approach completely subjected the mind to the laws of association. When the mind was presented with an image, this theory claimed, it operated as it did before any object confronting it, obediently perceiving what had been *given to it*. Thus it was necessary to ask, as did Descartes, whether we were dreaming or not — or, with Spaier nearly three centuries later, whether we were imagining or not. For Spaier 'the index of truth remains external to the representation itself, for comparison determines whether or not it should be incorporated into the grouping "reality".'[2] Images were distinguished from perceptions only by the introduction of 'an infinite system of references'. But this protracted analysis meant that our moment-to-moment judgments could never be more than probable. Every moment was rendered uncertain, an unverified pretension, a possible hallucination.[3]

For Sartre, the implications of this position constituted an obvious outrage to immediate experience. In fact, he argued, Spaier's problem was a false one: 'I am seated, writing, and see the things around me. Suddenly I form an image of my friend Peter. All the theories in the world are helpless against the fact that I *knew*, at the very instant

---

1. ɪ, p.6; ɪᴘᴄ, p.5.
2. ɪ, p.102; ɪᴘᴄ, p.95 (translation changed).
3. See ɪ, p.104; ɪᴘᴄ, p.96.

of the appearance of the image, that it was an image.'[4] Why was it necessary to undergo countless investigations in order to distinguish an image from a perception? We do so quite spontaneously. We know *at every moment* that we are imagining, in spite of the nonsensical claims of Hume, Taine, and Spaier. Thus, there was a basic, 'pre-predicative' difference between imagination and perception, rather than an initial identification. For Sartre, experience was an 'unimpeachable given' from which analysis should properly begin.

The thing-image theory distorted experience in a second way. For how could we *think* with those inert, passively received sense-data filling our heads? So long as the image was said to be a revised sense-perception, its appearance in consciousness must be governed by the physiological determinism regulating all such contents. The mechanical laws governing the external world would also govern consciousness, destroying thought as we know it. 'Thought, in short, could not function as the guiding theme around which images would be organized, as tools, as approximations. Thought would be strictly reduced to the sole function of grasping relationships between two sorts of objects: thing-objects and image-objects.'[5] For Hume, who followed this through consistently, consciousness was, therefore, a collection of inert objects moved about by mysterious and blind forces over which we have no control. The disturbing, yet entirely logical, outcome of the thing-image theory was stated by Sartre's former teacher, Alain: 'we do not think as we wish.'[6]

This was indeed consistent; but, Sartre insisted, it was not what really happened: for 'in such thought, bumping along and splintering, transfixed in all its processes by ever fresh appearances without logical inter-relations, who would recognize the faculty of reasoning, conceiving, devising machines, undertaking mental experiments?'[7] Against such patently wayward theorizing, Sartre affirmed the freedom and creativity of human thought.

The Image Described

What, then, was the reality of the image? Once we 'rid ourselves of the illusion of immanence' — of the illusion that the imagined sheet of

4. i, p.103; ipc, p.96.
5. i, pp.116-17; ipc, p.107 (translation changed).
6. i, p.117; ipc, p.108.
7. i, p.117; ipc, p.108.

paper had somehow entered the mind — the undeniable fact became manifest: if nothing was *in* consciousness, then its object must be outside, in the world. This was as true for imagining as for perceiving. 'In fact, whether I perceive or imagine that chair of straw on which I am seated, it always remains outside of consciousness. In both cases it is there, *in* space, in that room, in front of that desk. Now — and this is what reflection teaches us above all — whether I see or imagine that chair, the object of my perception and that of my image are identical: it is that chair of straw on which I am seated.'[8] Reflection taught a simple but central fact: that consciousness *aimed* at things beyond it, *directed* itself *outwards*. Consciousness was not self-enclosed: it was intentional. But if consciousness was typically directed outwards, what distinguished imagining from perceiving? It was simply that 'in one of the cases, the chair is "encountered" by consciousness, in the other it is not.'[9] In each case one tried to *see* the chair: when the chair was not actually present to perception one created an image. *How*, Sartre continued, were objects perceived? Never wholly and at a stroke: objects appeared 'only in a series of profiles, of projections'. To perceive, it was necessary to 'make a tour' of the object, to 'serve an apprenticeship'. 'The object itself is the synthesis of all these appearances. The perception of an object is thus a phenomenon of an infinity of aspects.'[10] Thus, a cube, for example, was never seen *as* a cube. Three of its sides would always remain hidden, its angles appear distorted, and so on. To perceive it was to 'learn' it, so as to hold in mind each profile as it was turned in the hand, mentally composing these separate impressions into a whole cube.

The process of *thinking* about the cube was quite different: 'I think of its six sides and its eight angles all at once; I think that its angles are right angles, its sides squared. I am at the centre of my idea, I seize it in its entirety at one glance.'[11] And in imagining too, 'the cube as image is presented immediately for what it is.'[12] Furthermore, 'the very act that gives me the object as an image includes the knowledge of what it is.'[13] It followed, then, that the image was poorer — pos-

8. *L'Imaginaire: Psychologie phénoménologique de l'imagination* (IP), Paris 1940, pp.16-17; *Psychology of Imagination* (PI), New York 1948, p.7.

9. IP, p.17; PI, p.7.

10. IP, p.18; PI, p.9.

11. IP, p.19; PI, pp.9-10 (translation changed).

12. IP, p.19; PI, p.10.

13. IP, p.21; PI, p.12.

sessed fewer attributes — than the object. 'In the world of perception every "thing" has an infinite number of relationships to other things. And what is more, it is this infinity of relationships — as well as the infinite number of relationships between the elements of the thing — which constitutes the very essence of a thing.'[14] Things 'brim over', they 'overflow' consciousness, constantly revealing new aspects. On the other hand, the image contained only such aspects and relationships as the subject chose to grant it. 'We must not say the other relationships exist in secret, that they wait for a bright searchlight to be directed upon them. No: they do not exist at all.'[15] The creator of the image has absolutely nothing to learn about it. Its 'sensible opacity' notwithstanding, the image really 'teaches nothing, never produces an impression of novelty, and never reveals any new aspect of the subject. It delivers it in a lump. No risk, no anticipation: only a certainty.'[16] Imagination, Sartre continued, was negative and primitive in character. The act of imagining 'can assume four forms and no more: it can posit the object as non-existent, or as absent, or as existing elsewhere; it can also "neutralize" itself, that is, not posit its object as existing.'[17] In any case, the image was *not* the object. The missing object, seen 'in image', was known with certainty to be *missing*, and its image as unreal. The image presented its object as *absent*, and itself, therefore, as *only* an image. At the heart of the experience of imagining was negativity, known and accepted as such from the outset.[18] Thus, for Sartre the traditional problem of Cartesian psychology simply did not exist. There could be no uncertainty concerning the status of a mental act whose conditions, modalities and results were known and accepted in advance.

The image was an act; it was a quasi-observation; and it presented its object as a nothingness. Its fourth trait was *creativity*. 'A perceptual consciousness appears to itself as being passive.'[19] But imagination was 'spontaneous and creative; it *maintains and sustains* the sensible qualities of its object by a *continuous creation*. In perception the actual representative element corresponds to a passivity of consciousness. In the image, this element, in what it has of the primary and incom-

14. IP, p.20; PI, p.11.
15. IP, p.20; PI, p.11.
16. IP, p.21; PI, p.13.
17. IP, p.24; PI, p.16.
18. See, for example, IP, p.25; PI, pp.17-18.
19. IP, p.26; PI, p.18.

municable, is the product of a conscious *activity,* is shot through and through with a flow of *creative will.*'[20]

There are many different kinds of image, and Sartre went on to describe these in a careful account of 'the image family' that ranged from the photograph at one extreme to the wholly mental image at the other, including also caricatures, signs, impersonations, schematic drawings and hypnagogic images. In every case, he argued, consciousness aimed at an object outside itself, was spontaneous, presented its object as not being present, and filled that object with its own pre-given knowledge. In every case, consciousness turned away from a realistic posture towards the world and created unreal objects. What differed from one form of imagining to the next was the nature and, so to speak, the quantity of the perceptual material — the analogue — present to consciousness. Moving from photograph to mental image, Sartre showed at each stage how, as more of the perceptual analogue dropped out, knowledge and spontaneity became more important, how, as the role of the analogue diminished, the role of consciousness — of outer-directed, intentional creativity — became more prominent.

Evaluating Sartre's Account

The main charge levelled in Sartre's historical critique of psychology was that theorists of imagination had consistently failed to examine, if not actively pre-judged, the data of experience. His second work on the subject, *L'Imaginaire,* embodied his own attempt to correct this longstanding failure by providing a meticulous rendering and analysis of the experience of imagining. Yet in the earlier *L'Imagination,* Sartre had already cast doubt upon his capacity for 'unprejudiced self-examination', at the outset making a major ontological statement: 'Never could my consciousness be a thing, because its way of being in itself is precisely to be *for* itself; for consciousness, to exist is to be conscious of its existence. It appears as a pure spontaneity, confronting a world of things which is sheer inertness. From the start, therefore, we may posit two types of existence. For it is indeed just insofar as things are inert that they escape the sway of consciousness; their inertness is their safeguard, the preserver of their autonomy.'[21] In this statement,

---

20. IP, p.27; PI, p.20 (emphasis added).
21. I, pp.1-2; IPC, pp.1-2.

contrary to his own first principle of analytic procedure, Sartre gave his own *a priori* account of what experience must be — and, as a later passage made plain, a glimpse of the general outlook that underlay his phenomenology of imagination: 'In the external world are inert objects which I can take hold of, move about, remove from a drawer or put back. We seem to be able to conceive an *activity* which operates on passive givens. But the mistake is easily detected. If I can pick up this book or that cup, it is insofar as I am an organism, a body also subject to the laws of inertia. The mere fact that I can oppose my thumb to my four fingers in a clutching gesture already presupposes the whole of mechanics. Here is only the appearance of activity. Hence it is impossible to assign to thought an evoking power over inert contents without at once materializing thought . . . That exists spontaneously which determines its own existence. In other words, to exist spontaneously is to exist for oneself and through oneself *(éxister pour soi et par soi)*. One reality alone deserves to be called "spontaneous": consciousness. To exist and to be conscious of existing are one and the same for consciousness. Otherwise stated, the supreme ontological law of consciousness is as follows: for a consciousness the only way of existing is to be conscious that it exists. It is therefore evident that consciousness can determine itself to exist, but that it cannot act on anything but itself. A sensory content may be the occasion for our forming a consciousness, but we cannot act by means of consciousness on the sensory content, dragging it from nowhere (or from the unconscious), or sending it back. If the image is a form of consciousness it is pure spontaneity, self-conscious so to speak, transparent to itself, and it exists only to the degree that it knows itself. It is not sensory content. It is perfectly futile to represent it as "rationalized", as "permeated by thought". There is no middle ground: either it is wholly thought, and one thinks *by means of* the image, or it is sensory content and one would think *on the occasion of* an image. In the latter case, the image will be independent of consciousness, *appearing* to consciousness according to laws peculiar to an image which is not consciousness. Such an image, which must be awaited, deciphered, and observed, is simply a *thing*. Any inert or opaque content takes its place, by the necessity inherent in its type of existence, among objects, that is to say, in the external world. That there are only two types of existence, as thing in the world and as consciousness, is an ontological law.'[22]

22. I, pp.124-126; IPC, pp.114-16 (translation changed).

A whole world-view was thus implicit in Sartre's study of imagination. Implicit, and also at stake; for as he went on to argue, it was the act of imagination, as he conceived it, that distinguished the first of these two types of existence — spontaneous consciousness — from the second — the inertia of things — and conserved it in its specificity. 'If we assume a consciousness placed in the very bosom of the world as one existent among others, we must conceive it, hypothetically, as completely subjected to the action of a variety of realities — without its being able to transcend the detail of these realities by an intuition which would embrace their totality. This consciousness could therefore contain only real modifications aroused by real actions and all imagination would be prohibited to it, exactly in the degree to which it was engulfed in the real. This conception of imagination enmired in the world is not unknown to us since it is precisely that of psychological determinism.'[23] And conversely, 'if it were possible to conceive for a moment of a consciousness which does not imagine it would have to be conceived as completely engulfed in the existent and without the possibility of grasping anything but the existent.'[24] Without this capacity, consciousness was 'crushed in the world, run through by the real'. Thus, in the opposition of things and consciousness, laws and freedom, inertness and spontaneity, the power of imagining was decisive. Imagination was the 'necessary condition' of freedom in the world.

The Lacunae of Sartre's Analysis

In every sentence of Sartre's carefully delimited study, the latent issue is that of human freedom. This theme will be explored, in due course. For the present, there remains the technical problem posed by these analyses of the imagination and its theorists. What were the effects of Sartre's philosophical presuppositions and ulterior concerns on the arguments of *L'Imagination* and *L'Imaginaire*?

It is evident, to begin with, that his definition of 'imagination' is extremely partial, and even distortive. The term 'imagination' has always included among its referents activities which are neither image-forming, in any important sense, nor constitutively negative in their relation to the real world — activities in which, on the contrary,

---

23. IP, p.233; PI, pp.266-67 (translation changed).
24. IP, p.237; PI, pp.271-72 (translation changed).

we mentally reconstitute a certain real world from the fragments directly available to us, or act directly upon the real world, intentionally and creatively.[25] But Sartre's 'brief history of the problem of imagination' is precisely restricted to the narrow faculty of image-forming. Moreover, this conceptual restriction is accompanied by historical omission.[26] The chief objects of discussion in Sartre's 'brief history', as given in the table of contents in *L'Imagination*, are 'The Principle Metaphysical Systems' (Descartes, Leibniz, Hume), 'Associationism' (Taine, Ferri, Brochard, Ribot), Bergson and Bergsonism, and the Wurzburg School. Two crucial names are missing from this list, the names of two thinkers who turned all previous thinking about imagination upside down, and effectively defined the terms of modern discussion of it: Kant and Coleridge. Many previous writers had spoken of the productive and reproductive imagination, of the faculties of creating anew (fantasy) and of recalling old perceptions (imagination). The tradition had spoken of a higher and a lower activity, the first (before Kant) being the safe, controlled ability to reproduce, and the second, the blind, chaotic, sensual power to make new things.[27] Kant continued the distinction in *The Critique of Pure Reason,* but subverted its established meaning, showing that the 'lower' faculty alone shaped the jumble of sense data encountered by us into a coherent whole.[28] After Kant, and especially with Coleridge, the honorific name of 'imagination' was given to the productive, spontaneous faculty, while the pejorative 'fancy' was attached to the routine, reproductive faculty. The imagination no longer merely reproduced what had already been experienced: it invented new objects and grasped their truth at the same time. The one-hundred-and-twenty-five-year span between Hume and Taine was in fact *the decisive period* in thinking about the imagination by English, German and French theorists, as the standard histories of aesthetics, literary theory and criticism bear out.[29] In Sartre's 'brief history' it is a complete blank.

25. See E.J. Furlong, *Imagination*, New York 1961.
26. 1, p.6.
27. Murray Wright Bundy, 'The Theory of Imagination in Classical and Medieval Thought', *University of Illinois Studies in Language and Literature*, XII, 2-3. (Urbana 1927)—an excellent but neglected historical study.
28. *The Critique of Pure Reason*, trans. Norman Kemp Smith, London 1961, p.81.
29. See Monroe Beardsley, *Aesthetics from Classical Greece to the Present: A Short History*, New York 1966; M.H. Abrams, *The Mirror and the Lamp: Romantic Theory and the Critical Tradition*, New York 1958; and René Wellek, *A History of Modern Criticism: 1750-1950*, Volume V: *The Romantic Age*, New Haven 1955.

Imagining versus Perceiving

My initial question was: what are the effects of Sartre's presuppositions on his study of the imagination? Do they distort his professed intentions? It is now possible to answer in the affirmative, and to say how and for what reason this distortion occurs. The exclusion of all imaginative activities except that of image-forming, and of that crucial moment in the history of thought where imagining and perceiving were seen as inseparable, was made in the interests of the stark conceptual opposition that rises steadily towards the surface of Sartre's analysis: 'the image and the perception', he concludes, 'far from being two elementary psychical factors of similar quality and which simply enter into different combinations, represent the two main irreducible attitudes of consciousness.'[30] The consequences of this opposition can be seen in Sartre's discussion of the 'external image', where he attempts to explain exactly what happens when I 'see' Peter in the photograph before me, or the person depicted in a painting. 'We become aware, somehow, of animating the photo, of lending it life in order to make an image of it.' Let us begin with our 'normal perception' of the photograph. 'As a perception, the photograph is but a paper rectangle of a special quality and colour, with shadows and white spots distributed in a certain fashion.'[31] Looking at it in this way, I see before me a real, existing object of the world. 'This photo, taken by itself, is a *thing*: I can try to ascertain the duration of its exposure by its colour, the product used to tone and fix it, etc.; the caricature is a *thing*: I can take pleasure in studying its lines and colours without thinking that they were intended to represent something.'[32] However Peter will not appear in the photograph or caricature, unless my attitude changes dramatically: 'an external object functioning as an image cannot exercise that function without an intention which interprets it as such.'[33] I must cease to see the shades, tones and lines *for themselves,* and look 'through' them to sight Peter. 'Through the photo, I envision Peter in his physical individuality. The photo is no longer the concrete object which gives me the perception: it serves as material for the image.'[34] For the image to appear the piece of paper must be 'animated by some help from me, giving it a meaning it had not as yet had. If I see Peter by means of

30. IP, p.156; PI, p.171.
31. IP p.32; PI, p.24.
32. IP p.31; PI, p.23.
33. IP p.32; PI, p.24.

the photo *it is because I put him there.*'³⁵

If I then relax this effort, the image will fade away. I shall once again see only tones and shades on the paper rectangle. Consciousness will revert to another plane: from imagination to perception. Thus, we can conclude that 'every object, whether it is present as an external perception or appears to inward sense, can function as a present reality or as an image, depending on what centre of reference has been chosen. The two worlds, real and imaginary, are composed of the same objects: only the grouping and interpretation of these objects varies. What defines the imaginary world and also the world of the real is an attitude of consciousness.'³⁶

How valid is Sartre's analysis? It is evident that its validity depends on the occurrence of cases where we do not bring knowledge and feeling to the act of perception. But is there any conceivable case where we do not 'animate' what we see, disengaging it from its surroundings and composing it into a coherent whole? We do not perceive without such activity. Thus, it is not that Sartre's account of how we come to see Peter in the picture is mistaken — it does seem to describe just what goes on. What is mistaken, rather, is to oppose this activity to a wholly factitious alternative, the supposed realistic, passive perception of the materials before us.

Sartre and Husserl

What was the source of this strange account of perception? Sartre's answer was clear and insistent: everything in his books on imagination — terms, lines of thought, examples — had been derived from the writings of Edmund Husserl. Even the critique of *a priori* theoretical construction and the affirmation of the criterion of experience had originated in Husserl. His declaration has found authoritative support. The historian of phenomenology, Herbert Spiegelberg, has praised these books for their fidelity to Husserl's thought. They are 'by far the most detailed and concrete phenomenological studies of the imagination we have. They are, on the whole, specimens of eidetic description in Husserl's earlier style.'³⁷

It will be instructive, then, actually to compare Sartre's account of

---

34. IP, p.35; PI, p.27.
35. IP, p.32; PI, 25.
36. IP, p.34; PI, 27 (translation changed).
37. *The Phenomenological Movement: A Historical Introduction,* The Hague 1960, Vol. II, p.498.

perception with Husserl's own discussion, in *Ideas*. 'Let us consider the engraving by Dürer, "The Knight, Death, and the Devil". We may distinguish first of all the normal perception, the correlative of which is the *thing* which is the "engraving", this sheet. In the second place, we find the perceptual consciousness in which, through these black lines and little colourless figures, "Knight on horseback", "Death", and "Devil" appear to us.'[38] The similarity is striking. There is no doubt that Sartre based his 'Peter' passage directly on this account. And it is this which makes the single, simple difference all the more fascinating: Husserl terms *both* ways of seeing 'perceptual' while Sartre reserves this term for the first, calling the second 'imaginative'.

Perception, as Husserl describes it, is a complex process. To begin with, we are assured by some sort of 'passive genesis' that 'the Ego always has an environment of "objects".'[39] Consciousness is scarcely spontaneous at this level: 'the individual object can "appear", one may be aware of it as apprehended, but without being spontaneously "busied with" it at all.'[40] So far, Sartre concurs. But for Husserl this is just the beginning of a rich and detailed account of what we actively *do* to perceive a world of objects, while for Sartre there is no more to be said about perception. Thus, we have seen him say that 'perceptual consciousness appears to itself as being passive';[41] and further, in a misleading comment on Husserl's notion of passive genesis, that 'all fictions would be active syntheses, products of our free spontaneity, and all perceptions, on the contrary, would be purely passive syntheses.'[42] In this way, perception is devalued, expressions like 'free spontaneity', 'creative will', 'continuous creation' and 'spontaneous and creative' being reserved for the discussion of image-forming. For Husserl, the presentation of bare materials to a waiting consciousness does not yet constitute an intelligible world of experience. This can only come into being through 'the Ego', in subsequent acts which could certainly be described as 'spontaneous', 'creative', and 'free'. From the outset the Ego has 'spontaneous tendencies to turn towards

38. *Ideas: A General Introduction to Pure Phenomenology*, trans. W.R. Boyce Gibson, New York 1931, §111, p.311; cited in I, p.149; IPC, pp.135-36.

39. Husserl, *Cartesian Meditations: An Introduction to Phenomenology*, trans. Dorion Cairns, The Hague 1960, § 38, p.79.

40. Ideas, §23, p.91.

41. IP, p.26; PI, p.18.

42. I, p.157; IPC, p.142.

the world and to grasp it'.[43] Syntheses, acts of belief and of valuation all are necessary in order for the finished world of experience to appear. Husserl speaks of the Ego's *free spontaneity and activity,* and affirms that it does not remain a 'passive indweller', that — on the contrary — it appears as 'a primary source of generation'. He distinguishes two components of what is, finally, the perceived world: the 'formless materials' and 'immaterial forms', the sensile *hyle* and the intentional *morphé.* The *hyle* includes all brute sensory contents — 'the data of colour, touch, sound and the like.'[44] By themselves these sensory materials are incomprehensible: meaning must be bestowed on them. 'Sensory data offer themselves as material for intentional informing or bestowals of meaning at different levels . . . '[45] Thus the 'material elements are "animated" through noetic phases, they undergo . . . "formal shaping" . . . [receive] "gifts of meaning" . . . '[46] The finished object of experience appears when the 'noetic' acts of consciousness, 'animating the material and weaving themselves into unitary manifolds, into continuous syntheses, so bring into being the consciousness of something, that in and through it the objective unity of the field of objects . . . may permit of being consistently "declared", "shown forth", and "rationally" determined.'[47]

Sartre's study acknowledged the inspirational role of Husserl's account, and appeared only to extend and supplement it. But it is now clear that Sartre in effect *dismembered* Husserl's analysis in order to establish a polar opposition between perception and imagination. He presented 'passive synthesis' — the first phase, according to Husserl — as the *whole* of perception, which thus lost its active, spontaneous character. The active consciousness was then redeployed in opposition to perception as the distinctive faculty of image-forming. Thus, the two interconnected aspects of perception, of our involvement in the daily world of experience, became for Sartre two wholly different *kinds* of consciousness: the one passively waiting for objects to come before it, the other actively conjuring up unreal objects; the one trapped in the world, the other free.

43. *Ideas,* §28, p.104.
44. Ibid., §85, p.246.
45. Ibid., §85, p.247.
46. Ibid., §97, p.285.
47. Ibid., §86, p.251.

Trapped or free: as question, as challenge, as predicament, this opposition was to be permanent in Sartre's thought. We shall see how, even as he insisted on the purest possible forms of human freedom, Sartre reverted again and again to images of an uninhabitable world. It is striking that Husserl, remaining strictly at the level of *a priori* consciousness, should have conveyed a sense of rich human creativity, while Sartre, the champion of activity, evoked a state of helpless immersion in things, mitigated only by the capacity to imagine the unreal. The distinctive tonality of Sartre's work — the affirmation of human creativity, counterpointed by an equally radical pessimism — was already present in these most technical of studies.

3

The Difficult Way or
the Magical Way?

How is Sartre's stark opposition of imagination and perception to be understood? We have already seen something of its biographical-historical moorings, in the boy brought up among books, in the young intellectual at once fascinated and repelled by the real world. We have also indicated its problematic relationship with Husserl's phenomenology of perception. It is necessary now to trace the roots and ramifications of this opposition in Sartre's early works, whose overall shape and sense of priorities it so evidently determined — in other words, to pass from technical questions concerning the formation of images, to the wider existential themes of his basic world-view.

The image of the world projected in these early writing is, strictly speaking, that of Newtonian mechanics: 'the ball is an inert body that remains still as long as no force arrives to set it in motion, but continues its motion into infinity if nothing impedes it.'[1] Things are passive, inert, acted on from outside, independent of our consciousness, governed by determinism. We become aware of this determinism not speculatively or theoretically, but in encountering things as part of an instrumental totality arrayed around us by our specifically human purposes. In *Esquisse d'une théorie des émotions* Sartre argues that the world appears 'as a complex of instruments so organized that if one wished to produce a determined effect it would be necessary to act upon the determined elements of the complex. In this case, each instrument refers to other instruments and to the totality of instruments; there is no absolute action or radical change that one can immediately introduce

---

1. I, p.121; IPC, p.111.

into this world. It is necessary to modify a particular instrument and this by means of another instrument which refers to other instruments and so on to infinity.'[2] Those familiar with *Being and Time* will recognize Heidegger here, but with an interesting qualification: insofar as we act in the world, we must submit to its ordered complex of laws, through a 'pragmatistic intuition of the determinism of the world.' For Heidegger, the key to the whole enterprise is human action: things are not independent entities confronting us, but rather our *equipment,* usable for specified purposes. But Sartre's focus is not trained on human actors but on the *pressures* and *demands* that that world imposes on them. According to this modified version, 'the world around us — what the Germans call *umwelt* — the world of our desires, our needs, and our acts, appears as if it were furrowed with strict and narrow paths which lead to one or the other determined end, that is, to the appearance of a created object. Naturally, there are decoys and traps scattered around here and there. This world might be compared to the moving of the coin-making machines on which the ball-bearings are made to roll; there are paths formed by rows of pins, and often, at the crossing of the paths, holes are pierced through. The ball-bearings must travel across a determined route, taking determined paths and without falling into the holes. This world is *difficult.*'[3] A four-page essay on Husserl's intentionality, written at the same time as these psychological books, reflected the same posture. In it, Sartre expressed enthusiasm at his encounter with Husserl, for now the academic philosopher could escape from the idealism that placed the real nature of the world outside of the world, in consciousness. Now reality might be seen 'on the road, in the city in the midst of the crowd, thing among things, man among men.' Phenomenology had enabled Sartre to look at *things,* not consciousness. 'Husserl has reinstated horror and charm to things. He has revived the world of artists and prophets: frightful, hostile, dangerous, with havens of grace and love.' Yet even here in spite of his enthusiasm and regardless of the 'havens of grace and love' that he discerned around him, the world as Sartre saw it was in the main a deeply inhospitable place. If he preferred direct knowledge of it to an idealist philosophy of consciousness, it was still a world in which we were 'abandoned . . . by our nature' — 'indifferent, hostile, and stubborn.'[4]

According to the *Esquisse d'une théorie des émotions,* we accept the world as instrumental totality and operate according to *its* laws and limitations. These laws and limitations appear more important to Sartre than the human purposes and actions which encounter them. The mechanical, law-governed universe troubles him yet he ignores the fact that we discover it in the process of gaining control over it, transforming it for our human ends. He pays no attention to the fact that we construct things to *fulfil* our purposes, to *meet* our needs, things that are helps as well as 'decoys and traps'. Above all, if the world is a coin-making machine, he does not see it is *we* who *build* the machine, that its difficulty is not given in the order of things, that we might dismantle it or build other machines for other purposes. Sartre confronts this humanly created world, then, not as a person engaged in action who takes stock of the paths and obstacles to action, who considers his purposes and the material at hand to fulfil them. Eager to place philosophy in the world, he also seems intimidated by the world, fearful of being immersed in it. Accordingly his psychological writings are actually devoted to exploring modes of *detachment.* Sartre's primary concern, in studying imagination and emotion, is to trace how we separate ourselves from the world, adopting a magical attitude in which the objects of our desires appear spontaneously and without effort, how we tear ourselves away so that consciousness is totally spontaneous, self-determining and free — how we escape into the *irréel,* into a world constructed by our imagination.

Transforming the World through Magic

The act of imagining, according to Sartre, is 'an incantation destined to produce the object of one's thought, the thing one desires, in such a manner that one can take possession of it.' He treats emotion similarly. Whereas earlier theorists, such as Freud and James, had treated emotion as 'externally' determined, as if by physiological events or unconscious process, Sartre argued that in fact emotion was an *act,* not a state. The thesis that 'states' of consciousness were in reality

4. 'Une idée fondamentale de la phénoménologie de Husserl: l'intentionalité', *Situations,* I, Paris 1947, pp.31,32.

acts, to be understood and judged as such, was of course central to all Sartre's work. His particular concern here was with the act of escape. We *choose* to be emotional when the world becomes too difficult: 'lacking the power and the will to accomplish the acts which we had been planning, we behave in such a way that the universe no longer requires anything of us.'[5]

Emotion and imagination are both magical transformations of the world. When engaging in them, we 'step' out of the difficult world of our real lives and into a domain ruled by our desires. Imagination 'transforms' a world which lacks the object I desire, and so 'it is the desire that constructs the object in the main.'[6] The world recedes and the image of the missing object appears. Emotion 'transforms' a world become too difficult, too demanding: 'when the paths traced out become too difficult, or when we see no path, we can no longer live in so urgent and difficult a world. All the ways are barred. However, we must act. So we try to change the world, that is, to live as if the connection between things and their potentialities were not ruled by deterministic processes, but by magic.'[7]

Emotion and imagination alike are spontaneous, self-determined, free acts in which we escape from a world 'ruled by deterministic processes'. If we refuse to engage in such magical acts, our only recourse is to submit to the demands, pressures and limitations, the causal order of the world. But for Sartre this implies accepting the world as given. Hence each fundamental attitude expels the other: 'there is emotion when the world of instruments abruptly vanishes and the magical world appears in its place.'[8] Emotion and imagination originate, then, in a rejection of the real world. 'To posit an image is to construct an object on the fringe of the whole of reality, which means therefore to hold the real at a distance, to free oneself from it, in a word, to deny it.'[9] Our choices are acceptance or withdrawal into fantasy. Real and unreal attitudes can never be reconciled; 'the real and the imaginary cannot co-exist by their very nature. It is a matter of two types of objects, of feelings and actions that are completely irreducible.'[10]

5. ET, pp.36-37; EO, p.65.
6. IP, p.162; PI, p.179
7. ET, pp.58-59; EO, p.33.
8. ET, p.49; EO, p.90.
9. IP, p.233; PI, p.266.
10. IP, p.189; PI, p.210.

It follows, then, that the magical attitude does not seek *really* to render our situation satisfactory, but only to diminish us, so that we become willing to accept an artificial solution: 'emotive behaviour is not on the same plane as the other behaviours; it is not *effective*. Its end is not really to act upon the object as such through the agency of particular means. It seeks by itself to confer upon the object, and without modifying it in its actual structure, another quality, a lesser existence, or a lesser presence (or a greater existence, etc.). In short, in emotion it is the body which, directed by consciousness, changes its relations with the world in order that the world may change its qualities. If emotion is a joke, it is a joke we believe in.'[11] The same is true of the image, which appears as a 'perpetual elsewhere', a 'perpetual evasion.' And, Sartre insists, I too become unreal in this process: 'the object as an image is an *irréel*. It is no doubt present, but, at the same time, it is out of reach. I cannot touch it, change its place; or rather I can well do so, but on condition that I do it in an unreal way, by not using my own hands but those of some phantoms which give this face unreal blows: to act upon these unreal objects I must divide myself, make myself unreal.'[12]

What is gained by this behaviour? In behaving magically, Sartre argues, we do not satisfy, but actually *change* and *limit* our needs.[13] Images deceive our desires, only appearing to satisfy them: 'this passive object, kept alive artificially, but which is about to vanish at any moment, cannot satisfy desires. But it is not entirely useless: to construct an unreal object is a way of deceiving desires momentarily in order to aggravate them. Somewhat like the effect of sea water on thirst. If I desire to see a friend I make him appear as an *irréel*. This is a way of *playing* at satisfying my desire. I play at it only because my friend is not there in reality.'[14]

But what, then, is the real efficacy of magical behaviour? It is, quite simply, that it provides security. Schizophrenics create and live in a fantasy-world first because they 'prefer a richness, a beauty, an imaginary luxury to the existing mediocrity *in spite* of their unreal nature'. But secondly, and more important, they 'adopt "imaginary" feelings and actions *for the sake of* their imaginary nature.'[15] When I

11. ET, p.34; EO, p.60.
12. IP, p.162; PI, p.178 (translation changed).
13. ET, p.22; EO, p.37.
14. IP, p.162; PI, pp.178-179 (translation changed).
15. IP, p.189; PI, pp.210-11 (translation changed).

consider the imaginary world, it becomes clear that 'none of these objects calls upon me to act, to do anything. They are neither weighty,
insistent, nor compelling; they are pure passivity, they wait. The
faint breath of life we breathe into them comes from us, from our
spontaneity.'[16] There is 'no risk, no anticipation, only a certainty.'[17]
This *irréel* is wholly unlike the real world, with 'its character of *presence*,
the sort of response it demands of us, the adaptation of our actions to
the object, the inexhaustibility of perception, . . . the very way our
feelings have of developing themselves.'[18] That world is 'alive, new,
unpredictable'. It makes demands on us, obliging·us constantly to
adapt to it, to cope with it. The healthy man is capable of responding
to these demands. But the morbid dreamer, the man who lives *in* imagination, wishes above all to escape them. He refuses to adapt his
feelings, which are 'solemn and congealed; they always return with
the same form and the same label; the sick person has had all the time
to construct them; nothing in them is left to change, they will not
stand for the least deviation.'[19] His fantasy world is carefully designed
to ensure his total control of the situation: 'It is a poor and meticulous
world, in which the same scenes keep on recurring to the last detail,
accompanied by the same ceremonial where everything is regulated
in advance, foreseen; where, above all, nothing can escape, resist or
surprise.'[20] We all resort to this world from time to time, but the morbid dreamer makes its sickly safety a way of life, in which he 'is able to
choose from the storeroom of accessories the feelings he wishes to put
on and the objects that fit them, just as the actor chooses his costume.
Today it is ambition, tomorrow sexual love. It is only the "essential
poverty" of objects as images that can satisfy the feeling submissively,
without ever surprising it, deceiving it or guiding it. It is only the
unreal objects that can come to nothing when the caprice of the
dreamer stops, since they are but his reflection; it is only they whose
consequences are no other than what is desired of them. . . .'[21]

The activity of the morbid dreamer is no more than the most ex
treme and consistent exercise of the choice open to each of us at every
moment: that of miserable escape from a demanding world. If the

16. IP, p.162; PI, p.78 (translation changed).
17. IP, p.21; PI, p.13.
18. IP, p.189; PI, p.211.
19. IP, p.190; PI, pp.211-12
20. IP, p.190; PI, p.212.
21. IP, p.190; PI, p.212.

demands of being-in-the-world are too great, we can always create 'phantom objects', 'strange creatures beyond the laws of the world of realities'. [22] The evasions to which these phantom objects invite us not only free us 'from our actual condition, our preoccupations, our boredoms; they offer us escape from every constraint of the *world*, they seem to present themselves as a negation of the condition of *being-in-the-world*, as an anti-world.'[23]

Absolute Freedom — to Withdraw

Sartre's argument, confident and powerful though it is, seems to end in a profound dilemma. Without 'magical' behaviour, we are abandoned to 'an indifferent, hostile, and stubborn world', obliged to obey its laws and yield to its demands. Yet the magical attitude also exacts a price from us, degrading consciousness and restricting us to an 'unnatural, congealed, abated, formalized' repertoire of response. Nevertheless, Sartre insists on the absolute freedom of consciousness, on its 'monstrous spontaneity', and on imagination as the modal activity of that freedom. Imagination is 'the whole of consciousness as it realizes its freedom,' he declares. It is 'the necessary condition for the freedom of empirical man in the midst of the world.'[24]

We are free because of our ability to imagine; consciousness 'is always free, it always and at each moment has the concrete possibility of producing the *irréel*'. [25] But, whatever Sartre may claim, this ability is not in any real sense, constitutive of freedom *in* the world. We are free to withdraw from a world that is lacking, that frustrates desire, and to achieve satisfaction in the imaginary. But beyond this inner freedom, without effect on the world, self-determination seems impossible. Imagination is the condition of my being free in the world, but I am free only to imagine — and too constant an exercise of this, my only freedom, leads directly, as Sartre himself argues, to the pathological.

This was the fundamental structure of Sartre's early studies of imagination. It fashioned the rigid bipolar logic of his analysis, governed his peculiar reading of Husserlian phenomenology and dictated

22. IP, p.175; PI, p.193.
23. IP, p.175; PI, p.194 (translation changed).
24. See IP, pp.236-37; PI, pp.270-71; and also Francis Jeanson, *Le Probème morale et la pensée de Sartre*, Paris 1947, p.96.
25. IP, p.236; PI, pp.270-71 (translation changed).

the omissions in his historical critique of theories of imagination. As we shall now see, it also explains why, having discussed the existential functions of imagination, Sartre went on to present a theory of art.

Is Art the Answer?
'La Nausée'

The theory of art outlined at the end of *L'Imaginaire* was, according to its author's own recollection, added as an afterthought.[1] This may well have been the case. Yet it was to be conserved as a central component of much of his subsequent work; and even in its first — fortuitous — setting, its significance was clear. It completed and gave practical anchorage to his studies of imagination by identifying the one objective human activity rooted in our ability to retreat to the *irréel*.

The theory was directly deduced from these studies, as we can see from a summary of its basic points. The aesthetic object which we appreciate — let us say, a painting — needs both artist and observer in order to come into existence. For the material object before us is not the aesthetic object. Art is an *irréel*, an imaginary object; and so, when I encounter the framed canvas covered by layers of paint, I am not yet in the presence of the aesthetic object. The material present to consciousness is rather an *analogue* which I must animate in order to make the aesthetic object appear. 'As long as we consider the canvas and the frame themselves, the aesthetic object "Charles VIII" will not appear. Not that it is hidden by the painting, but that it cannot present itself to a realistic consciousness (*une conscience réalisante*). It will appear at the moment when consciousness, in a radical conversion which implies the negation (*néantisation*) of the world, constitutes itself as image forming.'[2] The artist constructs not a 'work of art', but rather a material analogue which is *'visited* from time to time (each time the spectator takes the

1. *Sartre*, p.59.
2. IP, p.239; PI, p.275 (translation changed).

imaginative attitude) by an *irréel* which is precisely the depicted *object.*'[3]

The aesthetic object is always imaginary because it is never there before us. Even when listening to music, I directly perceive only the analogue, never Beethoven's Seventh Symphony itself. 'The Seventh Symphony is not at all *in time*. It thus entirely escapes the real. It presents itself *in person,* but as absent, as being out of reach.'[4] In other words, 'I really hear nothing, I listen in the imaginary.'[5] Sartre drew four consequences from this basic position. Aesthetic experience, outside of time and space, contains no sensual pleasure. Indeed, aesthetic contemplation cancels desire. Similarly, the real can never be beautiful because 'beauty is a value which can only be applied to the imaginary.' Furthermore, the experience of a work of art entails a temporary suspension of need and of the practical sense. And finally, aesthetics has nothing to do with morality, because morality implies being-in-the-world, not a negation of the world.

Many years later, Sartre stated that his intention in this discussion had been to combat 'a theory according to which the work of art was a real and metaphysical fact, concrete, a new essence given to the world.'[6] He had sought to remove all doubts — art is unreal and therefore we cannot save ourselves through it. But our own questions must be pressed. How does this theory fit into the overall intellectual structure to which it belongs? And is it consonant with experience? Not long ago, I entered the Detroit Institute of Arts and spent an hour with Bruegel's 'The Wedding Dance', all the time knowing that it was not a real wedding dance but an artistic representation. Did my consciousness operate 'a radical conversion which implies the negation of the world'? Can I say that my experience of 'The Wedding Dance' was 'constituted and apprehended by an imaginative consciousness which posits it as unreal'? Yes, and the effect of the painting may have been due to precisely this fact. I could leave an everyday life filled with trouble and uncertainty and enter the museum depressed and in disorder, to encounter there a clear, vital, harmonious — but unreal — world. I say 'world': it was the special aesthetic world of the museum, as experienced in a single painting.

3. IP, p.240; PI, p.275 (translation changed).
4. IP, p.244; PI, p.280 (translation changed).
5. IP, p.245; PI, p.280 (translation changed).
6. *Sartre,* p.59.

'The Wedding Dance', like all great art, is free from the clutter, the disorder, the externally imposed harmonies of daily life. 'A radical conversion', 'the negation of the world' — these terms are appropriate to describe my heightened experience before it. The experience was heightened *because* its 'object' was unreal; because on this canvas, a man living in Flanders four hundred years ago had been able to create just the world he wanted in just the way he wanted; because here in the museum, away from my daily struggles, I was able to look at his canvas and to see, in the fullest possible way, what was there. Sartre is correct to suggest that the experience of a painting is permeated with a sense of its unreality. It entails a rupture with reality because in the presence of art we relax our disposition to action, we only 'look at' the painting. Our activity lacks all practical consequence. Thus the painting is something more than the surface of specific designs and shapes before us. It becomes something to 'enter', to experience wholly in a way that temporarily 'leaves' daily life behind.

Sartre does well then, to call the time spent with a painting an 'induced dream'. For when I left the Institute of Arts and 'The Wedding Dance' that day, it was as if to 'wake up', to 'return', unhappily, to reality. But did I in fact *see* 'The Wedding Dance', or did I *imagine* it? Sartre's reply is unequivocal. The depicted subject is not there before me and will never appear to perception. It will appear only when I take up the imaginative attitude, ceasing merely to look at 'the brush-strokes, the impaste on the canvas, its grain, the varnish that has been spread over the colours'. [7] The beautiful object, 'The Wedding Dance' which gave me so much pleasure, appeared only when I stopped looking at the thing before me and instead turned it into an analogue. From those materials, on that surface, my imagination produced 'an unreal whole of *new things,* objects which I have never seen and will never see, but which are nonetheless unreal objects, objects which do not exist *in the painting* nor anywhere in the world, but which appear through the canvas and which have taken hold of it by a sort of possession.' [8] All art, as Sartre said of Beethoven's Seventh Symphony, is 'outside of the *real,* outside of existence',

According to Sartre, I stood before the object labelled 'The Wed-

7. IP, p.240; PI, p.275 (translation changed).
8. IP, pp.241-42; PI, p.277 (translation changed).

ding Dance' and actually saw nothing but the glass covering it, the strokes of colour, the lines, the frame. The scene appeared only when I assumed the imaginary attitude, and so created a synthetic imaginative whole that was not before me but was, strictly speaking, present only to my mind. Yet I did not seem to perform any special activity in seeing 'The Wedding Dance'. I did not feel more active or more spontaneous, I did not seem to be imagining rather than looking. Indeed I seemed precisely to be experiencing the object directly before me, and not something else, something unreal. Now, I am in fact spontaneous and creative when I see a painting — but when I look away from it I realize that I must be so in order to see *anything*. Turning to the grey chair behind me, I must sort and synthesize in order for the chair to appear. Passive optical registration of what is present would give me only an incoherent jumble of unknowns. In order to *see* anything, I must also think and imagine. Just as I do not 'simply' see a painting, I do not simply see the chair; and if I 'imagine' a painting, I also imagine the chair. Both acts are involved in any instance of perception. Hence, Sartre's sharp opposition is misplaced. Whatever the precise nature of 'aesthetic' activity, its distinguishing trait is not the transformation of the given object into an 'analogue' of something 'unreal'. In fact, the experience of 'The Wedding Dance' suggests that, far from *not* seeing, we see *more than usual*. How often do we stop to notice the colour of people's clothes, or to observe the ways in which people stand around at a party? Usually, in fact, we see very little. Perception is strictly governed — limited — by our practical purposes. But this changes when we enter a museum. We are there not to classify and select but to see fully, to let our powers of vision relax and play. Looking at 'The Wedding Dance', we are freer and more spontaneous than when we wait for a bus. But this is so because we are able to perceive, not because we stop perceiving. The experience of art involves a rupture with reality, but not the particular and total rupture posited by Sartre, and not for the reasons that he gives. When he points to the rupture as a fact of aesthetic experience he is quite convincing, but his explanation of it is based on an opposition between art and life that echoes and repeats the difficulties of the opposition between imagining and perceiving. This position was eventually to produce its own *reductio ad absurdum* in Sartre's work. Writing in 1948, he unhesitatingly rejected the entire history of Western sculpture. If art was an *irréel,* he reasoned, sculpture could not be sensuous; working in the mistaken belief that their aesthetic objects occupied space, 'for three thousand years sculptors have been carving only cadavers.'[9]

'La Nausée'

This rigid opposition between art and life offers the prospect of satisfying in the unreal world of art everything that is frustrated in life: it is precisely because art is in so many ways the opposite of an absurd world that Antoine Roquentin finds respite in it from his nausea. In this, *La Nausée* is a concrete exploration of themes so far only implied in Sartre's work. For our own purposes it is interesting equally for the ambiguities of its conclusion. Why, after the entire book has led him there, does Roquentin reject, or accept only ironically, the notion of art as consolation?

Roquentin is an intellectual who, after years of wandering, has come to rest in Bouville, a town by the sea, in order to write a biography of the Marquis de Rollebon, a diplomatic intriguer of the late eighteenth and early nineteenth centuries. Although only thirty, Roquentin is a man grown jaded; his loneliness is not intense or searching so much as a weary sense of *déjà vu*. Life offers him little; he asks less. The main supports of his daily existence are rooted in the past. For three years, he has been immersed in the life of a long-dead man. He remains attached to a woman whom he has not seen for four. Above all, he has had 'adventures', experiences whose special precision and coherence can be appreciated only in retrospect. Quite suddenly, however, without any will or action on his part, Roquentin sees these structures of evasion collapse, exposing the bare reality of existence. Immersed now in the present, he is possessed by intense, sickly-sweet, nameless sensations: by nausea. He gives up his increasingly fruitless attempts to control existence and experiences it directly: 'the word absurdity is coming to life under my pen; a little while ago, in the garden, I couldn't find it, but neither was I looking for it, I didn't need it: I thought without words, *on* things, *with* things. Absurdity was not an idea in my head, or the sound of a voice, only this long serpent dead at my feet, this wooden serpent. Serpent or

9. 'La Recherche de l'absolu', *Situations*, III, Paris 1949, p.292; trans. Wade Baskin, 'The Quest for the Absolute,' *Essays in Aesthetics*, New York 1963, p.84. Giacometti alone had understood that his art was imaginary, he declared.

claw or root or vulture's talon, what difference does it make. And without formulating anything clearly, I understood that I had found the key to Existence, the key to my Nauseas, to my own life. In fact, all that I could grasp beyond that returns to this fundamental absurdity. Absurdity: another word; I struggle against words; down there I touched the thing . . . .'[10] No conventional explanation could mitigate the fundamental, absurd contingency of the existent: 'this root — there was nothing in relation to which it wasn't absurd. Oh, how can I put it in words? Absurd: in relation to the stones, the tufts of yellow grass, the dry mud, the tree, the sky, the green benches. Absurd, irreducible; nothing — not even a profound, secret upheaval of nature could explain it. Evidently I did not know everything, I had not seen the seeds sprout or the tree grow. But faced with this great wrinkled paw, neither ignorance nor knowledge was important: the world of explanations and reasons is not the world of existence. A circle is not absurd, it is clearly explained by the rotation of a straight segment around one of its extremities. But neither does a circle exist. This root, on the other hand, existed in such a way that I could not explain it. Knotty, inert, nameless, it fascinated me, filled my eyes, brought me back unceasingly to its own existence. In vain to repeat: "This is a root" — it didn't work any more. I saw clearly that you could not pass from its function as a root, as a breathing pump, *to that*, to this hard and compact skin of a sea lion, to this oily callous, headstrong look. The function explained nothing: it allowed you to understand generally that it was a root, but not *that one* at all. This root, with its colour, shape, its congealed movement, was below all explanation . . . .'[11]

The Structures of Absurdity

It would be possible to return *La Nausée* to the period in which it was set and written — roughly speaking, from the Depression to Munich — to reflect on its almost total abstraction from history, compared with the later *Les Chemins de la liberté,* and perhaps to repeat the merciless judgment that Sartre himself finally passed on it: 'what I lacked [then] was a sense of reality. I have changed since. I have slowly

10.*La Nausée (*LN*)*, Paris 1938, pp.163-64; trans. Lloyd Alexander, *Nausea* (N), New York 1949, pp.173-74.
11. LN, p.164; N, p.174.

learned to experience reality. I have seen children dying of hunger. Over against a dying child *La Nausée* cannot act as a counterweight.'[12] It would also be possible to examine the complex literary constitution of the novel, in which the traditional device of the personal journal frames a text that at times recalls Zola (the Sunday ritual of the local bourgeoisie) and at others Flaubert (the character of the Autodidact), including naturalist description and an almost allegorical use of street and place-names, passages of philosophical speculation and of surrealist fantasy. However our main concern here must be with the role of *La Nausée* in the general development of Sartre's work, with the key themes of his early writings as they are deployed in his first novel.

The terms Sartre uses to describe existence fall into three distinct groups, connoting shapelessness, purposelessness and contingency.[13] Shapelessness: things threaten to grow, to spead, to swarm over us; they ooze, they are like paste, they are slack and bloated. As Roquentin describes things during his moments of nausea, they lose shape; they press up on all sides, defying order and regularity. He sees the underlying disorder: 'the root, the park gates, the beach, the sparse grass, all that had vanished: the diversity of things, their individuality, were only an appearance, a veneer. This veneer has melted, leaving soft, monstrous masses, all in disorder — naked, frightful, obscene nakedness.'[14]

Existence is meaningless, and so, superfluous. There is no reason for existing. Nothing has purpose, nothing is needed. Everything in the world is *de trop*. If there is no human network of purposes which gives things their function and meaning, neither is there any divine or natural plan which originates things as they are and defines their place in the world; nor is there even a biological order which lends the objects their individual shapes and properties, so that they might perform definite functions. 'Every existing thing is born without reason,

---

12. Interview with Jacqueline Piatier, 'Jean-Paul Sartre s'explique sur *Les Mots,*' *Le Monde*, 18 avril, 1964; trans. by Anthony Hartley, *Encounter* xxii, 6 (June 1964), p.62. In this context, it is worth mentioning the story 'L'Enfance d'un chef', where the fascist commitment of the protagonist is portrayed as an escape from contingency (*Le Mur*, Paris 1939; trans. Lloyd Alexander, 'The Childhood of a Leader,' *The Wall and Other Stories*, New York 1948).

13. This section draws on Francis Jeanson's excellent analysis 'Enfer et Bâtardise,' *Sartre par lui-meme*, Paris 1955, pp.114-44; trans. 'Hell and Bastardy,' *Yale French Studies*, 30, pp.5-22.

14. LN, p.162; N, pp.171-72.

prolongs itself out of weakness, and dies by chance',[15] Roquentin
decides. 'You couldn't even wonder where all that sprang from, or
how it was that a world came into existence, rather than nothingness.
It didn't make sense, the world was everywhere, in front, behind.
There had been nothing *before* it. Nothing.'[16]

The third aspect of existence is contingency. To detach things from
their functions is to say that nothing *must* be as it is. If there is no
human, divine, or natural order, neither is there a casual order.
Things just happen; anything can happen. Events follow each other
at random.

Art Quells Nausea

It is clear that *La Nausée* poses quite different problems from Sartre's
psychological writings. Yet all the works of the later 1930s have a
common theme: existence is fundamentally disturbing. Whether the
world be different, or simply absurd, we are tempted to escape from
it, and to relate to it through fantasy and illusion.

If existence as such is absurd, it follows that its basic nature cannot
be changed, but only hidden by our efforts to organize our lives, by
the pretence that we are needed, by the postulation of patterns and
laws. I cannot make my life into an adventure which has precision,
necessity and meaning, because these categories belong not to events
but only to our wishful thinking about them. Nature is not stable and
governed by law, no one is indispensable, no one has a right to exist.
La Nausée attempts to purge us of all such illusions, in the name of the
bitter truth of contingency. Roquentin is then faced with two pressing
problems: how to quell his nausea, and how to reorient himself for a
life without illusions. Old beliefs, old loves, old habits have fallen
away. He is alone in a cafe, listening to music.

> Some of these days
> You'll miss me honey

'What has just happened is that the Nausea has disappeared. When
the voice was heard in the silence, I felt my body harden and the
Nausea vanish. Suddenly: it was almost unbearable to become so
hard, so brilliant. At the time the music was drawn out, dilated,

15. LN, p.169; N, p.180.
16. LN, p.170; N, pp.180-81.

swelled like a waterspout. It filled the room with its metallic transparency, crushing our miserable time against the walls. I am *in* the music.'[17]

Roquentin's description of the music explains what has taken place: 'there is no melody, only notes, a myriad of tiny jolts. They know no rest, an inflexible order gives birth to them and destroys them without even giving them time to recuperate and exist for themselves. They race, they press forward, they strike me a sharp blow in passing and are obliterated.'[18] Art is outside of time. Unlike temporal events, musical notes are not disjunct and random, but connected and orderly. Each note is the result of the previous one, and vanishes to make way for the note that will succeed it. The melody is formed by an unnatural necessity. The overwhelming impression is of an internally-ordered sequence serving a single purpose, striving for a single effect.

Shapelessness is driven out, as are purposelessness and contingency. 'A few seconds more and the negress will sing. It seems inevitable, so strong is the necessity of this music: nothing can interrupt it, nothing which comes from this time in which the world has fallen; it will stop of itself, as if by order. If I love this beautiful voice it is especially because of that: it is neither for its fullness nor its sadness, rather because it is the event for which so many notes have been preparing, from so far away, dying that it might be born.'[19] The nausea is quelled, hands no longer appear flabby and gestures develop 'like a majestic theme'.[20] Roquentin's body comes to feel 'hard' and 'at rest like a precision machine'.[21] The music has driven out slackness and disorder by its own rigour and necessity — the rigour and necessity of something beyond mere existence. 'It does not exist. It is even an annoyance; if I were to get up and rip this record from the table which holds it, if I were to break it in two, I wouldn't reach *it*. It is beyond — always beyond something, a voice, a violin note. Through layers and layers of existence, it veils itself, thin and firm, and when you want to seize it, you find only existence devoid of sense. It is behind them: I don't even hear it, I hear sounds, vibrations in the air which unveil it. It does not exist because it has nothing

17. LN, p.37; N, p.34.
18. LN, p.36; N, p.33.
19. LN, pp.36-37; N, p.34.
20. LN, p.37; N, p.35.
21. LN, p.38; N, p.35.

superfluous: it is all the rest which in relation to it is superfluous. It *is* '.[22]

Roquentin's Ambiguous Turn to Art

The conclusion of the novel seems inevitable now: Roquentin will turn to art. But he does not, as we might expect, immerse himself in art as the only way of overcoming absurdity in his life. For after all, art does not really exist. In a late passage in his diary, Roquentin attacks the use of art as consolation: 'To think that there are idiots who get consolation from the fine arts. Like my Aunt Bigeois: "Chopin's Preludes were such a help to me when your poor Uncle died." And the concert halls overflow with humiliated, outraged people who close their eyes and try to turn their pale faces into receiving antennae. They imagine that the sounds flow into them, sweet, nourishing, and that their sufferings become music like Werther; they think that beauty is compassionate to them. The mugs.'[23]

Roquentin is waiting for the train that will carry him away from Bouville. He is thinking about music, in its opposition to existence. He bitterly admits having tried but failed to live in the imaginary. Then he shifts again and thinks of the composer and singer of *Some of These Days:* 'She sings. So two of them are saved: the Jew and the negress. Saved. Maybe they thought they were lost irrevocably, drowned in existence. Yet no one could think of me as I think of them, with such gentleness. No one, not even Anny. They are a little like dead people for me, a little like the heroes of a novel; they have washed themselves of the sin of existing. Not completely of course, but as much as any man can.'[24]

At this moment, then, he wonders if it might not be possible to justify his own existence in the same way? Not by writing history, as he had started out to do — 'history talks about what has existed' and 'an existent can never justify the existence of another existent'[25] — but by creating something *above* existence: 'a story, for example, something that could never happen, an adventure. It would have to

22. LN, p.218; N, p.233 (translation changed).
23. LN, p.217; N, p.232 (translation changed).
24. LN, p.221; N, pp.236-37.
25. LN, p.221-22; N, p.237 (translation changed).

be beautiful and hard as steel and make people ashamed of their existence.'[26] After everything that has passed, Roquentin seems about to accept illusions as the only solution: 'A book. A novel. And there would be people who would read this book and say: "Antoine Roquentin wrote it, a red-headed man who hung around cafes," and they would think about my life as I think about the negress's: as something precious and almost legendary. A book. Naturally, at first it would only be a troublesome, tiring work, it wouldn't stop me from existing or feeling that I exist. But a time would come when the book would be written, when it would be behind me, and I think that a little of its clarity might fall over my past. Then, perhaps, because of it, I would remember my life without repugnance. Perhaps one day, thinking precisely of this hour, of this gloomy hour in which I wait, stopping, for it to be time to get on the train, perhaps I shall feel my heart beat faster and say to myself: "That was the day, that was the hour, when it all started." And I might succeed — in the past, nothing but the past — in accepting myself.'[27] Having attacked all forms of fame or notability as an evasion of existence, Roquentin is now drawn to them himself. Having seen both his adventures and their rationale collapse, he is now ready once again to see his life as an adventure. Ironical and qualified as all this may be in Roquentin's mind, what is it if not consolation?

What are we to make of *La Nausée*, this unsparing dissection of illusions which seems finally to turn away from its own bitter conclusions yet without surrendering to the implications of its one, rigorously deduced affirmation? The *irréel* is a natural terminus of Sartre's thought. Why, then, does Roquentin hesitate before the one solution he so painstakingly develops?

The answer is obvious, and painful: art is not real. Roquentin emphasizes that writing a novel cannot really change his life, but only how he or others reflect on it. Art 'solves' life's problems, momentarily, but outside life itself, in the imaginary. *La Nausée*, which mocks and dissolves a hundred ways of escaping reality, can hardly endorse an escapist solution, however rigorously argued. *La Nausée* cannot simply endorse the aestheticist philosophy with which it coexists and to which its protagonist is drawn. For the dilemma so posed affects the

26. LN, p.222; N, p.237.
27. LN, p.222; N, pp.237-38.

novel itself. It is manifest in the paradoxical fact of its existence: as an inner record that establishes art as a palliative of existence and at the same time a *novel*, an *irréel*, whose single-minded purpose is to impose the truth of that existence, beyond all illusion. In its action, in its form, in its very existence, *La Nausée* condenses the central, unresolved tension of all Sartre's early work.

5

Is Art the Answer?
'L'Etre et le Néant'

L'Etre et le Néant, published during the German occupation of Paris in 1943, was Sartre's first major philosophical treatise. In it, the tensions we have so far sketched were lodged in the very structure of being. At the same time, however, Sartre concentrated the dynamism and energy that he had exhibited and insisted upon in his early writings and turned them towards the world.

Our activity in the world contains fundamental and irresolvable contradictions, yet we must actively assume this life because we are free only within it and are fully responsible for it. *L'Etre et le Néant* is most noted for its passionate argument against all determinism and for human freedom, and its exploration of the meanings of our involvement and action in the world. At its most profound, it was a strikingly original discussion of the ways in which individuals make themselves unique: of their consciousness, their subjectivity, their role as centres of meaning, sources of values, creators of possibilities. Deploying the concept of 'bad faith', it deepened the critique of illusions begun in *La Nausée*. We erect such illusions, Sartre now argued, in order to hide our fundamental freedom from ourselves. Within these arguments concerning human freedom, Sartre also set out the logic of human suffering. He now tried to show how conflicts with others, alienation from the world, and constant frustration of our own projects were all equally rooted in the very structure of existence. Not only total freedom and total responsibility, but also 'man is a useless passion' and 'hell is other people' — these were the key themes of Sartre's 'essay in phenomenological ontology'.

Two Regions of Being

Sartre's first major theme is the distinction between two mutually irreducible realms of being, the in-itself (*en-soi*) and the for-itself (*pour-soi*). The for-itself is not quite consciousness as I know it; the in-itself is not quite the object-world as I know it. Underlying the concrete relations *I* have with *things* are more basic relations. By acting on the in-itself, the for-itself emerges as consciousness oriented towards an object-world; by being acted on by the for-itself, the in-itself emerges as object-world. Thus, these technical philosophical terms are used to denote the ontological strata underlying the finished world of experience.

The in-itself is pure, opaque positivity of which, strictly speaking, we can say only that it *is*. 'Being is. Being is in-itself. Being is what it is.'[1] In itself it is neither possible nor impossible, necessary or unnecessary; it is beyond negation or affirmation, beyond passivity or activity. 'Being is *itself*. This means that it is neither passivity nor activity. Both of these notions are *human* and designate human conduct or the instruments of human conduct.'[2] Such categories as destruction, necessity, causality, quality, quantity, space, time, potentiality all imply the presence of human beings, all appear in the in-itself only through the for-itself. Here Sartre echoes the question of *La Nausée*: what is the world *before* we confront and categorize it? *Existence* has been transformed into the *in-itself*, but with a subtle difference. What Roquentin seeks to describe is strictly speaking indescribable, inaccessible to consciousness. The moment it becomes a phenomenon *for* consciousness — as having shape or shapelessness, for example — the in-itself has already been seen by the for-itself.

Consciousness and Nothing

In describing the for-itself Sartre is not always consistent. Often he substitutes 'consciousness' for 'for-itself,' implying a strict identity

1. EN, p.34; BN, p.lxvi.
2. EN, p.32; BN, p.lxiv.

between the two. When he is precise, however, he distinguishes them. For the time being I shall follow his own shifting terminology.

Consciousness is always consciousness of *something:* 'from the start it refers to the thing.'[3] Thus consciousness is relative and dependent: it arises on the foundation of a being which is not it, it is 'born *supported* by a being which is not itself.'[4] Consciousness 'can exist only as *engaged* in this being which surrounds it on all sides and which paralyses it with its phantom presence.'[5] Its dependence and relativity notwithstanding, consciousness is totally *self-determining:*'consciousness is a plenum of existence, and this determination of itself by itself is an essential characteristic . . . . The existence of consciousness comes from consciousness itself.'[6] But a consciousness which exists only to the degree that it reveals something else, which is absolutely self-determining, is itself *nothing*.

Engaged, self-determining, and nothing: these qualities signify, above all, that consciousness 'is nothing but the pure nihilation (*néantisation*) of the in-itself; it is like a hole of being at the heart of Being.'[7] This in turn means that consciousness arises only as the for-itself determines *not* to be the in-itself; that this happens only as it withdraws or detaches itself from the in-itself; that in so doing it *rejects* the in-itself, and in rejecting it, finds the in-itself lacking.

It is this peculiar relationship that gives birth to the concrete world of our experience. That is, the in-itself becomes a world of differentiated objects *only* through being 'negated' by consciousness. Thus, for example, if I look up at the night sky at a certain point in the lunar cycle, my sense perception, taken by itself, does not give me a crescent moon, for 'what is released to intuition is an in-itself which by itself is neither complete not incomplete but which simply is what it *is,* without relation with other beings'. The bare sense-impressions as yet have no meaning, are unrecognizable. I come to see the crescent moon only by relating these sense-impressions to something beyond themselves: 'in order for this in-itself to be grasped as the crescent moon, it is necessary that a human reality surpass the given towards the project of the realized — here the disc of the full moon — and

3. EN, p.712; BN, p.618.
4. EN, p.28; BN, p.lxi.
5. EN, p.134; BN, p.90.
6. EN, p.22; BN, p.lv.
7. EN, p.711; BN, p.617.

return towards the given to constitute it as the crescent moon.'[8]

Laing and Cooper's discussion of Sartre's later use of the term 'sur-pass' helps to illuminate the meaning of negation here. 'Surpass', *dépasser,* is the French equivelant of Hegel's *aufheben,* which carries the threefold connotation of transcending, negating, and preserving. That which consciousness transcends is negated, in the sense that its claim to be self-explanatory and fully adequate is rejected. It is left aside for a moment while consciousness grasps something new, a new totality. Then the original object is drawn into, and thus preserved in, the new totality as one of its components.[9] 'It is the full moon which confers on the crescent moon its being as crescent; what-is-not (in the sense that it has not yet come into existence) determines what-is.' The given in-itself leads 'outside itself to the being which it is not — as to its meaning.'[10] However, negation means more than this. The negative activity of consciousness, in which it detaches itself from the thing in order to identify it in terms of what it is not, is not mere-ly epistemological: It acts each time because the in-itself *lacks something.* At each moment consciousness makes an existential deci-sion, based on its needs and desires, to reject the in-itself, to go beyond it towards what is missing. Each situation is then defined in terms of the goal to be attained.

It is of decisive importance here to note that Sartre is not referring to this or that particular lack in our *already existing* world of experience, but to the very origin of that world. Before the for-itself emerges there is no world, only a brute, dumb in-itself. The for-itself emerges only by negating, rejecting the in-itself and going towards what it perceives it to lack: the world is 'constituted in its being by the lacked — that is, by what it is not'.[11] The human world is by nature lacking. 'Thus the world is revealed as haunted by absences to be realized, and each *this* appears with a cortege of absences which point to it and determine it.'[12] Man is a negative being; his world is a negative world. Transcendence of this world is 'a condition of the very rising up of the world as such.'[13]

8. EN, p.129; BN, p.86.
9. R.D. Laing and D.G. Cooper, *Reason and Violence: A Decade of Sartre's Philosophy, 1950-1960,* London 1964, pp.13-14.
10. EN, p.130; BN, p.87.
11. EN, p.130; BN, p.87.
12. EN, p.249; BN, p.199.
13. EN, p.53; BN, p.17.

Now a world seen as lacking *x* is a world in which *x* becomes a *value*. Value in general is the 'beyond' which I project and towards which I direct my action. Thus 'every value-oriented act is a wrenching away from its own being' towards *x*. [14] That which I value in a specific instance, which the for-itself sees as lacking, is its possiblity, The in-itself, 'being by nature what it is, can not "have" possibilities.'[15] Only the for-itself has possibilities, but in the sense that it *is* its possibilities. 'Thus the for-itself can not appear without being haunted by value and projected toward its own possibilities.'[16]

Existential Consequences: Freedom

Here then was Sartre's answer to the fundamental riddle of modern Western philosophy: does our consciousness shape the world or does the world shape our consciousness of it? Attempting to avoid both the idealism that reduced reality to human comprehension of it, and the mechanical materialism which would make of consciousness the passive recipient of a finished process, he affirmed that consciousness was dynamic, the bearer of all meaning, but that the world lay outside of it. His point was neither theoretical nor generic: the world was endowed with meaning not through the *a priori* constitutive acts of pure reason, but by the practical projects of individual con-sciousnesses.

'Practical': my account so far has not rendered the worldly tenor of *L'Etre et le Néant*. Its central theme, after all, is *liberté*. Most of the treatise is spent carefully laying the ontological groundwork for human freedom. No longer is freedom practically confined, as it was in *La Nausée* and the early psychological writings, to acts of escape. Sartre's premises are the same — freedom is the permanent ability to detach oneself from any situation, to simultaneously say no and go beyond; consciousness exists only by detaching itself, by defining itself in terms of what is missing, by perceiving what is lacking, by go-ing away from where it is towards its possibilities; freedom, simply, is not being determined by the given, but instead being able to detach ourselves from it in order to go beyond it towards value, toward what is lacking. But this is no longer an act of withdrawal in the margin of

14. EN, p.137; BN, p.93.
15. EN, p.144; BN, p.99.
16. EN, p.140; BN, p.96.

an already finished world. The world of experience is *based* on negation, has its *origin* in our freedom.

Ontology can — and must — now be written from the standpoint of
freedom. In order to determine what a brute existent is, consciousness must detach itself from it, seeing it as other than consciousness.
It must go beyond the in-itself towards its meaning, must see what is
lacking in it, in order to return to it with a grasp of its identity. To
grasp the world, then, one must first put oneself 'out of circuit' in relation to it. This happens spontaneously: 'what we call freedom is
impossible to distinguish from the *being* of "human reality." Man does
not exist *first* in order to be free *subsequently;* there is no difference
between the being of man and his being-free.'[17]

This is the richest and most controversial area of Sartre's early
thought — and in many respects, the most confusing. The confusion
springs from Sartre himself — from his attempt to go beyond the old
debate between determinism and free will while remaining an impassioned partisan in it, in a book that abounds in with extreme, outra-
geous — and incorrect — pronouncements about our illimitable freedom of choice. Twenty-five years later, Sartre expressed deep embar-
rassment at his early statements: 'the other day, I re-read a prefatory
note of mine to a collection of these plays — *Les Mouches, Huis Clos* and
others — and was truly scandalized. I had written: "Whatever the circumstances, and wherever the site, a man is always free to choose to
be a traitor or not . . . " When I read this, I said to myself: It's in-
credible, I actually believed that!'[18] *L'Etre et le Néant* contains
statements of the same order: 'The slave in chains is free to *break them;*
this means that the meaning of his chains will appear to him in the
light of the end which he will have chosen: to remain a slave or to risk
the worst in order to get rid of his slavery.'[19] Whether he accepts
slavery or tries to escape, only *he* can decide. 'It is therefore senseless
to think of complaining since nothing foreign has decided what we
feel, what we live, or what we are.'[20] Elsewhere in the book, this argument achieved its own, historically more concrete *reductio ad absurdum.*
The exclusion of Jews from 'Aryan' restaurants, Sartre wrote, 'can

17. EN, p.61; BN, p.25.
18. 'Itinerary of a Thought,' p.44.
19. EN, p.635; BN, p.550.
20. EN, p.639; BN, p.554.

have meaning only on and through the foundation of my free choice. In fact according to the free possibilities which I choose, I can disobey the prohibition, pay no attention to it, or, on the contrary, confer upon it a coercive value which it can hold only because of the weight which I attach to it.'[21] Indeed, in May 1941, as Sartre returned from internment, the Germans had begun to round up Jews in Occupied France. However free these Jews may have been, ontologically, 'to consider the anti-Semites as pure objects,'[22] it happened that at least twenty thousand of them were shipped to destruction as Sartre was completing his book.

Nevertheless, we should not fail to notice the bitterly anti-Nazi overtones of Sartre's strident insistence on our ability to choose, in any situation. This was patent in his play, *Les Mouches,* an allegory of the Resistance, in which he aimed to stir up rebellion, to destroy any and all arguments for quietism, for acceptance of the German occupation. Death, torture — these were no excuse, in the terms of *L'Etre et le Néant*: 'even the red-hot pincers of the torturer do not exempt us from being free.'[23] As he said in 1969, reflecting on these years, during the Resistance 'there was a very simple problem' — finding courage to resist. 'A Frenchman was either for the Germans or against them, but there was no other option. The real political problems, of being "for, but" or "against, but", were not posed by this experience. The result was that I concluded that in any circumstances, there was always a possible choice. Which is false. . . . '[24]

We Make Ourselves: Growing Points

Sartre's arguments for our choice, freedom and responsibility became famous after the Second World War as key themes of existentialism. But his analysis of human action had a more profound and, in the long run, more influential aspect — embodied in his apparently nonsensical claim that freedom is everywhere, whether the worker is simply at work in his daily tasks or rejecting his entire situation to become a revolutionary.

Was Sartre's early sense of 'freedom' so sweeping as to be mean-

21. EN, p.607; BN, p.524.
22. EN, p.610; BN, p.527.
23. EN, p.587; BN, p.506.
24. 'Itinerary of a Thought,' p.44.

ingless? As far as concrete social and political issues were concerned, yes. But beyond that there remained a fundamental thesis concerning human existence. That it was almost buried by his extravagant ethical claims was unfortunate; that he spent the rest of his career illuminating and deepening it is to our great benefit.

This is the side of Sartre's analysis of action which actually does point beyond the old debate over determinism and free will. What kind of 'freedom' is this, that is always ours — that is present whether the Jew is submitting to his fate or resisting it with all his might? What kind of 'freedom' is present in my act of simply opening my eyes and describing the objects around me? What kind of freedom is it that connects the epistemological fact of detachment, through which I establish a world around me, with the existential fact of my action in the world? This freedom is the substance of human reality. It is everywhere, in everything we do, at every moment. In this simple proposition, Sartre reopened an important pathway to human self-understanding. It centres not on arguments over our ability to choose, or our freedom, but rather on the fact that, regardless of all else, we make ourselves from what has been made of us. It is in this that human beings differ from stones and exist beyond the laws that govern them. We are, we may say, dialectical centres of intentionality, sources of laws. Our science may comprehend us, but it is *our* science, and *we* who comprehend. We produce the world, go beyond every given situation. Sartre's purpose is to give full weight to what is characteristically human in every situation while acknowledging that we certainly do not create, but are rather given, our individual points of departure. What we are given — our class, our nationality, our race, our very words, our historical situation, our family background — never affects us mechanically, never imprints itself on us as in a relation of cause to effect, never predestines us to act in a particular way. It becomes what it is for us by being drawn into us and thrown out as a new creation, our project.

In this conception, we can discern one of the intellectual continuities between the early and the later Sartre. For if initially he was intensely, demonstratively hostile to any suggestion of determinism, he was in the long run to accord the world its due role in the formation of the self. In the course of his explorations, he was brought to Marxism, seeing there a cogent account of history; and by the same process, the themes first developed in *L'Etre et le Néant* were released into Marxism, to produce a critical, searching dialectical thought whose effort, embodied in the later writings, to understand the relation between individuals and their societies remains a major theoretical challenge. Similarly, Sartre's insistence on 'existential psychoanalysis', however abstract and academic at first, heralded some of the most important recent trends in psychotherapy. If we fundamentally create ourselves, he argued, then neuroses are patterns of behaviour we invent in order to survive difficult situations. The inferiority complex, for example, was 'nothing other than the organized totality of my failure behaviour, as a projected plan, as a general device of my being.'[25] Mental illness is behaviour, and therapy would proceed by assisting us to recover our original layers of intentionality and to modify them by choosing new goals or new paths to our goals. [26]

The most striking example of the 'project' in *L'Etre et le Néant* is Sartre's discussion of the fatigued hiker. 'At first I resist and then suddenly I let myself go, I give up, I throw my knapsack down on the side of the road and let myself fall down beside it.'[27] Sartre reflects on what it might mean to be 'too tired.' One hiker may abandon himself to fatigue while another will avoid this at any cost. The fatigue itself could have been resisted longer. There is no adequate psysiological explanation for his being 'too tired.' It is clear then that his giving up can be understood only in relation to the 'organic totality of the projects which I am'[28] — that is, in terms of the projects in which, depending on their prior experiences, bodily fatigue is lent different meanings by different people. The hiker could indeed have kept going. *'But at what price?'* For some people the fatigue could be resisted or overcome only by directly subverting that 'organic totality of projects' — we might say, by threatening their identity.

This is the terrain of Sartre's 'existential psychoanalysis'. If we create ourselves, we do it according to a linked series of fundamental and secondary projects. We are not a collection of tastes, acts, and

25. EN, p.537; BN, p.459.

26. R.D. Laing's discussion of how the schizophrenic invents a false self pays homage to Sartre's discussion of bad faith. See *The Divided Self: An Existential Study in Sanity and Madness,* London 1959. For a more recent attempt to appy Sartre's thought to the theory and practice of psychotherapy see William V. Ofman, *Affirmation and Reality: Fundamentals of Humanistic Existential Therapy and Counseling,* New York 1976.

27. EN, p.530; BN, p.453.

28. EN, p.513; BN, p.454.

mannerisms but rather a whole which *we* continually unify. Any given action takes on meaning within this organic totality. A person's stuttering, to take Sartre's example, has meaning in terms of an original project of inferiority. To understand it is not to seek the 'complex' from which it issues, but rather the original choice that it expresses. I may cure my stutter, but if I do not also modify my primary project, I may simply create another infirmity to 'express the total end which I pursue'.[29]

This 'existential psychoanalysis' was hobbled at first by Sartre's hostility to Freudian psychoanalysis (and, ultimately, to determinism in general). He ignored the entire rich field of psychoanalytic concepts, especially those of the unconscious and repression, and, as we shall see, invented his own highly questionable ontological 'project of being' as the goal of psychic life. He insisted that individuals always acted totally freely, were free to renounce their original project at any moment and choose a new one. However, Sartre's actual analysis, which persisted into his later work, freed itself from and improved upon these theoretical positions. He successfully demonstrated that it was foolish to reproach the hiker with his free choice to keep walking, given his complex, structured relationship to this hike, his body, and his attitude about the world. We make ourselves, we may abstractly be able to change what we have made 'at any moment', but any such intention must reckon with the weight of our prior choices and the stakes we develop in them. Even while vehemently denying the existence of the unconscious Sartre presupposed and used the notion, meaning by it the hidden network of those early experiences and choices in which the self was created, the whole weight of its 'organic totality of projects'. What after all could it mean for him to acknowledge that 'when the psychoanalysis is close to grasping the initial project of the patient, the latter abandons the treatment and begins to lie'?[30] Later in his career, in the same way as he considerably narrowed the meaning and scope of social freedom, he discovered that his key insights were enriched, not threatened, by the understanding that 'consciousness plays the trick of determining itself by its forgetfulness.'[31]

In *L'Etre et le Néant* itself, Sartre developed only the main lines of his

29. EN, p.550; BN, p.471.
30. EN, p.554; BN, p.474.
31. 'Itinerary of a Thought,' p.48.

'existential psychoanalysis'. He was as yet unaware of its implications for psychotherapy, and the world counted for little in his scheme. However, he sketched an impressive critique of conventional biography as unwilling to grasp the person as project, as trying to explain people by interspersing accounts of external events with appeals 'to the great explanatory idols of our epoch — heredity, education, environment, physiological constitution.'[32] Existential psychoanalysis called for a more radical understanding of human beings, for a 'regressive psychoanalysis' that ascended from specific acts to the ultimate project, followed by a 'synthetic progression' that descended again from the project 'to the considered act and grasp[ed] its integration in the total form'. Sartre indicated, moreover, that he would exemplify and test this approach — in an analysis of Gustave Flaubert.

The Separation of Consciousness and Being: Contingency

These themes constitute the positive, enduring aspect of *L'Etre et le Néant*. We must turn now to examine their more sombre, negative counterparts in their intimate relation to the central propositions of Sartre's ontology.[33]

Creator of himself, giver of meanings to the world, 'man' is nevertheless 'a useless passion'. How can this be? If consciousness is necessarily free, if freedom is at the source of the world itself, then that negative totality which is the world must necessarily be radically separated from our consciousness of it. Consciousness can exist only as it sees the world as lacking, only as it rejects and surpasses it in order to give it meaning, only as it projects its possibilities as goals to be realized. Hence, consciousness is doomed to frustration. By nature consciousness is that which detachs itself from the world because the world is not enough; by its very nature the world is that which lacks. Neither consciousness nor the world could exist for one moment except in this negative relationship; this is the source of the 'problem' in *L'Etre et le Néant*, and of the gloom which pervades so much of it.

In seeing the world as lacking, consciousness also seeks to remove

32. EN, p.643; BN, p.559.

33. See Herbert Marcuse, 'Sartre's Existentialism,' *Studies in Critical Philosophy*, London 1972 — the most penetrating critique of *L'Etre et le Néant*.

that lack. It has projected certain possibilities and seeks to realize them. Success in this endeavour would mean overturning the original negative relation of the for-itself to the in-itself. The for-itself seeks 'a relation between the for-itself and in-itself in the mode of identity.'[34] Our goal is a new being, which would be a synthesis of the two modes of being, an *in-itself-for-itself*: harmony. However, if I contrast this goal with the self-origin of the for-itself, I become aware of 'the fact that things simply *are there* as they are without the necessity or the possibility of being otherwise and that I *am there* among them'.[35] The theme of contingency, so central in *La Nausée,* is here explained more precisely. The for-itself constitutes itself as consciousness of an in-itself which it did not create. Independent and prior in time, the in-itself appears as already there when the for-itself enters the scene and reveals it. Thus, in that primary act of consciousness, 'being apprehends itself as not being its own foundation, and this apprehension is at the basis of every *cogito*.'[36] In other words, consciousness arises as negation on the basis of a pre-given being, but never itself creates that being. Or to put it more existentially, 'the for-itself *is,* in so far as it appears in a condition which it has not chosen, as Pierre is a French bourgeois in 1942, as Schmitt was a Berlin worker in 1870; it *is* in so far as it is thrown into a world and abandoned in a "situation"; it *is* as pure contingency inasmuch as for it as for things in the world, as for this wall, this tree, this cup, the original question can be posited: "Why is this being exactly such and not otherwise?" '[37] It is posited in vain, for as we have seen, being does not create or 'found' itself; it discovers itself already there and waiting, without explanation, prior to any activity of consciousness. The emergence of consciousness in this contingent world 'refers indeed to the effort of an in-itself to found itself: it corresponds to an attempt on the part of being to remove contingency from its being.'[38] That is, this goal is posited in the very act in which the for-itself arises. The for-itself originates in 'a revolt of the in-itself, which nihilates itself against its contingency'.[39] The 'project of being' is not added to the world, after consciousness reveals it: it *is* the world. Consciousness withdraws from the in-itself

34. EN, p.132; BN, p.89.
35. EN, p.634; BN, p.549.
36. EN, p.122; BN, p.79.
37. EN, p.122; BN, p.79.
38. EN, p.127; BN, p.84.
39. EN, p.653; BN, p.566.

'to found being' and the world appears. The basic human project, of which all individual projects are variations, can now be characterized somewhat more clearly. 'Total being, the concept of which would not be cleft by a hiatus and which would nevertheless not exclude the nihilated-nihilating being of the for-itself, that being whose existence would be a unitary synthesis of the in-itself and of consciousness — this ideal being would be the in-itself founded by the for-itself and identical with the for-itself which founds it — *i.e.*, the *ens causa sui*.'[40] The goal of consciousness is to remove the world's independence and otherness, to recognize itself in the world. Humans have fashioned a common image for this mode of being: God. For God is precisely that being who is 'all positivity and the foundation of the world' and is at the same time 'self-consciousness and the necessary foundation of himself.'[41] 'Thus the best way to conceive of the fundamental project of human reality is to say that man is the being whose project is to be God.'[42] The human goal is 'the in-itself-for-itself, consciousness become substance, substance become the cause of itself, the Man-God.'[43]

The Perpetual Failure

But we fail. 'Human reality is by nature an unhappy consciousness with no possibility of surpassing its unhappy state'. The reason, rigorously deduced from the rest of the analysis, is that an in-itself-for-itself is contradictory. If the world originates in the withdrawal of consciousness from the in-itself, then any synthesis of for-itself and in-itself would cancel the very negation which makes the world appear, and so would cancel the world. Conversely, a consciousness that ceased to tear itself away from things would cease to be consciousness. We are condemned by the very structure of being itself: condemned to project new lacks, to tear ourselves away and point towards new possibilities. 'The for-itself is *effectively* a perpetual project of founding itself *qua* being and a perpetual failure of this project.'[44] There is no 'possibility of surcease from this perpetual flight'.

40. EN, p.717; BN, p.623.
41. EN, pp.133-34; BN, p.90.
42. EN, p.653; BN, p.566.
43. EN, p.664; BN, p.575.
44. EN, p.714; BN, p.620.

We cannot satisfy our desires, realize our projects, reconcile consciousness with being — not because of social or historical or material reasons, but because to *be* and to project goals are one and the same. To stop running is to cease to exist. 'Thus we run after a possible which our very running causes to appear, which is nothing but our running itself, and which thereby is by definition out of reach. We run toward ourselves and we are — due to this very fact — the being which cannot be reunited with itself.'[45]

This is the ontological core of *L'Etre et le Néant,* and the basis for one of its most celebrated declarations. 'Every human reality is a passion in that it projects losing itself so as to found being and by the same stroke to constitute the in-itself, which escapes contingency by being it own foundation, the *Ens causa sui,* which religions call God. Thus the passion of man is the reverse of that of Christ, for man loses himself as man in order that God may be born. But the idea of God is contradictory and we lose ourselves in vain. Man is a useless passion.'[46]

Bad Faith

The negative fact of our constant need to project new goals is at the the same time the positive fact of our irreducible freedom. But the goal, the in-itself-for-itself, becomes the perpetual snare of 'bad faith'. Bad faith is self-deception: specifically, the attempt to *be* something as if in a thinglike manner, as if I were an in-itself — as when I try to *be* a writer, or a waiter, or a homosexual, or indeed a sincere person, as if any of these were a *condition* I could absorb. It is bad faith to pretend that I am not free, to act as if what is really my choice is or could be a condition, to *become* a role as if I did not have to choose and recreate it at every moment — above all, to deny that I constantly escape myself, go beyond myself, project new goals. All determinisms are modes of bad faith, as is the simple statement, 'I can't help myself'. Bad faith denies the fluidity, the instability, above all the freedom by which we contantly make ourselves who we are.

I cannot escape this bad faith. To *be* sincere is itself a project of bad faith, an effort to reduce the constant flow of consciousness and its constant temptation to self-denial, to a 'state' of self-honesty. And, as

45. EN, p.253; BN, p.202.
46. EN, p.708; BN, p.615.

we have seen, the fundamental human project is always the in-itself-for-itself in one or another form. It is bad faith for the for-itself to try to *be* what it is, because it is 'as being the being which is what it is not', and which is not what it is, that the for-itself projects being what it is. The fundamental human project is always the in-itself-for-itself in one or another form. But, authenticity entails accepting who I am, the being who can never simply be itself, who is always beyond itself, who will always try, but fail, to come to rest.

Trying to Create the World

Man is a useless passion. Bad faith is inescapable. But there remains art. 'If I create a picture, a drama, a melody, it is in order that I may be at the origin of a concrete existence. This existence interests me only to the degree that the bond of creation which I establish between it and myself gives me a particular right of ownership over it.' In coupling creation with ownership, Sartre initiates an analysis which passes from the actual creation of objects — art — to knowing, play, and degraded forms of creation such as owning and destroying objects. In each case my goal is to overcome the ontological schism by taking possession of the object in the fullest sense — by making it *depend on me* for its existence. In an attempt to overcome the order of being, I seek to make the world *mine*. 'It is not enough that a certain picture which I have in mind should exist; it is necessary as well that it exist *through me*.'[47]

I want two things from the activity: first, 'to sustain the picture in being by a sort of continuous creation' so that it is *mine*, a perpetually renewed emanation of myself; and second, to create *an object* radically distinct from me. My goal is that it exist through me and yet by itself. It is *my* object because I conceive it, I give it an existence according to my plan; and yet it is *an* object, because I encounter it out there, independent and external. 'It is in order to enter into this double relation in the synthesis of appropriation that I *create* my work. In fact it is this synthesis of self and not-self (the intimacy and translucency of thought on the one hand and the opacity and indifference of the in-itself on the other) that I am aiming at and which will establish my ownership of the work.'[48]

I seek the same from knowing. I create and possess the world

47. EN, p.665; BN, p.576.
48. EN, p.665; BN, p.577.

through revealing it by my thought, my research. 'In knowing, consciousness attracts the object to itself and incorporates it in itself. Knowledge is assimilation.' I want *my* thought to be *true,* to be *objective.* That is, I want it to remain intact and independent of me, although mine, just as 'the mind is continually creating [the work of art] and yet it stands alone and indifferent in relation to that creation.'[49]

In play, too, I want the in-itself to be 'a sort of emanation of myself while still remaining in itself.'[50] To make a snowman, for example, is to impose a form, *my* form, on the matter so that the matter appears to exist for its sake. I have drawn the matter out of its absolute exteriority and indifference, and shaped it according to my own ends. I do the same in skiing: the snow becomes the field and support for my action, while apparently remaining itself. 'It is my field of snow; I have traversed it a hundred times, a hundred times I have through my speed effected the birth of this force of condensation and support; it is *mine.*'[51]

Failure Again

In each of these projects I try to overcome contingency. But 'this is precisely the project of the in-itself-for-itself,' which, we already know, is futile. The very notion of creation is contradictory.[52] Creation is emanation: what I create is *still* myself, and I can never create a self which is at the very same moment an *independent* object. At the end of the process, 'either I find only my pure subjectivity or else I encounter a naked, indifferent materiality which no longer has any relation to me.'[53] Subjectivity can never become objective without dissolving itself. 'The tragedy of the absolute Creator, if he existed, would be the impossibility of getting out of himself, for whatever he created could be only himself.'[54] As for ourselves, 'human reality therefore is by nature an unhappy consciousness with no possibility of surpassing its unhappy state.'[55]

49. EN, p.667; BN, pp.578-79.
50. EN, p.671; BN, p.582.
51. EN, p.674; BN, p.585.
52. EN, p.682; BN, p.592.
53. EN, p.681; BN, p.591.
54. EN, p.680; BN, p.590.
55. EN, p.134; BN, p.90.

Early in *L'Etre et le Néant*, Sartre hints that we may be able to escape
total frustration. He speaks there of beauty as an 'ideal fusion of the
lacking with the one that lacks what is lacking.'[56] Beauty represents
'an ideal state of the world, correlative with an ideal realization of the
for-itself; in this realization the essence and the existence of things are
revealed as identity to a being who, in this very revelation, would be
merged with himself in the absolute unity of the in-itself.'[57] *Merged,
unity, identity* — beauty, after all, involves the integration of formal and
sensuous dimensions in the same object: harmoniously shaped matter. Sartre re-states this elementary proposition of philosophical aesthetics in the terms of his own ontology: beauty is the reconciliation of
the for-itself and the in-itself. But the theses of *L'Imaginaire* still hold.
The beautiful is never real. To apprehend it we must relinquish the
realistic attitude. Hence, it is 'no more a potentiality of things than
the in-itself-for-itself is a peculiar possibility of the for-itself. It haunts
the world as an unrealizable.'[58]

Once again Sartre's argument seems to lead to art as refuge but
again he refuses this luxury. He rejects the escapist conclusions of his
thought. Philosophy, he reiterates, must be *in the world*. We have seen
his psychological writings attack the imaginary life yet incline towards
it as the only free life. *La Nausée* mocked the idea of art as consolation,
yet half-heartedly and ironically reverted to it at the end. In *L'Etre et le
Néant* he now argues that the world cannot really become beautiful.
Beauty is a value; values can never be fulfilled. 'To the extent that
man *realizes* the beautiful in the world, he realizes it in the imaginary
mode.'[59] We could experience beauty as real only if we could experience the world as a real harmony and interpenetration of consciousness and things. But this cannot be. To try to make it so is to
render one's life a useless passion.

But can we not, Sartre wondered at the end of *L'Etre et le Néant,* turn
our back on the hopeless goal of becoming the *ens causa sui?* Perhaps,
after all, a real-life solution may be possible. Is there not the possibility of an authentic life, in which freedom would exorcise the
'transcendent value which haunts it'?[60] Might freedom simply accept

56. EN, p.244; BN, p.194.
57. EN, p.244; BN, pp.194, 195.
58. EN, p.245; BN, p.195.
59. EN, p.245; BN, p.195.
60. EN, p.722; BN, p.627.

itself without bad faith? In the end, true to its own strong active impulse, *L'Etre et le Néant* directed its readers into the world, not away from it, asking whether freedom could not 'situate itself so much the more precisely and the more individually as it projects itself further in anguish as a conditioned freedom and accepts more fully its responsibility as an existent by whom the world came into being.'[61] Troubled by the persistent logic of his own thought, Sartre attempted in these concluding pages to press forward to a new horizon of hope. But as yet he could only pose questions.

61. EN, p.722; BN, p.628.

6

The Source of Sartre's Thought

Sartre's early writings displayed both original insight and weary deduction, energy and despondency, commitment to the world and a sense of being overwhelmed by it. We can discern two contrary impulses in them, the one leading towards the world and the other away from it, the one leading towards Marxism and the other to biographies of artists, the one leading him to political activism and the other to his study. These two impulses seem closely allied — not merely occurring in the same works, but apparently served by the same lines of thought. Sartre's theory of existential psychoanalysis stated that the intelligibility of any individual totality of behaviour was to be sought in the unitary project that was its source. Accepting this thesis, we should now ask: what was the common source of the contrary impulses in his own thought?

We have already seen the impact of phenomenology on the young Sartre. His early writings abound with enthusiasm for Husserl and, to a lesser degree, Heidegger. The publication of Husserl's *Ideas,* he wrote in *L'Imagination,* was 'the great event of pre-World-War-I philosophy.'[1] In *La Transcendence de l'ego* he applauded 'the phenomenologists' for having 'given full measure to man's agonies and sufferings, and also to his rebellions.'[2] In the 1930s, he described himself as a phenomenological

1. I, p.139; IPC, p.127.
2. TEC, p.104.

psychologist, carrying out Husserl's directives in the fields of imagination and emotion.[3]

What did Sartre find in Husserl? In the 1939 essay 'Une idée', he proclaimed his allegiance to Husserl's central insight, intentionality — referring also to Heidegger's theme of being-in-the-world — and to his effort to establish philosophy where it truly belonged, in the world.

According to his own self-interpretation, Sartre used Husserl to free himself from academic idealism — specifically that of Brunschvicg. Most of his key positions in 'Une idée' were formulated *against* a philosophy which would study the mind as the source and mainspring of the world and in so doing turn away from studying the world. The essay began by mocking 'alimentary philosophy', in which objects became mere contents of consciousness, which was envisaged as their receptacle.

Husserl, in contrast, never ceased to affirm that things could not be dissolved in consciousness. If I view a tree, it remains where it was, unchanged. Consciousness does not apprehend by 'digesting'. 'To know is to "explode towards", to break away from the moist gastric intimacy in order to go, down there, beyond self, towards that which is not self, beyond, towards the tree and yet outside it; for it escapes me and repulses me and I am no more able to lose myself in it than it is able to dilute itself in me: outside of it, outside of me.'[4] The consequences of this position were profound. The radical separation of consciousness from its objects was already obvious. Consciousness did not digest or assimilate its objects, but went out towards them; it was an act, a series of acts, but never a place. Viewed by itself, Sartre argued, consciousness was as 'clear as a great wind; there is no longer anything in it except a movement to escape itself.'[5] A consciousness that had nothing 'inside' was 'nothing but the outside of itself; and it is this absolute flight, this refusal to be substance, which constitutes it as consciousness.'[6] For Sartre, this was the 'profound meaning' of Husserl's discovery: consciousness was 'a connected series of explosions which tear us away from ourselves, which do not even allow a "myself" the leisure to form behind them.'[7] This totally active

---

3. I, pp.150-51; IPC, p.137. See also IP, p.14; PI, p.4; and the first chapter of *Esquisse*.
4. 'Une idée', p.30.
5. Ibid., p.30.
6. Ibid., p.30.
7. Ibid., pp.30-31.

consciousness was totally spontaneous, and such a consciousness was nothing at all. It existed only as it moved out of itself, towards objects. But if consciousness existed only as consciousness of objects in the world, if it had no 'world' of its own to dwell in and draw objects into, then it existed only among objects. Consciousness existed, as Heidegger said of *Dasein,* only in-the-world. And, according to Sartre, Heidegger knew that this was no passive waiting among objects. 'Understand this "being-in" in the sense of movement. To be is to burst into the world.'[8] By separating consciousness from its objects, Sartre claimed, Husserl had restored their independence and objectivity. Our various ways of becoming conscious ceased to be mere subjective reactions: 'they are only ways of discovering the world.'[9] Husserl called for a description of phenomena as they appear to consciousness, for there is no noumenon, no hidden being underlying the phenomena, to which we would react in a 'merely' subjective way. The world was simply as it appeared. The world implied by this condition was a highly specific one. For, as we have already seen Sartre say, the absolute separation of consciousness from the world meant that we were 'abandoned by our very nature in an indifferent, hostile, and stubborn world'.[10] We could no longer pretend that it was *we* who constituted the world, that some sort of pre-established harmony existed between it and ourselves.

Sartre's Self-Interpretation

The relationship between this notion of intentionality and the Husserlian original is much more problematic than Sartre admits — as any student of Husserl knows. Sartre in fact abstracts the idea of a relational and active consciousness from the complex context in which alone the idea made sense to Husserl. Consciousness was indeed a 'world' for Husserl, with its ideal entities, structures, and acts: not a container, but a structured means of shaping raw data into a finished world of experience, according to definite patterns and laws.[11] Sartre discards these highly differentiated modes of apprehen-

---

8. Ibid., p.31.
9. Ibid., p.32.
10. Ibid., p.31.
11. See for example the Third and Fourth Sections of Husserl, *Ideas,* especially pp.212-356.

sion precisely because they imply a consciousness possessing structures (and to that extent subject to laws), an ego, and an array of preconscious processes. In their place, he posits the empty acts of a 'nothing' engaged in 'bursting' forth towards the world. Sartre's formulation erases what was the central concern of Husserl: the entire cognitive pre-conscious dimension. He abstracts and retains only a skeletal and rudimentary form of intentionality — that of a bare consciousness approaching an *already existing* world. Setting out his basic terms at the beginning of *L'Etre et le Néant* Sartre clearly and self-consciously distinguishes between his view of intentionality and Husserl's. For him, the notion requires that consciousness be defined as transcendence — going beyond oneself towards the world. 'This was Husserl's essential discovery';[12] but he was to prove 'totally unfaithful to his own principle'. Strictly speaking, 'to say that consciousness is consciousness of something means that for consciousness there is no being outside of that precise *obligation to be a revealing intuition of something — i.e., of a transcendent being.*'[13] But by his erroneous focus on consciousness as constitutive, containing structures, ordered acts and a transcendental Ego, Husserl made the world come to depend on consciousness, rather than seeing consciousness as the spontaneous revelation of objects outside itself. The true goal of phenomenology was rather to explore the concrete, that is, 'man within the world in that specific union of man with the world which Heidegger, for example, calls "being-in-the-world".'[14] Thus, it was Heidegger who influenced Sartre to break with Husserl, to liberate intentionality and throw it in the world.[15] *L'Etre et le Néant* bears the traces of *Being and Time* on virtually every page. It begins, as Heidegger did, by describing the *question* as a basic and characteristic human posture. Heidegger's *Dasein* becomes Sartre's *pour-soi*, inauthenticity becomes bad faith, facticity and thrownness (*Geworfenheit*) become contingency. Sartre also takes over Heidegger's distinction between fear and anguish and his notion of *Dasein* existing in terms of its possibilities.

Heidegger emphasized Being-in-the-world, Husserl emphasized consciousness and its intentionality. Sartre's self-appointed task is to

12. EN, p.28; BN, p.lxi.
13. EN, pp.28-29; BN, p.lxi (emphasis added).
14. EN, p.38; BN, p.3.
15. See Francis Jeanson, p.138.

integrate the most fruitful themes of each into a total analysis, using each as a corrective to the other. Husserl is criticized for having 'shut himself up inside the *cogito*',[16] while Heidegger is taken to task for avoiding 'any appeal to consciousness in his description of *Dasein*.'[17] Sartre's goal is to study intentional consciousness in-the-world, among objects, amidst life struggles.

Consciousness and the World

This he does, insisting above all on the autonomy of consciousness — of necessity, since if it does not exist for itself and through itself (*pour soi et par soi*), then it necessarily exists as a thing; it obeys the laws of things, is determined by forces beyond its control; it is passive. But a spontaneous existent can tolerate no element of passivity, obey no laws, for it would then be determined *by* something else. It must be utterly spontaneous, having no structures, states, or contents. We have already seen Sartre's determination, in his early writings, to sweep consciousness bare of everything located in it by academic idealism, by theories of imagination or of emotion. Nothing could be permitted to qualify the 'monstrous spontaneity' of consciousness, which was either absolute or a mere thing. 'Any inert and opaque content takes its place, by the necessity inherent in its type of existence, among objects, that is to say, in the external world.'[18] The Husserlian transcendental Ego was subject to the same strictures, for, like the Freudian unconscious, it would make the conscious self the mere recipient of states constituted 'behind its back', rather than their absolute creator and support. Being unaware of the structures lying behind itself, consciousness would have no control over them. A transcendental Ego — any structure not immediately visible to consciousness — 'would slide into every consciousness like an opaque blade. The transcendental *I* is the death of consciousness.'[19]

This peculiar dynamic notion of consciousness leads to a specific conception of our relations with the world. And it is here that one aspect of Sartre's thought turns into its opposite. A wholly spontaneous consciousness cannot create or constitute the world. It may

16. EN, p.115; BN, p.73.
17. EN, p.128; BN, p.85.
18. I, p.126; IPC, p.116.
19. TEC, p.40.

only encounter things which are already there when it arrives. It may label them, but it hardly constitutes them in any deeper sense, because to be involved in the world is to become like it, passive, rigorously ordered — unfree. At this point Sartre diverges from Heidegger. Sartre argues that the existence of consciousness *depends on* the existence of things, while Heidegger's formula Being-in-the-world means that man and his world emerge simultaneously. For Heidegger, man is man *in so far as* he forms a world — a connected system of instrumental objects with himself as their centre of reference, and his survival as their ultimate purpose. All dualisms, such as subject and object, consciousness and things, man and nature, arise afterwards, on the foundation of Being-in-the-world, and fail to describe the underlying unity of man-in-the-world. 'The compound expression "Being-in-the-world" indicates in the very way we have coined it, that it stands for a unitary phenomenon. This primary datum must be seen as a whole.'[20] Heidegger then goes on to look at specific objects. Some are ready-to-hand — that is, they are usable. They exist as articulated, identifiable, useful pieces of equipment. On the other hand, an object may take on a 'pure' quality of being-just-present-at-hand when its primary character — its instrumental character — is disturbed. It may become unusable, or broken; or perhaps a necessary piece of equipment is missing. Only then, when its 'assignment' is disturbed, does the object stand out *by itself*, as conspicuous, as obtrusive, as obstinate. But as long as it remains usable the object 'holds itself in' — it is not noticeable for itself. Thus, on the primary ontological level, we focus on the task and not on the object itself.

Heidegger insists that pure thinghood, presence-at-hand — which Sartre regards as primary — is *not* the primary ontological character of entities: 'to lay bare what is just present-at-hand and no more, cognition must first penetrate beyond what is ready-to-hand in our concern. Readiness-to-hand is the way in which entities as they are "in themselves" are defined ontologico-categorically.'[21] Discussing how we first encounter an automobile's directional signal, Heidegger argues that we *do not* authentically see it if we regard it simply as 'a thing'. We more probably, and more authentically, regard it as a

20. Martin Heidegger, *Being and Time*, trans. John Macquarrie and Edward Robinson, New York 1962, p.78.
21. Ibid., p.101.

piece of equipment whose *specific* use we have not yet understood — 'as something ready-to-hand with which we have hitherto not known "how to begin" . . . not as bare thinghood presented for an apprehension of what is just present-at-hand and no more.'[22]

Sartre rejects this account. Taking the term being-in-itself (*être-en-soi, an-sich-sein*) directly from Heidegger, he reverses its meaning. He speaks of the priority and independence of 'the in-itself, which has no need of the for-itself in order to be.'[23] The in-itself simply is. It is prior to consciousness, which could not exist without it 'any more than a colour could exist without form or sound without pitch and without timbre.'[24] The in-itself is eternal and uncreated. 'Uncreated, without reason for being, without any connection with another being, being-in-itself is *de trop* for eternity.'[25] First it is there, and *then* consciousness encounters it, making of it what it will.

Thus, while Heidegger begins by focusing his attention on the active human project in terms of which things take on meaning, Sartre begins by stressing the primacy of the thing. For Sartre, Being-in-the-world comes to mean being among things which are at the outset uncreated, superfluous, with no reason for being. Or, as he declares in 'Une idée', we are thrown by our very nature into an inhospitable world. As long as it is seen in Heidegger's terms as emerging only with an instrumental totality arrayed around it, *Dasein* remains the starting point and the goal, *for whose sake* all tools exist and all actions are taken. Sartre, on the contrary, interprets *Dasein* as consciousness, but a very peculiar one — one which is totally spontaneous, empty, nothing. It cannot *act* on the world. The things around it are independent of consciousness and have no connection with it. They are simply there, present-to-hand, being-in-itself.

Erasing Consciousness

In banishing structures from consciousness Sartre displays a failure to understand why such structures were discovered or conceived initially: to explain how we operate and to explain reality 'out there'. Hume's scepticism perfectly separated consciousness from the things

22. Ibid., p.112.
23. EN, p.716; BN, p.622.
24. EN, p.716; BN, p.621.
25. EN, p.34; BN, p.lxvi.

of which it is conscious: he made clear that the structures we 'perceive' are not in the objects themselves. He demonstrated that the world, seen as completely independent of and beyond us, gives no hint as to how we experience it in a coherent and ordered way. In short, he showed that a world 'given', 'out there', contains in itself absolutely no reason for being intelligible to us. Philosophy had to look elsewhere to explain perception, cognition, and science: to the active, constitutive role of subjectivity. Now, by dissolving the structures of consciousness, Sartre disrupts all those concerns which originally prompted the search for such structures. How we come to have relatively secure knowledge of a world 'out there' — the central problem of rationalism from Descartes to Hegel — becomes wholly obscure. All is then objectivity, is reduced to what we are aware of at the moment, becomes equally inexplicable, equally unmotivated.

Sartre ejects into the world everything that 'idealism' explains through recourse to the structured activity of subjectivity. And therewith, the world becomes a moody, implacable given. Our own actions become completely arbitrary, because 'each instant of our conscious life reveals to us a creation *ex nihilo*.'[26] In his quest for total spontaneity, Sartre alienates us from the world and it from us at the outset. Yet in one sense or another we *create* that world: whether, on the epistemological level, by presenting ourelves with a coherent, intelligible world; on the ontological level, by arraying a world around us whose very being makes sense only with reference to our purposes; on the material level, by engaging in the social activity of labour to create the world we live in; or on the psychological level, by constituting the emotional tone and meaning of every moment of experience. The loss of this insight, borne in so many of the major currents in modern thought — those of Kant, Hegel, Marx, Freud, Husserl and Heidegger — is the real cost of Sartre's insistence on spontaneity.

Accounting for the World

Sartre is not unaware of this. In fact, he self-consciously resists any suggestion that subjectivity constitutes objectivity; 'the world has not created the *me*; the *me* has not created the world.'[27] And he self-

26. TEC, pp.98-99.
27. TEC, pp.105-106.

consciously presents us with a world of unexplained, absurd, meaningless things and actions — this is the gist of several of his stories and of *La Nausée*.

His purpose in doing so is to destroy the idealist notion that consciousness *is* the world. 'Une idée' is unequivocal in this respect: 'we have all read Brunshvicg, Lalande, and Meyerson, we have all believed that the spider-mind attracted things into its web, covered them with a white foam and slowly digested them, reduced them to its own substance. What is a table, a rock, a house? A certain assemblage of "contents of consciousness", an order to these contents. Oh, alimentary philosophy! Nothing seems more evident however: isn't the table the actual content of my perception, isn't my perception the present state of my consciousness?'[28] To suppose that consciousness constitutes the world, Sartre argues, is to destroy the worldliness of the world, to suppress its material reality and independence. To assert its worldliness, on the other hand, is to assert its total independence from consciousness.

But how could such a consciousness come to know and live in a world so drastically different and separate from itself? In order to explain our experience, a new being, quite familiar to traditional philosophy, must be posited prior to consciousness: the for-itself. The for-itself negates the in-itself — presumably in regular, patterned, predictable ways — and so there emerges an ordered, structured, world and a consciousness that comprehends it. But what is this if not the hidden return of pre-conscious constituting processes? Ejected at one moment of the argument, they are readmitted at another — for without them, a pure and clear consciousness would be left helpless before dumb, brute things.

But are we then to say that consciousness is the for-itself, and the world the in-itself? According to Sartre's insistent logic, yes: there are no special *a priori* structures, no pre-conscious processes, nothing *before* consciousness. But according to any logic of intelligibility, no: for without such structures it would be impossible to explain how the world appears as *already* structured, *already* intelligible. Thus, *L'Etre et le Néant* vacillates: now speaking technically of the for-itself and in-itself, as if these were *a priori* ontological and epistemological levels, now speaking of consciousness and the world, as if there were certain

28. 'Une idée', p.29.

specifically epistemological problems to be resolved on a technical level before any approach to people's actual struggles: and at other times speaking of people and things as if the whole matter were at bottom an everyday and worldly one. Only in this way does Sartre manage to account for all the things that are obfuscated by his insistence on the nothingness of consciousness.

From Absolute Objectivism to Absolute Subjectivism

Existential phenomenology as Sartre conceives it seeks to place consciousness in *direct contact* with a finished, given world. Without ceremony, consciousness is thrown into the world, to confront it immediately. 'Thus, in a stroke, those famous "subjective" reactions, hatred, love, fear, sympathy, which floated in the foul-smelling brine of mind, tear themselves away; they are nothing but ways of discovering the world. It is things which are suddenly revealed to us as hateful, sympathetic, horrible, lovable. It is a *property* of this Japanese mask to be terrible, an inexhaustible, irreducible property which constitutes its very nature — and not the sum of our subjective reactions to a piece of carved wood.'[29] Let us consider the implications of this thesis. I experience things directly as they are. Depending on no subjective structure through which to respond to the world, I am omniscient. But, at the same time, I become impotent before a world which is now completely reified — objective, independent of me, beyond my control. 'Everything happens as if we lived in a world whose objects, in addition to their qualities of warmth, odour, shape, etc., had the qualities of repulsive, attractive, delightful, useful, etc., and as if these qualities were forces having a certain power over us.'[30]

All the qualities of that world lie out of reach, *in* the world, by themselves. 'I pity Peter, and I go to his assistance. For my consciousness only one thing exists at that moment: Peter-having-to-be-helped. This quality of "having-to-be-helped" lies in Peter. It acts on me like a force.'[31] It is not my *feeling* about Peter and his danger that drives me to help him. 'There is an objective world of things and of actions, done or to be done, and the actions come to adhere as

29. Ibid., p.32.
30. TEC, p.58.
31. TEC, p.56.

qualities to the things which call for them.'[32] Sartre's formulations imply a positivism which makes it impossible ever to go beyond the given facts to their source: things are simply as they appear. Sartre appeals to 'the absolute law of consciousness for which no distinction is possible between appearance and being.'[33] Consciousness is completely aware of itself at every moment. I am aware of no subjective structures, therefore none exist. The individual is the first thing that is intuitively given. History, the ego, society — all must come later, since they do not *appear* until later. They are never primary, as the *cogito* is.

Now, such realities often are accessible to us, depending on what a certain historically constituted structure of experience makes self-evident and what it conceals. Sartre's approach allows no theoretical ground upon which to go beyond the distortions of experience, no theoretical platform from which to view the adequacy or inadequacy of our immediate consciousness of things, no way of arguing that something we do *not* immediately intuit may be more structurally important than something we do immediately intuit, no means of judging the relation between appearance and being. But the paradoxical effect of his argument is to invert its original terms. Subjectivity, which initially counted for nothing, becomes the supreme judge of experience: what *I see* is the truth. My perception of the world — not the world itself as it exists, as it really comes into being — becomes the measure of things. Sartre's argument suffers the fate of all positivism: in suppressing the subject, we forgo any chance of understanding the world and our relation to it, and instead, elevate a subjective impression of the world to the status of objective truth.

Absolute Freedom?

What then becomes of Sartre's argument that the spontaneity and autonomy of consciousness *depend on* its nothingness, emptiness and self-transparency? What of our absolute freedom?

The counter-argument advanced here brings us to a basic fact of experience: if we are free 'by nature', it is not at all in the absurd way the early Sartre suggests. What is at issue here is the very nature of consciousness — of that in us which projects goals, feels, thinks, plans,

32. TEC, p.56.
33. TEC, p.63.

reflects, orders experience, perceives the world, becomes self-aware, directs our work, communicates with others. The point of using such terms in speaking of 'consciousness' is that they serve to locate that constellation of faculties in the only place where it can actually exist: in our bodies, among other people, in the world. There is a decisive difference between saying *we* are in the world, and are conscious of it, and saying *consciousness* is in the world. *We* are materially, socially, historically conditioned: we can never be absolutely undetermined, absolutely spontaneous. All the modes of our awareness and cognition cannot but be affected by the process of which they are part, which they limit and which limits them, which they shape and which shapes them. But consciousness, as Sartre derives it from Husserlian epistemology, is hardly substantive enough to be part of such a process. It is, after all, a rather peculiar being. Sartre declares that 'any study of human reality must begin with the *cogito*', and goes on to focus on an unworldly, interior layer of consciousness originally abstracted by Husserl for epistemological purposes. Interiority, of course, is a necessary element at some stages of epistemological study. The world must temporarily be ignored if it is to be seen how consciousness assembles its cognizable sense of objects. This is why Husserl spoke of *bracketing* the world. But Sartre seizes on this inward aspect of consciousness and straightaway transposes it into a world of peeping Toms, dishonest homosexuals, and supercilious waiters. Interiority-in-the-world: it is a contradiction in terms. But this formulation (which is my own) conveys much of the sense of Sartre's enterprise. The incongruity that it evokes is the basis of his 'extreme subjectivism',[34] and the predicament of a freedom which, to the extent that it insists on its absolute character, is confined to the total, useless indeterminacy of the *irréel*.

Philosophy-in-the-World

This contradiction was also emblematic of Sartre's project as a philosopher in this first period. His purpose, made manifest in the short essay on Husserl, was to direct philosophy into the world. 'Une idée' rendered the significance of Husserl's thought in the most vivid

---

34. Theodor Adorno, 'Commitment', *New Left Review*, 87-88 (September-December, 1974), p.78.

and concrete terms. 'The philosophy of transcendence throws us on the highway, in the midst of menaces, under a blinding light.'[35] Consciousness was an 'escape' a 'refusal', a 'flight', a 'connected series of explosions'. The intent of Sartre's tone and idiom were reminiscent of a foregoing tradition of philosophical rebellion. Sartre too insisted that the language of literature, of the streets, was both appropriate and necessary in philosophical discussion of human life. Yet there was an important difference between Sartre and, say, Nietzsche. The purpose of Nietzsche's language was the transformation, the subversion of philosophical discourse. It was in its own way what Marx's social theory was in another: the end of philosophy as such. A glance at *L'Etre et le Néant* — or indeed *La Nausée* — reveals Sartre's distance from these thinkers in this respect. Like Husserl and Heidegger, he remained a philosopher, seeking the most general, timeless underlying structures of being, from which to deduce consequences for human life in the world. Truth was universal and *a priori*, and was unfolded in a systematic way by analysis of primary structures. Sartre's goal was to create a 'phenomenological ontology'. Thus, for all the vividness and concreteness of its illustrations and examples, his basic purpose — the search for *being* — was intelligible to rationalist philosophers who would have been initially disoriented by the writings of, say, Marx. In Marx, the search for timeless structures was abandoned in favour of the study of actual social activity in history. Sartre's break with tradition was more modest, accomplished not in the subversion of philosophy as such but in the elaboration of a new philosophical system. As Simone de Beauvoir remarked, the young Sartre wanted to bring philosophy into the world — to reform its stance and preoccupations, not to transform its nature. The systematic study of timeless universals was henceforth to illuminate our daily experience.

Philosophy-in-the-world: this intellectual orientation underlay the strange juxtapositions of the recondite and the everyday that characterized most of Sartre's early writings. *La Transcendence de l'ego* cited the commonplace — the desire to help Peter, waiting for a bus — in the service of technical arguments concerning the structure of the ego; and in *La Nausée,* ontological meditation was interwoven with incisive naturalist descriptions of everyday incidents.

35. 'Une idée', p.31.

The problem was, as Camus said of *La Nausée,* that the two dimensions of discourse were not integrated. Try as he might, Sartre only intensified the impression that he was lifting terms from a (properly) remote and (properly) technical realm of discourse and straightaway imposing them on worldly processes that had their own, quite different, dynamics. It may be possible, as Lenin suggested, to make a dialectical analysis of a glass of water. But such an analysis would neither apply philosophy to the glass nor read philosophy in it; rather, it would use the tools developed by dialectical thought — such as the notions of contradiction, change and history — to study this specific glass of water in its specific situation. Sartre's account of the dialectic between the self and the Other envisaged something quite different, showing, through the study of the structures of being, what forms human relationships *must take,* what their content *must be.* In the first case, philosophy provides tools to be applied to specific situations; in the second, answers to impose on them.

What then can we conclude about Sartre's existentialism in its first stage, that of philosophy-in-the-world? Sartre thrust into a finished and given world a totally spontaneous consciousness abstracted from technical epistemological analysis. He then studied these two terms, outside of history and social life, hoping to grasp their fundamental, timeless interrelations. However, such a consciousness could never be at home in the world. In one respect, Sartre detached it totally to preserve its freedom; in another, it was an alien being from the start. Isolated in its freedom, threatened by an overwhelming existence, consciousness could not 'act on anything but itself'. So, it transpired that the main motive of consciousness-in-the-world seemed to be to escape from the world: from *L'Imagination* to *L'Etre et le Néant* and, as we shall see, right down to *L'Idiot de la famille* — Sartre's existentialism was preoccupied with patterns of withdrawal, and with situations so adverse as to tempt us to withdraw.

At this point, our study of the structures and tensions of Sartre's early thought rejoins our description of his personal, political and intellectual starting points. Interiority-in-the-world and philosophy-in-the-world are appropriate characterizations of the projects conceived by the writer described in our first chapter. The radical separation which we have discerned at the root of Sartre's thought, between humans and their world, a separation which he postulated from the outset, and which he simultaneously contested and upheld, was inscribed in the biographical-historical and intellectual situation in which he began to write.

By 1943 Sartre's thought had not yet anchored itself in the world, although the whole of *L'Etre et le Néant* moved towards the exploration of action in the world. How were the questions posed at the end of that work — questions concerning an effective way of being in the world, without bad faith — to be answered? From now on, Sartre's dynamism was to be concentrated in an effort to overcome the radical separation that he postulated. But he had also, by 1943, created a formidable intellectual structure whose list was towards the *irréel*; and in this, as he later acknowledged, lay his 'ideological interest' — 'the fact of having written some books and of protecting them as an interest, of not renouncing them.'[36] The remainder of this study will follow Sartre's continuing effort to situate his thought in the world, on the basis of this intellectual structure, and will examine his complex record of success and failure in this attempt.

36. *Sartre,* pp.84-85.

Two

Discovering
the World

1

Turning Points

In October 1945, a new journal appeared in Paris: *Les Temps Modernes,*
so named in part because of the pleasing sound of its initials and its
allusion to Chaplin's last silent film.[1] It was launched with a powerful
and deeply controversial introduction written by its main editor, Jean-
Paul Sartre. The 'Présentation des "Temps Modernes" ' aligned the
journal with the Left and called writers to political commitment.[2]
Within a month André Gide fired off the first reply in the critical bar-
rage provoked by Sartre's notion of *engagement.* Sartre clarified and
deepened his argument in several subsequent essays, culminating in
the book length *Qu'est-ce que la littérature?*, which was printed in suc-
cessive issues of *Les Temps Modernes* from February to July, 1947. Thus,
the public storms that accompanied Sartre's and de Beauvoir's sudden
rise to fame in the autumn of 1945 were reflected in a smaller but no
less intense quarrel among writers. The very nature of literature
demanded political engagement on the side of the Left, Sartre now
argued — and he deduced this proposition from the basic principles of
his philosophy.

What was it that had so transformed the once reclusive Sartre by
1945? His own retrospective answer was simple: 'the war opened my
eyes.'[3] In 1947, he looked back on the years 'from 1930 on': 'historicity
flowed in upon us; in everything we touched, in the air we breathed, in

1. Simone de Beauvoir, *La Force des choses,* p.25; *Force of Circumstance,* p.14.
2. *Situations,* II, pp.9-30.
3. Philippe Gavi, Jean-Paul Sartre, Pierre Victor, *On a raison de se révolter,* Paris 1974,
p.24.

the page we read, in the one we wrote.'[4] External events, history, becoming overwhelming, compelled acknowledgement of their own reality. The world itself destroyed Sartre's illusions about isolated self-determining individuals and made clear his own personal stake in the events of his time. Sartre captured this enormous change in the first two volumes of *Les Chemins de la liberté,* written in 1939-1941 and 1943-1944 respectively, and explained it in a note he wrote for insertion in them: 'during the deceptive calm of 1937-38, there were people in certain circles who could still maintain the illusion of having their neatly walled-off and impenetrable histories. That is why I chose to narrate *The Age of Reason* in the conventional manner, showing only the relations between a few individuals. But when the days of September 1938 came, the walls came tumbling down. The individual, without ceasing to be a monad, becomes aware that he is playing in a more than individual game. He is still a window on the world, but he discovers unexpectedly that his life is taking on a general meaning and coming apart at the seams. It is a monad which has sprung a leak, and which will always keep on leaking even though it will not sink. To account for the ambiguity of this condition, I had to resort to the "wide screen" technique. All the characters in *The Age of Reason* will reappear in *The Reprieve,* only this time as lost people thwarted by a crowd of other people.'[5] The broad historical and intellectual outlines of Sartre's process of change are well described in Michel-Antoine Burnier's *Choice of Action* — his pro-Left but detached political stance in the mid-thirties, the shocking impact of Munich in September 1938, his return from mobilization and a prisoner-of-war camp, his activist and literary efforts during the Occupation, and finally, the decision to found *Les Temps Modernes.*[6] What, in each of these wartime experiences, led Sartre towards the political conversion announced in the first issue of *Les Temps Modernes?*

Two things stand out in Simone de Beauvoir's account of the time between Sartre's mobilization and departure for Alsace in September 1939, and the late spring of 1940. First, his military life displayed a striking continuity with his civilian past: above all, he kept on

---

4. QL, p.243; WL, p.207.
5. CRW, 45/61, p.113 (translation changed).
6. Trans. Bernard Murchland, New York 1968, pp.3-13. This detailed, informative study traces the development of Sartre's political positions and actions up to 1965.

writing. De Beauvoir quotes Sartre's description of his military life during the winter of the 'Phoney War': 'my work here consists of sending up balloons and then watching them through a pair of field glasses: this is called "making a meteorological observation." Afterwards I phone the battery artillery officers and tell them the wind direction: what they do with this information is their affair. The young ones make some use of the intelligence reports; the old school just shove them straight in the wastepaper basket. Since there isn't any shooting either course is equally effective. It's extremely peaceful work (I can't think of any branch of the services that has a quieter, more poetic job, apart from the pigeon breeders, that is, always supposing there are any of them left nowadays) and I'm left with a large amount of spare time, which I'm using to finish my novel. I hope it'll be out in a few months' time – I can't really see anything the censors could object to in it, apart from a lack of "moral health", and anyway I can't rewrite it.'[7] Military life turned out so unexpectedly normal, and even tranquil, that Sartre began to speculate whether modern war could be without slaughter 'just as a modern painting has no subject, modern music no melody and modern physics no solid matter.'[8] It permitted him still to occupy his time and mind with writing. And as usual, Simone de Beauvoir and Sartre read and commented on each other's work during their visits together.

Nevertheless, Sartre's mobilization led to profound changes in his outlook. Two new experiences in particular were decisive: his life was now fully in the grip of forces beyond his control, and he had become simply one man among others. He reflected on these experiences thirty years later: 'as for the fine little well-scrubbed atom I believed myself to be, powerful forces seized him, and sent him to the front with others without asking his opinion. The duration of the war, and above all of internment in Germany (which I escaped by passing myself off as a civilian) was for me the occasion for a lasting immersion in the crowd, which I believed I had escaped and which I had in fact never left.'[9]

In joining his unit, he was following orders: 'Sartre's action,' de

---

7. *La Force de l'âge*, p.440; *The Prime of Life*, p.340.
8. Ibid., p.430; p.333.
9. *On a raison de se révolter*, p.24.

Beauvoir wrote at the time, 'looks completely free and voluntary, yet obeys the dictates of an inflexible and self-generated compulsion that operates quite independently of the human will.'[10] Until August, 1944, they were to be governed by such compulsions: life lived under orders and under threat was no longer purely private and self-determined.

Sartre was also joining the crowd. This is strikingly conveyed by de Beauvoir's diary account of the end of Sartre's leave on February 15, 1940: 'Sartre gets into uniform again. We reach the station just before 9.15. Large notice up announcing that all trains for men going back from leave will depart at 9.25. Crowds of soldiers and their womenfolk making for the underground passage. Am reasonably calm, but the idea of this departure as part of a collective move I find distressing. The scene on the platform brings a lump to my throat — all these men and women with their awkward handshakes! There are two crowded trains, one on either side. The right-hand one pulls out, and a *long* line of women — some mothers, but mostly wives or girl friends — drift away, eyes glassy and red-rimmed: some of them are sobbing. A few elderly fathers among them, a dozen at most: this separation of the sexes is a primitive business, with the men being carried off and the women returning to town. There are very few tearful ones among those waiting for the departure of the second train, though some cling desperately around their lovers' necks; you can sense a warm, passionate night behind them, and the lack of sleep, and the nervous exhaustion that morning has brought. The soldiers make joking little remarks like, "Look at the waterworks!" but you can feel their closeness and solidarity. Just as the train is about to leave, a crowd of them jam the door of the carriage, and all I can see of Sartre in a dark corner of the compartment is his garrison cap, and his glasses, and an intermittently waving hand. The fellow in front at the door steps back and lets another take his place. The newcomer embraces a woman, then calls out, "Who's next?" The women line up and each takes her turn on the step, me among them. Then Sartre vanishes inside again. Violent feeling of collective tension in the air: this train's departure is really like a physical severance. Then the break comes, and it's gone. I'm the first to leave, walking very fast.'[11] The once isolated individual disappears in the crowd as his like-

10. *La Force de l'âge*, p.392; *The Prime of Life*. p.304.
11. Ibid., pp.443-44; p.343.

minded companion resists her own immersion. His fate, his chances, his risks are now the same as everyone else's.

These glimpses help to explain the change that de Beauvoir had seen in Sartre as they walked and talked during that February leave. 'Sartre was thinking about the post-war period; he had firmly made up his mind to hold aloof from politics no longer.'[12] Every man should 'shoulder the responsibility of his situation in life' by acting, he now believed. De Beauvoir emphasizes the depth of this change in Sartre — and in herself. It was time to give up escapism, to stop holding their 'situation at arm's length by means of fantasy, deception and plain lies'.

Sartre himself dates his political engagement from his next wartime experience, as a prisoner of war from June 1940 to March 1941.[13] He continued to work: three times a week he lectured on Heidegger to priests who were his fellow-prisoners; he went on planning the philosophical work which was to become *L'Etre et le Néant*; and he wrote a play, *Bariona,* which was performed by his fellow-prisoners at Christmas. But more important was his new-found sense of solidarity with his comrades, born of equality of situation, constant physical contact and perpetual communication.[14] Equally important, politics now became part of the substance of his life. Faced daily with their captors and with French collaborators and quietists, Sartre and other anti-fascists in the Stalag 'formed a sort of small, tight-knit fraternity, whose members were bound by an unspoken oath — never to compromise, to reject all concessions. Each member swore to keep rigorously to this rule when separated from the others.'[15] In his Christmas play about the birth of Christ and the Roman occupation of Palestine, Sartre spoke to his fellow prisoners about their common condition and sought to arouse their spirit of resistance to Nazism.

Thus, returning to Paris in March 1941, Sartre was determined to act. With de Beauvoir, Merleau-Ponty, and other students and intellectuals, he immediately took steps to form a Resistance group. The group was called 'Socialisme et Liberté', reflecting its concern to link the struggle for liberation to a fight for a democratic socialist society. They circulated news bulletins, made contact with other Resistance

12. Ibid., pp.443-44; p.343.
13. *Sartre,* p.68.
14. *Sartre,* p.67.
15. *La Force de l'âge,* p.493; *The Prime of Life.* p.381.

groups, and Sartre himself travelled to the Free Zone in an abortive effort to establish contact with a number of possible supporters and a larger central body. But most of the small groups that had sprung up immediately after the defeat soon disbanded, and Sartre approached the Communist Party to establish some sort of common front — again, without success. Rebuffed by the Communists, Sartre's group was now totally isolated at a time when tensions were rising and the Gestapo was beginning to arrest and deport resistance activists. Concluding that its slight efficacy bore no relation to the enormous risks its members ran, Sartre reluctantly decided to disband 'Socialisme et Liberté' in October 1941.

His isolation lasted until early in 1943, when PCF intellectuals invited him to join the writers' Resistance group, the Comité National des Ecrivains. For the rest of the war he participated actively in the CNE and its parallel theatre organization, writing for the underground *Les Lettres françaises* and attending many meetings. Such underground activities had, in de Beauvoir's words, 'an almost routine flavour about them',[16] and Sartre continued his other writing projects during the Occupation, but danger and fear remained real. Many of their friends and acquaintances — Communists and other activists as well as Jews — were arrested, deported, and killed. Gestapo torture was a daily reality that preoccupied everyone.[17] In mid-July 1944, a member of the *Combat* movement, with which they were associated through Albert Camus, was arrested, divulged names to the police, and then got word out to his comrades. Camus advised Sartre and de Beauvoir to move for the time being. They left Paris for four weeks, returning only when they heard that the American columns were nearing Chartres and that liberation was at hand.

All the Resistance groups in Paris had resolved that, whatever the risks and costs, the capital would be liberated by its own people. At Camus's request, Sartre wrote a series of articles on the insurrection for *Combat* between August 28 and September 4. Walking and cycling around Paris, Sartre gave a detailed description of the last days of the Occupation and the Allies' entry into Paris. In contrast with his stance in the days of the Popular Front, he was no longer an outsider. He identified himself with the crowd which 'had finally decided to take its destiny into its own hands.'[18] Reporting for a still-clandestine

16. Ibid., p.550; p.425.
17. See, for example, QL, p.246; WL, p.211.
18. From 'Colère d'une ville,' *Combat,* August 30, 1944; CRW, p.101.

newspaper, he was present at, part of, and was to be indelibly marked by, this festival of the oppressed, this great moment of collective life.

Turning Points: Literary

Sartre's literary and political activities did not develop in unison. *Les Chemins de la liberté,* begun in 1939, pondered new directions that its author had not yet taken. He had long been committed to the Resistance when the Occupation censors permitted Gallimard to issue *L'Etre et le Néant* — by which time he had already written in the clandestine bulletin of 'Socialisme et Liberté' and in the Resistance newspaper, *Les Lettres françaises.*

However there was one decisive literary indication of Sartre's development after 1939 in his turn to the theatre. In writing *Bariona,* Sartre was continuing his usual civilian activity. But for the first time he was also *acting* with his pen. We have already seen that, in one respect, writing books had had virtually the same meaning for Sartre when he was writing *La Nausée* as during his time at the Ecole Normale or indeed in his childhood. His audience was irrelevant, or perhaps a vehicle for his personal salvation; at best he wrote *against* his audience with the enormous missionary zeal of someone combating false truths. The experience of writing, staging and acting in *Bariona* transformed his attitude: it let him 'speak as a prisoner to other prisoners and bring up our common problems.'[19] Writing now became a direct, transparently social activity. Sartre never published *Bariona* or sought to have it publicly performed — 'because it was such a bad play', he later recalled. 'Nevertheless, on this occasion, as I addressed my comrades across the footlights, speaking to them of their state as prisoners, when I suddenly saw them so remarkably silent and attentive, I realized what the theatre ought to be — a great collective, religious phenomenon.' By 'religious', of course, Sartre had in mind neither God nor the church, but the process of reaffirming a deep, common social faith — in this case, the common spirit of resistance to Nazism.[20]

---

19. Interview by Paul-Louis Mignon, CRW, 68/487 and 62/368, p.412.

20. 'Forger des mythes', *Un théâtre de situations,* (TS), edited by Michel Contat and Michel Rybalka, Paris 1973, p.62; trans. Frank Jellinek, 'Forgers of Myths', *Sartre on Theater,* (ST), p.39. (In this volume Contat and Rybalka have faithfully and painstakingly collected and ordered virtually everything Sartre has said on theatre.)

Bariona deserves wider reading and close study. At its climax, the entire town population rises up suicidally against the Roman legions in order to create time for Joseph, Mary and the newborn Jesus to escape. *Bariona* reflected both the impossible situation of

Sartre's first publicly performed play, *Les Mouches,* was staged in Paris under the Occupation and was equally a political act. 'It was 1943 and Vichy wanted to mire us deeper in repentance and shame,' he recalled later. 'In writing *Les Mouches,* I tried with the small means available to me to help extirpate somewhat this sickness of repenting, this giving in to shame that they were trying to get out of us.'[21] In this version of Aeschylus's *The Libation Bearers,* a latter-day Orestes sets out to find his roots; decides to act and kills his father's usurper and his mother; refuses to become guilty as he rejects the authority of Zeus, and goes off alone, pursued by flies and furies demanding repentance. In this way, Sartre counselled rebellion under the very eye of the censor.

His next play, *Huis Clos,* first performed in 1944, was a somewhat timeless exploration of human relations, and seemed remote from political concerns. The hell of other people portrayed in it was an analogue of the philosophy of human relations expounded in *L'Etre et le Néant.* Nevertheless, as I shall argue later, *Huis Clos* is best viewed in the context of Sartre's consistent dramatic concern: the exploration of political action. For Sartre's plays — eight of them written after 1945 — form an impressive and, for France, unique body of politically committed theatre, evidence of the enduring effect of his wartime transformation.[22]

Turning Points: 'Les Temps Modernes'

The editorial group of *Les Temps Modernes* initially included Raymond Aron, Michel Leiris, Maurice Merleau-Ponty, Albert Ollivier, Jean Paulhan, Sartre and de Beauvoir — Camus declining membership because of his work at *Combat.*[23] The journal was an immediate success, achieving and maintaining a circulation of 11,000.

Christmas 1940, and Sartre's sense of the impasse of human existence. Yet, writing for and expressing the needs of the collectivity to which he suddenly belonged, speaking also of hope and collective action, Sartre wrote against his own world view, to encourage a spirit of resistance to the Germans' overwhelming power. Moreover, he had become close to several priests in his prison camp. Out of solidarity with them and a wish to unite all the French prisoners, he did not dare to attack their faith. Indeed, only the pretext of Christmas could have enabled the prisoners to stage so subversive a play. Obliged in these ways to treat Christianity positively, Sartre discovered in it currents of hope that he had previously mocked or overlooked.

21. 'Ce que fut la création des "Mouches" ' ('What the Staging of *The Flies* was Like'), *Le Figaro,* January 11, 1951; CRW, 51/37, p.88 (translation changed).

22. TS, p.12; ST, p.ix.

23. For this history, see Burnier, *Choice of Action,* pp.19-37.

The political character of the review was rapidly clarified as the Cold War set in. By the tenth issue, Aron and Ollivier had resigned. The editorial for December 1946, the first to be signed on behalf of the board as a whole, protested forcefully at the efforts of the French Government to re-impose colonial rule in Vietnam. *Les Temps Modernes* met the need for an intellectual rallying-point for non-Party socialists, establishing itself as a journal sympathetic to Marxism and Communism yet willing to analyse and criticize in a non-sectarian spirit.

Any randomly selected issue would show a broad range of articles and an impressive list of contributors. For example, No.156-157, published in early 1959 during the struggle over Algeria, included three articles on Algerian 'Myths and Realities', an inquiry by Serge Mallet into 'New Aspects of French Industry', an excerpt from Isaac Deutscher's biography of Trotsky, and an essay by Lucien Goldmann on reification. Through the years, Sartre and de Beauvoir were themselves to publish extensively in the journal, serializing many of their major works in it.

Sartre's activity as *directeur* was, by his own admission, inconsistent. He was deeply involved in the journal at the beginning, although Merleau-Ponty was its original political guide. Then, as Merleau-Ponty chose silence in response to the Korean War, the journal drifted aimlessly until Sartre asserted his pro-Communist direction and Merleau-Ponty departed. During the Algerian war Sartre was again intensely involved, making *Les Temps Modernes* a centre of resistance to French policy. The journal became important to him again after May 1968. More perhaps than any of his books, *Les Temps Modernes* incarnated Sartre's goal of intellectual commitment.

Turning Points: Intellectual

The third issue of *Les Temps Modernes*, published in December 1945, contained 'Portrait de l'antisémite', the first part of an essay that Sartre had written late the previous year. The full text of this work appeared in the autumn of 1946 as a book, *Réflexions sur la question juive*. In writing it, Sartre revealed his determination henceforward to confront the most difficult issues of his time.

France would have to come to grips with the single most shameful fact of the Occupation and Vichy years, Sartre insisted: its policies towards French and refugee Jews. Anti-semitism was still alive, and was deeply rooted in French society. Sartre incisively analysed the anti-semitic personality, and went on to sketch the authentic and inauthentic responses open to Jews — developing, as part of his discussion, a brilliant if partial explanation of the supposed Jewish love of rationalism. In conclusion, he rapidly sketched the only adequate basis for a definitive solution of the problem of anti-semitism: a classless society based on human solidarity.

This essay is striking for many reasons. More than anything he had yet written, *Réflexions sur la question juive* showed Sartre taking action as a writer in a sustained way. Second, it revealed for the first time his deep attachment to the oppressed. And third, the essay was Sartre's first effort to contribute specifically to social thought. However, for our own present purpose, the most pertinent feature of *Réflexions* is that it represented a systematic application to a social question of the categories of *L'Etre et le Néant*.

Sartre studied anti-semitism and the Jewish response to it as instances of individual choice, using *authenticity* and *bad faith, freedom* and *the situation,* as his central analytic categories. He understood Jewishness not as inherited biological or historical fact, but rather as existing only *in a situation*. In other words — those of the book's sharpest statement — Jewish identity was created by the anti-semite: 'it is neither their past, their religion, nor their soil that unites the sons of Israel. If they have a common bond, if all of them deserve the name of Jew, it is because they have in common the situation of Jew, that is, they live in a community which takes them for Jews.'[24] Thus, the basis of Jewishness was to be found in the dialectic of the self and the Other. Anti-semitism was a flight from freedom, an effort to attain the impenetrability of things.

Sartre himself later identified some of the severe limitations of his analysis, remarking in 1966 that it lacked any historical or economic dimension. This lack was evident in his focus on the *psychology* of Jew and anti-semite rather than on the concrete social issue and how to fight it. Thus, his newly acquired political radicalism was at odds with his habits and categories of thought. Yet it should be recognized that *Réflexions sur la question juive* was written in October 1944, after Sartre's basic philosophical categories had been defined but before they had

24. *Réflexions sur la question juive,* Paris 1946; trans. George J. Becker, *Anti-Semite and Jew,* New York 1948, p.67.

begun to be affected by his new political commitment. As a political analyst, he relied heavily on *L'Etre et le Néant,* and did little more than apply its theses to the social world. We know, however, that much of what we have studied there was incompatible with Sartre's enormous optimism in the period that saw the founding of *Les Temps Modernes.* Accordingly, Sartre's earlier insistence on the ontological character of human problems would have to defer to a new exploration of history and society. His desire to understand the world could not but be modified by his new-found urge to transform it.

The 'Presentation' of *Les Temps Modernes* revealed the depth at which Sartre had now begun to re-think himself: as an individual caught up in a certain history, as a writer and as an analyst of human life. Problems which he had earlier explained ontologically were now defined in social terms. Pessimism gave way before combative hope. Engagement was affirmed not only as a responsibility but as a condition of personal fulfilment. 'Since the writer has no means to escape, we want him to embrace his time tightly; it his unique chance: it made itself for him and he is made for it. One regrets Balzac's indifference to the 1848 Revolution, Flaubert's frightened incomprehension of the Commune. One regrets it for *them.* There is something there that they missed forever. We do not want to miss anything in our time. There may be some more beautiful, but this one is our own. We have only *this* life to live, in the middle of *this* war, of *this* revolution perhaps. Let us not draw the conclusion that we speak for a kind of populism. It is quite the contrary. Populism is the child of old parents, the dull off-spring of the last Realists. It is another attempt to get out of the game unharmed. We are convinced, on contrary, that one *cannot* get out of the game unharmed. Should we be mute and quiet as stones, our very passivity would be an action. The abstention of the man who would devote his life to writing novels about the Hittites would be, in itself, taking up a position. The writer is *situated* in his time. Every word has consequences. Every silence, too. I hold Flaubert and Goncourt responsible for the repression which followed the Commune because they did not write one line to prevent it. One might say that it was not their business. But was the Calas trial Voltaire's business? Dreyfus's condemnation Zola's? The administration of the Congo, Gide's? Each of these authors, in a special circumstance of his life, measured his responsibility as a writer. The Occupation taught us ours. Since we act on our time by our very existence, we decide that this action will be deliberate.'[25]

Political commitment, even when defended so eloquently as here, could not deepen and take effect in the ontological impasse of *L'Etre et le Néant*. How then was Sartre's new stance to be grounded, intellectually and in practice? We have seen his early sympathy for the PCF and the *idea* of socialism. But we have also seen his personal fear of social change and his indifference to Marxism as a theoretical guide to the understanding that he sought. How did he now regard Marxism, as theory and as movement, immediately after the Liberation? His attitude was ambivalent. Some years later, in the 1950s, he recalled the vague but persistent attraction that Marxism had exerted on him since the 1930s, and which had become clearer during the war: the attraction, not of a philosophical outlook, nor of a political movement, but of a unique combination of the two. 'I repeat it, it was not the idea which unsettled us; nor was it the condition of the worker, which we knew abstractly but which we had not experienced. No, it was the two joined together. It was — as we would have said then in our idealist jargon even as we were breaking with idealism — the Proletariat as the incarnation and vehicle of an idea.'[26] In other words, the theory by itself affected him far less than the fact of its connection with real political forces: the Party and the workers movement. As a philosopher, we know, he had been searching for *the concrete*. The war, the Occupation, and the Resistance led him to it, but in a way destined to turn his thinking upside down. Marxism claimed that its truth was verified *outside* of ideas: in the struggle, and eventual victory, of the proletariat. 'We wanted to fight at the side of the working class; we finally understood that the concrete is history and dialectical action.'[27]

The grasp of reality that Sartre had been seeking in his early period, it was now becoming clear, was attained in action. He had come to see this during the war years, in his relations with the PCF and his experience of the Resistance. The PCF, guided by a philosophy, was a well-organized and powerful machine, the leading force in the

25. 'Présentation des *Temps modernes*', *Situations*, II, pp.12-13; trans. Françoise Ehrman, 'Introduction to *Les Temps Modernes*', Eugen Weber, *Paths to the Present*, New York 1960, pp.433-34.
26. QM, p.24; SM, p.20.
27. QM, p.24; SM, p.20.

Resistance. In 1941 Sartre had been obliged to withdraw from political activity because it had rebuffed his lone attempt to set up a common front; two years later, when PCF intellectuals invited him to join the CNE and write for *Les Lettres françaises,* he responded eagerly. During the war Sartre had become an active supporter of socialism and revolution; the PCF, France's largest party at the time of the Liberation, was *the* party of socialism and revolution. However, as the solidary spirit of the Resistance began to wane, the PCF began to perceive Sartre's new philosophy as its competitor among young intellectuals. Its writers attacked Sartre for his recourse to Heidegger, a Nazi thinker; as a philosopher of quietism, despair and nihilism; as a writer preoccupied with filth and human wickedness.

Just enough of the old spirit remained for *Action,* a PCF weekly, to publish Sartre's reply to these attacks, in December 1944. In this essay, Sartre indicated his adherence to certain fundamental tenets of socialism. Like the PCF, he was fighting for the revolution; he 'subscribed completely' to the fact of the class struggle, and wanted to see an end to the privileges of capitalist society. At the same time he asserted a connection with Marx in his belief that men made themselves rather than fulfilling any pre-given essence, and in his central emphasis on action. Furthermore, with characteristic self-confidence, he presented his own philosophy as more adequate for revolutionaries than materialism, because it endowed human beings with responsibility for their lot and freedom to change it. Existentialism, then, was '*no mournful delectation but a humanist philosophy of action, effort, combat and solidarity.*' [28]

After months of silence, *Action* resumed the attack, this time with Henri Lefebvre indicting Sartre as an idealist, a subjectivist, and a part of the war machine against Marxism. *L'Humanité* followed suit, dismissing existentialists as lackeys of de Gaulle or of American imperialism. [29] Puzzled and hurt by these attacks, Sartre persevered in his project of articulating a pro-revolutionary but democratic politics aligned with yet independent of the PCF, accepting some Marxist ideas but still far distant from the theoretical core of Marxism.

28. 'A propos de l'éxistentialisme: mise au point', *Action,* December 29, 1944; trans. Richard McCleary, 'A More Precise Characterization of Existentialism,' CRW, vol. II: *Selected Prose,* p. 160.

29. This episode is related by Burnier, pp.39-51.

It was in this frame of mind that Sartre wrote 'Matérialisme et révolution' (1946), a striking attempt to cast his own philosophy as a suitable revolutionary alternative to Marxism. His central theme was the need to place the human impulse to transform and create — the impulse of freedom — at the heart of a revolutionary outlook; the need, that is, to supply what he found lacking in his reading of Marxism. This essay throws considerable light on Sartre's development in relation to Marxism. A rather abstract treatise on revolutionary thought, it was wholly lacking in historical and social analysis. Elsewhere, as an essayist calling for political engagement in writing, Sartre had begun to situate himself in his time; but as a philosopher he remained a stranger to the historical and social dimension. Furthermore, it gave no evidence of any real engagement with Marx's writings: in his critique of Marxism, Sartre was still in effect trying to steer between mechanistic materialism and idealism. He had read Stalin's *Dialectical and Historical Materialism,* and quoted it three times — more often than the writings of Marx or Engels. The impression thus given that Sartre had not yet seriously begun to read Marx in 1946 was confirmed by five footnotes added, and one expanded, for republication in 1949 in *Situations,* III.[30] Four of these indicated further reading of Marx. The most noteworthy of them distinguished Marx from the 'neo-Stalinist Marxism' of 1949, against which Sartre now claimed to have written his essay. In the expanded footnote, he added to a new bibliographical citation the distinction between 'the use made of ["objectivity"] today' and Marx's 'much deeper and richer conception', promising to develop this theme elsewhere.[31] Thus, it was only from around 1949 that Sartre was able to reflect on Marxian theory as distinct from the official Communist movement's version of it. This distinction was the fundamental precondition of his future intellectual development.

Towards 'Qu'est-ce que la Littérature?'

Thus, if Sartre was now a socialist activist, and a critic of the PCF and its philosophers, his relationship with Marxist theory had not yet

---

30. CRW, p.153. Contat and Rybalka call attention to these variants; close comparison of the two texts reveals still further alterations.

31. 'Matérialisme et révolution', *Situations,* III, Paris 1949, p.141; trans. Annette Michelson, *Literary and Philosophical Essays,* New York 1955, p.188.

become dominant among his intellectual concerns. His chief preoccupation was with the implications of his new political stance, and with the production of a body of work that expressed or explored it. Certain of the works of this phase have already been mentioned — the projected tetralogy of novels and the early plays. Others included the famous lecture, *L'Existentialisme est un humanisme*, the study of Baudelaire, two plays, *La Putain respectueuse* and *Morts sans sépulture* — and, above all, *Qu'est-ce que la littérature?*.

This crucial work set down the most important single conclusion reached by Sartre in the war years, in a sustained exploration and defence of the path of political commitment. But more than this — perhaps in consequence of the topic under discussion — *Qu'est-ce que la littérature?* referred back to his pre-war thought in a way that none of the works contemporaneous with it did. Sartre now reflected on virtually every important theme of his early thought and began to explore alternative solutions to the problems posed there. The relations between the pre-war theorist of imagination and the post-war exponent of *littérature engagée*, between the ontology of the first period and the politics of the second, now came into clear intellectual focus.

2

The Literary Kingdom of Ends

Why write? This is one of the organizing questions of *Qu'est-ce que la littérature?*. The question returns us to the ontological plane of *L'Etre et le Néant* but in such a way as to allow its transmutation into a field of social and historical action. In *Qu'est-ce que la littérature?* Sartre grants the individual an aesthetic satisfaction denied him by *L'Etre et le Néant*, a temporary resolution of his ontological struggles, whose purpose, however, is to propel him into a more concrete political struggle.

As in *L'Etre et le Néant*, Sartre maintains that I write in order to feel essential to the world. I want to see it as myself, and not as an alien and indifferent being; I want to overcome its self-sufficiency, to make it depend on me. 'If I fix on canvas or writing a certain aspect of the fields or the sea or a look on someone's face which I have disclosed, I am conscious of having produced them by condensing relationships, by introducing order where there was none, by imposing the unity of mind on the diversity of things.'[1]

But why should this impulse to mastery entail a retreat into art? Why do I not act directly on the real world itself? Again in keeping with *L'Etre et le Néant* Sartre depicts worldly work as fundamentally unsatisfying, in that it obliges me to substitute 'a set succession of traditional procedures for the free invention of means'.[2] I may produce an object, but I scarcely see myself in it. 'When it is a matter of pottery or carpentry, we work according to traditional norms, with tools whose usage is codified; it is Heidegger's famous "they" who are working with our hands.'[3] Even the artist fails in his project, but for the opposite reasons. Aesthetic joy 'is denied to the creator, insofar as he creates.'[4] As long as

1. QL, p.90; WL, p.33.
2. QL, p.97; WL, p.41.
3. QL, p.91; WL, p.34.
4. QL, p.107; WL, p.52.

I see the work as still mine, I 'can always change this line, that shade, that word.' I never see it as an independent object, about which I can say, 'I'm the one who did *that*.' For 'the writer meets everywhere only *his* knowledge, *his* will, his plans, in short, himself. He touches only his own subjectivity; the object he creates is out of reach; he does not create it *for himself*. If he re-reads himself, it is already too late. The sentence will never quite be a thing in his eyes. He goes to the very limits of the subjective but without crossing it. He appreciates the effect of a touch, of an epigram, of a well-placed adjective, but it is the effect they will have on others.'[5] I can see my novel as an independent object only if I re-read it much later, after I have forgotten what I meant and why I wrote it. But then it will no longer be *my* novel. Thus I remain at the border of the subjective and the objective without ever being able to contemplate the objective ordonnance which I transmit.'[6]

Nevertheless, art is not simply a useless passion. For after all, Sartre now affirms, the work of art does become an object, even if an 'unreal' one; and in this capacity lies art's 'answer' to *L'Etre et le Néant*. It is possible to overcome the ontological dualism, to create a world in which we see ourselves, and to enjoy our creation as an object. We do this 'in different degrees in experiencing all works of art, but especially in reading.[7] When I read, my consciousness creates an objective world, I become God-like. And in doing so, I feel genuine joy. Life's fundamental frustrations are overcome when I, the reader, create the aesthetic object.

The novel exists only as the reader responds to the words in the book, the 'solicitations to produce the object', and projects an imaginary world of people and actions beyond them. From the signs before me I create an imaginary world, a world which is objective and yet dependent on me for its existence: 'reading seems, in fact, to be the synthesis of perception and creation. It supposes the essentiality of both the subject and the object. The object is essential because it is strictly transcendent, because it imposes its own structures, and because one must wait for it and observe it; but the subject is also essential because he is required not only to disclose the object (that is, to make an object *be there*) but also so that this object might *be* absolutely (that is, to produce it). In a word, the reader is conscious of

5. QL, pp.92-93; WL, p.36.
6. QL, p.103; WL, pp.47-48.
7. QL, p.115n; WL, p.37n.

disclosing in creating, of creating in disclosing.'[8] The novel will not appear unless I create it: I am essential to the process. 'Raskolnikov, as I have said, would only be a shadow, without the mixture of repulsion and friendship which I feel for him and which makes him live.'[9] Yet the novel — brought to life by me, vivified by my feelings — is not me. I work within the given limits of an objective structure, for as we know, 'the words are there like traps to arouse our feelings and to reflect them towards us!'[10] The writer requires of the reader 'the gift of his whole person, with his passions, his prepossessions, his sympathies, his sexual temperament, and his scale of values.'[11] For the first time in any activity described by Sartre, the reader recognizes himself in an object. Like the objects of our world, 'the work seems to him as inexhaustible and opaque as things.'[12] Yet unlike the objects of the world, the novel 'has no other substance than the reader's subjectivity.'[13] Thus, subject and object are co-essential: here alone do I *found* an object, even if it is an *irréel*. Sartre now uses the most prized categories of the human project — *synthesis, totality, harmony* — to denote not an unattainable goal but an accomplished fact. The novel which I create-read is the for-itself-in-itself, the grand fusion, fully myself and fully beyond myself. In the creation of the aesthetic object the idea of God ceases to be contradictory and man ceases to be a useless passion.

The Structures of Aesthetic Joy

Art provides 'the sole case in which the creator gets any enjoyment out of the subject he creates.'[14] It is an experience in which we overcome our fundamental unhappiness. We suspend our constant projection of new goals, make a 'recovery of the world', and attain calm, harmony, totality and security. Art is also a locus of freedom, and the occasion of a 'pact of generosity' arising between persons.

The basic ontological fact is that consciousness exists only through detaching itself from being. But in reading I bring this process to a

8. QL, pp.93-94; WL, p.37 (translation changed).
9. QL, p.100; WL, p.44.
10. QL, p.95; WL, p.39.
11. QL, p.100; WL, p.45.
12. QL, p.96; WL, p.40.
13. QL, p.95; WL, p.39.
14. QL, p.108; WL, p.53.

momentary stop. I attain 'a transcendent and absolute end which, for a moment, suspends the utilitarian round of ends-means and means-ends.'[15] Here alone do I actually *attain a value*. The novel is not a tool, an instrument, which I use for this or that project. The imaginary world is itself an end, and instead of employing it for a purpose, consciousness seeks only to experience it for itself. 'I shall call this aspect of aesthetic consciousness the feeling of security; it is this which stamps the strongest aesthetic emotions with a sovereign calm.'[16] All opposition between myself and objects has ended. I no longer find them lacking, withdraw from them, project possibilities beyond them: consciousness comes to rest in the object it creates. The novel is, after all, a me-object, in which I have ceased to negate the object, in which the object has ceased to be alien, independent, and indifferent. My feeling of calm is due to the reconciliation of subject and object, of humans and their world, of consciousness and being. It has 'its origin in the authentication of a strict harmony between subjectivity and objectivity.'[17]

A New Direction?

Compared with the tenor of the early writings, the serenity of these passages is remarkable. But what is the substantive relation between the two? Has the conceptual structure of the early writings been transformed, or is it revealing hitherto unsuspected possibilities of development?

Sartre's exploration of freedom in aesthetic experience will answer this question. So far freedom has been specified in two ways: first, I am always able to withdraw and project a new situation, and second, nothing external determines my action. My negative power has a positive result in that I create myself in every situation. But I am still a useless passion, because my freedom is not effective in overcoming my fundamental alienation from the world. *Qu'est-ce que la littérature?* takes a new course, guided by an idea drawn from *L'Imaginaire*. Sartre now criticizes Kant for limiting imagination's freedom merely to revelling in itself, to 'giving itself its own law'. Kant 'forgets that the imagination of the spectator has not only a regulating function, but a

15. QL, p.107; WL, p.52.
16. QL, p.108; WL, p.53.
17. QL, p.108; WL, p.53.

constitutive one. It does not play; it is called upon to recompose the beautiful object beyond the traces left by the artist.'[18]

I actually *create* the object, and so am capable of *productive* freedom. The novel is an imaginary object, an aesthetic one, but it reaches beyond my own subjectivity and becomes indeed a wordly object. As I read, my freedom does not only appear to itself as pure autonomy but as *creative activity,* that is, it is not limited to giving itself its own law but *perceives itself as being constitutive of the object.* '[19] I am free not only to detach myself or create myself, but also to engage in satisfying, productive activity on something that goes beyond me. The novel has its source in my freedom as productive being.

A year earlier, in 'Matérialisme et révolution', Sartre had hinted at this new conception of freedom, describing work as a 'liberating relationship' between man and things.[20] But contrary to this more radical suggestion, he returns now to his earlier belief that I can be a successful producer only because of art's unreality. His original conceptual structure is thus preserved intact. Free to create a fictional world — which is, indeed, a useful one — I am not yet free to create a human one. Still, Sartre's new focus on the act of producing, whether the products be real objects or not, seems to mark a first step towards a redefinition of freedom, an effort to conceive of freedom if not yet as more real and tied to historical and social life, then certainly as more a matter of positive action in the world. The experience of art, Sartre now holds, is a way of recreating our world with ourselves as its source. In this respect it contrasts sharply with our experience of nature. Beautiful *natural* objects already exist and call upon us to play freely in *their* harmony. Freedom before such an object can only be conceived as 'subjective functioning' without effect on the object. But the work of art 'exists only if one *looks* at it'. At first it is 'pure appeal', 'pure exigence': I find before me only 'a task to be discharged'. In creating this unreal object, my freedom acts on the thing, and I am fully free. 'For freedom is not experienced by its enjoying its free subjective functioning, but in a creative act required by an imperative.'[21] The world is *there,* already given and indifferent. It 'appears as the

18. QL, p.97; WL, p.41.
19. QL, pp.107-8; WL, pp.52-53 (emphasis added).
20. 'Matérialisme et révolution', p.201; 'Materialism and Revolution', p.224.
21. QL, p.98; WL, p.42.

horizon of our situation, as the infinite distance which separates us from ourselves, as the synthetic totality of the given, as the undifferentiated ensemble of obstacles and implements — but never as a demand addressed to our freedom.'[22] In the experience of art, however, I overcome this alienation and the entire world comes to be based on my freedom. The specific people and objects I create stand against the background of an entire imaginary universe. For example, Van Gogh paints a red path. We then follow this path beyond the material limits of the painting, 'follow it among other wheat fields, under other clouds, to the river which empties into the sea, and we extend to infinity, to the other end of the world, the deep finality which supports the existence of the field and the earth.'[23] Through producing this or that object, 'the creative act aims at a total renewal of the world. Each painting, each book, is a recovery of the totality of being. Each presents this totality to the freedom of the spectator. For this is quite the final goal of art: to recover this world by giving it to be seen as it is, but as if it had its source in human freedom.'[24] In this brief, imaginary experience, the world becomes my task, and my freedom acts 'to make that unique and absolute object which is the universe come into being in an unconditioned movement.'[25]

Sartre's frequent references to 'joy' indicate how far he has come: I re-create the world in art and I feel joy. My new freedom, instead of being a burden, instead of tormenting me with constant reminders of what I lack — the freedom of the psychological writings, of *La Nausée* and much of *L'Etre et le Néant* — is now a source of pleasure. 'The recognition of freedom by itself is joy.'[26] This shift from *L'Etre et le Néant* is symbolized in Sartre's implicit reversal of his declarations that man is 'a useless passion' and that in trying to found the world 'we lose ourselves in vain'. The reader, we now see, must give himself over to the story, freely lending it his feelings and beliefs. In a free decision, he renders himself *passive* before the story, becomes spellbound by it. 'It is a Passion, in the Christian sense of word, that is, a freedom which resolutely puts itself into a state of passivity to obtain a certain transcendent effect by this sacrifice.'[27] Reading, we can now say, is a

22. QL, p.108; WL, p.53.
23. QL, p.106; WL, p.51.
24. QL, p.106; WL, p.51 (translation changed).
25. QL, p.109; WL, p.54.
26. QL, p.107; WL, p.52.
27. QL, p.99; WL, p.44.

supremely successful passion: 'the man who is reading has raised himself to the highest degree.'[28]

Old Conclusions or New Beginnings?

The change in Sartre's outlook is manifest in these passages. But we should ask whether, for all the novelty of its perspective, the conception of art expounded here is in any essential respect different from the earlier notion of art as consolation. And if his commitment to the real world prevented him at an earlier stage from surrendering to the logic of his analyses, how can Sartre now, as an avowed political activist, actually celebrate an apparently identical conclusion? In fact, the 'solution' of *Qu'est-ce que la littérature?* is radically distinct from that exemplified in Roquentin's music. Many elements survive from the first into the second, but their new context transforms their significance. To Roquentin, who could find no satisfactory course of action in a world that he found intransigently meaningless, art offered at least a semblance of salvation. Now it was a 'guiding thread' to political commitment. The unreal wholeness and freedom of art was no longer a refuge, but a prevision of socialism.

'Hell is other people': this famous line from *Huis Clos* summarizes Sartre's early view of society.[29] First staged in 1944, *Huis Clos* depicted conflict as the natural state of human relations, with sadism or masochism as their inexorable outcome. The play was composed according to the ontological analysis of *L'Etre et le Néant,* which concluded that there was no possibility of free individuals treating each other as such, whether in pairs, small groups or in societies. Sartre rejected this interpretation of his play at the time, unconvincingly; but as it turned out, he was in any case beginning to revise his earlier conclusions. The second chapter of *Qu'est-ce que la littérature?* posited the transcendence of this daily hell in the writer-reader relationship. Then, in its fourth chapter, originally published a few months afterwards, human conflict was re-located in history: it arose under certain conditions, Sartre affirmed, and could disappear given different conditions. Socialism could institute the Kantian kingdom of ends, where each would respect the other's freedom. We can best under-

28. QL, p.101; WL, p.45.
29. *Huis Clos, Théâtre,* Paris 1949, p.167; trans. Stuart Gilbert, *No Exit and Three Other Plays,* New York 1955, p.47.

stand this change in Sartre's thought if we return to his discussion of the self-Other conflict in *L'Etre et le Néant,* and then go on to see how he himself became its most telling critic after the War.

Master and Slave: 'L'Enfer C'est les Autres'

The point of departure for Sartre's analysis of human relations in *L'Etre et le Néant* is Hegel's dialectic of the Master and the Slave. *The Phenomenology of Mind* describes the development of self-consciousness as follows: consciousness begins in the attitude of sense-certainty, by seeing the things of the world as alien and independent and opposed to it, and then, after destroying their false objectivity, comes to recognize itself as lying behind the finished form of things. Self-consciousness is thus the height of knowledge: mind sees its categories, its laws, its activity as constituting the underlying meaning and nature of the world. At a certain stage in the process of self-awareness, consciousness needs to be recognized by *other* consciousnesses in order to be sure of itself; 'that is to say, it is only by being acknowledged or "recognized" ', only if objectified, that I am sure that *I* am, and of what I am.[30]

Hegel notes two ways in which this takes place. In one, I leave my mark on objects — making them, possessing them, consuming them. In the other, I have other persons recognize me. I come to see myself *in* the object I have created or consumed; or I try to have the other person recognize me and so give objective proof of what I am.[31] However, the other person is not a material object, but a free self-consciousness who also exists for himself. I cannot gain his recognition by working on him or consuming him, for as an inherently free and active self-consciousness he exists for himself and must do to *himself* whatever I wish done to him.[32] If he refuses to recognize me as a free self-consciousness, if instead he regards me as an object, then I lack his affirming, objectifying acknowledgement. A struggle necessarily follows. I demand that the other recognize me as free and, at the same time, yield up to me *his* freedom and existence for himself; and he wants the same from me. It appears that we cannot

30. G.W.F. Hegel, *The Phenomenology of Mind*; trans. J.B. Baillie, London 1931, p.229.

31. Ibid., p.232.

32. Ibid., p.230.

both be free at the same time in respect of each other. 'They must enter into this struggle, for they must bring their certainty of themselves, the certainty of being for themselves, to the level of objective truth, and make this a fact, both in the case of the other and in their own case as well.'[33] The struggle results in the victory of one over the other, and thus terminates in two opposed and complementary forms of consciousness: 'the one is independent, and its essential nature is to be for itself; the other is dependent, and its essence is life or existence for another. The former is the master, or Lord, the latter the Bondsman,' or slave.[34]

The Master is pure self-consciousness, existing for itself, free before all things and seeing all things as existing for it. The Slave, on the other hand, is 'not purely for [him]self, but for another, *i.e.*, as an existent consciousness, consciousness in the form and shape of thinghood'.[35] As Master, I have reduced him to a thing existing for me; I have cancelled his freedom and gained his recognition of mine. The Master alone exists for himself. The Slave is essentially a labourer working on objects for the Master, who appropriates and enjoys them without labour. The dialectic does not stop here. It proceeds to the point where free self-consciousnesses recognize and accept each other's freedom in a harmonious relationship of equality. 'The equality of selves,' comments Hegel's translator, 'is the truth, or completer realization, of self in another self; the affinity is higher and more ultimate than the disparity.'[36] Only the We of a much higher and later stage can realize this final goal — the free association of individuals. For Sartre, who devotes nearly a third of *L'Etre et le Néant* to the problem of human conflict, Hegel's analysis is far too optimistic. Hegel attempted to present a dialectic — an upward-moving process of development in which the original conflict would eventually be transcended in a harmonious relationship of equals. But in fact, Sartre says, I must move forever between the poles of Master and Slave, of sadism and masochism. 'While I attempt to free myself from the hold of the Other, the Other is trying to free himself from mine; while I seek to enslave the Other, the Other seeks to enslave me.

33. Ibid., pp.232-33.
34. Ibid., p.234.
35. Ibid., p.234.
36. Ibid., p.228

... Conflict is the original meaning of being-for-others.'[37] The Other need only look at me and I am fixed, robbed of my freedom — as is the other, in turn, under my gaze. 'Being-seen constitutes me as a defenceless being for a freedom which is not my freedom. It is in this sense that we consider ourselves as "slaves" in so far as we appear to the Other. But this slavery is not a historical result — capable of being surmounted — of a *life* in the abstract form of consciousness. I am a slave to the degree that my being is dependent at the centre of a freedom which is not mine and which is the very condition of my being. In so far as I am the object of values which come to qualify me without my being able to act on this qualification or even to know it, I am enslaved.'[38] I may rebel, trying to make the Other an object solely in order to escape objecthood myself. Thus begins an endless cycle of domination and counter-domination. 'All of men's complex patterns of conduct towards one another are only enrichments of these two original attitudes.'[39]

Can the circle be broken? Can we hope for changed relations in a different society? We have just now seen Sartre say that the problem is not at all historical. The issue turns instead on the very nature of consciousness as it stands before another consciousness; in so far as I act as a free, spontaneous subject, all things — including other people — are necessarily objects which I transcend towards my own projects; and in so far as I meet with a free spontaneous subject, I am threatened with objectification by it. But is there not, as Hegel suggested, a 'we' through which I might transcend this conflict to become part of a community of equals? It is not neccessary to posit a classless society: even Heidegger speaks of the *Mit-sein,* of being-with-others as a basic ontological structure.[40] Sartre is aware that being-with-others implies 'a sort of ontological solidarity for the exploitation of this world.'[41] 'The empirical image which may best symbolize Heidegger's intuition is not that of a conflict but rather a crew,'[42] that is, a cooperative human group. In *L'Etre et le Néant,* he agrees that individuals certainly do experience a 'we' — as when a group of people

37. EN, p.431; BN, p.364.
38. EN, p.326; BN, p.267.
39. EN, p.477; BN, p.407.
40. *Being and Time,* pp.149-168.
41. EN, p.302; BN, p.245.
42. EN, p.303; BN, p.246.

are spectators at a drama or an accident, or when individuals labour together or soldiers march in step. These experiences seem to overcome the original conflict and to reveal the 'we' as united in the process of directing itself outwards into the world. 'In this sense the ideal We-subject would be the "we" of a humanity which would make itself the master of the earth.'[43] Sartre has in mind the 'we' envisaged by socialism, but his analysis is somewhat uncertain. He concludes that I never really apprehend other subjectivities *as* subjectivities in this experience, but rather I feel myself slip into the collective. I remain radically separated from other subjectivities during the experience. The 'we' that I am aware of is thus not a genuine unity but a 'pure psychological subjective event in a single consciousness.'[44] It can never be guaranteed that anyone else feels the same way. Thus the experience is only a momentary one, inherently unstable and contingent. 'It comes and disappears capriciously, leaving us in the face of others-as-objects or else of a "they" who look at us. It appears as a provisional appeasement which is constituted at the very heart of the conflict. We should hope in vain for a human "we" in which the intersubjective totality would obtain consciousness of itself as a unified subjectivity. Such an ideal could only be a dream. . .'[45]

In the passages before and after this discussion, Sartre speaks of the proletariat. Both passages appear sympathetic to the possibilities of proletarian revolution and socialism, but their real thrust contradicts this hope. For the proletariat exists not as a 'we-subject', a free, united group of equals, but as an 'us-object', as objects dominated by a free and independent subject — the bourgeoisie. This us-object, which exists in shame and fear, can take upon itself a 'project of reversal' by which it would liberate 'the whole "us" from the object-state by transforming it into a we-subject.'[46] But this is enormously difficult. The oppressed class can, in fact, affirm itself as a we-subject only in relation to the oppressing class and at the latter's expense; that is, by transforming it in turn into 'they-as-objects' or 'them'.[47] Socialism, as a community of equals, could maintain itself only in the face of an enemy. A society of free men treating *all* other free men as free is thus

43. EN, p.498; BN, p.425.
44. EN, p.497; BN, p.425.
45. EN, pp.500-501; BN, p.428.
46. EN, p.494; BN, p.422.
47. EN, p.494; BN, p.422.

impossible. 'The essence of the relations between consciousness is not the *Mit-sein*; it is conflict.'[48]

Literature: The Pact of Freedoms

By 1947, we have already seen , Sartre had come to believe that man as 'useless passion' was transcended in art. So too was man as relentless enemy of each and every other. Just as the reader's productive freedom overcame his alienation from the in-itself, so, in Sartre's conception, the cooperative relationship between writer and reader reconciled the self and the Other. If we constitute the work of art from the materials left for that purpose by the artist, then its existence depends on our collaboration. Hence, 'there is no art except for and by others.'[49] The writer *needs* the Other for his work to be completed. 'If the author existed alone he would be able to write as much as he liked: the work as object would never see the light of day and he would either have to put down his pen or despair.'[50] The success of the author's enterprise depends on the reader's freedom. His work is not a finished object but an appeal: to my spontaneity, my inventiveness, my freedom to lend my feelings. Therefore, he cannot seek to act upon me — to treat me as an object — without frustrating his own project. He cannot try to manipulate or overwhelm me, for either act, if successful, would destroy my ability to create the aesthetic object from the signs he has fashioned. The author's relationship to me can only be based on recognition of my freedom and spontaneity. 'If I appeal to my reader so that we may carry the enterprise which I have begun to a successful conclusion, it is self-evident that I consider him as a pure freedom, as an unconditioned activity; thus in no case can I address myself to his passivity, that is try to *affect* him, to communicate to him, from the very first, emotions of fear, desire, or anger. There are, doubtless, authors who concern themselves solely with arousing these emotions because they are foreseeable, manageable, and because they have at their disposal sure-fire means for provoking them. But it is also true that they are reproached for this kind of thing, as Euripides has been since antiquity because he had children appear on the stage. Freedom is alienated in the state of passion; it is abruptly engaged in partial enterprises; it loses sight of its task which is to produce an absolute

48. EN, p.502; BN, p.429.
49. QL, p.93; WL, p.37.
50. QL, p.93; WL, pp.36-37.

end. And the book is no longer anything but a means for feeding hate or desire. The writer should not seek to *overwhelm*; otherwise he is in contradiction with himself; if he wishes to *make demands* he must propose only the task to be fulfilled.'[51] He should demand that I freely loan my feelings, always recognizing that I may withdraw them at any moment, and that only on this condition can the materials before me be transformed into the 'free dream' which is the work of literature. He should understand that I must give myself generously and not mechanically: ' . . . the reader's feelings are never dominated by the object, and as no external reality can condition them, they have their permanent source in freedom; that is, they are generous — for I call a feeling generous which has its origin and its end in freedom.'[52]

We have already seen Sartre compare the aesthetic object to beautiful natural objects. He speaks, following Kant, of the *purposiveness without purpose (finalité sans fin)* of the latter. I find the natural object constructed in an orderly, harmonious way, *as if* some will had intended it for a purpose, yet I view it without regard to any utilitarian purpose.[53] Beautiful natural objects have the *appearance* of finality, but standing before them, I never feel that my freedom is being called upon to act because I do not feel that a *creative will* lies behind these relations, demanding that I bring them into being. In nature there is only 'an appearance of order', an 'illusion of a calling forth which seems to solicit this freedom and which disappears immediately when one regards it,'[54] leaving only an occasion for capricious musing. 'No sooner have we begun to run our eyes over this arrangement, than the call disappears; we remain alone, free to tie up one colour with another or with a third, to set up a relationship between the tree and water or the tree and the sky, or the tree, the water and the sky. My freedom becomes caprice. To the extent that I establish new relationships, I remove myself further from the illusory objectivity which solicits me. I *muse* about certain motifs which are vaguely outlined by the things; the natural reality is no longer anything but a pretext for musing.'[55]

51. QL, pp.98-99; WL, p.43.

52. QL, p.100; WL, p.45.

53. See Immanuel Kant, *Critique of Judgment,* trans. J.H. Bernard, New York 1951, Sections 10 and 11.

54. QL, p.102; WL, pp.46-47.

55. QL, p.102; WL, p.47.

Everything changes when the spectator stands before an object made by a human being. For he knows with a deep security that what he sees or reads has been intended. 'However far he may go, the author has gone further. Whatever connections he may establish among the different parts of the book — among the chapters or the words — he has a guarantee, namely, that they have been expressly willed. As Descartes says, he can even pretend that there is a secret order among parts which seem to have no connection. The creator has preceded him along the way, and the most beautiful disorders are effects of art, that is, again order.'[56] It may be difficult to grasp the artist's intentions — we often must speculate about what exactly is meant in this or that perplexing passage. But these problems are beside the point. We may or may not fully grasp what the artist meant, but we are absolutely certain that he did mean something. In experiencing nature, we may discover harmony, yet we know that this is entirely by chance. But in a novel in which, say, the protagonist is required by the layout of the city to cross a certain park, there are no accidents: 'the park came into existence only *in order to* harmonize with a certain state of mind, to express it by means of things or to put it into relief by a vivid contrast, and that state of mind itself was conceived in connection with the landscape.'[57]

The freedom of the writer-reader relationship is necessarily reciprocal. Recognizing that a human will intended all that I read, I must regard the writer as free. It would destroy my entire experience to see him as passive, dependent, determined by forces beyond his control, or writing mechanically or automatically. 'If I were to suspect the artist of having written out of passion and in passion, my confidence would immediately vanish',[58] and with it, my experience of the novel as an aesthetic object. If I regarded the writer as a passive being, I would thereby place his work in 'the chain of determinism'. The novel would appear then as an object of nature, written by accident or chance — a fit object of musing, and perhaps analysis, but no longer a novel, an imaginary object which I freely create. If I regard the writer as object, approaching him in order to control and dominate, I deprive myself of that 'free dream', of the planned human world that awaits me. This experience can be realized only if I

56. QL, p.103; WL, p.48.
57. QL, p.104; WL, p.49.
58. QL, p.104; WL, p.49.

approach the novel in a spirit of generosity, according to the Kantian moral dictum, treating other humans not as means but as ends.

I regard the creation of the aesthetic object as a *task,* expressly imposed on me by the artist, but find no such demand in any natural object. I create the aesthetic object, and so engage my freedom, only as I see it to be willed *by* someone — by a free Other. Aesthetic collaboration necessarily suspends the self-Other conflict. For the process to take place, I must recognize my own *and* the Other's freedom: 'reading is a pact of generosity between author and reader. Each one trusts the other; each one counts on the other, demands of the other as much as he demands of himself. For this confidence is itself generosity. Nothing can force the author to believe that his reader will use his freedom; nothing can force the reader to believe that the author has used his. Both of them make a free decision. There is established a dialectical going-and-coming; when I read, I made demands; if my demands are met, what I am reading provokes me to demand more of the author, which means to demand of the author that he demand more of me. And vice-versa, the author's demand is that I carry my demands to the highest pitch. Thus my freedom, by revealing itself, reveals the freedom of the other.'[59]

Towards Socialism

The aesthetic dimension is a community of free equals. This may mean one or other of two things. *Either* no such actual community is possible, and so the experience of art offers a rare and unreal moment of harmony between myself and the Other, as it does between myself and the literary world I create; *or* such a community may indeed be possible under different social forms, and the experience of art offers us a prevision of it. *L'Etre et le Néant* argued unequivocally that 'we shall never place ourselves concretely on a plane of equality; that is on the plane where the recognition of the Other's freedom would involve the Other's recognition of our freedom.'[60] But *Qu'est-ce que la littérature?* registers a drastic shift in Sartre's judgment of the self-Other conflict. The optimism of his aesthetic argument is extended on to the 'concrete' plane of social life, as he drops his earlier negative attitude towards Kant's moral theory.

If the world is not really 'the city of ends that it ought to be, it must

59. QL, p.105; WL, p.49-50.
60. EN, p.479; BN, p.408.

at least be a stage along the way; in a word, it must be a becoming and it must always be considered and presented not as a crushing mass which weighs us down, but from the point of view of its going beyond towards that city of ends.'[61] Conflict is central to human relations today. But it is the oppression of class society and not the nature of consciousness that makes it 'quite impossible to treat men as ends in contemporary society.'[62] The city of ends is at present 'a feeble abstraction', but it can be made real through 'an objective modification of the historical situation' — through the struggle for 'the freedom of the person *and* the socialist revolution.'[63]

The theoretical foundations of Sartre's new commitment were as yet slender, but they supported a seemingly decisive shift. A year earlier, in 'Matérialisme et Révolution', Sartre had repudiated the social and political perspectives of *L'Etre et le Néant,* and accepted, in very revealing terms, the possibility of a classless society which would abolish 'the oppressive relationship between men so that the slave's will and that of the master, which exhaust themselves in struggling against one another, can be turned back wholly upon things. The liberated society will be a *harmonious* enterprise of exploration of the world.' At the same time, Sartre expressed dissent from the official Marxism of the Communist Party — a revolutionary determinism which, although capable of achieving 'a more rational organization of society', was 'not based on the mutual recognition of freedom'.[65] Above and beyond the rational organization of the community, Sartre maintained, socialism would institute 'a new humanism, . . . experienced as such by a free subjectivity', which the Marxism of the Communist Party failed to pursue or even understand. This new 'reign of freedom' would arise because the socialist revolutionary 'demands the liberation of his whole class and, more generally, of all men'.[66] Sartre's definition of the revolutionary act was in striking opposition both to the Marxism of the PCF and to the terms of *L'Etre et le Néant*: 'it springs from a recognition of other freedoms and it demands recognition on their part. Thus, from the beginning, it places itself on the level of solidarity.'[67]

61. QL, p.110; WL, p.56.
62. QL, p.297; WL, p.269.
63. QL, pp.296, 298; WL, pp.268,270.
64. 'Matérialisme et révolution', p.201, 'Materialism and Revolution', p.224.
65. Ibid., pp.208,201; pp.228,224.
66. Ibid., p.216, p.234.
67. Ibid., pp.217-18; p.234.

This solidarity was not only that of the we-subject *against* their oppressors, a solidarity which, failing the appearance of another, 'external' enemy, would vanish after the revolution. What Sartre envisaged
here was the liquidation, and not merely the redirection, of the self-
Other conflict. His emphasis was quite Marxist: the liberation of the
proletariat would secure the liberation of *all* men — or, in his own
terms, this particular act of liberation required all individuals to
recognize each other's freedom.

What did Sartre concretely mean by talking of men's mutual
recognition of freedom in a socialist society? His guide at this point
was Kant. Beyond the self-Other conflict, once thought to be basic,
Sartre envisaged an ideal relationship. The actual relationship — conflict — turned out to be rooted in class society: the 'mutual
recognition of freedom' could only issue from socialism. No longer
regarded as human destiny, the self-Other conflict now appeared in
both a Marxist and an ethical light. Sartre showed how the act of
labour already manifested human freedom — the power to shape, control and change things — even if the capitalist system denied this at
other levels by treating men as objects.[68] In a socialist revolution,
men would collectively repudiate their status as things for other
humans and assume the determining, shaping role implied from the
start by the creative act of labour. 'The declaration that "we too are
men" is at the bottom of any revolution.'[69] Socialism would introduce
a community of producers, which would be by definition a community of ends — of humans respecting each other as fully free, self-
determining individuals. *Only* socialism could achieve the community
of ends. The Others would recognize my freedom and I theirs only
insofar as we all together controlled the process of production and the
society itself. Fully democratic control over all social institutions
required the 'mutual recognition of freedoms' at all levels of decision-
making. The Other would recognize my right to control as I
recognized his: in a fundamentally democratic society neither would
have any need to see the Other as an object, to dominate him. The
freedom of each single individual was bound up with the freedom of
all others. In 'Matérialisme et révolution' Sartre demanded that
revolutionaries recognize this community of ends as the goal of

68. See ibid., pp.198-206; pp.22-228.
69. Ibid., pp.188-89; p.217.

all their actions — carrying them far beyond mechanical and deterministic philosophies which denied human freedom.

Freedom on Many Levels

How, then, does *Qu'est-ce que la littérature?* define the relationship between literature and socialism? The author-reader community realized as I read a novel is the formal incarnation of socialist society. Our recognition of the Other's freedom on the aesthetic level implies our concrete recognition of the Other's freedom on the social level. The realm of art is an island of equals in any society; its principles are those of a truly free humanity. The aesthetic community temporarily overcomes the struggle between individuals and realizes the Kantian imperative: 'let us bear in mind that the man who reads strips himself in some way of his empirical personality and escapes from his resentments, his fears, and his lusts in order to put himself at the peak of his freedom. This freedom takes the literary work and, through it, mankind, for absolute ends. It sets itself up as an unconditioned exigence in relationship to itself, to the author, and to possible readers. It can therefore be identified with Kantian *good will* which, in every circumstance, treats man as an end and not as a means. Thus, by his very exigence, the reader attains that chorus of good wills which Kant has called the City of Ends, which thousands of readers all over the world who do not know each other are, at every moment, helping to maintain.'[70] These readers are experiencing the same kind of human relationships as will obtain under socialism. Thus, 'although literature is one thing and morality a quite different one, at the heart of the aesthetic imperative we discern the moral imperative. For since the one who writes recognizes, by the very fact that he takes the trouble to write, the freedom of his readers, and since the one who reads, by the mere fact of his opening the book, recognizes the freedom of the writer, the work of art, from whichever side you approach it, is an act of confidence in the freedom of men.'[71]

Sartre's Key Terms in 1947

We shall soon see the important role allotted to literature in the struggle for socialism. But our main interest for the moment is in assessing

70. QL, p.293; WL, pp.264-65.
71. QL, p.111; WL, pp.56-57.

the alterations that have occurred in Sartre's conceptual structure. The ontology of *L'Etre et le Néant* has begun to open up — if not to history and society at least to an historically and socially framed set of ethical choices. Human relationships now have two basic possibilities, and we must struggle towards the better. Both 'Matérialisme et révolution' and *Qu'est-ce que la littérature?* indicated and explored this new view of human relations; but while the former saw the possibility of ending our inbuilt alienation from the world, the latter, a year afterwards, rehearsed and elaborated Sartre's original theme of an ontological impasse. What is the explanation of these inconsistencies in Sartre's immediately post-war writings?

As our discussion of the self-Other conflict should make clear, Sartre had no intention at this stage of abandoning his 'ideological interest' in the philosophy which reached mature expression in 1943. He approached new questions, social and political questions, but using instruments carefully refined over a period of years. Quite characteristically, and in spite of his new activist political orientation, Sartre *deduced* socialism from his own central concepts. In these respects, historical reality seemed so far to be a catalyst inducing the appearance of new alternatives in Sartre's ontology rather than an agent of real conceptual transformation. Even in his description of 'the situation of the writer in 1947' (Chapter Four), Sartre's main ideas were drawn from his rather timeless and abstract description of human relations as they appear in art.

In other words, the early Sartre was for the most part still present in 1947. The political activist still operated within the conceptual structure explored in Part One of this study. If he was becoming optimistic, his thought was no less rooted in a fundamental pessimism. If he was now exploring new possibilities in human relations, and was tentatively hopeful that socialism would abolish the self-Other conflict, he was still committed to the fundamental dualism between the for-itself and the in-itself. If he now engaged in political activity, it was as a writer.

At the same time, Sartre now displayed more clearly than ever the strength of his intellectual drive towards the real. And the fertility of his basic ideas was borne out in his critique of Marxist orthodoxy. Unhistorical though it remained, there was something compelling about Sartre's argument. At stake in it was a vision of man which he insisted must animate any revolutionary politics. Men and women were not passive and totally determined by history, but however alienated, were already shaping the world. They were capable both of taking it back into their own hands and of controlling it. This insight related Sartre's self-created socialist theory to Marx's early writings and to a dialectical impulse in Marxism that he had yet to encounter and understand. Labouring to create an alternative to what he knew as Marxism, Sartre fashioned for himself the beginnings of a dialectical conception of human creativity — even if he kept it separate from history and society, presenting it as a kind of philosophical imperative — and held to this conception in so far as the Marxism he encountered denied the spontaneous and potentially or actually self-determining character of human activity.

Neither 'Matérialisme et révolution' nor *Qu'est-ce que la littérature?* was as clear or systematic as the preceding pages may have suggested. Sartre was now in the midst of an intellectual upheaval and his purpose in writing these texts was exploratory; not to set down the results of finished reflection and study but to reach for and examine ideas that were now only emerging. He was defending his now well-known and controversial philosophical theses, testing them in areas that he had left underdeveloped so far, and exploring the implications of his new found commitment. Above all, the concern of the later and longer of the two, *Qu'est-ce que la littérature?*, was to explore, define and defend a project that appeared diametrically opposed to everything that he had previously written about art and its role in human existence: the project of political engagement in literature.

Literature and Revolution

In claiming that the literary and the real 'cities of ends' were animated by the same principle, Sartre revoked his earlier separation of art, the *irréel*, from real life. Literature was now a 'conducting wire' leading to socialist democracy.[1] Sartre demanded that writers do more than offer their readers a fleeting experience of the imaginary city of ends — that they show how it implied another, a real city which could only be brought about through social change. In this perspective, he outlined specific literary themes, criteria for judging literature, and the relationship to be sought between writer and audience.

The very nature of literature demanded such *engagement*. A writer who became a fascist or a collaborator, Sartre had written in *Les Lettres françaises* in April 1944, betrayed the very principles of art.[2] Reiterating this thesis now, he extended it to include writers who withdrew into visions of the eternal. Literature was a social art with a definite function and effect, an act always situated in a given society at a given time, and whose deepest meaning was human freedom. A literature fully aware of itself would accept its function, would immerse itself in the issues of the day, and this always from the standpoint of the oppressed.

Action by Disclosure

Sartre begins *Qu'est-ce que la littérature?* by deepening the familiar theme of art as a 'mirror', using the concepts of *L'Etre et le Néant*. Psychological or social determinism, fatalism, the notion of destiny are all modes of bad faith in which I lie to myself about my terrifying

1. QL, p.296; WL, p.268.
2. 'La Littérature, cette liberté' ('Literature, That Freedom'), *Les Lettres françaises*, 15, p.8; CRW, 44/45, p.94.

freedom to create myself, to change and assume new patterns of behaviour. (I may also attempt to hide an identifiable pattern in my behaviour, such as homosexuality, by claiming that my actions are random, disconnected, and without meaning). Whether proclaiming my helplessness or denying my behaviour, my bad faith is an avoidance of myself as I am. But in reading a novel I see myself; and this self-confrontation is precisely the function of literature. I see my own patterns of conduct and my own freedom as I assume them in the act of reading. Reading is thus a cognitive act — not in the sense that I learn something *new* about the world or myself, but because I encounter what I have tried to keep hidden from view all along. In reading I become self-conscious. This process has two aspects. In the first, which Sartre defines through the concept of bad faith and the self-Other dialectic, I feel as if I have been seen by the Other, 'caught in the act' as when peering through a keyhole. 'If you name the behaviour of an individual, you reveal it to him; he sees himself. And since you are at the same time naming it to all others, he knows that he is *seen* at the moment he *sees* himself. The furtive gesture which he forgot while making it, begins to exist beyond all measure, to exist for everybody; it is integrated into the objective mind; it takes on new dimensions; it is retrieved.'[3] Another person has seen me for what I am and fixes my pattern of behaviour in describing it. He sees me, and before him my behaviour appears objective. I can no longer pretend that it exists only as I want it to appear, that it is other than it really is, that it is only temporary or that circumstances forced me into it. Through being seen, my bad faith is shattered and I see myself as I am. Looked at, I look at myself.

The second dimension of the act of reading distinguishes it radically from being surprised at the keyhole. I myself create the novel. I freely bring about this self-revelation. It can never be imposed by another person. I can put the novel down, I can skip over the disturbing passages, I can read it rapidly or without interest. Moreover, Sartre implies, the picture taking shape in my imagination depends on me in an even deeper way. At the most profound level, the novel *is* *me*. Raskolnikov and Porfiry cannot exist unless I lend them my feelings. Unless I project my own experience and feelings into the characters, they cannot live. This suggestion is left largely undeveloped in Sartre's analysis, but its implication is clear. I do not merely observe someone else's picture of a pattern of behaviour that I happen to share with the protagonist. I myself participate in creating that protagonist's action. The novel is *my* subjectivity become objective. Seeing myself in the novel is not a subjectivist error or a mere after-effect of literary experience but a constitutive moment of the very act of reading. I see myself and see myself as *seen*. In making this possible, the writer is politically engaged in 'a certain method of secondary action which we may call action by disclosure'.[4] Why should we call it action? Because seeing myself, the free assumption of this or that pattern of behaviour, is a decisive moment of my action. In order to explain this, Sartre distinguishes between my ordinary or immediate state and the reflective state. Ordinarily I am immersed in my spontaneous activity; I do not see my activity as it is, from the outside, with the Other's eyes. 'But spontaneous behaviour, by passing to the reflective state, loses its innocence and the excuse of immediacy: it must be assumed or changed.'[5] In other words, when a reader recognizes his pattern of dishonesty and evasion, he can no longer hide it from himself. In spite of all his efforts, it has appeared for what it is, seen by the Other and willingly created by himself. 'After that, how can you expect him to act in the same way? Either he will persist in his behaviour out of obstinacy and with full knowledge of what he is doing, or he will give it up.'[6]

This is the heart of Sartre's theory of literature as critical mirror. Reflection is a moment of action, not a detached contemplative activity. For through reflection — and through it alone — I correct, judge, and change myself. Only when I step back and look at myself do I know what I am doing. Reflection is 'an essential condition of action.'[7] Only this 'reflective revolution' frees me from my immersion in the instrumental chain of the world and allows me to see my activity and its meaning.[8] Such self-discovery is the business of literature. 'To speak is to act: anything which one names is already no longer quite the same; it has lost its innocence.'[9] To write is to act. Art, an *irréel*, turns out to have a vital function in the real world. In this way, Sartre reverses the trend of his earlier thought, carrying us

3. QL, p.72; WL, p.16.
4. QL, p.73; WL, p.17.
5. QL, p.142; WL, p.90.
6. QL, pp.72-73; WL, p.16.
7. QL, p.197; WL, p.153.
8. Cf. EN, p.252; BN, p.201.
9. QL, p.72; WL, p.16. See also EN, pp.116-118; BN, pp.74-76.

beyond his rigid separation of the imaginary and real worlds. But there are two equally striking lines of continuity. First, art becomes a mode of action precisely *because* it is an *irréel*. As the concluding chapter of *L'Imaginaire* had already indicated, it is in the very act of projecting an *irréel* that we detach ourselves from the real world, free ourselves from it, and see it as a whole. As long as we maintain a realistic attitude we are immersed in events, unable to see ourselves. Thus art's very 'unreality' is what makes it a source of change through reflection and self-knowledge. And second, art is in some sense all-powerful here, as it was earlier. Again and again we have seen Sartre say that, as an *irréel*, art momentarily solves life's basic problems. He now argues that literature, as a decisive moment of action, has the power to change what people do. In either case, words and their peculiar power are at the heart of Sartre's world view. Even as he becomes politically engaged, aesthetics remains at the centre of his thought.

Revealing This Society

One might accept Sartre's principle of disclosure yet insist that what must be disclosed are the permanent weaknesses of the species, the unchanging problems of any society. This was his own course in *La Nausée* and *Huis Clos*. The socio-historical situation and its issues were marginal to these works. Why should the writer orient himself to the specific society in which he lives and turn to social rather than purely individual problems?

We have already seen Sartre discover society and history. On the theoretical level his political conversion led him slowly to change his notion of the *situation*. One of the most promising lines of *L'Etre et le Néant* had spoken of man exercising his freedom in a given situation which included his past, his present environment, his fellow humans, and the prospect of his death. But this account lacked all clarity concerning the relative importance of these dimensions and laid primary emphasis on our ability to act within any situation. In the introduction to *Les Temps Modernes,* Sartre began to emphasize the historical and social dimension of the 'situation'. 'Man *is* only in a situation: a worker is not *free* to think or to feel like a bourgeois.'[10] Now, accordingly, he insisted that the writer and reader were born into a given class at a given historical point in the development of their society.

10. 'Présentation', p.22; 'Introduction,' p.441.

There is no pure 'man' and there is no pure 'literature'. Each book appeals to the whole life of the particular society in which and for which it was written. 'Hence, in each one there is an implicit recourse to institutions, customs, certain forms of oppression and conflict, to the wisdom and the folly of the day, to lasting passions and passing stubbornness, to superstition and recent victories of common sense, to evidence and ignorance, to particular modes of reasoning which the sciences have made fashionable and which are applied in all domains, to hopes, to fears, to habits of sensibility, imagination, and even perception, and finally, to customs and values which have been handed down, to a whole world which the author and the reader have in common. It is this familiar world which the writer animates and penetrates with his freedom. It is on the basis of this world that the reader must bring about his concrete liberation; it is alienation, situation, and history. It is this world which I must change or preserve for myself and others. . . .'[11]

Action by disclosure is, then, directed at a given class at a given point in the life of a given society. The writer not only shatters the bad faith of this or that isolated individual. He also presents the society, and especially its ruling class, with the image it tries to hide from itself. 'If society sees itself and, in particular, sees itself as *seen*, there is, by virtue of this very fact, a contesting of the established values of the regime. The writer presents it with its image; he calls upon it to assume it or to change itself. At any rate, it changes; it loses the equilibrium which its ignorance had given it; it wavers between shame and cynicism; it practices dishonesty; thus, the writer gives society a *guilty conscience;* he is thereby in a state of perpetual antagonism toward the conservative forces which are maintaining the balance he tends to upset. . . .'[12]

It is necessarily an act of contestation to present a class society as it really is, to present the ruling class as it really is, because any class society is naturally dishonest with itself. Its bad faith may lie in proclaiming the universal equality of men while maintaining their inequality, or in proclaiming the right to property while it sanctions the vast majority's lack of it; at all events, its ideology is at odds with the facts of its social reality. But it does not yet see itself as dishonest: it

11. QL, p.119; WL, p.64.
12. QL, p.129; WL, p.75.

has a good conscience. Now when the writer reflects the society's own image, and asks it to assume it, he makes the contradictions apparent. By penetrating the mystifications of ideology, the writer threatens the society's equilibrium. Because he presents things as they are, he naturally opposes all modes of self-deception. He is the natural enemy of any class society.

If I ignore the social struggles and issues of the day I do not thereby become neutral. Writing remains action, and so, also, is silence. 'This silence is a moment of language; being silent is not being dumb; it is to refuse to speak, and therefore to keep on speaking.'[13] To refuse, to escape into eternal values or to see art as existing for its own sake, is tacitly to accept the established society. By not revealing and thus helping to change this or that aspect of a society's life, the writer uses his influence on behalf of the existing order. To help maintain the existing order writers need not sing its praises: it is enough that they do not speak out against it.

The world's hunger, the atomic threat, the alienation of man — these are the realities of our situation. To remain silent about them is to accept them, as does the writer who spends his life writing novels about the Hittites. When the writer remains silent about the epoch's central problems it may well mean that 'the ruling classes have directed him into frivolous activities without his knowing it, for fear he might join the revolutionary troops.'[14] The imperative is not, finally, to *become* engaged, but to become aware of being engaged already. For we have already taken sides, whether we admit it or not: 'if every man is embarked, that does not at all mean that he is fully conscious of it. Most men pass their time in hiding their engagement from themselves. That does not necessarily mean that they attempt evasions by lying, by artificial paradises, or by a life of make-believe. It is enough for them to dim their lanterns, to see the foreground without the background and, vice-versa, to see the ends while passing over the means in silence, to refuse solidarity with their kind, to take refuge in the spirit of pompousness, to remove all value from life by considering it from the point of view of someone who is dead, and at the same time, all horror from death by fleeing it in the banality of everyday existence, to persuade themselves, if they belong to an oppressing class, that they are escaping their class by the loftiness of

13. QL, p.75; WL, p.19.
14. 'Présentation', p.12; 'Introduction', p.435 (translation changed).

their feelings, and, if they belong to the oppressed, to conceal from themselves their complicity with oppression by asserting that one can remain free while in chains if one has a taste for the inner life. Writers can have recourse to all this just like anyone else.'[15] Sartre's demand is that writers and readers 'achieve the most lucid and the most complete consciousness of being embarked.'[16] Aware that writing is in fact an action, and silence no less so, the writer should understand that his words are 'loaded pistols'. 'If he speaks, he fires. He may be silent, but since he has chosen to fire, he must do it like a man by aiming at his targets, and not, like a child, at random, shutting his eyes and firing merely for the pleasure of hearing the gun go off.'[17] Becoming aware of his influence, the writer must decide that this influence shall be deliberate and conscious; he must be responsible for his actions.

Now the writer who is not in bad faith, who has become aware of his own situation, cannot really write about anything he pleases, just as he cannot be anyone he pleases. It would be senseless, for example, to write a charming and heartbreaking love story amid the debris and disorder of France in 1947. And the self-conscious writer will see, as a man and as a writer, that not all values and all causes are equally legitimate. Because his writing is by its very nature an act of confidence in the freedom of men, he will want to engage himself on their side.

Freedom for All

Does the aesthetic city of ends necessarily imply the freedom of all other people? Is it not possible to write for a small circle — the ruling elite and their professional and intellectual supporters — to speak of them as free, and to accept the oppression of everyone else? And why — to take up Sartre's wartime argument — is it impossible to write a good novel advocating oppression?

Sartre admits that any writer chooses and thus limits his audience, speaking to certain specific groups. Richard Wright, for example, does not try to reach those who cannot possibly be affected by his work, say Frenchmen or Southern racists. But beyond a specific and limited group, composed of black intellectuals and sympathetic

15. QL, pp.123-124; WL, pp.69-70.
16. QL, p.124; WL, p.70.
17. QL, p.74; WL, p.18 (translation changed).

whites, Wright still addresses everyone. 'The illiterate Negro peasants and the Southern planters represent a margin of abstract possibilities around his real public. After all, an illiterate may learn to read. *Black Boy* may fall into the hands of the most stubborn of Negrophobes and may open his eyes. This merely means that every human project exceeds its actual limits and extends itself step by step to the infinite.'[18]

Any book implies a readership of *all* humans, even if abstractly and in the distance. People may learn to read, may be drawn in by it and see themselves. All people — even the most vicious racists — freely make themselves and thus may conceivably change. This means that every novel is potentially a concrete, if unintended, relationship between the writer and all other people. I might enter the city of ends with anyone. This holds even for a racist novel. A black may read the book, and in so doing exercise his power of free, self-determining creativity. Having entered the city of ends with me, he would read that I consider him an inert, passive object, capable only of being directed from without. It is a contradiction. The mutually respectful relationship on which the novel rests belies the way I have depicted him and what I would do to him. My novel denies the very principles which make its existence possible.

While his argument remains abstract and timeless in temper, Sartre now introduces the historical dimension into the centre of his analysis. He undertakes an extended history of the relationship between writer and reader in France from the twelfth century to the present, which shows how the audience of literates broadened and how, by the mid-nineteenth century, the writer could ignore the proletarian masses only by betraying his craft. Literature can appear now as the 'common and forever renewed experience of all men' only because reading and writing are no longer the special preserve of a few.[19] 'To-day we consider reading and writing as human rights and, at the same time, as means for communicating with others which are almost as natural and spontaneous as oral language. That is why the most uncultured peasant is a potential reader.'[20] Anyone can read: this is the central fact today. It visibly confirms a human freedom which the existence of classes tries to deny. All humans are now recognized to be capable of creating that imaginary object, the novel,

18. QL, p.127; WL, p.73 (translation changed).
19. QL, p.131; WL, p.77.
20. QL, p.131; WL, p.78.

and all can equally enter with me — and with each other — into the aesthetic city of ends. If I advocate the oppression of any portion of humankind I am simply denying in my words the very fact which I recognize in my writing. This is the concrete historical reason why in my writing 'I feel that my freedom is indissolubly linked with that of all other men.'[21]

From the time of Flaubert, Baudelaire, and the Symbolist poets, writers have faced two publics — an actual public which does in fact read their works and for whom they directly write, and a virtual public, the oppressed masses. This split readership exists only because classes exist. In such a situation, the writer can become truly universal only by placing himself on the side of the vast majority. Their freedom does not demand anyone else's oppression, but rather a classless society. The freedom of the ruling class, however, *requires* that the many be oppressed. There are, then, two reasons why the writer who is aware of himself and his craft will place himself on the side of the masses. First, their cause is the only one which truly involves freedom for all; and second, this freedom is the concrete realization of the formal reader-author relationship in a society where all can read. In such a society, the distinct historical possibility exists that all humans can be free.

Literature in a Classless Society

Sartre's argument culminates in the claim that literature can 'only realize its full essence in a classless society'.[22] There, the writer will become the 'mediator' — the agent of self-consciousness — *for all*. Only in this society will the writer's *subject* — human freedom — and his potential *public* — the whole body of free people — coincide. No longer will the 'virtual public' remain 'like a dark sea around the sunny little beach of the real public' while the writer confuses 'the interests and cares of man with those of a small and favoured group.'[23] No longer torn between the bourgeoisie and the proletariat, the writer would no longer need 'to deny that he is in a situation, he would no longer seek to soar above his times and bear witness to it before eternity, but, as his situation would be universal, he would express the hopes and

21. QL, p.112; WL, p.58.
22. QL, p.194; WL, p.150.
23. QL, p.194; WL, p.150.

anger of all men, and would thereby express himself completely'.[24] Only in a classless society would literature be truly able to be itself, to 'enjoy its essence'. 'Literature in this classless society would thus be the world aware of itself, suspended in a free act, and offering itself to the free judgment of all men, the reflective self-awareness of a classless society. It is by means of the book that the members of this society would be able to get their bearings, to see themselves and see their situation.'[25]

To be fully effective, then, the writer needs a fully democratic socialist society. He 'must write for a public which has the freedom to change everything; which means, besides suppression of classes, abolition of all dictatorship, constant renewal of frameworks, and the continuous overthrowing of order once it tends to congeal.'[26] In a class society, institutions become rigid in an attempt to keep the class structure frozen and to protect the interests of the ruling class. Humans may become self-aware in a class society, but its fixed forms and institutions keep them from acting on that awareness. Once classes are eliminated, however, society will be able to respond immediately and flexibly to new human goals, new human projects, and develop institutions as they are needed, destroying old institutions as they become petrified and useless.

Because a free society has no 'stability' in the traditional sense it elevates the writer beyond all previous expectations. In 'a collectivity which constantly corrects, judges, and metamorphoses itself, the written work can be an essential condition of action, that is, the moment of reflective consciousness.'[27] 'In short, literature is, in essence, the subjectivity of a society in permanent revolution.'[28]

The Power of Words

Calling for *engagement* in writing, Sartre also demands that we who read, who read *him,* should become engaged. His argument itself attempts to demonstrate that words can lead to change, that the reflection they induce is a decisive moment of action. In writing he

24. QL, p.194; WL, p.151.
25. QL, p.196; WL, p.152.
26. QL, p.196; WL, p.153.
27. QL, p.197; WL, p.153.
28. QL, p.196; WL, p.153.

tries to compromise his readers, show them to themselves, to prompt
them to change their behaviour or at least be troubled by it. We can
experience directly as we read the enormous faith that Sartre places in
the power of words. He was later to become disillusioned — and
perhaps we can already see why. We have noted Simone de
Beauvoir's reflection that Marxism or psychoanalysis 'might have
clarified our thinking in the thirties', but that they lacked either. Still
lacking some such clarification, Sartre's argument remained suspended. While demanding engagement of this abstract figure, *the
writer,* Sartre put little weight on the underlying forces — material,
psychological, or social — which actually lead people to see this or that
reality, to adopt or change a course of behaviour.

This was of course strictly in keeping with his earlier rejection of
pre-conscious and unconscious structures, and with his entire line of
thought from *La Transcendence de l'ego* to *L'Etre et le Néant.* It was notable
here, in 1947, that while certain lines of his thought began to shift,
Sartre stood fast in, and acted out of his belief in the transparency of
consciousness. If consciousness was totally free and spontaneous, if
no internal or external forces shaped our perceptions, feelings, or
actions, then indeed a passionate argument might demand, and
perhaps win, commitment from us. By systematically undervaluing
the weight of the internal and external world, Sartre now overvalued
the power of words.

In part, of course, Sartre's faith in words was the index of his complete dependence on them, in his increasingly adverse political situation. The solidarities of the Resistance had passed with the euphoria
of the Liberation. The PCF had emphatically rejected Sartre, leaving
him politically powerless and isolated. His new situation was described by de Beauvoir: 'suspect among the bourgeoisie and cut off
from the masses, Sartre was condemning himself to a future without a
public; from now on he would have merely readers. He accepted this
solitude willingly, because it titillated his love of adventure. Nothing
could be more despairing than this essay, and nothing more high-
spirited. By rejecting him, the Communists were condemning him to
political impotence; but since to name is to unmask, and to unmask is
to change, Sartre extended his notion of commitment still further and
discovered a *praxis* in writing. Reduced to his *petit-bourgeois* singularity, and rejecting it, he was aware of himself as "an unhappy consciousness", but had no taste for jeremiads and was confident of being

able to find a way of going beyond this state.'[29]

In effect, Sartre was calling on words to remake his situation. So, for all its force, his vision was an abstract one. If his exploration of the social meanings and conditions of writing was fertile and provocative, it was unmistakably redolent of philosophy-in-the-world. Yet the activist energy of these years was unmatched in Sartre's work, and impelled him to his highest pitch of productivity. In *The Writings of Jean-Paul Sartre*, Contat and Rybalka record 135 pages of entries for the 1945-49 period, compared with ninety-two and ninety for his next two most productive half-decades. Sartre's hope for the power of words might eventually bring him to disillusionment, but its immediate result was an impassioned effort to realize *une littérature engagée*.

29. *La Force des choses*, p.146; *Force of Circumstance*, p.131.

Three

Changing the World

In the Mesh of History

Early one July morning in 1961, Sartre and Simone de Beauvoir were at the latter's apartment packing for a summer holiday in Rome when Sartre's mother phoned to tell them that a plastic bomb had exploded in the entrance hall of his apartment building. As a leading public supporter of Algerian self-determination, Sartre had become a target of the right-wing campaign of terror that mounted as the colonists' position deteriorated. The damage was not serious, and Sartre and de Beauvoir were able to go on their way to Italy. However, returning to Paris in the autumn, they discovered that assassination attempts had spread, and Sartre began to receive threatening letters from Oran. For safety they moved temporarily into a furnished apartment rented in his secretary's name. When, in early January 1962, a shop on the corner was blown up, Sartre and his friends immediately — but mistakenly — concluded that the attack had been aimed at him. As de Beauvoir remembers, 'most of the left-wing journalists, political figures, writers and university teachers had by now been the target of a bomb attack.' It was no surprise, then, that on January 7 a second bomb exploded at Sartre's apartment, this one more effective than the first. It blew up the entire floor above, tearing off the door of Sartre's apartment and destroying a cupboard on the landing. A wall collapsed on the upper floors, leaving staircase hanging in space. The courtyard was strewn with rubble. 'We went up the service stairs,' de Beauvoir wrote, 'passing tenants coming down with suitcases in their hands. The vanished cupboard, the staircase open to the sky — even though I'd been told, I couldn't believe my eyes; inside the apartment, there were papers all over the floor, doors torn off, walls, ceilings and floors covered with a sort of soot.'[2]

1. *La Force des choses*, p. 641; *Force of Circumstance*, pp. 613-614.
2. Ibid., p.639; p.611.

What had Sartre done to provoke this attack? He had published articles in *Les Temps Modernes* supporting the Algerian Revolution, signed petitions and issued statements of solidarity, testified at trials on behalf of Algerian militants and their supporters, sponsored solidarity organizations and spoken at demonstrations. Most recently, in Rome a month earlier, he had called a press conference to declare his support for the liberation movement. In sum, he had done everything in the power of a left-wing intellectual to support the Algerian struggle, condemn French use of torture, and encourage insubordination in the army.

As far as we can learn, the bombings seem to have affected Sartre little. Yet, they symbolized much of the reality of individual political commitment. Most obviously, they signified that commitment meant far more than simply acting on the world. The world resists. No project of commitment can be so easily carried out, is without consequences. The bombings showed that the events and forces which Sartre sought to act upon and influence would in turn have their own power over him. To be directly threatened as Sartre was in 1939-41 and again in 1961-62 was only one form of history's peculiar power. He encountered, and was fundamentally marked by, many others: the Cold War, the revelations about labour camps in the USSR, the Korean War, the French war in Indochina, the execution of the Rosenbergs, the insurrection in Budapest and the Soviet invasion of Hungary, the Algerian war of independence, de Gaulle's return to power, the Cuban Revolution, the American war in Vietnam, the Soviet invasion of Czechoslovakia. And winding through this history was the abiding presence and changing politics of the French Communist Party.

The developing writer whose strengths and limits we have so far explored had now overcome his initial separation from this historical world. As a result of the war, Occupation and Liberation he would fully *enter* this history; not to venture an occasional comment, but to launch a sustained effort as a writer and activist, seeking to influence real events and admitting them as vital terms of his thought. We have seen Sartre choose to liquidate his fascination with the *irréel* as an alternative, his distance from history, in order to become fully real and to live his history explicitly. History was no longer his background: it became his element, his hope, his rage, his chance of thinking clearly, his risk of confusion and bad faith. Correspondingly, history now becomes a central theme of our analysis and critique of his writings.

How far did Sartre remain bound by his original 'ideological interest'? This crucial question is henceforward both theoretical — addressed to the logic of his writings — and historical — concerned to measure their adequacy to the objective situations in which they intervened. In studying Sartre's development from 1947 to 1962 we will be able to observe exactly how far he reconstructed his original terms into concepts capable of comprehending and intervening effectively in the human world, and how far he remained rooted in his isolated individualist and potentially aestheticist origins. His development in these fifteen years both showed the ultimate limits of his achievement and illuminated the historical — political and cultural — conditions that imposed them. The deepest interrogation and critique of Sartre must now simultaneously become an interrogation and critique of the specific period of history he lived. How otherwise could we evaluate his success and failure in a period when he devoted himself to influencing the PCF, to lecturing the USSR, to struggling with every available weapon for Algerian independence? Turning now to the decisive stage of Sartre's career, we will first examine the key steps in his political development from 1947 to 1962. A broad view of Sartre's political evolution must obviously include his plays, essays, and theoretical development. But I shall begin with Sartre as activist, in the broadest sense: with his changing sense of political priority, and his changing relationship to the PCF and the USSR. This examination will set out the objective limits within which Sartre thought, created and struggled, and trace his growth as a political actor in relation to them.[3] The following three chapters will focus specifically, and in greater depth, on the key areas of his writing during this period: his plays, political essays, and social philosophy.

The Apprenticeship to Realism: A Third Way?

Two armies had liberated Europe from Nazism in the name of two antithetical systems. While the British and American forces had swept through Western Europe and installed pro-capitalist regimes, the Red Army had set up pro-Communist governments in the countries

---

3. Rossana Rossanda has perceptively if somewhat abstractly sketched Sartre's political trajectory from the 1930s to the 1970s, mentioning some of the strengths and weaknesses I discuss below. See 'Sartre's Political Practice', Ralph Miliband and John Saville, eds., *The Socialist Register 1975*, London 1975.

under its tutelage. At this stage of his activity, Sartre's main political idea was to steer between the victorious powers: his goal was a neutralist, socialist Europe. He foresaw that politically and culturally France would be dominated by the great powers unless the *European* working class could create a distinct socialism for the continent. He spoke and wrote eloquently for French and European independence from the United States *and* the ussr, in the interests both of peace and of a genuinely democratic but not reformist socialism.[4] Thus his first major political undertaking after founding *Les Temps Modernes* was the Rassemblement Démocratique et Révolutionnaire (rdr): a would-be revolutionary socialist organization independent of the Communists.

Why should Sartre have tried to call a *new* movement into being? What motivated his attempt to find a 'third way'? Why could he not simply endorse the ussr and join the pcf? There were, of course, his deep theoretical differences with orthodox Marxism during these years and, as he himself later reflected, the fact 'that I would have had to disavow *L'Etre et le Néant* to enter the Party.'[5] We may recall that if the pcf attracted Sartre, its own intellectuals kept him at a distance or attacked him, except for a brief period during the war. Just the same, in 1947, in the concluding section of *Qu'est-ce que la littérature?*, Sartre undertook a principled and objective analysis of the relationship between writers and the pcf.

To be a committed writer meant to want to speak above all to the proletariat, which 'demands the right to make history at the moment that we are discovering our historicity'. Otherwise engagement was an abstraction, an appeal limited from the outset to other *petit-bourgeois* intellectuals. But unfortunately 'these men, to whom we *must* speak, are separated from us by an iron curtain in our own country; they will not hear a word that we shall say to them. The majority of the proletariat, straight-jacketed by a single party, encircled by a propaganda which isolates it, forms a closed society without doors or windows. There is only one way of access, a very narrow one, the Communist Party.' To be committed, then, and be effective, entailed the writer's joining the Party. 'But can he become a Communist and

---

4. See 'Défense de la culture française par la culture européenne' ('Defending French Culture by Defending European Culture'), *Politique étrangère,* 14th year, no. 3 (June 1949); crw 49/186, pp.225-229.

5. *Sartre,* p.85.

remain a writer?'[6] Party intellectuals were forced to justify many distasteful policies in the late 1940s: the Rajk and Kostov trials, the Comintern's break with Yugoslavia, the existence of forced-labour camps in the USSR.[7] They were obliged to renounce all intellectual autonomy and agree to speak on behalf of any policy decided by ruling Party circles. Sartre's friend Nizan had been one such intellectual, and had been shattered by the Hitler-Stalin pact. Sartre linked the Party's treatment of its intellectuals with its abandonment of its revolutionary purposes. 'The politics of Stalinist Communism are incompatible in France with the honest practice of the literary craft,' he declared.[8] The political conservatism of the Party was the fundamental reason why the committed writer should not join it. Literature was by nature contestation and heresy; it must call everything into question. But Stalinist conservatism had long since stopped doing so. By 1947 Sartre had already had three years of personal exposure to the Party's methods of stifling intellectual opposition, including 'persuasion by repetition, by intimidation, by veiled threats, by forceful and scornful assertion, by cryptic allusions to demonstrations that are not forthcoming, by exhibiting so complete and superb a conviction that, from the very start, it places itself above all debate, casts its spell, and ends by becoming contagious; the opponent is never answered; he is discredited; he belongs to police, to the Intelligence Service; he's a fascist.'[9] If not joining the PCF meant being cut off from the proletariat, joining it would mean becoming part of a propaganda machine which negated 'the very meaning of writing'.[10]

The point was, Sartre knew, that the choice was an impossible one. Remaining outside the party was the only way to remain committed to socialist revolution and democracy. At the same time, the PCF, hostile to both and to Sartre's intellectual independence, would continue to revile and slander him. As independent socialists in 1947, as existentialists and not Marxists, Sartre and his close comrades had 'fallen outside of history and were speaking in the desert'.[11] Until the

6. QL, p.277; WL, p.247.

7. The outrages of official Communism in this period are catalogued in David Caute's comprehensive if somewhat unbalanced study, *Communism and the French Intellectuals 1914-60,* New York 1964, pp.162-196.

8. QL, p.280; WL, p.250.

9. QL, p.280; WL, p.251.

10. QL, p.295; WL, p.267.

11. QL, p.289; WL, p.260.

Cuban Revolution, no party, movement, or country gave what Sartre considered anything like adequate expression to the values that he upheld. Socialism, the vision of human liberation, democracy and plenty, was realized in partial, primitive social forms whose progressive content was nearly cancelled by their oppressive features. Yet to be a socialist entailed commitment not only to ideas, but to a real, historical movement of liberation. At *Les Temps Modernes*, first Merleau-Ponty, then Sartre, struggled with this intolerable dilemma. Reflecting later on the period when the existence of the Soviet labour camps became known, Sartre described the options as they then appeared: 'Either the USSR was not the country of socialism, in which case socialism didn't exist anywhere and doubtless, wasn't possible: or else, socialism was *that,* this abominable monster, this police state, the power of beasts of prey.'[12]

How was it possible, in such straits, to develop a sense of socialism as the real historical possibility of freedom, democracy, and national self-determination? One way was to create an organization which would struggle for a socialism based on such principles. The 'Appel du Comité pour le Rassemblement Démocratique Révolutionnaire' gave voice to Sartre's commitment to socialism and democracy, peace and neutrality: 'between the corruption of capitalist democracy, the flaws and weaknesses of a certain sort of social democracy, and the limitations of Stalinist communism, we think that a free people's assembly for revolutionary democracy is capable of giving new life to the principle of freedom and human dignity by linking them to the struggle for social revolution.'[13] Obviously this was an ideal solution — to place socialism on the agenda, but 'on the basis of the heritage of political liberties common to all civilized peoples'; to recognize that class-based parties already existed, but ask them to 'come together in the International Revolutionary People's Assembly'.[14] The hopes embodied in the appeal were quickly dashed by a series of spectacular events. Early 1948 saw the coup in Prague and the beginning of Marshall aid to Europe. In the United States, the military draft was resumed. Berlin was blockaded by the Red Army in June, and this was countered by the massive British and

---

12. 'Merleau-Ponty', *Situations,* IV, Paris 1964, p.237; trans. Benita Eisler, 'Merleau-Ponty,' *Situations,* New York 1965, p.275.
13. Reprinted in full in CRW, 48/167, pp.207-210; see p.210.
14. CRW, p.209.

American airlift until May, 1949. The NATO Treaty was signed in the same month. That autumn the Soviet Union exploded its first atomic bomb, and the Chinese Revolution came to a victorious conclusion. The Cold War fell like a shroud over Europe and nowhere created such polarization as in France. And, as we now know, during this period a systematic American campaign of financing Washington's friends and subverting its enemies reached into every contested country.

This was the context in which the RDR was born, briefly flourished, and died. Led by Sartre, Gerard Rosenthal, and a former Trotskyist, David Rousset, it was doomed from the outset. Sartre laboured on its behalf for well over a year, but by 1949 its course was alarmingly clear. Rousset and Georges Altmann, editor of *Franc-Tireur,* travelled to the United States to get financial aid from the CIO, whose reputation in France as a 'left-wing' union disguised the extent to which it had become a Cold-War tool of the American government. Rousset returned with a project for 'study courses' devoted to 'peace'; Altmann sang the praises of a United States allegedly heavily influenced by workers and their unions. Sartre became suspicious of his colleagues' intentions and began to discern the hand of the American Embassy in the RDR's planned 'International Day for Resistance to Dictatorship and War.' He decided not to attend, and with Merleau-Ponty and Richard Wright sent a telegram to the meeting criticizing the State Department. Attended by ten thousand people on the eve of May Day, the meeting in fact turned out to be pro-American. One speaker justified the atomic bomb, another was Walter Reuther of the UAW-CIO. The RDR began to split open as Sartre remained insistently neutralist. He was strongly against the Atlantic Pact while Rousset refused to see it as a menace. Sartre's friends began to question the movement's finances, as well as Rousset's efforts to obtain financial aid from the CIO. Extremely disillusioned, Sartre resigned in October. [15] His unpublished note, quoted by de Beauvoir, revealed his reaction to the subsequent dissolution of the RDR: '*Circumstances merely appeared to be favourable to the association. It did answer to an abstract need defined by the objective situation, but not to any real need among the people. Consequently they did not support it.*'[16]

15. See Burnier, *Choice of Action,* pp.54-66 and de Beauvoir, *La Force des choses,* pp.189-94; *Force of Circumstances,* pp.171-77.
16. Ibid., p.194; p.177.

We cannot improve on Sartre's critique of the RDR: organized from above, it originally embodied excellent ideas; yet it was a rather abstract and naive effort to conjure up a movement which nobody wanted. Hindsight tells us that the RDR was doomed from the outset to split Eastwards and Westwards. But hindsight often distorts: the RDR was an impossible project in what was in reality an impossible situation. We can hardly fault an activist committed to revolutionary and democratic socialism for attempting to create an alternative before accepting the facts of the Cold War. Sartre acted in good faith, only to see the RDR's original purposes subverted by the pro-American camp, quite certainly with its political support and quite possibly with financial aid as well. His political baptism could only have strengthened his hostility to capitalism and the West. Another unpublished comment was a terse statement of the lesson to be drawn from the experience: *'Splitting up of the RDR hard blow. Fresh and definitive apprenticeship to realism. One cannot create a movement.'*[17] He now had two options: to remain in political limbo, or to do whatever was necessary to align himself with the PCF.

At this time too, Sartre was learning the same lesson from the early performances of *Les Mains sales*. The Communist Hoederer is certainly one of Sartre's most positive dramatic creations. But an opposing faction of the Proletarian Party has assigned the bourgeois intellectual Hugo to kill him. Hugo discharges his assignment, but out of jealousy, not political conviction — and does so only shortly before the USSR orders the adoption of Hoederer's united-front policy. The play is clearly critical of Hugo throughout, but in identifying with him the audience cannot avoid being critical of a Party leadership that merely parrots Soviet policy, resolves internal differences through assassination, and falsifies history to avoid admitting its own mistakes. The charged political situation of 1948 determined the response to the play. However balanced *Les Mains sales* may appear thirty years later, it was universally seen at the time as an attack on the Communists. From the beginning it threw the Party into a rage.[18] The bourgeois press, in de Beauvoir's words, waited to see the Communists' reaction and then 'buried Sartre in bouquets'.[19] Sartre was deeply shaken by both the bourgeois celebration and the Communist

17. Ibid., p.194; p.176.
18. Burnier, p.45.
19. *La Force des choses*, p.168; *Force of Circumstance*, p.151.

outrage unleashed by *Les Mains sales,* as his hasty retreat made plain. He strongly opposed any anti-Soviet rendition of the play, and immediately sought to have the American performance blocked. Later, as he drew closer to the Communists, he banned it in Austria, Spain, Greece and Indochina.

In an interview given in 1964, Sartre referred to the historical situation for his explanation of these events, emphasizing that the *audience* of the time had assigned the play its objective meaning. 'There is nothing to be done about it; if the whole of the French bourgeoisie makes *Le Mains sales* a hit and if the Communists attack it, that means that something has really happened. It means that the play has become anti-communist of *its own accord,* objectively, and that the author's intentions no longer count.'[20]

But this interpretation told only the externals of the story, as Sartre's interviewer astutely pointed out. Sartre had written an honest, independent play, deeply critical of specific aspects of Communist practice and not unsympathetic, in the end, to Hugo's critique of the Party. But he understood neither the Party nor the historical situation if he assumed that the PCF could see *Les Mains sales* as anything but a declaration of war, and if he thought the bourgeois press and audience would see anything else in it but an attack on Communism. Between the programmatic declaration of *Qu'est-ce que la littérature?* and his first practical venture in committed writing, *Les Mains sales,* the Cold War had supervened, remaking his field of action and the meaning of his intervention in it. In France, *Les Mains sales* became Sartre's most widely performed play. The 1951 film version was picketed by PCF militants and shown under police protection, while Sartre declared: 'I wash my hands of it.'[21] In 1952 he forbade performances of the play in any country without the approval of the local Communist Party. 'I do not disown *Les Mains sales,*' he said two years later, 'but I regret the use to which it has been put. My play has become a political battlefield, an instrument of political propaganda.'[22]

The Intolerable Contradiction: Choosing Sides

The fate of the RDR and the strange career of *Les Mains sales* show how

20. Interview with Paulo Caruso, March 4, 1964: TS, p.251; ST, p.212.
21. Interview in *Paris-Presse,* 'L'Intransigeant', June 7, 1951; CRW, p.603.
22. *Le Monde,* September, 25, 1954; CRW, 48/153, p.191.

difficult it was for Sartre in the late 1940s to become a committed intellectual while remaining independent of both the PCF and anti-Communism. In his later account of the political intinerary he shared with Maurice Merleau-Ponty, Sartre defined the overwhelming problem of that time: how to function as 'fellow-travellers without anyone's having invited them on the trip'.[23] How, that is, could one be an independent and critical socialist intellectual in 1948, functioning alongside and in alliance with the PCF? 'We had to defend Marxist ideology without hiding our reservations and our hesitancies. We had to go part of the way with people who, in turn, treated us like police-intellectuals. We had to thrust and parry without being insulting or severing relations; criticize freely but with moderation those cadavers who didn't tolerate a single disagreement; affirm, in spite of our solitude, that we were marching along at their side, at the side of the working class.'[24]

Sartre had been attacked by the PCF as an agent of the government and Wall Street for his role in the RDR. Such slanders were not new. Since 1945 *L'Humanité* had referred to Sartre and his colleagues at *Les Temps Modernes* as Gaullist or American agents, and a number of more philosophically inclined PCF writers, including Roger Garaudy, Jean Kanapa and Henri Lefebvre had laced their attacks with outright vilification. The months before the appearance of *Les Mains sales* had seen insinuations about Sartre's and de Beauvoir's private life in the PCF weekly *Action,* a heavily distorted portrait of Sartre in *Les Lettres françaises,* Kanapa's violent attack on *Situations,* I, and a campaign by Elsa Triolet for a boycott of the writings of Sartre, Camus and Breton. 'The situation could scarcely have been any worse,' Simone de Beauvoir observed;[25] but with the appearance of *Les Mains sales,* it did indeed worsen further. The play was reviewed in *L'Humanité* as the work of a 'nauseating writer', a 'scandal-mongering playwright'.[26] A Russian critic wrote: 'for thirty pieces of silver and a mess of American pottage, Jean-Paul Sartre has sold out what remained of his honour and probity.'[27] In the following year the Communist attacks on Sartre multiplied: where in 1945 he and his

23. 'Merleau-Ponty', p.221; 'Merleau-Ponty', p.259.
24. Ibid., p.221; p.259.
25. *La Force des choses,* p.167; *Force of Circumstance,* p.150.
26. CRW, 48/145, p.187.
27. *La Force des choses,* p.168; *Force of Circumstance,* p.151.

colleagues at *Les Temps Modernes* had tried to be 'everyone's friends', by 1950 they were isolated and 'were looked upon by everyone as enemies'. [28] Sartre had become in the words of André Gorz, 'the most denounced, the most hated man in France.'[29] By 1952 Sartre had in spite of himself become in the only eyes that counted, those of the PCF, an enemy of the working class. 'And the contradiction that was tearing him apart,' de Beauvoir recalled, 'had by then become intolerable.'[30] As he himself wrote in unpublished notes: 'I was a victim of and an accomplice in the class struggle: a victim because I was hated by an entire class. An accomplice because I felt both responsible and powerless . . . I discovered the class struggle in that slow dismemberment that tore us away from them [the workers] more and more each day . . . I believed in it, but I did not imagine that it was total . . . I discovered it against myself.'[31]

Taking Sides: the Early 1950s

All the while the Cold War was growing more intense. In June 1950 in Korea, it had exploded into actual fighting, apparently at the initiative of the Communists. The existence of the Soviet camps had been sensationally revealed in the Paris press the previous autumn with David Rousset's voice among the loudest in denunciation. Capitalist-Communist tension was reaching its peak in France as military service was extended to eighteen months. And of course, France was fighting its futile war to regain control over Vietnam, opposed only by the PCF and a handful of independent leftists like Sartre. Merleau-Ponty, political editor of *Les Temps Modernes,* counselled that the journal remain silent now that the Soviet Union seemed to have chosen war.[32] Sartre's friends, Camus among them, began to talk obsessively about whether to stay or leave when the Russians invaded Paris. For Sartre such 'intellectual games . . . by pushing things to extremes, revealed to each man the necessity to choose, and the consequences of his choice.'[33]

28. Ibid., p.217; p.199.
29. *Sartre,* p.79.
30. *La Force des choses,* p.280; *Force of Circumstance,* p.261.
31. Ibid., p.280; p.261.
32. 'Merleau-Ponty', p.236; p.274.
33. Ibid., pp.247-8; p.286.

Many were politically broken by the strain. Of the group originally invited to collaborate on *Les Temps Modernes,* for example, Raymond Aron became a political 'realist' — that is, cynical about the chances for socialism — and rallied to the capitalist powers in the Cold War as an editorialist for *Le Figaro.* By 1961 he had gone so far as to contribute an approving preface to Herman Kahn's *On Thermonuclear War.* Camus pretended to stand above all parties but became a bitter anti-Communist. Born in Algeria, he refused to speak out against the French during the Algerian War. And Merleau-Ponty, after pioneering the development of a non-party Marxist theory, was deeply disillusioned by the Korean War, as well as by the failure of the French proletariat to remain revolutionary. But rather than become an anti-Communist he 'took refuge', in Sartre's words, 'in his inner life', taking new and wholly unpolitical paths of intellectual exploration.[34]

Sartre, however, did not become cynical or disillusioned. Characteristically, he placed himself at the point of greatest contradiction and attempted to think forward from it. In *Le Diable et le bon Dieu,* first performed in 1951, he grappled with questions of morality, idealism and realism in political action. Whereas, in *Les Mains sales,* Hugo had never understood 'the imperatives of concrete action',[35] Goetz now slowly moved from doing evil abstractly, to doing good abstractly, to acceptance of the need to struggle in the real world amidst real people. Sartre's notes show that he had reached the same point as his protagonist and was able now to accept a collective discipline without denying his own liberty. 'After ten years of rumination, I had reached a breaking point: one light tap was all that was required.'[36] This 'tap' came after the Ridgeway riots at the end of May 1952, with the ludicrous arrest of the Communist leader, Jacques Duclos, as part of a deliberate government attempt to suppress the PCF.

The Communists had been part of the post-Liberation coalition governments, reaching their peak of more than 28% of the vote in 1946. But their intransigent stance at a time of sharpening international polarization, including their opposition to the colonial war in

34. Ibid., p.235; p.273. Sartre was being too indulgent; we shall see Merleau-Ponty arrive at a 'new liberalism' after leaving *Les Temps Modernes.*
35. TS, p.270; ST, p.228.
36. *La Force des choses,* p.280; *Force of Circumstance,* p.261.

Vietnam when the Communist defence minister had formal charge of prosecuting it, led to their expulsion from the government in 1947. From then on the PCF, representing the majority of French workers, was the pariah of French politics. The ruling parties further manipulated the situation against the PCF in preparation for the 1951 elections. Its share of the vote dropped only slightly from 1946 as the anti-Communist scare reached its height, but under the new electoral law, over a quarter of the popular vote gained the party only a sixth of the assembly seats.

It was in this setting that the US General Matthew Ridgeway, former head of command in Korea, came to Paris in May 1952 *en route* to assuming command of NATO. In a great display of militancy, the PCF organized a protest demonstration which led to street rioting. The police retaliated with suppression of the riots and the trumped-up arrest of Duclos. In this major clash between the Communist Party and the State even the most farcical details were enveloped in the climate of international Cold War: two dead pigeons, meant for dinner, were confiscated from Duclos's car and publicly presented as carrier pigeons used for coordinating the riots.

Reading about this in Rome, Sartre was impelled to a decisive conversion. The obvious frame-up of Duclos brought to a head his slowly accumulated disgust at his own class. 'In the name of those principles which it had inculcated into me, in the name of its humanism and of its humanities, in the name of liberty, equality, fraternity, I swore to the bourgeoisie a hatred which would only die with me. When I returned precipitately to Paris, I had to write or suffocate. Day and night, I wrote the first part of *Les Communistes et la paix*.'[37] He now gave up trying to remain independent of the blocs. Both *Les Communistes et la paix* and his 'Réponse à Camus' made clear, in de Beauvoir's words, that 'the post-war period was over. No more postponements, no more conciliations were possible. We had been forced into making clear-cut choices. Despite the difficulty of his position, Sartre still knew he had been right to adopt it.'[38] As he later wrote, he decided 'to accept the point of view of the USSR in its totality and count on myself alone to maintain my own.'[39] Critical independence of the PCF and insistence on democratic and revolu-

37. 'Merleau-Ponty' p.249; pp.287-88.
38. *La Force des choses*, p.281; *Force of Circumstance*, p.262.
39. Ibid., p.282; p.262.

tionary principles were no longer his guiding theme: in the real world of the class struggle and the Cold War, he decided that it was far more important to take sides. Korea, Vietnam, McCarthyism, the Duclos arrest — these events made any neutral or intermediate position impossible. In spite of the labour camps and all else about the USSR, and the PCF which dishonoured or indeed vitiated the cause of socialism, Sartre violently rejected his own class. If it was necessary to choose, he would side with the proletariat and its actual representatives.

Accordingly, he formulated a new principle: whatever his criticisms might be of the PCF and the USSR, they both fundamentally represented the oppressed and exploited masses. Anti-Communism he henceforth regarded as simple treason to the masses. 'An anti-Communist is a rat. I couldn't see any way out of that one, and I never will.'[40] Sartre was emphatic that to side against the Party at this moment of history, was to side *with* the exploiting class. The socialist movement, he wrote in 1956, was the absolute standard of reference by which any political undertaking must be judged, 'because, to the exploited, exploitation and the class struggle are their reality and the truth of bourgeois societies . . . It is the movement of man in process of developing himself. The other parties believe that man is already developed.'[41] In other words, Sartre abandoned any and all forms of neutralism. The existing forms of socialism were privileged: to understand socialism 'it is necessary to marry its movement and adopt its objectivity.'[42] Its leaders were also privileged, in that their crimes, mistakes and abominations deserved the severest criticism and condemnation. 'The greatness of their undertaking and the weight of their responsibilities deprive them of *all mitigating circumstances*.'[43] Sartre refused to set himself up, as Merleau-Ponty had done after 1952, as a neutral judge of both East and West, Communism and capitalism. He rejected any 'eagle's eyrie from which the evolution of peoples' regimes and of capitalist democracies could be jointly appraised.' He fully accepted as his own the point of view of socialism, however grotesque it might be, even if it had become 'that bloody monster which itself tears itself to pieces'.[44]

40. 'Merleau-Ponty', pp.248-9; p.287.
41. *Le Fantôme de Staline, Situations,* VII, Paris 1965, p.148 (FS); trans. Irene Clephane, *The Spectre of Stalin,* London 1969, p.4 (SS) — translation changed.
42. FS, p.281; SS, p.90.
43. FS, p.282; SS, p.90.
44. FS, p.236; SS, p.61.

Ironically, even in this choice Sartre was not a free agent. Certainly he had come to affirm the 'realistic' necessity of fully endorsing the PCF and the USSR: but his ability to make this more than a rhetorical gesture depended on the Party. We may recall that the PCF kept Sartre on the sidelines during the Occupation until 1943 when it approached him to join the CNE and work on *Les Lettres françaises*, and that in 1945 the Communists broke suddenly with him after allowing him space in *Action* to argue his point of view. In *Entretiens sur la politique* Sartre recounted the cat-and mouse game the PCF played with him after 1945, offering discussion, then breaking off; friendly Party intellectuals expressed their personal sympathy as the Party press was slandering him. In 1950, while travelling in Africa, Sartre was prevented from making contact with revolutionary leaders from the Ivory Coast because of the Communists' hostility to him. Finally, in late 1951, a PCF threatened with total isolation approached him anew, this time as part of its efforts to create a united front of intellectuals opposed to the war in Indochina. A PCF sailor-militant, Henri Martin, had been jailed for passing out peace leaflets, and the Communists launched a broad-based struggle to free him. Sartre jumped at the chance to work closely with the PCF and took charge of the project which resulted in the book *L'Affaire Henri Martin*.

Sartre's and the PCF's attitudes had now changed. He became active in the Peace Movement and the France-USSR Association. He would not write another *Les Mains sales*; in fact, his next play — and one of his most directly partisan — *Nekrassov*, guyed the anti-Communist hysteria promoted by the bourgeois press. For the next four years Sartre scarcely criticized the PCF or the USSR. Indeed, his new-found determination to accept the contradictions of the time and take the side of Communism led him to some of his most naive and ill-considered political statements. For example, his uncritical enthusiasm for the Communist-sponsored Peoples' Peace Congress in Vienna in late 1952 is embarrassing to recall today, as are his ingenuous descriptions of life in the USSR in 1954, after his first visit — he went so far as to claim that he had found complete freedom to criticize, and that the Soviet elite, subject to such criticism, had no special privileges.[45] In *Les Communistes et la paix*, he made exaggerated claims for the PCF's relationship with the French proletariat, arguing that the Party was the exact and necessary expression of the class.

45. See CRW, 54/260, pp.302-303; for Sartre's later view of this see 'Autoportrait à soixante-dix ans,' p.220; 'Self-portrait at Seventy', p.86.

The Mid-1950s: High Hopes, New Stature

Sartre's new, positive attitude towards the USSR and the PCF was intimately connected with another major historical event: the death of Stalin in 1953. Although this passed without mention by either Sartre or de Beauvoir, by the next year the post-Stalin thaw had gone far enough for them to visit the USSR for the first time. Sartre's excessively laudatory remarks upon returning reflected his discovery of a new zone of hope: the Communist world. By 1957 he had also visited Czechoslovakia, China, Yugoslavia, and Poland. At this time too, as the Socialist world began to slough off the dead weight of Stalinism, Sartre became a leading Marxist thinker in his own right. In a criticism of Party intellectuals in early 1956 he concluded that 'Marxism in France has come to a halt'.[46] His essay was an attempt to encourage the Party to undertake, and also to begin on his own, the kinds of intellectual work that would set it on the march again. His new posture was one of hope: the hope inspired by the thaw, by Khrushchev's startling revelations at the Twentieth Party Congress, by first-hand experience of the Chinese Revolution. It seemed possible now that the terrible nightmare was at an end and that socialism was about to become democratized and humanized.

This was the spirit of Sartre's response to the Soviet invasion of Hungary in the autumn of 1956. A new national and popular revolutionary movement led by Communists was crushed by Soviet tanks. Sartre unflinchingly condemned it as a crime, and severed relations with the PCF and all his friends among Russian writers 'who are not denouncing (or cannot denounce) the Hungarian massacre'.[47] He was also active in persuading the National Council of the Peace Movement and the board of directors of the CNE — both broad groups with strong PCF participation — to criticize the invasion. At the same time, his basic hopes remained unaffected. The invasion hearkened back to Stalin; it represented socialism's past, not its future. *Le Fantôme de Staline,* published in early 1957 in the special Hungarian issue of *Les Temps Modernes,* appealed to the Soviet leaders as comrades who had misunderstood their own and their people's real interest, suggested that the first phase of socialist development had necessarily to be brutal but had now created the basis for a democratized socialism and called upon the French Communists and

46. 'Le Reformisme et les fétiches', *Situations,* VII, Paris 1965, p.117.
47. CRW, 56/289, p.334.

Socialists to form a Popular Front. Thus in response to the Hungarian events, Sartre not only refused to become disillusioned with Communism, but forefully denounced the intervention in the name of socialism.

Sartre's itinerary in these years closely paralleled that of the Italian Marxist philosopher, Lucio Colletti. Forced by the Cold War to choose, Colletti joined the PCI without illusions. Unlike Party intellectuals of long standing, he experienced Stalin's death and Khrushchev's 'Secret Speech' not as disasters, but as a liberation. These years severely shook or broke the faith of many lifelong Communists, but both Sartre and Colletti for the first time dared to hope that Communism might free itself from this brutal past which they did not share. And so, after Hungary, Colletti rose in a PCI which had lost most of its professors, while Sartre probed yet more deeply into the causes of Stalinism and struggled yet more vigorously to create a living Marxism.[48]

Le Fantôme de Staline showed that Sartre had come through his period of strongest loyalty to the PCF and the USSR with his critical judgement actually strengthened. To his indomitable independence he had added during this period a sufficiently sure grasp of Marxism and socialist history to enable him to stand on his own as a Marxist thinker, and to judge the USSR in terms of it own theory.

The attitude of the PCF had also changed by now. Sartre could no longer be disregarded by them or dismissed as an 'intellectual cop'. His growing stature and the continuing thaw in the Cold War ironically make his 'broken' relations with the USSR and the PCF far more cordial than his best efforts at rapprochement had been in the years before 1950. Garaudy, who had insulted him as a 'grave-digger' in 1946, now remained friendly after Hungary in spite of his criticism — indeed within a few years Sartre was to take the stage with Garaudy before six thousand people for a debate on the dialectics of nature. More immediately important, however, was his trip to Poland in January 1957 to make contacts and encourage the thaw taking place there. At the request of a Polish journal he agreed to write the essay on 'existentialism in 1957' which, later that year, became *Question de méthode*. In this essay, published in Polish in April as *Les Temps Modernes* was publishing its Polish issue, Sartre refused to

48. See Lucio Colletti, 'A Political and Philosophical Interview', *New Left Review* 86 (July-August 1974), pp.3-5.

spare 'lazy' Marxism. Examining the development of Marxism historically, he tried to explain why existentialism — as the outlook representing the claims of the concrete individual — must continue to exist separate from but alongside an arrested orthodox Marxism. At the same time he expressed his deep conviction that Marxism could be reconstructed along what he now understood as its original lines.

The Late 1950s: Algéria, de Gaulle and the Turn to the Third World

From around 1954 to 1959, then, Sartre's rising political spirits reflected the end of the worst phase of the Cold War, Khrushchev's American visit, and the great economic and technological advances of the Soviet Union. His great hope remained that Stalinism was now obsolete and that perhaps 'de-Stalinization will de-Stalinize the de-Stalinizers.'[49] This failed to happen. Sartre said nothing about the shipwreck of de-Stalinization after 1960, about the absence of further reforms in the USSR. The new opportunities of the 1950s had led, after all, to bureaucratic socialism without terror. Moreover, as the great events of the late 1950s drew his attention back to France, it became clear that the end of the international Cold War had failed to unfreeze the politics of his own country. His effort, at the end of the still-hopeful essay on Hungary, to free the PCF from its past of Stalinism and isolation,[50] was cruelly mocked by PCF support for Mollet's special powers to crush the Algerian insurrection in 1956, the putsch in Algiers in 1958, and de Gaulle's return to power the same year. Both the PCF and the working class remained passive over Algeria. De Gaulle's 80% majority in the referendum of September 1958 allowed him to carry along the vast majority of Frenchmen into his project of modernizing French capitalism and the bourgeois state.

Sartre played an admirable role in the struggles against de Gaulle and on behalf of the Algerians. Moreover, he was now an independent political agent. For the first time, his work as activist was not fundamentally conditioned by the attitude and action of the PCF. In breaking with the Communists on Hungary he had also chided them

49. FS, p.261; SS, p.77 (translation changed).
50. See Rossanda, 'Sartre's Political Practice', p.65.

for their passivity and moderation with regard to Algeria.[51] He intensified his own involvement in the Algerian struggle at the same time as the PCF was voting special powers to Mollet; he was one of the first to sign the 'Manifesto of the 121' while the Communists criticized its initiators and signatories. Whenever possible he joined with Communists in joint action over de Gaulle's return to power or the war. But he criticized their reluctance to fight, and he himself took an increasingly militant stand on Algeria.

Les Temps Modernes became a centre of intellectual opposition to the war and de Gaulle, and issues were regularly seized by the authorities, first in Algeria and then in France itself. Sartre himself was responsible for a number of articles and interviews which fell victim to the censors, and the journal likewise printed a steady stream of materials attacking and compromising the government. Sartre wrote repeatedly in support of the Algerians, against torture, and against de Gaulle. He testified at trials of Algerian and pro-Algerian militants, struggled to build anti-war and anti-de Gaulle coalitions, sponsored and attended demonstrations. By 1959 he had taken a decisive new political direction, going beyond a 'peace' position and advocating support for the Algerian 'enemy', the FLN. In signing the 'Manifesto of the 121' he deliberately courted arrest and imprisonment. And then, as the struggle was drawing to its close in 1961 and 1962, came the bombings of his apartment. Again and again in reading de Beauvoir's account of this period, we have the sense of a small, brave and intensely committed group acting virtually alone, occasionally joined by the Communists, opposed by near-unanimous public opinion.

Besides this militant refusal to compromise, Sartre's writings of this period reveal the dissipation of his hopes for both East and West. Franz (France?) the hero of *Les Sequestrés d'Altona* (1959), is a torturer who, unable to redeem himself, ends in suicide. Sartre's preface to the new edition of Paul Nizan's *Aden, Arabie* attacked the Left's resignation and acquiescence in 1958 and looked to the emergence of a new generation and a new movement.[52] However the most striking essay of these years signalled his discovery of a new zone of hope just as Europe was coming to appear hopelessly compromised. His preface to Fanon's *The Wretched of the Earth* proclaimed passionate solidarity

51. See FS, pp.299 300; SS, pp.102 3.
52. See 'Paul Nizan', *Situations*, IV; *Situations*, Greenwich, Conn., 1965.

with revolutionaries throughout the Third World: 'we know that it is not a homogeneous world; we know too that enslaved peoples are still to be found there, together with some who have achieved a simulacrum of phoney independence, others who are still fighting to attain sovereignty and others again who have obtained complete freedom but who live under the constant menace of imperialist aggression. These differences are born of colonial history, in other words of oppression. Here, the mother country is satisfied to keep some feudal rulers in her pay; there, dividing and ruling she has created a native bourgeoisie, sham from beginning to end; elsewhere she has played a double game: the colony is planted with settlers and exploited at the same time. Thus Europe has multiplied divisions and opposing groups, has fashioned classes and sometimes even racial prejudices, and has endeavored by every means to bring about and intensify the stratification of colonized societies.'[53]

Sartre's powerful, violent essay established him as one of the West's leading spokespersons for the Third World. It was directed *against* the West, against his readers. 'With us, to be a man is to be an accomplice of colonialism, since all of us without exception have profited by colonial exploitation.'[54] We are all exploiters, he insisted, there is a colonial settler in every one of us. It was only through a violent offensive against us, their oppressors, that the colonized peoples would recover their humanity: 'by this mad fury, by this bitterness and spleen, by their ever-present desire to kill us, by the permanent tensing of powerful muscles which are afraid to relax, they have become men: men because of him [the Western oppressor] and against him.'[55] Sartre identified a new reality in the world: that 'in the past we made history and now it is being made of us.'[56] The direction of history had changed, and while the West might resist, watch and wait, it could no longer impede it. Those whom we had made our objects and beasts of burden were now taking aim — at us.

This essay was a masterpiece of self-flagellation: we are all guilty, Sartre declared; we deserve to have our history stolen from us, and the natives' violence against us is their only way of achieving full

---

53. 'Les Damnés de la terre', *Situations*, V, Paris 1964, p.171; trans. Constance Farington, 'Preface', Frantz Fanon, *The Wretched of the Earth*, New York 1965, pp.9-10.
54. Ibid., p.187; p.21.
55. Ibid., p.178; p.15.
56. Ibid., p.189; p.23.

humanity. If he had indeed discovered a new zone of hope, he had done so only through great physical distance or self-denial. His hope for the Third World was inseparable from his despair about his own society. He was to maintain these new political postures in the 1960s, combining relative indifference to changes in the Soviet camp and a deep disillusionment with France and the PCF with hopes for the emergence of a new Left and vigorous solidarity with movements for national liberation.

Achievement and Disillusionment

Sartre came to maturity as a political intellectual between the immediate post-war years and the end of the Algerian war. Across this period, he maintained an unshakeable dedication both to the democratic and humanistic commitment that had drawn him to socialism, and to the ideal of effective action in the political world. Yet he refused to make a fetish of either, seeking rather to situate himself directly in the tension between them. He could tell, for example that *Les Temps Modernes* in 1952 was running the risk of becoming 'moralistic' — a remote, abstract guardian of principle. When the Cold War imposed on those who remained political the choice of becoming pro- or anti-Communist, he embraced the existing socialist society, monstrosity that it was, as the only alternative to siding with the ruling class. But when the USSR acted in fundamental violation of its own principles, he did not hesitate to denounce it. And at this point he began new project, trying to understand why the Soviet Union had developed in this way and to reopen Marxist theory. Within stringent historical confines, he continued to develop his socialist perspective. If the failure of the RDR taught him much about his own and history's limits, he still refused to permit the eclipse of the very reasons for his commitment. While he was for a short time an uncritical apologist of the PCF and the USSR, he asserted an authoritative independent position after 1956. Nothing — neither personal danger nor total isolation — could induce him to acquiesce in the outrage of the Algerian war, indeed, the struggle seemed to foster his own growth. In the end, for all his schooling in realism, Sartre's hallmarks during the 1950s were his growing radicalism, his deepening sense of socialist principle, and his towering independence and integrity.

The symbol of all this was his refusal of the Nobel Prize in 1964.

His statement of rejection evinced an unpretentious but total commitment to socialist values as living principles of personal conduct. In refusing the prize Sartre was insisting on his need to remain independent: 'the writer should refuse to let himself be transformed into an institution.'[57] What was important was what the writer said, not who he was. 'I want to be read by people who feel like reading my books. Not by celebrity collectors.'[58] Sartre sought to avoid entering the elite class of cultural notables, to avoid being seen as an institution who happened to have 'extremist' ideas, and who by becoming a notable would be forgiven his 'controversial political past'. He sought to scuttle this kind of 'objective salvaging' operation — in the name of political commitment and of the struggles to which his life had become devoted. To accept this literary coronation would have been to permit the cultural notables, and the bourgeois they represented, to say: 'finally he's on our side. I could not allow that.'[59]

Sartre's second reason for refusing the Nobel Prize was that it had become, in the context of the Cold War, 'an honour restricted to Western writers or Eastern Rebels'.[60] He would have been glad to receive the prize during the Algerian War, for 'it would have honoured not just me but the freedom we were fighting for. But nobody offered me the prize then, only now, after all the fighting is over.'[61] However honourable the intentions of the Swedish Academy, the Nobel Prize had come to be seen as supporting the interests of bourgeois society: Sartre refused to lend legitimacy to so tendentious an accolade by accepting it.

But if he had 'come through' in the years between the end of the Second World War and the Algerian war, what was the reason for the disillusionment expressed in a 1960 interview which Contat and Rybalka rightly describe as 'essential to an understanding of Sartre'?[62] Speaking to Madeleine Chapsal, Sartre freely communicated his sense that something had gone wrong: his project of engaged writing had failed. Had anything changed as a result of his writing? 'Not a thing', Sartre replied. 'On the contrary, ever since my

57. CRW, 64/410, p.452.
58. CRW, 64/411, p.454.
59. CRW, p.455.
60. CRW, 64/410, p.453.
61. CRW, p.453.
62. CRW, 60/334, p.375.

youth I have experienced utter impotence, but that's neither here nor there. You could say, if you like, that to begin with I wrote a few books which weren't directly concerned with social problems; then came the Occupation — people began to think it was necessary to act. After the war, we felt once more that books, articles, etc. could be of use. In fact they were of no use whatever. Then we came to feel — or at least I did — that books conceived and written without any specific relation to the immediate situation could be of long-term use. And these turned out to be just as useless, for the purpose of acting on people — all you found was a distortion of your own thoughts and feelings. You find your own words turned against you and changed out of all recognition by a young man taking a casual swipe at you. Fair enough — I did the same myself. That's literary action for you — you can see that it doesn't produce the results you wanted it to.'[63] What was the meaning of this seeming admission of failure?

We have seen some of its historical causes: the faltering of de-Stalinization, the war in Algeria, de Gaulle's rise to power, the prostration of the PCF and its 1961 electoral disaster. But Sartre was speaking here of *his own* ineffectiveness, and not only history's cruel denial of his hopes. In *Les Mots,* published in 1963, Sartre sounded the same note. It was not a passing mood: *Sartre on Cuba,* a collection of reports first printed in *France-Soir,* also expressed the self-doubt of a radical intellectual. Several years later, in the aftermath of May 1968, he condemned the 'classical' model of the left-wing intellectual and struck out in a wholly different direction. Does anything in the career I have just summarized explain such a startling shift of perspective? Sartre's great achievement, after all, had its other side. We shall see that in some subtle but fundamental way he never found a comfortable role as political intellectual, and that on the theoretical level, he never fully transcended the basic limits and contradictions of his thought. In order to demonstrate this, it will be necessary to return to our study of Sartre's key terms and their propensities, this time in the context of his plays, political essays, and social philosophy. As we move from one area to another of his writing during this period we shall be able to identify both his achievement and the roots of his disillusionment.

63. 'Les Ecrivains en personne', *Situations,* IX, Paris 1972, p.25; trans. John Matthews, 'The Purposes of Writing', *Between Existentialism and Marxism,* London 1974, p.21 (translation changed).

2

Engaged Theatre

Sartre as engaged writer was, above all, a playwright. His very first lectures on theatre presented it as a locus of conflict and action — not reflection or psychological exploration.[1] The supreme question of his own theatre was that of choice — choice in situations, amidst events. He wrote for the stage in order to *act* in history, to engage his audience in issues of collective concern, and to change — or explore what it means to change — social reality. Here, as much as in the novel, the basic theses of *Qu'est-ce que la littérature?* were the working precepts of artistic composition.

Sartre's plays confirmed his break with the timeless concerns of *L'Etre et le Néant* and *La Nausée*. They were specifically of the present, plays that took sides on contemporary issues. They enacted sharp denunciations of mid-twentieth-century capitalism, racism in the American South, German and French fascism, war and imperialist expeditions, torture and doctrinaire Communism. On the other hand, they also included affirmations of an undoctrinaire revolutionary realism that accepted people as they were and acknowledged the necessity of violence in the process of their social liberation.

These plays met the demand for commitment. Franz, appealing to the crabs in his room (*Les Sequestrés d'Altona*); the intense triangle of Hugo, Hoederer, and Jessica (*Les Mains sales*) — these are powerful moments of theatre, as is Goetz's decision to take command of the peasant army in *Le Diable et le bon Dieu* and Henri and Julie's decision in *Mort sans sépulture* to lie to their torturers and live. Their power lies in their historicity: Franz, sick with guilt at having served as a torturer on

1. See TS, p.30-33; ST, pp.14-17. See also ibid., p.61; pp.38-39.

the Russian front; Hugo's tragic unwillingness to accept, and see the connection between, self-acceptance, personal warmth and political realism; Henri and Julie overcoming their guilt and self-hatred sufficiently to be able to think politically and serve the Resistance; and Goetz's intense illumination that helping people begins by accepting them as they are, by accepting the reality we live and seek to change. Commitment is never a given here; it is always in question. Sartre brought his pressing personal theme onto the stage, there to voice its rich and complex tensions.

The plays place the individual in history, among others, and subject him to, or demand from him, violent action. How can the individual become a real historical actor, free from mystification, capable of effective action yet genuinely working towards positive goals? This was Sartre's own question after 1940, and his theatre presented both its deepest philosophical meanings and its most accessible, everyday incarnations. It was, therefore, intimately associated with the themes and concerns that we have already identified and explored. The individual whom Sartre's plays plunge into action is, after all, Roquentin — one conscious of being *de trop,* cut off from commitment, an intellectual isolated from others, unsure of how to act, caught up in questions of personal salvation.

'Les Mouches'

Orestes, the protagonist of *Les Mouches*, is such an individual. *Les Mouches* deserves its reputation as a play of the Resistance. It stressed what was politically the most demanding theme of *L'Etre et le Néant* — that humans are always free to resist — and did so in a way that enabled it to elude censorship. Sartre's first political message to his fellow-countrymen was that it was an act of bad faith to accept the regime of guilt and penitence, and that the only authentic course was that of struggle. Nevertheless, as I indicated earlier, the conception of freedom developed in *Les Mouches* faithfully reflected the contradictory position Sartre had arrived at by 1943. It expressed both the energy and the hopelessness of *L'Etre et le Néant,* both the activism and the isolation of 'consciousness-in-the-world'. *Les Mouches* re-located this ontological predicament in a situation demanding action.

Orestes does not kill Aegistheus and his mother, Clytemnestra, for any of the motives originally presented by Aeschylus: not to avenge his father, or to claim his throne, or even to liberate the Argives from the usurper. Although he proclaims his mission as liberator at several places, the claim remàins hollow and rhetorical.[2] He is too well aware that he is a total stranger to Argos: 'these folk are no concern of mine'.[3] Orestes begins as a young scholar having no bonds with anyone in Argos but his sister Electra, and from the start is burdened by his empty, detached freedom. 'Some men are born engaged', he laments, 'a certain path has been assigned them, and at its end there is something they *must* do, a deed allotted.'[4] Rootless and aloof, he kills for one reason: in order to lay claim to something of his own, even — or perhaps especially — if it be a crime. It is as if Sartre had turned Roquentin away from writing and towards action. Orestes acts ostensibly under the pressure of events, but ultimately for the old reason: so that he will no longer be *de trop*. In his personal drama of alienation Orestes tries to earn a sense of belonging, to acquire a weight of his own, by heaping upon himself all the crimes of Argos. 'The heavier it is to carry, the better pleased I shall be; for that burden is my freedom.'[5] He will *own* his crime: unlike the people of Argos, unlike Aegistheus and Clytemnestra themselves, Orestes will claim it without guilt. And so he will have no need to repent or to pretend that someone else has done it.

Electra, on the other hand, shrinks from her role as accomplice and embraces Zeus's regime of penitence. She has wished for her mother's and Aegistheus's death in her every waking moment, but passively and strictly in the imaginary. Orestes's act explodes her fantasy. Electra discovers that she wanted them not to die but to live on as objects of her hatred. She will now wholly give herself over to guilt.

Guilt (and Oreste's freedom from it), violence (and his proud owning of it) and the passage from aloofness to engaged freedom: these are central themes of *Les Mouches*. They begin to define what Pierre Verstraeten describes as the original problematic of Sartre's theatre.[6]

---

2. Francis Jeanson makes this abundantly clear in *Sartre par lui-même*, pp.18-20. Jeanson argues that 'the work of Sartre in its totality could without exaggeration be considered as the commentary, critique, and transcendence of the conception of freedom this play proposes' (p.24). This excellent little book is the pioneering study of Sartre's theatre: it sketches broad and basic Sartrean preoccupations — even if it too often uncritically adopts Sartre's own point of view.

3. *Les Mouches*, p.26; trans. Stuart Gilbert, *The Flies, No Exit and Three other Plays*, p. 63.

4. Ibid., p.24; p.61 (translation changed).

5. Ibid., p.84; p.108.

This problematic defined Sartre in 1943: fully a stage beyond the internalized and metaphysical ponderings of *La Nausée* yet still marked by aloofness and unreality. The tension of this problematic is best registered in the most puzzling aspect of *Les Mouches*: Oreste's final departure from Argos. To be sure, Orestes spurns Zeus's offer of the throne of Argos — his own throne — in exchange for repudiation of his crime. But this is a device: Jeanson has found more telling, internal reasons for Orestes's departure. First, it stems from what is, finally, the personal rather than political character of his engagement.[7] His crime does not lessen his distance from the Argives and make him 'a man among men'. His 'coronation' is to be stoned by the angry crowd, who are too miserably comfortable in subservience and penitence to applaud his act. If at the end 'all here is new, all must begin anew',[8] this is true only for Orestes. Sharing nothing with this mob, Orestes remains detached even in his new-found situated freedom and refuses to claim his throne. He refuses any commitment which deeply links him with other people or creates permanent relationships of dependency. His ideal of freedom, even after the murders, remains aloofness and independence.[9] But why, then, does he call the Argives 'my people' and tell then, 'I love you, and it was for your sake that I killed'?[10] The question must be referred to the specific history of Orestes's creator. For Sartre in 1943 engagement did not yet mean solidarity and collective '*work* which should be accomplished patiently in history, in the relative, through uncertain and groping acts, none of which are truly good, none truly evil.'[11] Political action in *Les Mouches* was accordingly, rather a single hero's blind and theatrical gesture, his defiance of Zeus, his freeing people by example and contagion; his need of others was primarily a need for verification of his own act. Did *Les Mouches* faithfully reflect

6. See Pierre Verstraeten, *Violence et éthique; Esquisse d'une critique de la morale dialectique à partir du théâtre politique de Sartre*, Paris 1972, pp.7-31. This original book is by far the best full-length study of Sartre, even if it is somewhat abstract, limits itself to certain aspects of Sartre's theatre, and exaggerates the achievements of his dramatic project. Verstraeten probes deeply into Sartre's plays and elicits some of their key lines of development. This chapter is indebted to his penetrating discussion.

7. Jeanson, *Sartre par lui-même*, p.19.

8. *Les Mouches*, p.108; *The Flies*, p.127.

9. Jeanson, p.19.

10. *Les Mouches*, *Théâtre*, p.108; *The Flies*, p.126.

11. Jeanson, p.21

Sartre's own attitudes at the time? According to his famous essay, 'La République du silence', written immediately after the Liberation, it did. In this essay, Sartre described the Resistance as an individual, not a collective struggle. He saw it as a new kind of experience in which the fighters were *alone* in all circumstances. 'They were hunted down in solitude, arrested in solitude. It was completely forlorn and unbefriended that they held out against torture, alone and naked in the presence of torturers, clean shaven, well-fed, and well clothed. . . . Alone. Without a friendly hand or a word of encouragement. Yet, in the depth of their solitude, it was the others that they were protecting, all the others, all their comrades in the Resistance. Total responsibility in total solitude — is this not the very definition of our liberty?'[12]

It is not, unless in exceptional conditions. This vision of heroic isolation excluded the sense of solidarity in struggle, the sense of direct mutual dependence that members of the Resistance certainly shared. But this dimension of the struggle lay beyond Sartre's reach in the first years of his political involvement. It was this partial vision that *Les Mouches* reflected: an isolated hero commits a liberating murder and then marches off guiltlessly on his *own* path, pursued by the outraged flies and furies of remorse, watched by an astonished crowd. Yet Orestes's spectacular act was, for Sartre, a declaration of engagement. Orestes defied Zeus (and by implication, the German conquerors). The blood on his hands symbolized concrete historical action.

Orestes represented an answer to Roquentin's total detachment, but one that fell short of full engagement in history.[13] In introducing the problematic of Sartre's theatre, *Les Mouches* reasserted the problem of his entire career: given his starting points, the basic terms of his outlook and his concrete historical situation, how was effective engagement possible? Could the stiff, rhetorical, abstract Orestes of 1943 be transformed into a convincing and historical 'man among men' who acted *with* people and *for* them, stayed among them to fight for their common goals, understanding that action was 'patient work' and not theatrical gesture?

12. 'La République du silence', *Situations*, III, Paris 1949. p.13; trans. Ramon Guthrie, 'The Republic of Silence,' *The Republic of Silence*, A.J. Liebling, ed., New York 1947, p.499.
13. Verstraeten, p.27.

'Huis Clos'

A year later Sartre wrote his only wholly non-political play, whose answer to this question was given in its most notorious line: 'Hell is other people' — which is to say, in effect, 'Hell is ourselves.' Utterly estranged from anything like common goals, Garcin, Estelle and Inez have been thrown together for all eternity as each other's torturers. *Huis Clos* has already been cited as expressing Sartre's pessimistic view of the relation between the self and the Other. Twenty years after its composition, in a preface to a recording of the play, Sartre insisted that ' "hell is other people" has always been misunderstood. It has been thought that what I meant by that was that our relations with other people are always poisoned, that they are invariably hellish relations. But what I really mean is something totally different. I mean that if relations with someone else are twisted, vitiated, then that other person can only be hell.'[14] However, this was said after a further eight plays and many years of struggle with his original view of human relations. To be sure, Garcin does not say '*Other people* are hell', but rather 'hell is other people' — a far less categorical claim. But a play erects a total world, its own world. Were it to portray its only Jew as a money-grubber we would rightly think it anti-semitic, if its only woman were portrayed as susceptible to fainting fits, or its only black as shiftless, we would rightly think it sexist, or racist. If the playwright has an alternative version, this can only have countervailing effect if suggested or presented within the world of the play. It tells us nothing about *Huis Clos* when Sartre claims, twenty years later and outside the play, that other human relations are possible. In itself, *Huis Clos* contains not even the hint of an alternative. Sartre's attempt at clarification does not address the fact the he places his three characters in hell: Garcin, the pacifist-coward, Inez, the sadist-lesbian, and Estelle, murderess-coward, who is totally self-centred and entirely dependent on others' view of her. Garcin wants to be alone to hide from his own cowardice; Estelle desperately needs his interest and approval. Just as they begin to accept each other's self-deceptions, Inez breaks in with the icy truth. None of the three can rest, be left alone, or not affect the others. With classical simplicity and power, Sartre portrays them as unable to do anything but torture each other. Arguing abstractly, Sartre may claim that 'of their own

14. TS, p.238; ST, p.199.

free will they put themselves in hell.'[15] But they act out of necessity. *Huis Clos* presents these particular characters and no others; it gives no hint that they might possibly act otherwise; and contains no explanation for their behaviour that suggests an alternative. The door suddenly flies open and they have the chance to leave — but for where: somewhere else in hell? Each *chooses* to remain with the others. But when they are at their most real, arguments for their freedom seem quite rhetorical: Inez, Garcin, and Estelle *need* each other, *need* their particular hell. They are stuck. 'Well, well,' Garcin says at the end, 'let's get on with it.'[16]

If *Huis Clos* presents this brutal vision so effectively it is because it is such an accomplished play. It totally lacks the stiffness and rhetorical flavour of *Les Mouches*. Built upon a powerful image of hell as a Second-Empire drawing-room containing two other people, the play has a sureness of touch missing from any of Sartre's later plays until *Les Sequestrés d'Altona*. The characters are realistically drawn without artifice, incongruence or superfluity.[17] It is worthwhile to speculate on what lay behind the artistic difference between Sartre's classic existentialist play and his first engaged play. If the drama of timeless pessimism is so much better than its predecessor, it is because Sartre was intellectually so much more at home in it. Engagement was not a given for Sartre, but a project whose strains we have already seen dramatized in the person of Orestes. The issues raised by *Les Mouches* would have to be worked through and mastered before Sartre's historical and committed characters could attain the realism of the timeless, isolated individuals of *Huis Clos,* before rhetorical flourishes could become human speech, and dramatic gestures, comprehensible social acts. It was to be fifteen years before Sartre developed an engaged theatre that approached the artistic quality of *Huis Clos*.

Huis Clos adds a key question to that posed by *Les Mouches*: is it possible to develop human relations that are not infernal? By placing his original vision on the stage, Sartre put it in the context of action, and subjected it to renewed reflection. Just as virtually every one of his

15. TS, p.239; ST, p.200.

16. *Huis Clos*, p.168; *No Exit*, p.47.

17. See Dorothy McCall's judgment in *The Theatre of Jean-Paul Sartre*, New York 1969, p.125. This is a useful but uneven book; McCall misleadingly groups Sartre's plays thematically rather than according to his development and lacks an adequate grasp of the political issues involved, but generally has a sure sense of dramatization and character.

plays presented and recast the theme of human action, so they also worked and reworked the theme of human relations until the negativism of *Huis Clos* had been superseded by the more positive approach of his retrospective comments in 1965. 'Hell is other people' was not Sartre's last word on human relations, but his first.

'La Putain Respectueuse' and 'Morts sans Sépulture'

Sartre's next four plays, and the screenplay, *L'Engrenage*, took him significantly beyond these dramatic starting points. In *La Putain respectueuse*, for the first time, he presented a concrete historical situation. In so far as social issues figured in *Les Mouches*, they were refracted through Orestes's self-centred quest for a positive identity. But Lizzie, Fred, the Senator and the hunted black man are above all social beings whose words and actions are shaped by the socio-historical setting: the American South of the 1930s. In fact, the plot is taken from the Scottsboro Case of 1931 in Alabama. Here is no timeless drama of consciousness, but the interaction of people firmly set in a very definite social structure — Southern aristocrat, poor white, and black. Indeed, the characters remain virtual stereotypes, never emerging as more than generic social determinations. This aspect of the play defined the limit of its artistic achievement. But it was due to Sartre's effort to break new ground. His energy in this simple play was not concentrated in his customary philosophical exploration of moral issues, but rather in an attempt to capture the *social* dimension of consciousness and action: the aristocrat who arranges things by appealing to his family's rootedness and superiority; the unnamed Negro who momentarily defends himself but cannot bring himself to shoot whites; the poor white woman who momentarily identifies with the Negro but ultimately succumbs to the mythology perpetuated by her social superiors.

If *La Putain respectueuse*, attempted one kind of development beyond *Les Mouches* and *Huis Clos, Morts sans sépulture,* first performed on the same occasion in 1946, attempted another. This play ends tragically, as do many of Sartre's engaged plays, but its core action is affirmative: Henri and Julie overcome the shame, despair and isolation of their situation, and decide once again to live and struggle. The two protagonists are captured when their *maquis* unit fails in its mission. They are tortured by their Vichy captors and Julie suffers the added violence of rape. Henri, with Julie's assent, strangles her fifteen-year-old brother François when it is realized that he will talk under torture and betray their leader, Jean. Unlike Canoris, the Communist militant, Julie and Henri are reduced to despair by the torture that drives their comrade Sorbier to leap from a window to his death. Sick with guilt and shame, they come to hate themselves so much as to look forward to death. However, at Canoris's urging, they decide in the end that life is worth living, that as Canoris says, 'we have no right to die for nothing.'[18] Resolving to serve the Resistance, they lie to their torturers in order to protect Jean, withstand the 'look of triumph' in their torturers' eyes, and, in this spirit, submit to eventual death. Their death is shocking, but a victory nevertheless, for it now signifies resistance rather than defeat, solidarity rather than self-hatred.

In this play there is room only for deliberate and affirmative political acts or for resignation, and no one chooses resignation. Isolation, the sense of superfluity and aimlessness — these are not ontological states, but specific conditions imposed by the situation, which Henri and Julie eventually overcome. Their decision to lie to protect Jean is the most unambiguously positive moment in Sartre's theatre until Goetz's conversion at the end of *Le Diable et le bon Dieu*. *Morts sans sépulture* moves towards the presentation of real, non-rhetorical collective action based on solidarity, and in this, achieves an advance over its predecessors.

Yet the protagonists' decision is taken amidst appalling extremes of personal terror and degradation. Sartre was right to insist that the play is really about torture — and also, therefore, that the political situation is merely the 'frame'. *Morts sans sépulture* was not, in fact, 'a play about the Resistance'. Moreover, Sartre has written, the play was a failure, because 'the victims' fate was absolutely predetermined, no one could suppose that they would talk, so there was no suspense, as it is now called.'[19] The play's weakness lies equally in its characters: the torturers are never developed as characters, and the victims are, like Lizzie in *La Putain respectueuse*, impossibly lucid and rational.[20] *Morts sans sépulture* suffered at once from an excess of 'reality' — the

18. *Morts sans sépulture*, *Théâtre*, Paris 1946, p.246; trans. Lionel Abel, *The Victors, Three Plays*, New York 1948, p.26.

19. TS, p.242; ST, p.203.

20. See McCall, pp.52,86.

extremism of the situation — and a dearth of moral-psychological probability. In this play and in its companion, Sartre pressed more strongly than ever towards a theatre of historical situations. In both, the difficulty he experienced in presenting realistic historical individuals and actions was evident. The assurance of *Huis Clos* had not yet been recovered.

'L'Engrenage'

L'Engrenage, a little-known screenplay written in 1946 but never filmed, was adapted for the stage first in Switzerland, Italy and Germany, finally appearing in Paris in 1969. Originally called 'Les Mains sales', it portrayed the fate of a socialist revolution in a small, non-industrialized but oil-rich eastern European country bordering on a threatening capitalist power. Its leader, Jean Aguerra, is overthrown in a coup by forces wishing to realize the original aims of the revolution: nationalization of the foreign-owned oil industry, freedom of speech and press, and election of a parliament. Aguerra has betrayed these promises and become a bloody tyrant: his campaign of terror included attempts at a bloody forced collectivization of agriculture, and brought about the death of his former best friend and comrade-in-arms, Lucien Drelitsch, thrown into a concentration camp for violating a decree on press censorship; and he leads a life of drunkenness and debauchery. Aguerra, deposed, is brought to trial, and the story unfolds in a threefold movement.

An overwhelming personal and political indictment is presented which he mostly accepts, scarcely moved by it to defend himself. At the same time, the compelling reasons for Aguerra's brutal policies become clear, both in flashbacks and in the situation faced by the new government: the neighbouring power will invade if its oil concessions are nationalized; a free press and parliament would certainly raise the demand for nationalization and must therefore be suppressed. It emerges that Aguerra's sole goal was to buy time. If the revolution can hold out until the great power is drawn into the anticipated war with another state, the thirty-five enemy divisions will be withdrawn from the border, and the revolution's goals can be carried out. 'In a few years the deported will be able to return home. They will be able to nationalize oil and men will be happy.'[21]

21. *L'Engrenage*, Paris 1948, p.188; trans. Mervyn Savill, *In the Mesh*, London 1954, p.125.

On a third level, these political reasons become the basis of Aguerra's personal appeal to Hélène, Lucien's widow, for understanding and forgiveness. In his only serious defence of himself, we see him as detesting violence but absorbing it into himself and using it as the only means of struggle against oppression. He is totally committed to the survival of the revolution, but his violence has consumed him and, succumbing to self-hatred, he has sought relief in alcohol and debauchery. At the end of the play, these three themes are reunited: Aguerra is condemned to die by the court, forgiven by Hélène — and by history — and François, the new leader, submits as he must to demands from the oil cartel and the foreign ambassador that the oil concessions must not be nationalized.

In *L'Engrenage,* for the first time, history — the 'frame' of *Morts sans sépulture,* present but fixed and frozen in *La Putain respectueuse,* obviously behind but not actually present in *Les Mouches,* and totally absent from *Huis Clos* — became the theme of Sartre's theatre. *L'Engrenage* was thus a turning point in his development as a dramatist. In every succeeding play, history was to permeate his characters and their actions. [22]

This screenplay also broached a topic which was to be central in virtually all of Sartre's plays: that of violence. Aguerra has embarked, deliberately and with open eyes, on a course of systematic terror, which he sees as a lesser evil than foreign invasion. He has 'dirty hands' and hates himself for it, but he believes that one who wants to abolish poverty in his historical situation can take no other course. Developing Sartre's theme, Pierre Verstraeten has argued that the problem of violence is central in any effort to come to grips with history: indeed, he *identifies* history with violence. He traces in Sartre's plays the development of an ethic of worldly action whose essential structure is 'the conflict between a dialectical vision and two visions which ought to be transcended: the ethical vision and the realistic vision.'[23] The dramatic and political mainspring of *L'Engrenage* is the struggle between the partisan of an idealist and purist revolutionary morality, Lucien Drelitsch, and a more realistic advocate of revolutionary effectiveness, Jean Aguerra.

In the person of Lucien, the ethical vision refuses all traffic with violence. It insists that the non-violent and humane society of tomor-

22. See Verstraeten, p.35.
23. Ibid., p.18.

row can never be built by violence and inhumanity today — only clean hands can ensure clean hands. It is an idealism that insists on acting as we ought, regardless of consequences. The dialectical vision, on the other hand, insists that violence and inhumanity are all around us and within us, that we tacitly sanction them, partake of them, and benefit from them even as we pretend to keep our own hands clean. Furthermore, violence and inhumanity can be abolished only by a sustained political struggle against their cause, class society. This is a struggle to the death in which all available means must be utilized, and whose prime criterion is victory. If Aguerra's dialectical vision sounds more compelling than Lucien's ethical alternative this is because it is contructed as such. There is no authentic conflict of equals in *L'Engrenage*. Lucien is absolutely moralistic about the revolutionary situation, while Aguerra truly understands it. The real and pertinent conflict is within Aguerra himself. Although he does what must be done, he is torn by the contradiction between his humane intentions and their inhumane results, by the need to become brutal in order genuinely to do good in history. This struggle is represented as the real meaning of history. Jean internalized this objective tension and it destroys him in the end. Yet he succeeds: he buys time and protects the revolution.

L'Engrenage attempts to take the full weight of history, its ability to find and shape the people who do its work, its ability to transform the meaning of their acts into the opposite of what they intended. Nevertheless it has certain decisive weaknesses in common with the coeval *Morts sans sépulture*: although history is placed at the heart of the action, its specifics are scarcely made convincing or real. The 'situation' is schematically drawn, too simply dependent on the threatening foreign power. The same oversimplifications make the characters unconvincing. Lucien is politically unbelievable — a revolutionary who insists on non-violence, remains on the central committee of the revolutionary party, and preserves his purity while his comrade, Aguerra, carries out politically and morally distasteful tasks on his behalf. The character of the latter, on the other hand, is unconvincing in a different direction: both a monster and a completely committed, ultimately humane revolutionary, sickened by but willing to do the violence to which history summons him, Aguerra is most deeply flawed in his complete lucidity — as if his political and moral degeneracy was psychologically compatible with a clear and honest insight into the process of self-destruction, or a cogent view of the historical process and his own contradictory role in it. His strength as a character, however, is that these tensions are charged with historicity: not personal eccentricity but the unbearable contradictions of his position make him into the man we see brought to trial.

This is not true of the action as a whole. The play's peculiar set of personal relationships — characteristically reminiscent of *Huis Clos* — are superimposed on, not integral to, the story's significant historical tensions. Jean loves Hélène who marries Lucien: all are on the central committee, except Suzanne, who acted as Jean's nursemaid and becomes his chief accuser at his trial. Jean destroys Lucien but wins Hélène's forgiveness, and Suzanne succeeds in destroying Jean. Important as these personal relationships are, they never lose the timeless quality of *Huis Clos,* and unlike Aguerra's own tensions never become charged with concrete historical meaning. It is as if two quite distinct actions unfold — the personal *and* the political, rather than a single, deeply integrated and historically situated struggle. But to make engagement real in the theatrical context entails the integration of concrete history into the most intimate substance of characters, their actions and the issues embedded in them. This was the challenge that Sartre's theatre had yet fully to meet.

'Les Mains sales'

Les Mains sales, which exploded on the Paris stage in April 1948, was the first dramatic success of Sartre's engaged theatre and its most popular product. It is perhaps Sartre's most exciting drama, charged with tension and ambiguity; and furthermore, it is politically and personally rich at the same time, depicting individuated characters whose actions embody significant historical issues. [24]

This judgement may seem inapposite on a first reading of the play. Hugo is apparently another Orestes: alienated, *de trop,* able to experience himself only through other people's eyes, given to rhetoric and gesture rather than real action, and contemptuous of those he would help. And as with Orestes, his main passion is seemingly to *save himself,* to establish *his* identity through a spectacular, bloody crime.

---

24. See Philip Thody's acute discussion in *Sartre: A Biographical Introduction*, London 1971, p.92. This informed and detailed little book is especially good on Sartre's politics and literary works.

But Hugo differs from Orestes in one decisive respect. He has committed himself to a life of political action: this is his goal, the lens through which he sees himself and the measure of his inadequacy. This crucial circumstance sets Hugo in a context which, first of all, deprives him in advance of any absolute role in the drama. In *Les Mouches* Sartre spoke *through* Orestes whose alienation, by and large, can hence be regarded as the frame of reference of the play as a whole, not a posture to be explored and criticized in terms of one or more alternatives. But in *Les Mains sales,* the existentialist hero has ceased to be Sartre's philosophical point of reference. The 'Orestes figure' has become a tormented young man searching for his identity in the context of a new reference-point, the undoctrinaire Communist, Hoederer. The philosophical-moral-political framework of *Les Mains sales* is Hoederer's commitment to a socialist future, his love of people, his human warmth and directness, his sense of realism, effectiveness and flexibility, his refusal to posture, his sense of historical perspective. [25]

Hoederer is, as critics have noted, the one positive character in Sartre's plays. [26] It was through his committed humanism that Sartre was able for the first time to contest the Orestes figure of Hugo, to point to an authentic satisfying course of action; and through Hoederer's generous approach to the tormented adolescent bent on killing him that he was able to point beyond the self-Other conflict. [27] In *Qu'est-ce que la littérature?* the idea of socialism brought Sartre beyond the theoretical impasse of his early work; in the delineation of the socialist Hoederer, he glimpsed individual human possibilities beyond the personal shortcomings of his early characters.

Furthermore, in representing the alienated man as an *adolescent,* Sartre begins to explore the causes of his condition. Why is gesture Hugo's most appropriate mode of action? In part, the reasons stem from Hugo's bourgeois background: his rebellion against his rich father, his guilt at never having known hunger, his sense of not belonging in the Party and need to win a place there, the abstractness and one-sided purity of his commitment, his self-absorption. In so delineating Hugo, Sartre achieved a major advance. He historicized

25. *Les Mains sales*, Paris 1948; trans. Lionel Abel, *Dirty Hands, No Exit* and *Three Other Plays*.

26. See Thody, p.93; and McCall, p.73.

27. See Jeanson, p.40.

many of the characterizations of *Les Mouches* and began to explore their concrete social origins. Even the most intimate tensions of *Les Mains sales* are implicated in wider historical antagonisms. Hugo, trying to escape his background, seeks to kill Hoederer in order to prove to himself and to his Party mentors, Louis and Olga, that he is real; Jessica, coming from the same background as Hugo and as a woman at least equally unsure of her own reality, lives for make-believe and is drawn to seduce Hoederer so as to win confirmation from a real man.

Yet there are also dramatic weaknesses which reveal that Sartre had not yet completely synthesized historical and personal concerns. The characters, it might be said, stand as individuals on the threshold of historicity. All exhibit a certain thinness, a slightly stereotyped quality, and remain, therefore, not fully integrated. Jessica, for example, is more complex than most of Sartre's female characters, but she shares with them a typical lack of identity, an inability to confront the man's world on anything like its own terms or even to be aware of this as an issue. Sexuality and irrationality are her main dimensions. Hugo's naiveté and political ignorance are improbable in the editor of the party paper. And his confrontation with Slick and George casts him as too adolescent, them as too brutish to be credible. Too often the dialogue of the play is stiff and awkward, abstracted equally from either the political or the personal.

Yet on balance, *Les Mains sales* is one of Sartre's greatest dramatic achievements. In order to appreciate this, however, it is necessary to free the play from the confusion surrounding its political meaning.[28] From the play's first appearance onwards, Sartre disowned its political content by claiming (for example) that *Les Mains sales* was 'not a political play *in any sense*'.[29] This process continued through the remarkable interview in 1964 in which Sartre persisted in holding Hugo completely in the wrong even while Paulo Caruso confronted him with the play's objective thrust: to make the audience sympathize with Hugo *against* the Proletarian Party.[30] The politics of *Les Mains sales* have been confused largely by Sartre's and Simone de Beauvoir's

28. McCall, for example wrongly sees the play's political theme as confused (*The Theatre of Jean-Paul Sartre*, p.64); while Thody accepts its critique of official Communism but fails to understand that Hoederer stands for a humanistic, non-doctrinaire Communism (*Sartre: A Biographical Introduction*, pp. 89-90).

29. TS, p.246; ST, p.207.

30. TS, pp.250-67; ST, pp.211-25.

statements *about* it. Taken in itself, the play is politically quite clear. It sharply criticizes the orthodox Communists, Louis and Olga, for making Hoederer, an opponent on tactics, into an enemy who must be assassinated. It criticizes them for being doctrinaire, incapable of flexibility or creative thought; for falsifying history after pretending to denounce political deception; and for using people as if they were machines. Hoederer, on the contrary, respects his opponents and wishes to struggle politically with them; and analyses situations rather than apply formulae to them, having a strong appreciation of reality even while remaining committed to the goal of socialism. He accepts the idea of lying as a political tactic, as the situation dictates and within the framework of a broader revolutionary morality, and he has a genuine regard for people. Finally, while the orthodox faction are quite willing to use Hugo's immaturity for their own ends, Hoederer, at the risk — and eventual loss — of his life, offers Hugo a relationship of genuine respect, in full knowledge of his intentions.

Between the poles of these two very different types of Communist, Hugo is struggling to establish his identity, to overcome his feeling of utter inadequacy, to become real and effective. Chance — or rather Jessica's own yet deeper sense of unreality — leads him to discover her with Hoederer, just as he comes to accept the latter's offer of help. And so he commits the murder whose motivation eludes him until the final moment when Louis's men come to apprehend him. But is his suicide merely a repetition of his act of murder — an adolescent gesture expressing an inability to change and, more generally, total personal failure?[31] He is ready to rejoin the party and return to work until he hears the news that Hoederer's oppositional line is now Party policy, having been ordered by the USSR; Hoederer is to be rehabilitated and his murderer, who killed him for obscure personal reasons, is presumed dead. Hugo's response combines theatrical posturing with a real critique of the Party. If his approach is clearly wrong, so too is the Party's. Sartre later justified the Party's falsification of the past as 'an imperative of praxis,'[32] suggesting that had Hugo really understood Hoederer he would have accepted Olga's view, changed his name, and stayed in the organization. But if Hoederer advocated though never actually practised temporary compromise and deception in the name of revolutionary goals, he also

31. See Jeanson, p.44.
32. TS, p.257; ST, p.217.

stood for a humaneness and undogmatic outlook notably lacking in Louis and Olga.

The play clearly does not vindicate the dominant party faction. It shows them rather as Stalinist hacks parroting the twists and turns of an externally imposed line, and as subjecting Hugo to his fatal dilemma: either submission to their cynicism and dogmatism, or the persistence of his personal sense of unreality and dependence on gesture. A Communist like Hoederer posed a genuine alternative, but necessity — both Hugo's and that of Olga and Louis — the necessity of the orthodox Party faction entwining itself with that of the bourgeois intellectual unsure of his own reality, led to his murder. Thus, the audience identifies with Hugo not merely because his is the last voice of the play, but because of his despair, his inability to find an authentic alternative, his wish to redeem not himself, but Hoederer. Rehabilitation and the change of line are insufficient: Hugo demands that the death of this humane and undogmatic revolutionary be redeemed in a more fitting way. But what paths are open? The way of the Party leadership is to assassinate and then to rehabilitate, to falsify history. But acquiescence in this is not merely 'growing up': it is also giving up. To do so is to risk destroying one's integrity in the name of the very ideals that sustain it. For Hugo to refuse Olga's offer, then, is not merely weakness: it reveals, positively, his dogged attachment to some residue of his positive reasons for joining the Party. But he has no exit. In order to affirm Hoederer against the Party, Hugo uses the only way open to him, a false one, and the only language available to him, also false. Inevitably then, the main focus of identification is not the specific character of his gesture, but its underlying sense of protest against Party orthodoxy and its cynical affirmation of Hoederer.

It should by now be obvious that the political achievement of *Les Mains sales* is inseparable from its dramatic achievement. But one cannot lay it down or leave the theatre without a feeling of futility similar to that produced by *Les Mouches* or *Huis Clos*. For after all, even this exploration of effective engagement leaves 'no exit'. The one fully positive character in Sartre's theatre is assassinated both by intention and by accident, the dominant party faction adopts his line on orders from the USSR, Hugo learns nothing and kills himself. If the major concern of the Sartrean theatre was to explore the prospects of acting humanely and effectively in the world, it must be concluded that by the time of *Les Mains sales* this goal had not been achieved.

But might it be that Sartre was delineating not his own limits but the limits of effective action in 1948, in a society where the Communist Party was the only significant potentially revolutionary force? Were not his own perspectives, for the first time, beginning to coincide with the objective historical situation? Was it possible for Sartre to dramatize possibilities beyond those historically present? As we know, during the Paris run of *Les Mains sales,* Sartre actively tried, and failed, to create in the RDR a 'third way'. His failure led him back, after 1949, to the PCF as the only possible route to personal political involvement. This returns us to perhaps the most interesting fact about *Les Mains sales,* that Sartre in a certain sense 'rewrote' it after it appeared, both denying its criticism of the Communist Party and trying to control where and how it could be performed. He had been compelled to choose between swallowing his criticism of the PCF or becoming defined as its enemy. History imposed a kind of submission — which concretely entailed, among other things, denying the critical meaning of his own play. In dealing with the Communists' response to *Les Mains sales*, then, Sartre took precisely the unsettling path that Hugo had refused. But in following it, he learned a lesson beyond Hugo's grasp, the lesson that Hoederer stood for in the abstract; and in the process he transformed the moral and political framework of *Les Mains sales. Le Diable et le bon Dieu* was the dramatic fruit of this transformation. As he himself observed in 1951, 'Goetz is a Hugo who is converted.'[33]

'Le Diable et le bon Dieu'

Goetz's conversion is one of the high points of Sartre's theatre, and of his entire career. Step by step, we have followed the slow transformation of the Sartrean protagonist. Orestes was a Roquentin thrown into history; Hugo was Orestes committed to the revolution; and Goetz is a Hugo who matures into a whole and responsible being. By the final curtain Goetz has overcome, one after another, his thirst for absolute evil, then for absolute good and finally for asceticism. Realizing that God is dead, Goetz for the first time discovers his *need* for other people and resolves to pursue liberation with them. In Goetz's transformation, an engaged individual takes shape from one who had been absorbed in moral dilemmas. Goetz goes beyond

33. TS, p.270; ST, p.228.

unreal gestures and acting for others and begins to act for authentic reasons; he gives up his obsession with personal salvation to join with the struggling masses; he abandons the demand for immediate liberation and accepts the exigencies of a prolonged struggle; he accepts solidarity in this struggle as the only way of loving his fellow humans as long as they are unfree; and he takes his place as a leader, recognizing in this role his only way of being 'a man among men' until genuine equality is possible. In Goetz, Sartre rendered dialectical the vision of *Qu'est-ce que la littérature?* and 'Matérialisme et révolution': the city of ends was attainable only in history, only through a long-range revolutionary project which both kept the humane society as its motivating principle and fully acknowledged the violence of present society.

Pierre Verstraeten rightly sees Goetz's conversion as the decisive step in the evolution of Sartre's ethics. Hoederer had understood and advocated a dialectical ethics, one which accepted violence as vital in the struggle to suppress the causes of violence. But his ideas were presented schematically, not arrived at through lived experience as in the several stages of *Le Diable et le bon Dieu*: 'Goetz, by his commerce with failure, solitude, nothingness, is able to assume the contradictory practice imposed by the situation; he can decipher the necessity of transcending all morality, as well as all violence, at the same time as the impossibility of transcending it in present circumstances; he is capable of confronting and operating a synthesis which detotalizes itself before his eyes; he can lead a contradictory enterprise: a dialectic which de-dialecticizes itself in the very moment it constitutes itself.'[34] Goetz understands, through his own experience, both the goal of a non-violent future and the need to use specific forms of violence to achieve it: he is no longer either a cynical realist or a naive idealist. He no longer resigns himself and the world to pure evil, or pretends that pure goodness is possible. He attempts with full awareness to accept *revolutionary* action: to utilize violence without thereby destroying the revolutionary goal.

Goetz gives up trying to be *good*: that project was based on, and supported, the world's evil. He gives up trying to help people: that project had contempt built into it. His love for the poor had been totally abstract as well as condescending. More, it had been fundamentally self-centred: his goal was to win, earn *their* love: 'I wanted

34. Verstraeten, p. 115.

pure love: ridiculous nonsense. To love anyone is to hate the same enemy. Therefore I will adopt your hates.'[35]

Thus, Goetz learns the only love possible in a time of social upheaval: solidarity. This is not love itself: it will remain 'too early' for love until conditions are created which make it possible. In joining with others to create those conditions, Goetz cannot yet be a 'man among men' — his dream as it was Oreste's — for the insurrectionaries do not need one more militant, but, 'in this period of reflux, a leader, hard, and intransigent. Goetz is this leader; it is therefore as such that he will serve these new brothers in misfortune — that is, *in still denying them*, in the anticipation of a long term where all constraint will be abolished.'[36]

Goetz is presented to the captains as their new leader:

NASTI: . . . I have news for you which is worth a great victory: we have a general, and he is the most famous military leader in Germany.

A CAPTAIN: This monk?

GOETZ: Everything except a monk! (*He throws off his robe and appears dressed as a soldier.*)

THE CAPTAINS: Goetz!

KARL: Goetz! For God's sake! . . .

A CAPTAIN: Goetz! That changes everything!

ANOTHER CAPTAIN: What does it change, tell me? What does it change? He is a traitor. He's probably drawing you into a fine ambush.

GOETZ: Come here! Nasti has named me chief and leader. Will you obey my orders?

A CAPTAIN: I'd rather die.

GOETZ: Then die, brother! (*He stabs him.*) As for you others, listen to me! I take up this command against my will, but I shall be relentless. Believe me, if there is one chance of winning this war, I shall win it. Proclaim immediately that any soldier attempting to desert will be hanged. By tonight, I must have a complete list of troops, weapons, and stores; you shall answer for everything with your lives. We shall be sure of victory when your men are more

35. *Le Diable et le bon Dieu,* Paris, 1951, p. 275; trans. Kitty Black: *The Devil and the Good Lord,* New York 1960, p.145.
36. Verstraeten, p.105.

afraid of me than of the enemy. (*They try to speak.*) No. Not a word. Go. Tomorrow you will learn my plans. (*They go. Goetz kicks the body.*) The kingdom of man is beginning. A fine start! Nasti, I told you I would be a hangman and butcher. (*He has a moment of weakness.*)

NASTI: (*laying his hand on Goetz's shoulder*): Goetz . . .

GOETZ: Never fear, I shall not flinch. I shall make them hate me, because I know no other way of loving them. I shall give them orders, since I have no other way of obeying. I shall remain alone with this empty sky over my head, since I have no other way of being among men. There is this war to fight, and I will fight it.[37]

One central fact about *Le Diable et le bon Dieu* prevents acceptance of it as the fulfilment of Sartre's theatrical project: it is not, for all the importance of its ideas, a dramatic success. We have just seen Goetz kill the captain in demonstration of his willingness to be violent in the pursuit of good. But this killing lacks dramatic necessity. It is a rhetorical device chosen to make a point, rather than a 'natural' development of the play's action. Similarly, Goetz's final statements are too abstract, too general. They show that an intellectual problem has been resolved and a moral choice made, but not that a concrete person has changed. They lack detail and individuality, as does Goetz himself throughout the play. His remarks show that the main action is a philosophical struggle, not concrete individual life-experience. If performing before God transforms all Goetz's acts into rhetorical gestures, Sartre is able to show this to us and make it intellectually comprehensible, but not to bring it to life before us as a dramatically credible obsession. In the same way, the evil with which Goetz grapples is abstract and remote; and his own evil is unmotivated, has no effect on him, is instantly forgiven and easily abandoned.[38] We need not quarrel with Sartre for placing God at the centre of *Le Diable et le bon Dieu,* but rather for his manner of doing it. Having predicated the whole play on belief in the existence of God, Sartre suddenly has Goetz undergo conversion at the end and cease believing — an unmotivated conversion lacking continuity with Goetz's past, and only now posed as a central theme. The play works best as a drama of ideas — and even then it does not adequately explore its own chosen

37. *Le Diable et le bon Dieu,* pp.281-82; *The Devil and the Good Lord,* pp.148-49.
38. See McCall, pp.38-41.

themes. The problem here is not one of detail: it lies at the core of the play, in its characters, its language, its issues. Sartre's most positive, most ambitious, most spectacular play is also his stiffest and least convincing. In *Les Mains sales,* Hugo *is* the young bourgeois intellectual filled with revolutionary righteousness and the need to be seen. In *Le Diable et le bon Dieu,* however, the 'truths' stand out: they are abstract, not adequately integrated into character and event. Goetz makes little sense as a person: he is above all the bearer of a theme. The characters scarcely interact, their words scarcely affect others. They are interconnected as ideas, as components of a problem, but not as individuals. It is fitting that *Le Diable et le bon Dieu* should have been set in the sixteenth century, turning on religious and other questions remote from Sartre. This historical distance from our own time and its issues betokens the distance within the play itself, between its half-realized characters and events and its profound dénouement.

'Kean' and 'Nekrassov'

However one may criticize it, no one can see or read *Le Diable et le bon Dieu* and not understand it as a *beginning.* The Party of Louis and Olga has become the peasant organization headed by the one-dimensional yet admirable Nasti. The oppressive demand that Hugo stifle himself and all he values has been transcended by the realistic appreciation that only in the struggle can Goetz fully become himself. Goetz is no longer against the struggle, or above it, or outside it: he is now with the peasants, in the midst of it. He is ready to begin afresh.

Simone de Beauvoir has said that Goetz represented the transcendence of the contradiction that had torn Sartre since his politicization — the contradiction between his commitment to freedom, and the 'discipline of solidarity with all men'. In *Le Diable et le bon Dieu,* Sartre brought his reflection on commitment to a close by resolving on a realistic revolutionary stance: acceptance of the collective struggle, with all its limitations, as the locus of effective individual engagement. 'I made Goetz do what I was unable to do,' Sartre wrote in his unpublished notes. By the next year, de Beauvoir continued, he 'had reached the same point as Goetz: he was ready to accept a collective discipline without denying his own liberty'[39] — that is by aligning

39. *La Force des choses,* pp.262, 280; *Force of Circumstance,* pp.243,261.

himself with the Communists, as the only possible revolutionary force.

This new revolutionary-realist commitment had a striking effect on Sartre's plays. In fact the period between 1952 and 1956, when his relations with the PCF were at their closest, was the only time when his drama was not primarily reflective. The plays of these years did not meditate upon action and its consequences; they seemed themselves to *be* actions.

Neither *Kean* nor *Nekrassov* is very profound; compared with the rest of Sartre's theatre, both are positively light-hearted. *Nekrassov* is Sartre's only wholly comic drama, and in adapting *Kean,* Sartre altered Dumas's original to heighten its comedy and minimize its melodramatic elements. Equally important, neither was publicly very successful; they are, besides *Morts sans sépulture*, the two least known of Sartre's plays. To be sure, both plays treat serious issues, but by presenting rather than exploring them. The Sartre who adapted *Kean* was clearly on the side of reality rather than gesture; the Sartre who wrote *Nekrassov* was unambiguously opposed to the anti-Communist manipulations of the bourgeois press. He posed no great moral-political dilemmas and no genuine ambiguities which could not be resolved on the stage.

Kean depicts the actor's decision to leave the stage and become real. At the beginning of the play, it is shown that Kean is not a man, but an actor. He can do nothing in his private life but play roles, conjuring up grandiose and dramatic feelings without experiencing them himself, living in the illusion of wealth while owning nothing and indebted to everyone. He attracts vacuous aristocrats who value his glamour and reward him by supporting, befriending, or falling in love with him. This life of grand gestures has rendered Kean incapable of knowing who he is. In a moment of insight he sees what it has meant: 'You cannot act to earn your living. You act to lie, to deceive, to deceive yourself; to be what you cannot be, and because you want to forget yourself. You act the hero because you are a coward at heart, and you play the saint because you are a devil by nature. You act a murderer because you long to poison your best friend. You act because you are a born liar and totally unable to speak the truth. You act because you would go mad if you didn't act. Act! Do I know myself when I am acting? Is there ever a moment when I cease to act?. . .'[40]

Kean lives in the *irréel*, as do Goetz, Hugo, and in a sense, Orestes. In play after play, Sartre explored this preference for the world of fantasy and gesture, and the reasons why its emptiness came, sooner or later, to weigh so heavily. In his first novel, Sartre sought to dispel Roquentin's illusions, but, paradoxically, left him no alternative to the imaginary; nearly twenty years later, *Kean* opened the passage to the real world. The play traces Kean's collapse as an actor, both onstage and off. Caught in a complicated love affair, he breaks down during a performance, departs from his scripted role and publicly insults the Prince of Wales and other notables. In the wake of this disaster, he decides to leave England and the stage — and the imaginary — to live as Mr Edmund; to become sober, to marry and settle into an ordinary life. Saying goodbye to noble gestures and overwhelming passions, Kean finally finds his own bearings in the real.

Kean presents a clear and unambiguous choice. The real world seems less grand than the *irréel,* but is infinitely preferable to it. As with Goetz, people are central to Kean's life and decision. Like Goetz he changes, but this time the familiar Sartrean theme is rendered crisply and conclusively. *Kean* is as light and bracing as *Le Diable et le bon Dieu* is dense and ponderous. The whole play, in short, is charged with the optimism and energy of Goetz's conversion.

Nekrassov, Sartre's one wholly comic play, is also perhaps his most wholly political. It contains no personal or philosophical explorations: its characters *are* identical with their actions and social positions. *Nekrassov* is also Sartre's most 'Brechtian' play, vigorously poking fun at the capitalist press, its personnel and practices.

The delightful first meeting between Inspector Goblet and the journalist Sibilot, for example, is one of the play's best touches, deftly situating both men as *petits bourgeois*. Goblet, searching for the swindler de Valera, has entered Sibilot's apartment and immediately feels at home:

40. *Kean,* Paris 1954, p.81; trans. Kitty Black, *Kean, The Devil and the Good Lord and Two Other Plays,* pp. 199-200.

INSPECTOR (*with a sweep of his hand*): The furniture: nineteen twenty-five?

SIBILOT: Ah, 1925? Oh, yes.

INSPECTOR: The Decorative Arts Exhibition, our youth . . .

SIBILOT: The year of my wedding.

INSPECTOR: And mine. Our wives chose the furniture with their mothers; we weren't even consulted. The in-laws lent the money. Do you like those 1925 chairs?

SIBILOT: You know, in the end one no longer sees them. . . .

They go on to confide in each other: each one sadly admits his professional-social servility. Goblet recognizes in Sibilot 'a face like mine. A sixty-thousand-francs-a-month face'. Each one recognizes in the other his essential self, his *petit-bourgeois* self, and responds accordingly. 'My poor Sibilot,' says the Inspector:

SIBILOT: My poor Inspector. (*They shake hands.*)

INSPECTOR: Only we can appreciate our poverty and our greatness. Give me a drink.

SIBILOT: Gladly. (*He fills two glasses.*)

INSPECTOR: (*raising his glass*) To the defenders of Western culture. (*He drinks.*)

SIBILOT: Victory to those who defend the rich without loving them. (*He drinks.*). . .[41]

To criticize these characters as too generic or stereotypical would be misguided. Sibilot and Goblet are intentionally made interchangeable, not distinctly individual *petits bourgeois*. Sartre's purpose here was to distill each man into his class identity and function as his deepest self.

He achieved a number of such satirical-political successes in *Nekrassov*: the fall of Mouton after de Valera-Nekrassov ingeniously omits him from the Soviet list of victims; the come-down of the Lilliputian Palotin; Demidov, the Communist so pure as to become a rabid anti-Communist, and his exchanges with de Valera-Nekrassov; the scene where de Valera convinces Palotin that he is Nekrassov because Palotin *needs* him to be; the story of the suitcase filled with radioactive dust; the obsessive anti-Communism of *Soir à Paris*; the

41. *Nekrassov*, Paris 1955; trans. Sylvia and George Leeson, *Nekrassov, The Devil and the Good Lord and Two Other Plays*, pp.339-42.

reduction of de Valera, the master manipulator, to a cog in the capitalist machine which comes to dominate the stage; and finally, the improbable transformation of Sibilot into the powerful editor of *Soir à Paris*.' Sartre himself later criticized *Nekrassov* as only half-successful because it focused too much on de Valera and not enough on how he became 'enmeshed in the paper's machinery'.[42] This self-criticism was excessive. Certainly Sartre toyed with making de Valera into his traditional dramatic hero, preoccupied him with the hero-impostor dilemma, but he did not succumb to this temptation. He went on instead to show, with marked success, the system creating, swallowing up and recreating its personnel. Whatever its faults, *Nekrassov* remains Sartre's most underrated play.[43]

It may be that Sartre's negative attitude towards the play was conditioned by its unusual position in his theatre as a whole. *Nekrassov* after all — and not coincidentally — is both uncharacteristically political and at the same time, was 'welcomed unreservedly by the Communists, the CGT and the TEC [the PCF-sponsored play-going society]. Their papers wrote about it, seats were set aside for them at cheaper prices.'[44] In fact, its lack of resemblance to his usual theatre notwithstanding, *Nekrassov* marked Sartre's closest approach to being an activist playwright connected with a movement. Had he continued to develop in the direction indicated by it, perhaps it would now be better known and less harshly judged by its author. But in fact it represented the outer limit of his theatre, a rare moment of political integration.

'Les Sequestrés d'Altona'

The mood of Sartre's next play was strikingly at odds with his earlier optimism. In fact, *Les Sequestrés d'Altona* invariably provokes comparisons with *Huis Clos*: its five characters seem locked away from the world, bent on judging and destroying each other. Sartre himself saw it as a kind of *historical* variation on the earlier play, in which 'characters are dominated, gripped by the past throughout just as they are by each other.'[45]

Sartre's apprenticeship to history, completed formally in *Le Diable et*

42. TS, p.297; ST, p.252.
43. See CRW, 55/265, p.307.
44. TS, pp.69-70; ST, p.45.
45. TS, p.314; ST, p.268.

le bon Dieu, only now bore fruit artistically. In *Les Sequestrés d'Altona,* he recaptured the dramatic power of *Huis Clos,* the ease and sureness of touch he had shown when not preoccupied with the theme of engagement. Now, depicting the inferno of the twentieth century, Sartre wrote a play to rival his depiction of the timeless hell. In *Les Sequestrés d'Altona,* for the first time since *Huis Clos,* Sartre created individual characters fully integrated in word and deeds with their situation.

What does it mean to call *Les Sequestrés d'Altona* an 'historical *Huis Clos*'? The play's entire action turns on the experience of Nazism and the Second World War in the family of a wealthy industrialist. The Gerlach family, Germany's largest shipbuilders, is dying — the old man has throat cancer, while Franz is locked in his room, mad with guilt and pride and waited on by Leni, who ministers both to his madness and to his sexual needs. A supreme realist, the father wants to settle the family accounts before he dies, and so induces Werner's wife, Joanna, to see Franz to arrange one last meeting of father and eldest son. Joanna's presence fascinates Franz and brings him back to reality — the reality of his own wartime role as Nazi collaborator and then torturer, and the post-war reality of Germany's recovery. Leni, willing to see Franz die if she must lose him to Joanna, reveals each of these, telling the true story of Franz to Joanna, and the truth of 'the German miracle' to Franz and so banishing the madness which conceals his guilt from him. The play ends with the fall of the house of Gerlach: Franz and his father commit suicide together, Leni moves into Franz's room, and Joanna and Werner leave the family home and shipbuilding empire.

The play's most significant personal tensions are, at root, historical: the Gerlach family's power and sense of superiority; the old man's opportunistic decision to collaborate with the Nazis, to the point of selling them land for a concentration camp; the Protestant morality in which Franz so fervently believed. Franz was broken by the sight of the Rabbi whom he had rescued being killed by ss men summoned by his father, and by his subsequent exemption from punishment, as a Gerlach. Forced to enlist in the army, his sense of powerlessness, combined with an ingrained passion for power, made of him 'the butcher of Smolensk', a torturer of partisans. These events, far in the past, are the truth that Franz lives with and yet tries to escape by his flight into the imaginary. He hides in the *irréel* by defending his century against the judges of the future, by deceiving himself about Germany's fate (he is convinced that it still lies in ruins and that its people are starving) and by lying about his own role (he claims to feel guilty for not having done enough to avert Germany's defeat). At the same time, his father has become unnecessary to a capitalist economy dependent now on managers and technicians — the family firm will continue in spite of the old man's death. Yet everyone in the family has been broken by his once awesome power. Leni is a misfit who feeds off Franz's madness, and Werner knows only submission to his father's will. By the play's end, collaboration with the Nazis, the transformation of capitalism and its own related internal decay bring the house of Gerlach to destruction. 'Hell', still a central image in Sartre's work, is no longer simply 'other people': it is the curse of a particular history, the inability to overcome the specific evils that certain human beings have done to others in the twentieth century.

Sartre's overriding concern in *Les Sequestrés d'Altona* was to explore the individual as historical agent. His achievement was to make a particular individual, Franz, come alive *as* and *because* he embodied a vital historical issue, to show both his individual actions as they arose from historical forces and the historical forces as they were affected by the action of individuals like him. Sartre's treatment of Franz's guilt revealed how far he had advanced in his understanding of the relationship of individuals to history. Franz is not a Nazi and not a mass murderer. In wartime, in exceptional circumstances, he has tortured and murdered. But these are emphatically *his* acts. By denying Franz the evasions of 'collective guilt', or obedience to higher orders, Sartre left him unable to displace responsibility for his acts on to Hitler, the military command structure or Germany as a whole. He chooses sequestration and madness as his only alternative to confronting what he himself has done, to an immersion in guilt which could only end in his suicide. How did Franz come to torture and murder to begin with? His attempt to save the Rabbi was prompted not by human sympathy for prisoners (whom he despised) but by pride and a desire to redeem his father: by the arrogance inbred in the scion of one of Germany's leading families. Thwarted and defeated, the son of the all-powerful industrialist himself counted for nothing, not even forced to bear the consequences of his moral act. Raised to value power but discovering himself powerless, he became an officer of a regime based on a cult of power. In this way, Franz absorbed Nazism into his very character, and became an eager collaborator: 'I was Hitler's wife. The rabbi was bleeding and I discovered at the heart of my powerlessness some strange kind of approval. *(He is back again in the past.)* I have supreme power. Hitler has changed me, made me implacable and sacred, made me himself. I am Hitler, and I shall surpass myself. *(Pause. To the* FATHER*)* No rations left. My soldiers were prowling around the barn. *(Back in the past.)* Four good Germans will crush me to the earth, and my own men will bleed the prisoners to death. No! I shall never again fall into abject powerlessness. I swear it. It's dark. Horror has not yet been let loose. . . . I'll grab them quickly. If anyone lets loose, it will be me. I'll assume the evil; I'll display my power by the singularity of an unforgettable act; change *living* men into vermin. I alone will deal with the prisoners. I'll debase them into abject wretches. They'll talk. Power is an abyss, and I see its depths. It is not enough to choose who shall live and who shall die. I shall decide life or death with a penknife and a cigarette lighter. *(Distractedly.)* Fascinating! It is the glory of kings to go to hell. I shall go there. *(He stands as though in a trance, downstage.)*[46]

Why is there no exit at the end, no possibility of redemption? Why can Franz only die, Franz who has been torturing himself for thirteen years? He knows himself completely at the end but cannot accept himself. For even now he remains in some sense 'Hitler's wife' — not merely because he has a portrait of Hitler on his wall, or wears a tattered military uniform, but above all because of his enormous pride.[47] Old Gerlach, with his characteristic pragmatism, condemns Franz's crimes as individual murders of a common criminal who only 'risked prolonging the massacre and hindering reconstruction'.[48] But Franz had been raised as a prince; and, defending himself before the tribunal of the thirtieth century, he dementedly adopts this role: he 'alone speaks the truth: the shattered Titan, the eyewitness, ageless, regular, secular, *in saecula saeculorum*. Me. Man is dead, and I am his witness.'[49] A prince locked in his own bedroom, still insane with pride and lust for power and, in the post-war capitalist world, utterly impotent and useless — Franz must die because of his guilt and because

. 46. *Les Sequestrés d'Altona,* Paris 1960; trans. Sylvia and George Leeson, New York, 1961, pp.163-4.

47. See McCall, p.137.

48. *The Condemned of Altona.* p.170.

there is nothing left for a prince to do. Produced by the twentieth century, for a moment its active agent, he is also its victim.

Negativity and History: The Limits of Sartre's Theatre

Why did *Les Sequestrés d'Altona,* Sartre's last and in many respects his best major play, end so negatively? Why did Sartre's theatre culminate in an historical *Huis Clos* rather than an historical *Le Diable et le bon Dieu?* Was Sartre rendering his own negativity in historical terms, giving political coloration to the dilemmas that had engaged him since the thirties, or was he discovering, and rendering in terms appropriate to them, fundamental negativities *of the twentieth century?* Why did his theatrical project lead to Franz, someone who has embraced the *irréel,* overwhelmed by the weight of his acts? We have seen that Goetz's past violence left no strain: forgiveness was not even an issue. Why then was there no exit for Franz?

First performed in 1959, *Les Sequestrés d'Altona* was designed to call attention to the torture then being perpetrated by the French in Algeria. 'My subject,' Sartre writes, 'is a young man returning from Algeria who has seen certain things out there, has perhaps had a share in them, and keeps his mouth shut.'[50] He went on to identify the specific motivation of the play: 'the political situation in France makes it imperative to recover such people for society and despite the filthy brutalities they may have perpetrated.'[51] By 'recover' Sartre meant, very specifically, to make active in the struggle against the war. But this play about a family beyond redemption, whatever else it may do, explores no alternatives to Gerlachs' destruction, explores no basis for a positive struggle. Franz is emphatically *not* recoverable.

As with *Huis Clos* and *Les Mains sales,* Sartre's statements about his intentions distract us from what his play actually presents on the stage. He suggested, for example, that he had created a German bourgeois family in order to clarify the issue of collaboration with the Nazis, and that this choice was meant to heighten his audience's identification with the issues and ultimately, their self-understanding. But, after all, who are the Gerlachs? A family of shipbuilders employing tens of thousands, who despised the plebeian Nazis yet accepted

49. Ibid., p.58.
50. TS, pp.305-6, 31, p.259-60.
51. TS, p.306; ST, p.260.

their regime because it expanded the navy and conquered foreign markets. The Nazis served the Gerlachs' interests just as they served the Nazis. Thus the family's guilt extends beyond Franz's actions, into the heart of its economic empire, and the social order at whose head it stands. It is doubly condemned by history, having once eagerly collaborated with Hitler and now been rendered anachronistic by the economic and technical growth of post-war Germany. We may indeed sympathize with Franz as much as we condemn him—an important achievement of the play—but we can feel little sadness at the fall of the house of Gerlach. Long before the first act the family has lost all vitality. Franz becomes a war criminal because of its displacement, which leaves his power-lust no other means of satisfaction. *Les Sequestrés d'Altona* is a play of indictment, not of struggle. Unlike *Le Diable et le bon Dieu*, it contains no hopeful anticipation of the future, no sense of historical possibility. Its only question is, how will the doom of the Gerlachs be played out?

Sartre had earlier resolved the problems of effective revolutionary action in the abstract; he had now integrated individuals into history, in concrete representations. But he never created a modern-day Orestes who stayed with his people, a Hoederer who lived, a Hugo who changed, a Goetz after his conversion—or a Franz who was recovered 'for society'. Here we reach the conclusion of Sartre's project in the theatre, and its political limits as an intervention in history.

Sartre created a rich and original body of plays, a connected series of explorations into some of the most profound dilemmas of his time. To mark its incompleteness is not to detract from its achievement. However, it is impossible to overlook the shift that occurred in Sartre's concerns after 1955, when he completed the last of his three most 'positive' plays. Why did he return to his earlier negativity? Why did his work in the theatre come finally to close with *Les Troyennes*, a play that concluded:

> Soon you are going to pay.
> Make war, imbecilic mortals,
> ravage fields and cities,
> violate temples and tombs,
> and torture the vanquished.
> You will die from it.
> All of you.[53]

52. ᴛꜱ, pp.303-4; ꜱᴛ, p. 257-8.
53. Euripides, *Les Troyennes,* adaptation de Jean-Paul Sartre, Paris 1965, p.130.

Sartre had evidently not abandoned struggle: but his point of view had shifted with his mood. His attention, in his last two plays, was focused now on the enemy—capitalists, collaborators, European colonialists. At the same time—and this is the most important shift—he deliberately constructed *Les Sequestrés d'Altona* so that his audience would identify the enemy as itself. Franz-France. Was it France whose crimes were so great that it must hide in madness, so great that Sartre must uncover them through images of Nazi Germany? This was precisely the point: Sartre was writing about the war in Algeria from the point of view of a European sympathetic to the Algerians. By 1959 his theatre no longer explored questions of action and effectiveness on behalf of those in or near a revolutionary movement. In drawing the audience to identify with Franz, Sartre was suggesting that *they* were the enemy. His adaptation of Euripides made this explicit:

> Men of Europe.
> You despise Africa and Asia
> And you call us barbarians, I believe,
> But when vainglory and greed
> Throw you on our land,
> You pillage, you torture, you massacre.
> Where are the barbarians then?[54]

One of Sartre's main reasons for translating *The Trojan Women* was to present a 'denunciation of war in general and colonial expeditions in particular.'[55] Three other considerations stood out in his comments: his interest in this play, which 'ends in total nihilism', after it had already been newly translated and performed during the Algerian war;[56] his scholarly approach to problems of translation; and his change of focus from the Greeks to Europeans in general. The play's action takes place after the fall of Troy, and portrays the terrible fate of the Trojan women and Hector's child. Its bitter mood continues the gloom of *Les Sequestrés d'Altona*: the war is over, we are witnessing a further stage of disaster, and more misery and retribution are to come. But why did Sartre turn to Euripides for this story, why at this point become a translator, why become so uncharacteristically fascinated with scholarly questions? Furthermore, why did he now search for *continuity* with the past, and why depict such generaliz-

54. Ibid.
55. TS, p.364; ST, p.313.
56. TS, p.365; ST, p.314.

ed and motiveless suffering unredeemed by any struggle to end it?

Sartre's shift, and his inability to go further than Goetz's new beginning before relapsing into the mood of his two final plays, was conditioned by events in France after 1955: the PCF's automatic support for the Soviet invasion of Hungary, the Communist Deputies' vote in the National Assembly for emergency powers to prosecute the war in Algeria; the PCF's generally passive attitude towards the Algerian struggle; de Gaulle's assumption of power in 1958 with only token opposition from the Left; and the subsequent referendum confirming the Fifth Republic. De Beauvoir has recalled that those opposing the war felt their isolation keenly, that they grew to be hated by—and themselves to hate—their fellow-countrymen. The years between 1956 and 1962 are revealed as the most dismal of all in her memoirs, unredeemed even by victory in Algeria: 'for seven years we had desired this victory; it came too late to console us for the price it had cost.'[57] Sartre no longer felt in solidarity with the Left, 'that corpse, lying on its back and full of worms' which 'was so characterized by assent that one day in the autumn of 1958 it expired murmuring a final yes.' Worse still, by 1960 he had come to feel deeply pessimistic about the efficacy of his own efforts: 'fifty years of living in the backward province which France has become are very degrading. We shouted, protested, signed and countersigned. We declared, according to our habits of thinking, "It is not permissible…," or, "The proletariat will not tolerate…." And now at last, here we are. So we have accepted everything. Shall we communicate our wisdom and the glorious fruits of our experience to these unknown young men? Sunk lower and lower, we have learned only one thing—our basic impotence. This is the beginning of Reason, I agree, of the fight for life. But our bones are old, and at the age when most people think about writing their will, we are discovering that we have done nothing. . . .'[58]

This self-lacerating vision also recalls Sartre's original negativity. 'Man is a useless passion'—this, after all, was one of his basic tenets. We have now seen that although his plays carry him beyond it, they in some sense remain entangled in the problematic to which it belonged. He certainly took giant strides forward from his timeless

57. *La Force des choses*, p.671; *Force of Circumstance*, p.642.
58. 'Paul Nizan', *Situations, IV*, pp.138, 143; *Situations*, pp.123, 126.

pessimism, from his sense of the world's overwhelming weight. Yet the world's negative aspects remained overwhelming, and action could never merge with positive struggle and fully drawn characters. A token of this ultimate defeat is that play after play remained preoccupied with the *irréel*: not only Orestes and Electra, but also Hugo, Goetz, Kean, de Valera, and Franz were haunted by the *irréel*. Sartre never entirely abandoned his old refuge; from beginning to end and in spite of profound changes, we almost never witness a struggle whose key question is not the character's problematic relation to action in the real world. In relation to the crucial question—how far has Sartre been able to transform his thought to accommodate his new activism?—the testimony of the plays is deeply equivocal. They struggled to reach the world, and to re-orient their audience in it. But the very tenacity of this struggle, and its concluding pessimism, signified that in some sense the original Sartrean problematic prevailed.

Inasmuch as his original limits could have been overcome only in a dialectic with history, it is difficult to conceive of Sartre's fully transcending his original dilemmas and moving towards a concrete, historically rooted revolutionary optimism in the Europe of the late 1950s and early 1960s. Whether the ultimate limits of his theatre were those of his original problematic, or of the historical situation in which he laboured, or, more likely, of the interaction and mutual reinforcement of the two as his dramatic project struggled to break new ground, Sartre ceased to write plays and to meditate on problems of individual-revolutionary ethics. Deeply disappointed in his political hopes for Europe, he now turned to a direct and passionate practice of solidarity with the revolutionary struggles of the Third World. The place of this phase in his political writing, and its substantive relationships with his work as a whole, will be analysed in the course of an examination of his political essays.

3

Sartre as Political Thinker

The political essays reveal a new capacity in Sartre, one which reached maturity only in the fifties. In a world of fateful events, something important happened and Sartre would respond. Immediately he mastered several major writings on the particular issue and wrote a thorough, well-informed and penetrating essay. At the same time, he made no effort to devise a long-range project of political analysis and research directed towards any specific political goal. He seemed rather to be everywhere, responding swiftly to everything. If writing was action, then he acted by defining a position to be taken at the present moment, rather than developing the intellectual apparatus necessary for any longer-term effort of orientation. In short, these political writings were a kind of journalism.

Yet Sartre's journalism was like no other. Not limited to describing events, he used scholarship extensively, and laboured in every essay to explain the deepest meaning of his subject. Sometimes this effort brought him to important insights, as in his discussion, in *Les Communistes et la paix*, of how the French Communist Party had managed to lift the proletariat out of passivity. But at other times it produced turgid, chaotic analyses in which all sense of the issue was lost. Struggling to grasp the essence of events, Sartre would make one false start after another before finding his direction. Refusing to confine himself to a modest journalistic role, Sartre the political essayist failed to develop the ordinary discipline of the genre. Invented dialogues, extensive arguments with opposing positions, long passages of historical background, philosophical excursions, such abstractions as *the* French or *the* Russian worker, lengthy reconstructions of events—all these devices found their places in his essays. Usually he laboured least and reached his best when he was most purely the moralist. The beginning of the essay on Fanon was a case in point. He was not yet trying to explain reality; his purpose was simply to arouse the conscience of his audience, to induce a sense of complicity with the white settlers. 'Have the courage to read this book,' he exhorted them, 'for in the first place it will make you ashamed, and shame, as Marx said, is a revolutionary sentiment.'[2] But this was uncharacteristic. Usually the direct human appeal was replaced by argument, analysis, mock dialogue. Very often Sartre did not so much recount events (such as the abortive PCF demonstration of June 4, 1952) as argue about them. Too often there was little ease or lucidity in these writings, but instead a struggle to get to the event, as if from the outside. In the end, however, when the event was grasped and deciphered, Sartre would take his stand.

It was usually a courageous one. We have seen him, in 1948, try to create a 'third way' in the face of growing Cold-War polarization, and again in 1956, in the name of socialism. We have seen his defence of and alignment with the PCF in 1952 and his condemnation of the Soviet invasion of Hungary. He supported Yugoslavia against the Soviet bloc in 1950,[2] worked against French colonialism in Vietnam in 1951-52, and condemned the US for the Rosenberg executions in 1953.[3] In 1955 he reported warmly on his trip to China[4] and in the following year he analysed colonialism as a system.[5] After 1958, he attacked Gaullism in France and the colonial cause in Algeria, becoming one of the first major Western partisans of revolution in the Third World.[6] In the same capacity he wrote in support of the Cuban Revolution in 1960, and a year later he published his famous preface to Fanon's *Damnés de la terre*.

A 'fresh and definitive apprenticeship to realism'—Sartre's summary of his experience in the RDR foreshadowed the broad lines of his political growth from *Qu'est-ce que la littérature?* to the end of the Algerian war. It should be added, however, that his slowly strengthening sense of reality was intimately connected to and

1. 'Les Damnés de la terre,' p.175; Preface to *The Wretched of the Earth*, p.12.

2. 'Faux savants ou faux lièvres,' *Situations*, VI, Paris 1964.

3. 'Les Animaux malades de la rage', *Libération*, June 22, 1953; trans. 'Mad Beasts,' CRW, vol II, pp.207-211 (See also vol.1, 53/240, p.285).

4. 'Sartre Views the New China', interview by K.S. Karol, *New Statesman and Nation*, December 3, 1955.

5. 'Le Colonialisme est un système', *Situations*, V.

6. See his series of articles in *L'Express*, collected in *Situations*, V; and also his essay on torture in Algeria, 'Une Victoire', *Situations*, V; trans. John Calder, 'A Victory', introduction to Henri Alleg, *The Question*, New York 1958.

developed *in terms of* his strengthening revolutionary outlook. Sartre's development was twofold. He grounded himself more firmly in reality at each stage, deepening his capacity to understand events and situations; and he steadily clarified and demarcated his own role as thinker and writer. In this way he developed, with all his faults, into a mature and authoritative political commentator.

Yet by the end of the period it was noticeable that here too disillusionment was setting in. Examination of Sartre's trajectory as political essayist will throw light on this disillusionment, as well as on his remarkable successes. This section will focus in some depth on one extended essay from each of four stages of Sartre's political development: the pre-Cold War socialist-neutralist period of *Les Main sales*; the phase of alignment with the Communists heralded by *Le Diable et le bon Dieu*; the hopeful period after Stalin's death, when Sartre became a Marxist and an independent and critical fellow traveller, attacking Soviet intervention in Hungary; and finally, his turn towards the Third World at the time of the Algerian War. Each stage yielded a book: *Entretiens sur la politique, Les Communistes et la paix, Le Fantôme de Staline*, and *Sartre on Cuba*. In passing from one to the next we shall see the remarkable changes and equally striking constants in Sartre's development as a political thinker.

Neutralism and Idealism

Sartre's understanding of the RDR, contemporaneous and retrospective, suggests two things: first, that he began his career as a political commentator immersed in the *ought* as opposed to the *is*; and second, that his self-appointed role as thinker and writer at this time was to *create* a movement. *Entretiens sur la politique* sketched an organization that was not 'the expression of a class, but which, placed on the border between middle classes and working class, sought rather to realize contacts between the two classes which on many points, have the same interests.'[7] In keeping with most of Sartre's political writings between the Liberation and the high Cold War, the book was guided by this vision. For all their analyses of French society, these discussions with Rousset and Rosenthal scarcely descended to the world of real forces, real limits and real possibilities. Instead the three in-

7. Sartre, David Rousset, Gerard Rosenthal, Paris 1949, p.36.

terlocutors painted an inspiring picture of a new left-wing structure which would be free of the effects of the Communist Party and would mediate between the PCF and the rest of the Left. Certainly the RDR's reason for insisting on internal democracy were persuasive: the proletariat would be schooled in democratic deliberation and the exercise of power and thus prepare itself to direct society. The RDR would provide a 'true concrete experience of democracy' by creating 'a permanent contact between the base and the directing committee on the one hand, and on the other hand between the separated elements of the base.'[8] These ideas were valid, but the RDR was nonetheless a project of intellectuals, hatched from their vision of the ultimate political goal, or from their critique of Communism, but without roots in an actual movement. Sartre sounded rather like his own character, Hugo, when he insisted that tactics be evaluated according to whether they were a 'stage on the way to emancipation' of the proletariat, and rejected tactics that might lead to provisional success but were incompatible with this emancipation.[9] Hugo after all corresponded to a certain side of Sartre himself. The ideas of the RDR were naive because they bore no relation to any force or class in French life. Just as the ultimate critique of Hugo was his suicide, so failure was the ultimate critique of the RDR project. However, we should be alert to the temptation of overly criticizing the Sartre of the 'third force' in the name of his later realism as Sartre himself did with Hugo. His situation, like Hugo's, deserves greater sympathy. We have seen that the realism available to Hugo was not Hoederer's but that of Olga and Louis. The realism available to Sartre in 1948 would have meant abandoning fundamental socialist values just as he was developing them. It is to Sartre's great credit that he came to socialism by way of its loftiest hopes and, as we shall see, remained a major force for socialist hope on into the 1970s. Sartre's abstraction in this period was necessary if he was to identify himself with peace, independence from the two blocs, and above all with belief in revolution and democracy—in short, if he was to think beyond the dominant alternatives of 1948. *'It is not true,'* declared the RDR's 'Appel', *'that a generation must be sacrificed in order to redistribute the products of labour equitably.'* And 'it is not true that socialism must put on either an anaemic or a savage mask.'[10] Perhaps

8. Ibid., p.28.
9. Ibid., p.23.
10. 'Appel du Comité pour le RDR', CRW, 48/167, p.209.

to think such thoughts required a certain detachment, idealism, and even unreality at a time when reality stood so far from theory, and so much at odds with the traditional substance of socialist hope.

But as history can make idealists of people who sincerely hope to understand and change reality, so Sartre brought his old habits of unreality with him into his encounter with the political world. Until the RDR was founded, Sartre's political work had been done with his pen. In formulating the project of engagement he had only begun to rethink the basic terms of his stance towards reality. Now he sought to go further, to build an actual organization without yet reconsidering the dualism that led to philosophy-in-the-world. It is little wonder then, that the engaged intellectual's initial impulse should have been to create a movement corresponding to his ideas. Sartre's first sustained action suggested an idealist and magical effort to transform the real world from the outside, rather than a patient concrete *praxis*.

Realism and Communism

His next step inverted the terms of the first. Sartre now became a realist with a vengeance, attaching himself decisively to the Communists and arguing for the necessity of their hegemony over the working class. *Les Communistes et la paix*, Sartre's first serious approach to the PCF, explored the Party's relationship to the proletariat and attacked one by one the arguments which would distinguish or separate the two. 'Realism' was indeed his new watchword. He now demonstrated how far he had come since 1948 as he scorned those whose hopes and project he had then shared. He dismissed the plan for a Popular Front, from his new emphasis on what was historically possible, as 'both totally reasonable and totally absurd.'[11] Similarly, he interrogated Georges Altmann, an early supporter of the RDR who turned rightwards towards the United States, on his vision of 'a daring social democracy': but where is the basis for such a course? Where is the political team that will apply it? Where is the majority that will carry it into power?[12] At the same time he mocked the 'possibilism' of such groups as the Trotskyists who hoped and worked for a more democratic and revolutionary party at the head of the workers.

11. *Les Communistes et la paix, Situations*, VI, (CP), Paris 1964, pp.230-31; trans. Irene Clephane, *The Communists and Peace with an Answer to Claude Lefort*, (CPA), London 1969, p.104.

12. CP, p.85; CPA, p.4.

Sartre's systematic justification of the PCF was undisturbed by any note of criticism. The Communists, for their part, welcomed Sartre to their side. No less an ideological enemy than his former student Kanapa called Sartre's support 'courageous' and 'generous'.[13] Thus began the first phase of a relationship that persisted, unbroken even by Sartre's formal withdrawal in 1956 after the Soviet invasion of Hungary, until the late 1960s.

In accepting the PCF as it was, Sartre seemed to relinquish his earlier democratic and revolutionary hopes. Indeed he went much further, furnishing theoretical justification of the very nature and structure of the PCF. He deployed extended economic, social and historical arguments in an attempt to establish the Communists, *especially* in their negative traits, as the necessary and exact political expression of the proletariat. At the beginning of *Les Communistes et la paix* he spoke of 'that incurable vice' of the Communists: 'I wonder if it is not simply the peculiar nature of the proletariat.'[14] He sought to demonstrate this total identity of Party and class in the four essays that he wrote over the next two years. The Party, he argued with a strange intensity, was exactly as it must be: authoritarian, bureaucratized, centralized, consisting of paid militants who act *on* the class. It was the only possible Communist Party.

By turns violent, brilliant or Jesuitical, these essays were Sartre's first sustained effort to comprehend concrete social reality. This fact alone marked *Les Communistes et la paix*, and Sartre's answer to Claude Lefort's criticisms of its first two parts, as a kind of conversion. The essays developed in two overlapping waves. First, Sartre presented the theoretical argument for his identification of the PCF with the proletariat. Second, he tried to show the social and historical basis for this identification.

The Party, so his argument went, did not so much express the working class as *make* it exist. Alone, without the Party, the workers remained separated, discouraged individuals without hope or direction. Each one was a man of the 'mass' — totally absorbed in personal concerns, 'he will become a *different* man only by a kind of conversion'.[15] Only under the urging and leadership of the Party —

13. Mark Poster, *Existential Marxism in Postwar France: From Sartre to Althusser*, Princeton 1975, p.163.

14. CP, p.87; CPA, p.6.

15. CP, p.247; CPA, p.114.

indeed, following its orders—did the atoms making up the mass discover their solidarity, their collective consciousness. Only then did they become the subject of history rather than its object—*a working class* rather than dispersed individuals wholly shaped and dominated by bourgeois society. And without the Party? 'If the tie of solidarity is broken the worker would continue to be a producer, a manual worker, a wage-earner, but he would no longer be a proletarian, that is to say, an active member of the proletariat.'[16] In other words, class was not a pre-existing entity. 'Classes do not exist, they are made'[17] — made in 'an epoch-making operation which reflects an intention: it can never be separated from the concrete will that animates it nor from the ends it pursues.'[18]

In the intervals between actions, what was it that kept the worker from sinking back into the mass, completely losing his sense of collective needs and collective struggle—especially given the exhausting and isolating conditions of his work? Sartre's answer was: only an organization 'which shall be the pure and simple incarnation of *praxis.*'[19] The worker's condition made it necessary that this organization remain independent of and external to his daily life, that it become an authority giving orders, that it consist of paid specialists such as the militant who could help 'his comrades define the sense of [their] ambiguous experience.'[20] Organization, links between workers widely separated, clarity about goals, the power of analysis, the determination to struggle—if these were to be kept alive among the workers they must be maintained *outside* the workplace. Thus the Communist Party, and specifically the PCF of the 1950s, *was* the working class; 'the Party forms the social frameworks of working-class memory, it is the sketch of their future, the organ of their action, the permanent link which struggles against their massification; it is the *perspective* from which the proletariat can put itself back into society and in its turn take as object those who make an object of it: it is the tradition and the institution. But the *content* of these empty forms will come to birth, by the very linkage of the movement which the masses make in order to draw nearer to one another; it is by being brought

16. CP, p.206; CPA, p.88.
17. CP, p.206; CPA, p.88.
18. CP, p.207; CPA, p.89.
19. CP, p.247; CPA, p.115.
20. 'Réponse à Claude Lefort,' *Situations*, VII, Paris 1965, p.32.; CPA, p.223.

into touch that particular interests are changed into general interests, it is through this that isolated individuals become *an undertaking.*'[21] This suggestive line of thought was Sartre's first formulation of what would become key concepts in the *Critique*. Even when all possible criticisms of these concepts and their obvious limits of application are made — and in a moment I will take up some of them — they still contain an important insight. As Sartre develops the concepts of the 'series' and the 'group' it will become clear how useful they are for understanding massification in some of its most seemingly democratic forms — public opinion polls, for example, or elections — and for understanding revolutionary upheavals.

Aware that theoretical insights into group processes could not alone account for history, Sartre tried to discover the basis of massification in the specific history of class struggles in France and in the particular development of French capitalism. This part of the essay was Sartre's first effort at a Marxist analysis of society, and perhaps one of the first such studies of a specific society since the Bolshevik Revolution. He carefully traced the specific development of French capitalism in the nineteenth and twentieth centuries, arguing that the French bourgeoisie had deliberately chosen an anti-development and under-consumptionist Malthusian course in response to the revolutionary threat from the proletariat. This important line of thought was also to be carried into the *Critique* and, much later, to become central to Sartre's explanation of the misanthropy of Gustave Flaubert. Now he went on to describe the massive industrialization, beginning in the early twentieth century, which created a de-skilled working class that now needed the PCF to give it shape and coherence. Dispersion, exhaustion, passivity, ignorance and lack of confidence — these were necessary traits of the unskilled proletariat created by twentieth-century French capitalism.

Had Sartre at last satisfied his persistent drive to reach reality? Did *Les Communistes et la paix* signify that Sartre had overcome the attitudes that had long separated him from social and political reality — isolation, individualism, dualism, idealism, interiority, and a fascination with the imaginary? Had he now reworked his thought into an effective and flexible instrument for understanding reality?

21. Ibid., pp.60-61; CPA, p.242.

Was he now able to take his place in the real world, a 'man among men'? If it marked a political conversion, did *Les Communistes et la paix* also mark an intellectual conversion for Sartre, or at least the completion of the transformation begun in 1940?

We may certainly begin to apply the label 'Marxist' to Sartre in this period. And we have seen the contemporary *Le Diable et le bon Dieu* present his new revolutionary realism — but of principle only: he had developed a new attitude but not made it come alive on the stage in 1951, and indeed remained unable to do so in his future plays. Sartre claims that *Les Mots*, begun in 1953 while he was still engaged in *Les Communistes et la paix*, reflected his awakening from idealism, his renunciation of literature as salvation.[22] But a close look at *Les Communistes et la paix* reveals it as a partial awakening, an incomplete renunciation. Sartre had become a revolutionary realist in a way still deeply conditioned by his early relation to reality. It was, first of all, perhaps, the worst-written of all of his essays. It is turgid and repetitive — oppressively so. Sartre argued on and on about the meaning of the events of May 28 and June 4, but made no attempt to depict the events themselves. He was clearly more concerned to write against *other writers* than to present reality. His writing consequently exhibited a leaden, remote, often unreal quality, as if he could only make contact with political reality through the most extreme verbal exertions. The related 'Réponse à Claude Lefort', one of his most ill-tempered writings, leads the reader to speculate that Sartre's alignment with the Communists could only be accomplished by considerable internal violence.

The political and theoretical limitations of *Les Communistes et la paix* were identified in two important contemporary criticisms, the first, political reply by Ernest Mandel in 1953, the second, two years later, Merleau-Ponty's political and philosophical analysis of Sartre's ultra-bolshevism. These two essays deserve special attention, for their penetrating insight into Sartre's political and philosophical postures at the time of his conversion to Marxism. We can discern, in their light, how the problematic of *L'Etre et le Néant* was borne by Sartre into his subsequent political thought and action. Mandel, responding with great dignity and theoretical acumen to Sartre's dismissal of 'Trotskyist possibilism', focused on the uncritical, irrational quality of

22. *Sartre*, pp.110-111.
23. Ernest Mandel, *La Longue Marche*, p.87.

Sartre's adherence to the PCF, and his 'rigid system of real-only-possible-realist' which allowed no room to evaluate any particular Party policy in terms of its alternatives.[23] Sartre's strange bow to realism suspended him in a kind of fatalism according to which 'all politics effectively applied at a given moment becomes by this fact alone the only possible politics.'[24] Thus the proletariat had refused to turn out for the June 4 demonstration not because the Communists were wrong, or had followed a wrong course since the Liberation, but because, discouraged and weakened, the workers remained stuck in their isolation and did not even exist as a class. Mandel, to the contrary, insisted on evaluating the Party. 'The first criterion of an effective politics,' he affirmed, 'is to know if it is based on a correct or false analysis of reality.'[25] He criticized the PCF for acting from a false analysis, for retarding the development of working-class power and class-consciousness, and took Sartre to task for his submission to the party line. Indeed three of his most acute criticisms bore footnotes to *Entretiens sur la politique* and Sartre's 1950 essay on Yugoslavia, which had blamed the Stalinist bureaucracy for destroying revolutionary subjectivity. Mandel was concerned to raise the consciousness of the proletariat: nothing in *Les Communistes et la paix* remotely alluded to this. He was concerned with the goal of socialist revolution: Sartre not at all, it seemed. Mandel based himself on laws of development, on a commitment to evaluating the possible courses of socialist politics, on the history of the working class and socialist history, and above all on a belief in the combativeness of the proletariat; for all of these, Sartre had substituted the immediate and direct action of the Communists to create an active class from the passive, dispersed mass of labouring individuals. But, Mandel replied, the class persisted, it had a history, it underwent and integrated into its consciousness defeat and disillusionment as well as achieving victories and self-awareness. Properly guided, and entering favourable historical circumstances, it would become freely aware of its own power, its own needs, and its revolutionary opportunities. To place the locus of class and class consciousness *outside* it, to make these depend on the great moments of action led by the PCF was 'simply to reduce this concept to the absurd.'[26]

24. Ibid., p.85.
25. Ibid., p.80.
26. Ibid., p.100.

How is one to explain Sartre's fatalism, his continuing distance from historical analysis, his refusal to make an objective evaluation of the PCF? One of Mandel's formulations pointed forward to Merleau-Ponty's critique: 'Marx is a dialectician; you are a metaphysician balanced between the absolute and nothingness. There is the difference.'[27] Mandel's political critique overlapped with the far less engaged and (perhaps consequently) philosophically more penetrating essay by Merleau-Ponty. Sartre's former close colleague, now withdrawn from the fray, brilliantly if obliquely traced the very faults of *Les Communistes et la paix* criticized by Mandel to the persistence in Sartre's political thought of the ideas of *L'Etre et le Néant*. Further, he showed that Sartre's attitude towards the world was still marked by a derealizing tendency that undermined any project of commitment. Not a Marxist, Merleau-Ponty argued, Sartre subjected Communist practice to an analysis based on *his own* outlook. In the process the concepts of Marxism were reduced one by one to the terms of the Sartrean drama: 'the conception of Communism that Sartre proposes is a denunciation of the dialectic and the philosophy of history and substitutes for them a philosophy of absolute creation amidst the unknown.'[28] The Party in relation to workers isolated and inert before the former galvanized them — did not this vision suggest the for-itelf appearing on the margin of the in-itself? 'It is precisely that the Party, like the militant, is pure action. If everything comes from freedom, if the workers are nothing, not even proletarians, before they create the Party, the Party rests on nothing that has been established, not even on their common history.'[29] Sartre's ontological dualism become political analysis ignored the meanings that pre-existed the Party, the ebb and flow of history, the intentions and motion already inherent in the social whole, the fact that the workers' 'landscape' was 'animated'. In this unMarxist philosophy 'in which meaning, seen as wholly spiritual, as impalpable as lightning, is absolutely opposed to being which is absolute weight and blindness,'[30] there was no growth or development of the class over time. 'The workers' unity

27. Ibid., p.100.
28. Maurice Merleau-Ponty, *Les Aventures de la dialectique,* Paris 1955, p.138; trans. Joseph Bien, *The Adventures of the Dialectic,* Evanston 1973, p.101.
29. Ibid., p.147; pp.107-108.
30. Ibid., p.168; p.124.

is always to be remade',[31] in a series of magical acts in which conversion alternated with atomization. 'Reading Sartre, one would believe that the Party's action is a series of *coups de force* by which it defends itself against death.'[32]

Certainly, Sartre had announced his agreement with the Party on specific areas 'reasoning from *my* principles and not theirs'.[33] But this was precisely the problem: 'Contrary to appearances, being-for-itself is all Sartre has ever accepted, with its inevitable corollary: pure being in-itself.'[34] His basic philosophical premiss was precisely what led him to focus on bursts of action, not the articulated relationships of human action and history; to focus on pure intentions, rather than submit their results to evaluation: to hypothesize an identification, not an exchange between those who give and those who receive politics; to speak of the workers *obeying* the Party rather than critically appraising it; to focus on separate and distinct actions at each moment, rather than the slow historical process of the 'coming-to-be of meaning in institutions.'[35] His fundamental difference with Marx was that for him 'the relationships between classes, the relationships within the proletariat, and finally those of the whole of history are not articulated relationships, including tension and the easing of tension, but are immediate or magical relationships of our gazes'.[36] With Sartre we were not in a complex historical situation but in 'the magical or moral universe'.[37]

Above all, Sartre remained where he had begun: in the *cogito*, looking out on the world of action. And so *commitment* remained his unresolved problem. It was not that the writer's peculiar action — of unveiling — could ever become transformed into action itself, or that anything could remove the inherent difficulty of achieving a balance between seeing and doing. But Sartre's difficulties went beyond these: he mistakenly '[dreamt] of touching the things themselves through action,'[38] while remaining a writer. As in *L'Etre et le Néant*, choice became the paramount act of the for-itself. And it was a choice bet-

31. Ibid., p.199; p.148.
32. Ibid., p.158; p.116.
33. CP, p.168; CPA, p.62.
34. *Les Aventures de la dialectique*, p.190; *The Adventures of the Dialectic*, p.142.
35. Ibid., p.168; p.124.
36. Ibid., pp.206-7; p.153.
37. Ibid., p.207; p.154.
38. Ibid., p.241; p.179.

ween things, the only way of making direct contact with the thing itself. Thus we must ask 'whether commitment as understood by Sartre does not transform the relationships of action into relationships of contemplation'.[39] The writer who wanted to act and who understood his task of unveiling, who accepted the inherent necessity of encountering history in indirect and symbolic ways, 'would act more surely by accepting this kind of action which is eminently his, by reporting his preferences, his internal debates with Communism than by bringing to others the austere news of the choice he has made, out of duty, between existing things.'[40] The *need to choose* which registered in so much of Sartre's politics thus sprang from his continuing desire to 'reach' reality across an unbridgeable distance. And the intellectual distortions caused by it stemmed from his continuing tendency to impose philosophy on the world, so becoming 'impervious to experience'[41] and, in this case, transmuting Communism 'into Sartre'.[42] Failing to realize that philosophy must develop *new* categories, raise and answer questions when encountering history, Sartre simply *substituted* philosophy for the 'servitudes and virtues' of action. Political action as conceived by Sartre became 'commitment': a series of brief confrontations which were always in some sense *outside,* which never took charge of the world, never moved '*within* situations and facts'.[43] His fellow-travelling posture was derived from his basic outlook: 'sympathy for communism and unity of action with it on certain particular points represent the maximum possible action in a conception of freedom that allows only for sudden interventions into the world, for camera shots and flash bulbs. Today, as yesterday, commitment is action at a distance, politics by proxy, a way of putting ourselves right with the world rather than entering it; and, rather than an art of intervention, it is an art of circumscribing, of preventing intervention.'[44]

Sartre's 'commitment' was 'an attitude, not an action': it expressed 'the principle of changing oneself rather than the order of things.'[45] Commitment was Sartre's way of overcoming, again and again, the

39. Ibid., p.241; p.179.
40. Ibid., pp.241-2; pp.179-80.
41. Ibid., p.248; p.184.
42. Ibid., p.252; p.187.
43. Ibid., p.258; p.191.
44. Ibid., p.259; pp.192-93.
45. Ibid., p.260; p.193.

distance he himself created, and its difficulties arose from 'the uneasiness of a philosophy confronted with a type of relationship to the world — history, action — that it does not want to recognize. For commitment in Sartre's sense is the negation of the link between us and the world that it seems to assert; or rather Sartre tries to make a link out of a negation'[46] — the negation which we have already discerned at the heart of Sartre's thought.

This realism without possibilities, based as it was on Sartre's extreme pessimism concerning the proletariat, was animated by no vision of socialism or democracy or the end of alienation. Both critics commented on his flirtation with the imaginary, on his vision of political action as a kind of 'theatre'.[47] His political 'realism' recalled the earlier apolitical pessimism of the thirties. In the end, as Merleau-Ponty commented, Sartre's 'extreme realism cannot be distinguished from an extreme idealism'.[48]

Merleau-Ponty's pioneering essay showed that Sartre's central categories entailed limitations that would deeply affect his future development, and began the important task of relating the weaknesses of Sartre's political posture to the weaknesses of his philosophy. But as Simone de Beauvoir argued in a lengthy refutation, Merleau-Ponty tended to address himself to a 'pseudo-Sartre'. It was not, as she tirelessly insisted, that a fair reading of Sartre would show him meeting in advance all of Merleau-Ponty's objections (she herself by and large opposed stray pronouncements by Sartre to what Merleau-Ponty with greater perception regarded as key themes of Sartre's thought, and in so doing occluded the real tensions and contradictions in the latter's work).[49] Rather, Merleau-Ponty created his 'pseudo-Sartre' by ignoring the many positive aspects of Sartre's essays, as well as the changes he had undergone since the early 1940s. In over a hundred pages of intensive, brilliant but puzzling analysis, he made no allowance for the transitory character of Sartre's essays, for the emerging tension between the 'old' and the 'new' Sartre. The strongest part of de Beauvoir's reply shows why: in calling for 'a new liberalism' at the end of his book, Merleau-Ponty had, she insisted, changed

46. Ibid., p.260; p.193.

47. See for example, ibid., p.262; p.195.

48. *Les Aventures de la dialectique*, p.227; *The Adventures of the Dialectic*, pp.168-69.

49. Simone de Beauvoir, 'Merleau-Ponty et le Pseudo-Sartrisme,' *Les Temps Modernes* 114-115 (June-July 1955).

camps. While he evaluated Sartre in terms of Marx, he had himself abandoned his own Marxist commitments. Yet in spite of his political retreat, Merleau-Ponty still confronted the committed Sartre with a fundamental crux: effective commitment necessitated the transcendence of Sartre's basic attitude towards reality, as expressed in *L'Etre et le Néant*. If *Les Communistes et la paix* could be so devastatingly — and convincingly — ascribed to his ontology, and if the problems of the one so clearly stemmed from the problems of the other, then Sartre the political thinker would sooner or later have to come to terms with his own most deeply anchored assumptions. The re-considerations of *Qu'est-ce que la littérature?* would have to develop into a full-scale philosophical transformation.

Hungary and Dialectics

By the early 1950s Sartre had become a Marxist; and, his four years of uncritical fellow-travelling ended, he forcefully denounced the Soviet invasion of Hungary in the name of socialism. What did *Le Fantôme de Staline* reveal about his development as a political thinker?

It was indeed Sartre's first political essay of real stature. He now understood the necessity of *explaining* events in and for themselves, no longer refracting — and distorting — them through philosophical categories. To be sure, he did not operate *without* categories, but here for the first time his Marxist analysis let events stand out on their own, often brilliantly illuminating them. The confused picture of Hungary in October-November 1956 began to come clear, as Sartre patiently assessed the relative weight of classes and parties and explained both their unity against the USSR and the potential differences within the insurrectionary movement.

Was socialism threatened in Hungary? If a new government centred on the Communist opposition accepted the redistribution of land by the peasants alongside the established socialization of industry, and if both the insurrectionary movement and the USSR grasped the necessity of giving oppositionist Communists a decisive mediating and governing role — no. Yet, in so far as a government called into being through free elections would cast the discredited Communists into a decidedly minority position, and in so far as a new government that let Hungarian society develop freely would undermine the authoritarian socialism imposed from without by the USSR — in that sense, there was indeed a threat. Sartre's detailed analysis showed simultaneously how the developing situation threatened almost every step the Soviet Union had taken in Hungary since 1945, why it entailed real risks for those committed to socialism, and yet why it was the only acceptable route for Hungary. It became equally clear that any denunciation of the USSR must reach back at least to the policies of industrialization and collectivization imposed on Hungary since 1949. Sartre himself went still further, trying to explain the historical roots and meaning, in the Bolshevik Revolution and the process of building 'socialism in one country', of Stalinization and the creation of those contradictory entities, the 'Peoples' Democracies'. He argued that Stalinism and oppressive Communism, this 'bloody monster which itself tears itself to pieces', had fulfilled whatever historical function it might have had and was ready to give way to a new era of democratization and trust.

Equipped now with this historical understanding of the conditions for socialist democracy, Sartre transcended the antinomies of his earlier political positions. Socialist ideals — which have meaning only as definite historical intentions — found their embodiment in deeply contradictory realities. Backwardness and isolation had doomed the Soviet Union to a socialism of terror and the cult of personality. But reality must always be judged in terms of its concrete alternatives: today democratization was possible, in a secure, developed socialist nation. The state of Soviet socialism in 1957 called for a new evaluative framework, one of whose terms must be democracy. Sartre the dialectical analyst now criticized the political realists just as four years earlier, precisely in the name of 'realism', he had criticized those whom he regarded as the political idealists. He attacked the argument of those 'in certain progressive and Communist quarters' who sought to establish the necessity of the Soviet invasion: their argument 'is said to be Marxist: I believe it to be much older than Marx; it can be summed up thus: "what must be must be." '[50] No, he insisted, there was no inevitable rightness or even regrettable necessity about Soviet actions.

Sartre was now so far from *Les Communistes et la paix* that he forcefully pleaded the importance of judging *all* Communist actions and policies. The aim of Communism, 'to give justice and freedom to

50. FS, p.155; SS, p.9 (translation changed)..

all men,'[51] radically distinguished it from any politics aimed at preserving class domination. No one need *condemn* colonialism, for the only way to deal with such a system is to struggle to abolish it. On the other hand, as he had already argued in opposition to Merleau-Ponty, socialism '*is privileged, in that,* to understand it, it is necessary to marry its movement and adopt its objectives; in short it must be judged in accordance with what it wants and its means in accordance with its aim, while all other undertakings are estimated according to what they do not know, what they neglect or what they reject.' These arguments revealed the full extent of Sartre's development. But why was it necessary so to emphasize this judicial attitude towards socialism? Very simply, so that the movement would be impelled to become all that it potentially was: the concrete reality of human liberation. As humanity's only hope, socialism could not be cynically abandoned, even when it became a nightmare: 'to preserve hope, it is necessary to do exactly the opposite: to recognize, in spite of the mistakes, the abominations, the crimes, the obvious privileges of the socialist camp, and to condemn with so much the more strength the policy which puts those privileges in danger.'[52]

Henceforward, Sartre attacked the orthodox again and again — but no longer, as in 'Matérialisme et révolution', from the outside. He now stood firmly within the socialist movement and Marxism, and, for the first time, evaluated politics with genuine power and authority. After criticizing Communist defenders of Russian intervention, Sartre went on to attack the Party as 'an outfit with hardening arteries which can no longer make recruits among the young, and whose middle-agedness rises year by year'.[53] He lashed the Party intellectuals for their theoretical indolence, their recourse to mythology rather than Marxism, their readiness to suppress rather than try to interpret new experience: they were 'pompous asses who take the class struggle for a Platonic Idea or who make it intervene like a *deus ex machina.*'[54] Whereas in 1952 *they* had been the acknowledged Marxists, approached by Sartre from his own, existentialist starting-point, the mid-fifties saw the assertion of a new relationship: the Party intellectuals were *false* Marxists, dogmatists and schematizers, in opposition

51. FS, p.280; SS, p.89.
52. FS, pp.282-3; SS, p.91.
53. FS, p.184; SS, pp.27-28.
54. FS, p.176; SS, p.23.

to whom Sartre sought to grasp, and be faithful to, the Marxian dialectic. Sartre decided to study Hungary rather than theorize about who the insurrectionaries *must be*; he likewise tried to study the development of the Soviet Union to account for its contradictory behaviour. And so his political writing gave birth to a new goal: not merely to take a position on the event, but to understand it — in Merleau-Ponty's words, to *unveil* political reality. At this point Sartre entered, and began to be a force within, Marxist thought.

Nevertheless, *Le Fantôme de Staline* retained some of the troubling traits of his earlier work. His analysis of Hungary and discussion of Soviet development were such as to make a stand, a further act of 'commitment', superfluous. Why *condemn* the Soviet regime after showing that its own past, its international situation, its reading of events, its very *raison d'être* as ruling bureaucracy, all demanded intervention to cut down a revolution in Hungary? 'No one,' Sartre insisted, 'has the right to say that events in Hungary made intervention inevitable.'[55] Yet his own analysis unveiled one necessity after another. Using language unfamiliar to *L'Etre et le Néant* he spoke of the 'necessity' of the Nagy regime and its programme; he stated that, 'beginning in 1930 the Soviet leaders in the name of the proletariat, were compelled to exercise an iron dictatorship over a hostile peasantry'; that a mood of pessimism *necessarily* resulted from 'the exercise of dictatorship and the internal contradictions of bureaucracy';[56] that 'it became necessary to create a working-class elite' in the USSR; that Russian socialism *had to be* oppressive.[57] Sartre's own careful analysis failed to discover the basis for any alternative to Soviet intervention. Such a basis would have had to reside in the facts themselves, not in any theoretical argument against determinism. But as he presented them, the facts all spoke in favour of the Soviet invasion.

The more Sartre decided to reveal events rather than argue *about* them, the more he presented them in their *necessity*, and so cancelled his own role as independent political agent. As Merleau-Ponty suggested, the one form of commitment was quite different from the other. But they overlapped in *Le Fantôme de Staline* and, in the end, Sartre's earlier version of commitment caused the essay to lose its way. His account of the internal situation in Hungary was detailed,

55. FS, p.215; SS, p.47.
56. FS, pp.225,234; SS, pp.54,60.
57. FS, pp.227,236; SS, pp.55,61.

concrete and illuminating. Turning then to explain Soviet motives, Sartre began to lose focus: his account of Stalinist Communism, for all its merit, was more abstract and less specifically informed. Therewith, his concern became more universalist, redolent of the philosopher imposing his categories on politics. However brilliantly, he tended to invent rather than encounter reality. Thus, it never became clear, specifically, *why* the ussr had invaded Hungary. Thus too, in his great optimism he devised an ideal Soviet policy whose concrete possibility he did not convincingly establish. And he too quickly seized on the Soviet Union's new strength as a reason for demanding a democratic policy — the basis also for his argument that the invasion was not inevitable. He addressed himself to the Soviet rulers, calling on them to adopt a more trusting line, rather than examine either their immersion in the Cold War or their stake in keeping Soviet society *as it was*. His failure to analyse closely either the international or the domestic basis of Soviet politics created the false impression that Soviet policy-makers enjoyed a wide area of freedom to act without endangering their own interests or those of the Soviet Union as they perceived them. Beyond the various necessities, all represented as now past, Sartre mistakenly projected the present as a new field of indeterminacy in which Soviet leaders could choose a truly positive course; they were culpable because they had chosen the less progressive of the available actions. Sartre's conclusions disclosed an inability to bring his newly-acquired Marxism to bear on precisely the problem that had always most occupied him: the discovery of a course of action in the present.

Sartre strayed still further when he turned at the end to France and its Communist Party, presciently projecting an intelligent policy of Socialist-Communist alliance without beginning to analyse concretely the class basis, nature, structure, and interests of its proposed constituents in 1957. His great hope for Communism in Eastern Europe led him to try to unblock French politics. But what began as a cogent Marxist analysis of reality ran aground as Sartre returned to the existential politics of choice and assertion. 'Whatever happens, we must back it: the *Front Populaire* or stagnation — we must choose.'[58] Sartre cited the response of an imagnary interlocutor and went on to analyse 'the disastrous practice of the cp'.[59] The intermingling of the new and

58. fs, p.292; ss, p.98.
59. fs, p.296; ss, p.101.

the old in Sartre's political writing — his growing authority as a Marxist analyst and a familiar tendency towards self-distancing and unreality — were manifest.

The constants criticized by Merleau-Ponty persisted alongside and within Sartre's evolution into a Marxist political thinker. In both form and content, Sartre's essay was at its best describing the situation in Hungary itself. But it was constructed as an argument against *other writers,* and ended up at an uncomfortable distance from its own subject-matter. As *Le Fantôme de Staline* proceeded, Sartre seemed more and more outside events, seemed more and more to be labouring to grasp them.

Cuba and Revolution

Three years later, by the time of his 1960 trip to Cuba, Sartre had discovered the Third World, solidly aligning himself with revolutionary movements for independence and socialism. At the same time he had become independent and critical of official Marxist theory, as well as Communist and Soviet practice, and was especially disillusioned with the PCF. Deeply depressed by events in France, he and Simone de Beauvoir travelled to Cuba to try to 'shake ourselves out of our inertia'. [60] What he found there was the first actual embodiment of his own political stance. Cuba confirmed and strengthened his revolutionary commitment.

However, Sartre's Cuba essays were atypical. They first appeared in *France-Soir,* France's largest bourgeois newspaper, and were no doubt inspired by the tension between Cuba and the United States. Sartre's prospective audience was not the usual small Left-intellectual sector, but a popular readership of over a million: he appears to have seen a chance to win support for revolutionary Cuba and written accordingly. Thus his series of articles avoided any explicit reference to socialism; they carefully, if implicitly, distinguished the guerrillas from Communism and Marxism; and Sartre's usual extended theoretical explorations were absent. Indeed 'Ideology and Revolution', the theoretical last chapter of the English version, never appeared in French; and while he authorized translations of the *France-Soir* series into Spanish, Portuguese, Italian, Polish, Turkish, German and Rus-

60. De Beauvoir, *La Force des choses,* p.511; *Force of Circumstance,* p.487.

sian, Sartre never consented to their being republished in book-form in French.[61] Very simply, they were composed as a journalistic report, which on tactical grounds concealed the full extent of their author's political identification with the Cuban Revolution.

Nevertheless *Sartre on Cuba* has much to tell us. It revealed Sartre's intellect at work once more in an extended effort to understand a single event. It showed the extent of his assimilation of Marxism, his strengthening grasp of historical reality, his changing sense of the role of political intellectuals — and as well as these, the extent to which his earlier limitations persisted in the mature Marxist. For all its tactical and journalistic character, *Sartre on Cuba* marked the point Sartre had reached as a political thinker by 1960.

Most striking and successful was Sartre's attempt to describe the reality of revolutionary Cuba as it might appear to a French bourgeois. The first report shrewdly began by placing readers in the midst of Havana, but at an appropriate distance from the real social locus of the revolution: 'This city, so easy to understand in 1949, has confused me. This time I failed to understand a thing. We are living in the fashionable district. The Hotel Nacional is a fortress of luxury, flanked by two square notched towers. Two qualities are required of its clients who come from the Continent: fortune and taste. As these are rarely reconcilable, if you have the first, they will grant you the second without looking too closely. In the hall I often meet tall "Yankees" (they are still called that in Cuba, unless one terms them "Americans"), elegant and sporty. I look with surprise at their chilled faces. What's crushing them? Their millions or their feelings? In any case, it's a problem which doesn't concern me. My millionaire hotel room would hold my Paris apartment. What can one say about it? There are silks, folding-screens, flowers in embroidery or in vases, two double beds for me, all alone — all the conveniences. I turn the air conditioning all the way to enjoy the cold of the rich. While it's 86° in the shade, I approach the windows and, shivering sumptuously, I watch the passers-by perspire.'[62] Such signs of luxury, as the rest of the chapter explains, 'were really signs of dependence and poverty.'[63]

The second chapter looked into Cuba's recent past under Batista. Then Sartre turned to the cane fields, initiating a close analysis of

61. See CRW, pp.375-85.
62. *Sartre on Cuba*, (SC) New York 1961, p.7.

Cuba's past which reflected his own political outlook. Brief but detailed, these three chapters were an excellent introduction to Cuban economic and social life. In them Sartre spelt out the semi-colonial relationship between American corporate interests, Cuba's latifundistas and comprador bourgeoisie, and the Cuban masses. 'Cuba is an underdeveloped country, I'll grant you that, but that's because other countries, with Cuban complicity, have prevented its development.'[64] Or rather, Cuba had become economically developed — strictly according to the needs of the United States economy. The country exported massive amounts of semi-refined sugar and imported almost everything it needed, from rice to automobiles; and in eagerly accepting and administering this situation, Cuba's rulers kept most of the population in a state of constant under-employment, illiteracy, hunger and disease. The next two chapters dealt with the recent past — the guerrilla movement. The following three surveyed the revolution's economic, social and political forms. After describing the revolution's youthful energy, and rebellious, individualist qualities, Sartre went on to discuss Fidel Castro's political outlook and style.

Looking at Cuba today, what did Sartre see? The dawn-till-dawn energy of the revolution, its youthfulness, its commitment to rebellion and individualism, its humanism, its rejection of ideology, its devotion to removing hunger and raising production. He presented a kaleidoscope: Fidel complaining about warm lemonade at a public beach and Che taking a shower; the young ministers staying up all night, the agrarian reform; Castro's humane intentions and the young rebels with beards. And then, in 'Ideology and Revolution', actually written before the first sixteen chapters, he formulated the theoretical thesis that the ideology of the revolution developed first in action: 'deeds produce ideas'.[65]

In these articles Sartre completed a stage begun in *La Fantôme de Staline*: Rather than philosophize about reality, he sought to unveil it. Perhaps the requirements of newspaper reporting created a further pressure in this direction. At any rate, the Cuban Revolution appeared in Sartre's vivid, committed account as a real event, not a drama taking place among intellectuals. He did not argue, but

63. sc, p.12.
64. sc, p.36.
65. sc, p.151.

reported. Yet his analysis and perspective showed forth in the facts themselves. Sartre was closer to the world he was writing about now than at any time since becoming politically engaged. His self-imposed role was not simply to announce his stand but to reveal Cuba.

However, the faults of his earlier political writing persisted. The opening paragraphs, for all their refreshing concreteness, tended to present *Sartre seeing Cuba* rather than Cuba itself. 'This time,' he tells us, 'I failed to understand a thing'; or he professes not to be concerned about the Americans, having gone out of his way to concern his readers. These authorial intrusions were not designed to establish a frame of reference that would make clear how he saw what he saw; they were quite random, personal, idiosyncratic. *He* failed to understand a thing (Why? We do not know); *he* did not worry about the Americans (Why? We do not know). Seeming to confide so much, Sartre in fact revealed virtually nothing — we are left to puzzle over *his* attitudes at the expense of the Hotel Nacional. It was as Merleau-Ponty had perceived: in a sense, Sartre remained in the *irréel* even after his break with it. Instead of letting himself be governed by a rigorous, objective logic, he persisted in remaking reality. The real event still tended to be converted into a literary one.

Again and again we read invented dialogue and action: 'People in the cities shrugged their shoulders furiously. "It's Castro playing his pranks again. This time he's going to lose. He thought he was making a surprise attack but the surprise was on him — it was an act of desperation".'[66] Inflated passage follows inflated passage, rhetoric taking the place of analysis: 'A field of sugar cane, in my opinion, is not exactly gay. In Haiti I saw some that were said to be haunted. I recall the red earth of a broken-up road, and the dusty rotting of the cane in the sun. In Cuba, I recognize with the same respect the impenetrable multitude of these stalks. They press one against the other, they embrace one another, one would say that they entangle themselves around their neighbors, and then from time to time one discovers a fissure between them, a high tunnel, black and deep. All the gradations of green — dark green, acid green, cabbage green, coarse green, blue green — assault the observer as far as the eye can reach. Each year, they cut the stalk; it does not have to be replanted for five years. This obstate fecundity gives me here, as in Port-au-

66. sc, p.18.

Prince, the feeling of being present at the ceremonies of a vegetable mystery.'[67] This is a literary language, and accomplished as it is, that is the problem. *Sartre on Cuba* exhibited an odd alternation between literary and theoretical approaches. Again and again, by what appeared to be 'merely' stylistic devices, the precise, objective quality of the real world tended to disappear into a quite idiosyncratic, semiliterary 'world'. Sartre seemed to remake reality in order to present it, seemed to *de-realize* reality, turning it into an object of his imagination that met *his* needs, obeyed *his* laws.

This, of course, refers only to one tendency in Sartre's reports on Cuba. It might be said that this tendency arose from their character as political journalism, or, at the limit, that it was a residue from the early Sartre, a cause of needless difficulty, but nothing more. However I would argue that it was the sign of more substantive problems. How did Sartre the socialist present the Cuban Revolution? He indicated that although the leaders disclaimed interest in ideologies, the necessities of Cuban life led them towards socialism. For example, 'the co-operative, in Cuba, was inscribed in the nature of things. Cane, in any event, needs the wide open spaces. The fallow lands of the old latifundias, naturally, are abolished — they are given to other growers for them to plant other crops. But the plantation itself, with its millions of green stalks, cannot be divided without pulverizing sugar production. Is one going to encumber it with 20,000 small isolated producers, opposed by competition, by interests, by diversity of tools and techniques? And how could one indicate, in this virgin forest, the frontiers of each property? There is also the factory, which passes on the orders and awaits the harvest. What good does it do to possess privately if you have to cut the stalks together and hold the means of transport in common? Cane requires this unity of common enterprise. Formerly it was the feudal community of the destitute, of the enslaved journeymen, in debt, without land; tomorrow it will be the production co-operative.'[68]

Sartre was fully aware of what was taking place: an agrarian reform which for the most part removed land from the hands of private individuals and foreign corporations and placed it under the control of the co-operatives. This was only one of several decisive initiatives: others included government intervention to determine rents, wages, and the

67. sc, p.21.
68. sc, p.75.

costs of electricity; a shift in the basis of power from the foreign-equipped army to the rebel forces; a shift of social weight from the American corporations and native bourgeoisie and latifundistas to the peasantry; a planned economy designed to increase production; and massive government investment to create new, public economic sectors, such as popular tourism. All these indicate that in the spring of 1960 the Cuban Revolution was moving clearly in the direction of socialism. Sartre chose to minimize their significance for obvious tactical reasons, to win support for a threatened Cuba. In refusing to call the trends he reported 'socialist', Sartre was trying to combat anti-Communism — not through dissimulation, but by arguing that 'Cuba's situation alone' imposed these measures. His constant justification of revolutionary acts in terms of Cuba's situation was aimed against explanations based on the 'Communist conspiracy'.

But Sartre went much further than tactics alone dictated. Besides trying to protect and support Cuba, he also reconsidered the relationship between theory and practice. In Cuba, he claimed to have found revolutionaries whose actions stemmed from the concrete situation that they confronted, not from abstract and general theories. 'It's not principles or opinions which count,' he affirmed.[69] What counted were the necessities of the situation. The co-operatives instituted by the agrarian reform did not spring from someone's socialist vision, but were 'inscribed in the nature of things'. The planned economy did not result from any ideological commitment of the leadership, but 'had been imposed because the circumstances require it'.[70] The urgency of Cuba's economic tasks made elections impossible: 'the situation imposed' its political structures on Cuba.[71] Sartre's undoctrinaire Cuban revolutionary refused to generalize: 'his unique and singular problem is the island and what has to be done there.'[72] General ideological principles — *ideas*, specifically, Marxist ideas — would divert him from it and, in any event, would be a luxury amid such pressing demands: 'not a minute for theory, not an action which isn't founded on experience.'[73] Sartre praised the leadership *because* it did not know where it was going, had no ideological line and

69. sc, p.75.
70. sc, p.81.
71. sc, p.85.
72. sc, p.80.
73. sc, p.97.

was uninterested in broad laws of history. The implied contrast was everywhere, and too strong to ignore: Sartre preferred Cuba's pragmatic leaders to a group of trained and disciplined militants whose fixed goal was to institute socialism. He preferred their pragmatism to theories that saw all specific situations as opportunities for confirming their own line and furthering their own goals. The rebels cared about the people, about their own specific situation, and not primarily about any set of abstract principles.

We can see in this approach Sartre's maturing critique of orthodox Communism, present in *Le Fantôme de Staline* and formulated more clearly in 1957 in *Question de méthode*. In the latter work, he attacked the 'lazy Marxism' that dissolved the specificity of people and events into formal categories of thought. The use of Marxist concepts as a set of labels doing service for specific knowledge, rather than as a system of regulative ideas deployed in specific studies, was an *a priori* method. Such a method 'does not derive its concepts from experience — or at least not from the new experiences which it seeks to interpret. It has already formed its concepts; it is already certain of their truth; it will assign to them the role of constitutive schemata. Its sole purpose is to force the events, the persons, or the acts considered into prefabricated moulds.'[74] The issue was not a complicated one. 'What is necessary is simply to reject apriorism.'[75] Sartre claimed not to be rejecting Marxism, but only the work of 'today's Marxists'[76] — those who had all the answers about the Hungarian Revolution before they knew anything about the events, those who thought it sufficient to type Valéry as a *petit-bourgeois* intellectual without understanding him individually. He advocated a Marxism that respected the irreducibility of facts, events, individuals, which rejected all forms of idealism and returned constantly to its own point of departure: 'there are only men and relations between men.'[77] The goal of *Question de méthode* was 'to reconquer man within Marxism'.[78]

But *Sartre on Cuba* overshot this goal, and was in fact at variance with it. In an important sense, Sartre's position here was *anti*-Marxist. The demands of the situation were *opposed* to theoretical

74. QM, p.34; SM, p.37.
75. QM, p.36; SM, p.42.
76. QM, p.41; SM, p.50.
77. QM, p.55; SM, p.76.
78. QM, p.59; SM, p.83.

analysis, the specific was *opposed* to the general, practice was *opposed* to theory. Sartre admired the Cuban revolutionaries *not* for carrying out this proposed project of joining the general and the specific, theory and practice, but for choosing the latter over the former. Circumstances dictated actions and ideology: this was the ground of his praise for the Cuban leaders. Sartre's Marxist analysis, for all its lucidity, was reserved for the book's background chapters; it was never deployed in the present and used to appraise the current situation. As in *Le Fantôme de Staline,* Marxism was apparently of no use as a guide in the present.

How much of this 'anti-Marxism' can be explained by Sartre's desire to win support for Cuba from those who would normally be anti-Communist? In fact, very little. In an interview broadcast throughout Cuba but not in France, Sartre took the same position, arguing that 'the originality of this Revolution consists precisely in doing what needs to be done without attempting to define it by means of previous ideology.'[79] Similarly, it was the one chapter of *Sartre on Cuba* never to appear in France that elevated the rejection of *a priori* concepts and a revolutionary programme to the level of principle by arguing that the Cubans were quite right to develop ideology only through their own experience.

What does this tell us about Sartre's attitude towards Marxism? In writing about Cuba, Sartre was not saying that relevant aspects of socialist analysis could fruitfully be applied to the Cuban situation, but rather that no previously conceived general analysis could be used to understand the country. He was suggesting not that socialist theory was a body of historically-grounded specific insights and general lines of analysis, but rather that it was a set of abstract principles that did not fit reality. He was not saying that conventional Marxist ideology could not be proclaimed in Cuba for a series of specific historical reasons — its proximity to the United States and its consequent domination by anti-Communism, the peasant basis of the revolt, the belated role of the Communist Party in the insurrection — but rather that the politics of practice-before-ideology, in which 'deeds produce ideas', was to be generally preferred to some more dialectical relation of theory and practice.

Nowhere in his writings on Cuba did Sartre conceive of Marxism

79. From a March 10, 1960, interview, cit. Leo Huberman and Paul Sweezy, *Anatomy of a Revolution,* New York, 1960, p.145.

as a set of intellectual-political tools which could — or had ever been able to — incorporate a systematic historical analysis of a situation, a grasp of its key contradictions and main tendencies of development. Such a set of tools would include precise studies of the specific problems at hand and would discover general lines for their transformation. Basing itself rigorously on the concrete situation, such a Marxism would claim the right to guide political practice. Sartre gave no hint that such a Marxism had ever existed, that it had actual achievements to its credit, and that it had at times been able to achieve a close interaction between theory and practice. For him it was once again either — or: prefabricated ideologies, where the programme was contrived in advance, or ideas spontaneously generated by the situation. We are, in a familiar fashion, forced to choose.

It is, after all, a striking conclusion to this discussion of Sartre's development as a political writer: a 55-year old Marxist philosopher, having spent his entire adult life struggling first to grasp and then to change reality, visits a great revolution and apotheosizes its lack of theory. How, after his shifts, did he see himself in the situation, how did he perceive his own role as an intellectual? We have seen Sartre move step by step from attempting to create a movement to unveiling social and political reality. We have seen his intellectual-political acumen increase at each stage. Yet in his book on Cuba, the newly Marxist thinker was anti-Marxist, and this out of a kind of anti-intellectualism. Marxism emphasizes the role of thought in guiding action; Sartre having earlier made thought a form of action, now made action all-important.

Perhaps, then, the requirements of solidarity were not the only reason for Sartre's uncritical endorsement of the Cuban revolution. If thoughts spring from actions, only those who act can judge them. Intellectuals dispose of no independent means of evaluation. Perhaps their role is merely to be intelligent publicists, observers, journalists or propagandists. Certainly they have no right to guide the activists.

An odd paradox appears. In the last pages of *Qu'est-ce que la littérature?*, Sartre projected a political writing task so grandiose as to stagger the imagination — to make people change, to make them want socialism. 'All power to words' would be its appropriate watchword. By the time of his visit to Cuba, he had apparently turned around completely: power resided exclusively with action. Over time, one term of the basic contradiction had produced the other. The all-powerful writer who took on too grand a task called forth the humble witness who could only approve what the real activists were doing. The old, abiding problem of Sartre's work had reproduced itself, this time in reverse. The link between imagination — or theory — and reality — or practice — still eluded him, making an effective role as a writer impossible.

To discover the ultimate cause of Sartre's frustration as a political thinker — and as a playwright — we must return to his basic attitude towards reality, to his philosophy. *L'Etre et le Néant* synthesized Sartre's fundamental outlook as of 1943. To understand the theoretical reasons why Sartre could not complete the transformation suggested in *Qu'est-ce que la littérature?* we must now study the Marxist Sartre's philosophical *magnum opus,* completed shortly before his trip to Cuba in 1960: the *Critique de la raison dialectique.*

4

Individualist Social Theory

By 1957, Sartre had acquired considerable political experience, and become a confident proponent of a Marxist position. He now went a step further, and from 1957 to 1959 he worked intensively on a major philosophical project, the *Critique de la raison dialectique*. His stated purpose in writing the *Critique* was to 'raise one question, and only one: do we now possess the materials for constituting a structural, historical anthropology?'[1] — to ask 'whether there is any such thing as a Truth of humanity (*une Verité de l'Homme*)'?[2]

Why should these questions lead to a critique of dialectical reason — 'critique' in the Kantian sense of determining the nature, conditions, and limits of this form of reason? If a structural, historical anthropology is possible, the dialectic will be its principle of intelligibility; that is, any Truth of humanity will be dialectical. This associates the undertaking with Marxism: for the dialectic is, after all, central to Marxism both as a logical form by which to approach human reality, and as the substance of that reality. Marx had derived the dialectic from Hegel, re-located it in the material world, and used it to explain human history. But he did not explain why history *should be* dialectical. Sartre's goal, building on the actual theoretical and practical achievements of Marxism and attempting to overcome its current impasse, was to lay a philosophical basis for the dialectic, to *found* it.

1. CRD, p.9; trans. Alan Sheridan-Smith, *Critique of Dialectical Reason*, I: *Theory of Practical Ensembles*, (CDR) London 1976, p.822.
2. CRD, p.10; CDR, p.822.

The dialectic emerges from, and *is itself*, human activity. From the very outset the *Critique* maintains a sharp distinction between the ways in which we understand the human and the physical worlds — between dialectical reason and analytical reason. The dialectic is the *only* adequate means, Sartre insists, of understanding human reality, from the practical activity of a single individual to the vast course of world history. Furthermore, we do not *submit to* the dialectic, as a reading of Stalin's *Dialectical and Historical Materialism* might lead us to believe: if there is a dialectic it is 'no more than ourselves.'[3] It is our practical activity, or *praxis*, that totalizes the world around us, projects a goal on the basis of what has already been achieved, and transcends the practical field towards new ends.

Thus, in seeking to establish the 'validity and limits' of dialectical reason as the logic of human *praxis*, Sartre was acting as Marxism's Immanuel Kant. But after all, it was the author of *L'Etre et le Néant* who now proposed this decisive project within Marxism. Did this mean, as many writers have claimed, that Sartre was trying to *reconcile* Marxism with existentialism?[4] The fundamental issue, rather, was lived reality: if any intellectual project of 'reconciliation' was possible it was because experience already united the two modes of thought. Sartre's purpose was to explain human reality, regardless of the label borne by his tools. If his earlier thought lacked a necessary socio-historical dimension which he now drew from Marxism, it was equally the case that Marxism as he encountered it lacked a grasp of the specificity of individual experience, which he now sought to bring to it.

He had somewhat one-sidedly initiated this philosophical project in 1946 with 'Matérialisme et révolution', and carried it further with the 1952-54 essays on the Communist Party. The object of these writings, philosophically speaking, was to locate *subjectivity* within history in general and the revolutionary project in particular: to establish the centrality of creative human activity, first against Marxism and offering existentialism as a substitute, but as Sartre developed and deepened his understanding of Marxism, he came to accept it as 'the untranscendable philosophy for our time'[5], and to regard existentialism

---

3. CRD, p.134; CDR, p.39.

4. As Fredric Jameson acutely points out in *Marxism and Form*, Princeton 1971 (p.206), such an approach caricatures and distorts the issue by treating intellectual systems mechanically. One of the best studies of the *Critique*, this essay elucidates its relationship with *L'Etre et le Néant*.

5. CRD, p.9; CDR, p.822.

as a still-necessary ideology *within* it. Thus he intended 'not to reject Marxism in the name of a third path or of an idealist humanism, but to reconquer man within Marxism',[6] not to abandon his focus on subjectivity or individual experience, but to comprehend both concrete individual experience and human activity in general within a social and historical framework.

Thus Sartre posed anew the classical question of social theory: how can we understand both concrete individuals *and* the social world to which they belong? And can we understand each in terms of the other? That is, in Sartre's terms, how do separate individual acts combine to produce a constituted social world? Sartre never doubted that the multiplicity of individual *praxes* produced this world. He repeatedly warned against the 'hyper-organicism' which would tear society away from its individual foundations, and make it an autonomous force obeying its *own* laws and acting upon *us*. Against this, he proposed to *explain* social groupings by deconstructing the larger wholes into the multitude of acts which compose them. A third, intimately related question was: how is it that our individual acts do in fact become forces which seem to take on a life on their own? Why is human life in history an inferno of class oppression and class struggle? Attempting to answer this question, Sartre brought two novel emphases to the discussion of social life: the fact of 'scarcity', and the way in which, under conditions of scarcity, our own product became a vast 'practico-inert' field which in turn imposed its power on us.

The questions posed by Sartre in the *Critique* are fundamental. Yet it is clear that they are *his* questions, marked in their very formulation by the problematic governing all his past work. The themes of *L'Etre et le Néant* recur: the rejection of determinism in the name of free human activity; the individual as the decisive reality; human life as an overwhelming hell. Yet they have evidently been deepened: human freedom is now seen as practical activity; the *praxis* of each is related to the *praxis* of all; and the inferno in which we live is one constituted historically, by human acts. The *Critique de la raison dialectique* is Sartre's greatest contribution to Marxist philosophy and social theory. As such, it is of decisive significance in any study of his development. It is the point at which we can most pointedly ask how fully he accomplished the passage from 'Man is a useless passion' and

6. QM, p.59; SM, p.83.

'Hell is other people', and also the point of departure for discussion of his later evolution in the sixties and seventies.

A Badly Written Book

Let us begin by observing Sartre at work in the *Critique*. In the long passage that follows he begins his analysis of scarcity.

' . . . The whole human adventure — at least until today — is a fierce struggle against *scarcity*. Thus, at all levels of worked and socialized matter we find again at the base of each of its passive actions the original structure of scarcity as first unity coming to matter from men and returning to men through matter. For our part, the contingency of the relation of scarcity does not trouble us: certainly, it is logically possible to conceive, for other organisms and on other planets, a relationship to an environment which would not be scarcity (although we are quite incapable of *merely imagining* what it might be and, in the hypothesis that other planets would be inhabited, the most likely conjecture is that living beings would suffer from scarcity there as here); and above all, although scarcity might be *universal*, it varies within a given historical moment. According to considered regions (and certain reasons of these variations are historical — overpopulation, underdevelopment, etc. — therefore are fully intelligible at the interior of history itself, while others — for a given state of technical development — condition history through social structures without being conditioned by it — climate, richness of the subsoil, etc.). But it remains that three quarters of the population of the world are undernourished, after thousands of years of history; thus, in spite of its contingency, scarcity is a fundamental human relation (with nature and with men). In this sense we must say that it makes us *these* individuals producing *this* history and who define themselves as men. Without scarcity we can perfectly conceive a dialectical *praxis* and even labour: nothing would prevent, indeed, the products necessary to the organism from being practically inexhaustible while in spite of everything, a practical operation would be necessary to tear them from the earth. In this hypothesis, the unity of human multiplicities turned upside down by the counter-finality of matter would necessarily subsist: for it is to labour that it is linked as to the original dialectic. But what would disappear is our character as *men*, that is, since this character is historical, the very singularity of our History. Thus, any man whatsoever today ought to recognize in this fundamental contingency the necessity which (through thousands of years and very directly, even today) imposes on him being exactly who he is. We shall study, in the progressive moment of experience, the problem of contingency in History and we shall see that the problem is above all important in the perspective of a future of man. In the case which occupies me, scarcity appears less and less contingent to the degree that we ourselves engender its new forms as the environment of our life on the base of an original contingency: one can see there, if one wishes, the necessity of our contingency or the contingency of our necessity. It remains that an effort at critique should distinguish this particularized relation from the general relation (that is, independent of any historical determination) of a dialectical and multiple *praxis* with materiality. However, as scarcity is a determination of this general relation, as it only manifests itself to us through it, it is proper in order to keep from wandering to present scarcity first and to leave the universal relations of the dialectic with the inert to be extricated afterwards. We shall describe the relation of scarcity briefly, for the reason that everything has already been said; in particular historical materialism as interpretation of *our* history has provided desirable precision on this point. What has not at all been tried, on the contrary, is studying the type of passive action which materiality as such exercises on men and on their history in returning a stolen *praxis* to them under the form of counter-finality. We shall there further insist: History is more complex than a certain simplistic Marxism believes, and man has to struggle not only against nature, against the social environment which has engendered him, against other men, but also against his own action insofar as it becomes other. This type of primitive alienation expresses itself through other forms of alienation but it is independent of them and on the contrary itself serves permanent anti-*praxis* as a new and necessary moment of *praxis*. Without an effort to determine it, historical intelligibility (which is evidence in the complexity of a temporal development) loses an essential moment and is transformed into unintelligibility.'[7]

---

7. CRD, pp.201-202; CDR, pp.123-25. I have used my own translation here in order to retain the original sentence and paragraph structure.

The first noteworthy feature of this passage is that it is all drawn from one paragraph, seventy-two lines in the original. Its length is typical of the *Critique*. Let us summarize its content. 1. Scarcity exists as a long-standing and virtually irremediable relationship of humans to nature. 2. It is only a contingent and specific instance of the basic human relationship with nature; but, 3., it is contingent in a special sense, since scarcity leads to our particular history and makes us a specific kind of people. 4. Were scarcity overcome, our labour would still result in 'counter-finality', a 'passive activity' of worked matter reacting against its workers. 5. The *Critique* will first briefly discuss scarcity, then move on to the basic human relation to nature.

Here are five fairly comprehensible introductory propositions. Why does Sartre's paragraph appear so dense and require such an effort to decipher? Let us trace its development. In the first two sentences, Sartre makes the point that scarcity has long been a fundamental fact of life. His thought now drifts sideways, in the process stating an integral point — that scarcity, while not built into human life as such, has become a dominant fact of our life. From the phrase, 'for our past' onwards, the paragraph begins to wander, occupies us with alternative views, elaborating them and indicating their peculiar problems. His prose actually breaks down in the sentence which begins 'according to considered regions' and then plunges into a parenthesis from which it never emerges again. At last, Sartre returns in force to his point. ('But it remains that three quarters of the population of the world are undernourished . . . '). Yet here too his thought refuses to move directly forward; again he is conceiving alternatives. This time he returns to the vision of plenty, no longer to show that it is conceivable and thus that scarcity is only contingent, but now for the purpose of arguing that in conditions of plenty, certain problems (about which, at this point in the *Critique*, we cannot conceivably know) would subsist while our fundamental character as *men* would disappear. Our fundamental character: the book has not discussed it yet, except in an aside: 'in this sense we must say that [scarcity] makes us *these* individuals producing *this* history and who define themselves as men' — an undeveloped but obviously important idea thrown out while another is being developed. Sartre returns again to his original topic ('In the case which occupies us . . . '). Now he presents a new idea, namely that we build the structures of our world on the original contingency of scarcity, in the process making scarcity less contingent. This idea is intriguing, but it is mystified rather than clarified by Sartre's coy and paradoxical suggestion that one may 'see there, if one wishes, the necessity of our contingency or the contingency of our necessity'. He now changes the direction again: it remains — apparently — to raise the question of how to proceed. Yet he returns to the significant idea, suggested five long sentences earlier, that within the universal relations proper to *praxis* as such, scarcity engenders its specific kind of *praxis*. He indicates that he will first discuss scarcity, and then *praxis* in general. A further change of direction then follows; outlining the future course of his analysis, Sartre indicates that he will not say much about scarcity, since Marxism has already illuminated it (a claim he will confound within twenty-five pages) but will later discuss the anti-*praxis* that simplistic Marxism ignores — this refers forward to an as yet unwritten and unread analysis of the practico-inert, of which the reader can have no inkling. By the end of the paragraph even the most tenacious reader is likely to be lost — the more completely since the next sentence returns to the idea of scarcity.

Thus, the argument undergoes no fewer than five changes of direction. It does not develop. Rather, it darts back and forth briefly raising a series of related issues, but solving every problem encountered in the same way: by assertion. Instead of patiently developing its ideas, Sartre's prose asserts, obscurely raises questions which threaten the assertion, wanders into parentheses, and then back out to the original point. It is an undisciplined, almost incoherent style of writing in which everything must be said, more or less at once, and never otherwise than by a kind of fiat. These pages are representative of the work as a whole. The *Critique* contains examples of controlled writing and careful thought — for example, the discussion of the *praxis*-process of colonialism in Algeria near the end of the book — but by and large it is undisciplined, self-indulgent, confused and confusing.

Why is the *Critique* so badly written, so nearly bordering on a kind of intellectual chaos? Simone de Beauvoir has revealed something of Sartre's personal state as he laboured on the book in early 1958. 'It was not a case of writing as he ordinarily did, pausing to think and make corrections, tearing up a page, starting again; for hours at a stretch he raced across sheet after sheet without re-reading them, as though absorbed by ideas that his pen, even at that speed, couldn't

keep up with; to maintain this pace I could hear him crunching cor-
ydrame capsules, of which he managed to get through a tube a day.
At the end of the afternoon he would be exhausted; all his powers of
concentration would suddenly relax, his gestures would become
vague, and quite often he would get his words all mixed up. We spent
our evenings in my apartment: as soon as he drank a glass of whiskey
the alcohol would go straight to his head. "That's enough," I'd say to
him; but for him it was not enough; against my will I would hand him
a second glass; then he'd ask for a third; two years before he'd have
needed a great deal more; but now he lost control of his movements
and his speech very quickly and I would say again: "That's enough." '[8]
The years of the struggle over Algeria were enormously trying for
Sartre and de Beauvoir, and, in the latter's words, 'Sartre protected
himself by working furiously at his *Critique de la raison dialectique.*' The
disorderly style of the book was, in part, the necessary price of this
resort, the visible trace of the stress to which Sartre was subjected as
his political hopes for France drained away.

A further, more radical cause of difficulty was embedded in the
Critique itself: not only in the enormous, perhaps overwhelming difficulty of the undertaking — nothing less than to render history intelligible as a human undertaking, even in its most infernal dimensions — but also, and precisely because of this ambition, in the problematic that organized it. Were Sartre's analytic categories adequate
to such an undertaking? Or was he attempting to square the circle, to
understand social being using concepts that implicitly denied its reality? Could the *Critique* accomplish its goals, given its own starting
points? It is one of the least confident of Sartre's writings, and its
stylistic torsions and disorders testified also to the presence of racking
and perhaps unresolvable internal tensions.

Praxis and the Adventure of the 'Critique'

Sartre's analysis begins, familiarly, with lone individuals labouring
on the world in isolation from each other. Humans labour on the
world, a world of scarcity, in order to transform it to meet their
needs. In the process they totalize the world before them, elaborate a
more or less coherent view of it and determine what it lacks; they then

8. *La Force des choses,* p.407; *Force of Circumstance,* p.385.

set projects and go beyond the given world, transforming it so that the need is met. This process is dialectics, the principle of the activity and of its intelligibility, the logic of *praxis*. Sartre repeatedly attacks two distortions of intelligibility: the tendency of Engels and, later, of official Soviet Marxism to raise the dialectic beyond humans and so take it from their hands, and the conviction held by proponents of 'analytical reason' that reality is merely an agglomeration of discrete units whose interrelations are external and secondary. Against the latter Sartre affirms that the world is indeed an internally connected whole-in-the-making; and in opposition to the first, he insists that this dialectic exists only because humans continually create the world.

At the outset, we perform our *praxis* alongside each other but in separation, engaged in a common practical field but dominated by the Other. Our basic social state is one of *seriality*. Sartre describes seriality in its many forms: waiting for a bus, reading the newspaper on the bus, listening to the radio, the 'top ten' records, public opinion, and conformity. Every form of seriality reveals me as a mass man: I alienate myself from my own purposes and, separated from but alongside other people, adopt the conduct that I expect them to adopt. The serial individual acts by himself, but as *others* would want him to. Standing alongside each other, we only appear to act together: each of us is dominated and radically isolated.

The dialectic of the group is introduced with Sartre's depiction of how, in an insurrectionary situation such as the storming of the Bastille, separate individuals overcome their seriality and combine under threat to form a fused group. In a radical rupture reminiscent of the for-itself's negation of the in-itself, the literary 'pact of freedoms' between writer and reader, or the PCF's activity in creating a working class, they cease to be passive and isolated and instead become participating members of a group acting towards a common goal. After overcoming the external threat, the group turns inwards to guard against the possible defection of its members, who are always free to leave. The members swear an oath of loyalty and so impose inertia on themselves and try to limit their own freedom. The pressure applied by the group's members to each other leads to a state of terror. They threaten anyone who defects, and cement the loyalty of everyone else. As it seeks to stabilize itself, the group assigns specific functions to individuals. The group becomes an organization, supervising a distribution of tasks to meet the common interest, common danger, and common need. Each individual now controls a small corner of the world, but does so for the benefit of the organization and not himself.

The group still exists to meet the common needs of its members, who still freely decide to join and remain in it. But to preserve itself, it has taken on considerable inertia. Created when its members entrust their freedom to the group, the apparatus for preserving the group becomes a power over them, begins to resist change and solidifies into an institution. An authority establishes itself over the group's members, and then narrows its own base. Individuals relate to the authority by obedience. Those in positions of authority, fearful lest the individuals organize themselves, seek to keep people separated from each other in order to guarantee their obedience and powerlessness. And so we move, inexorably, from the revolution to Stalin, from the collective act of individuals altering history to the collective submission of individuals to their product — all without ever leaving the domain of intentional human activity, the domain of *praxis*.

Scarcity and Human Relations

All praxis unfolds in a world of *scarcity* and in a *practico-inert* field, which together frustrate it. These two categories are fundamental to Sartre's analysis. They drive it forward, impart to it much of its peculiar tone, and, ultimately, lead it astray. In order to understand the *Critique* it is essential to define and evaluate their precise role.

Scarcity is a central fact of human history, Sartre maintains. Very simply, '*There is not enough for everybody*'. To a person living among others this fact means that 'the consumption of a certain product elsewhere, by others, deprives him *here* of an opportunity of getting and consuming something of the same kind.'[9] Where there is not enough food there are too many people. Under conditions of scarcity, 'each person is the inhuman man for all the Others'.

The Other is a perpetual potential enemy as long as there are too many of us for the available means of sustenance. He may lay claim to what we both need, marking me as expendable in his eyes. Inhumanity does not arise from any 'human nature'; it is interiorized scar-

9. CRD, p.204; CDR, p.128.

city: 'Nothing — not even wild beasts or microbes — could be more terrifying for man than a species that is intelligent, carnivorous and cruel, which can understand and outwit human intelligence, and whose aim is precisely the destruction of man. This, however, is obviously our own species as perceived in others by each of its members in the context of scarcity.'[10]

Scarcity need not even be directly involved for the Other to become a terrifying enemy. In a general environment of scarcity there is always someone who does not have enough, someone who is treated as, and therefore becomes, an anti-man. In such a situation, any freedom is a hostile force because it can be my own undoing. 'In other words, it is undeniable that what I attack is man as man, that is, as the free *praxis* of an organic being. It is man, and nothing else, that I hate in the enemy, that is, in myself as Other; and it is myself that I try to destroy in him, so as to prevent him destroying me in my own body.'[11]

For scarcity to have its terrible effect direct violence need not be necessary. 'It merely means that the relations of production are established and pursued in a climate of fear and mutual mistrust by individuals who are always ready to believe that the Other is an anti-human of an alien species.'[12] Apportioned out among members of society, scarcity becomes institutionalized in societies divided into classes. Historical materialism correctly describes this environment: all the structures of social life are determined by the society's mode of production. Even socialism has not discovered how to supersede this fundamental determination of human life, 'except possibly through a long dialectical process of which we cannot yet know the outcome'.[13] Scarcity, in short, is the principle of negativity in history: 'This provides a foundation for the intelligibility of that accursed aspect of human history, both in its origins and today, in which man constantly sees his action being stolen from him and totally distorted by the milieu in which he inscribes it. It is primarily this tension which, by inflicting profound dangers on everyone in society, by creating diffused violence in everyone, and by producing the possibility for everyone of seeing his best friend approaching him as an alien wild

10. CRD, p.208; CDR, p.132.
11. CRD, p.209; CDR, p.133.
12. CRD, p.221; CDR, p.149.
13. CRD, p.213; CDR, p.139.

beast, imposes a perpetual statute of extreme urgency on every *praxis*, at the simplest level, and, whatever its real aim, makes the *praxis* into an act of aggression against other individuals or groups.'[14]

This passage seems to fulfil Sartre's post-war promise, as presented for example in *Qu'est-ce que la littérature?* He has not abandoned his earlier sense of an ontological — and inevitable — basis for human struggle; he has however deepened it, and rendered it material and theoretically contingent. Here, as elsewhere in the *Critique*, Sartre has pressed the original idea beyond its given form and has grasped its social and historical truth. The Other continues to be my enemy, but now for intelligible — and ultimately suppressible — historical reasons. André Gorz argues that in this conception Sartre has given us the keys to a realistic understanding of the miseries of human history. Gorz's excellent defence of the *Critique* argues that an activist Marxist thinker might build on it to show how the underlying scarcity, for example, reproduces itself at other social levels and becomes displaced from one society to another. He emphasizes that Sartre's grim analyses point to facts of life which Marxists cannot wish away: famine, violence, 'the reign of necessity'. It is now possible to untangle a history filled with violence, slavery, war, massacres, and genocide by pointing to the ultimate and objective threat every human holds for every other human.[15]

However this terrifying picture is simply wrong: wrong because the *Critique* shows no sense that humans are also deeply connected for *positive* reasons. On perhaps the most fundamental level, humans do not encounter each other primarily as threat. We produce *our* food *together*, build *our* houses *together*. Even in the most alienated and exploitative division of labour, we work collectively, assist each other. As farmers, factory workers, tradespeople, teachers, we produce for each other so that others may produce for us. Sartre's analysis of the class struggle gives the impression that the goal of the capitalist is primarily to destroy his workers, not to exploit their labour — for which their continued survival is necessary. He wholly ignores the fact that even the most exploitative society could not last a single day were it not also co-operative. Above all a society must feed, clothe, and house its members. The society may indeed be unable to produce

14. CRD, p.223; CDR, p.150.
15. André Gorz, 'Sartre and Marx', *New Left Review*, 37 (May-June 1966).

enough for all to live decently, but its scarcity — and how it is distributed — can only be understood in a context which includes existing social means of arranging the common struggle for survival and an existing level of productive capacity. These have required co-operation at every step of their history.

At root, even the most exploitative societies are contradictory, not merely negative, as Sartre's emphasis would lead us to conclude. In one fashion or another we collectively organize to do the work needed to get our collective living. We may not produce enough, and we may fight over our product. I may succeed in imposing on you a given social form of antagonistic co-operation so that I benefit relatively and you suffer relatively from the scarcity. We then co-operate as I exploit you and you accept your lot or wait to resume the struggle. Helper *and* threat, you are both the key to my life and the prospect of my death. I depend on you and fear you. Our relationship must be contradictory, at least until the end of scarcity — or its more or less equal distribution — and the end of class society.

Scarcity has no meaning prior to social life in history. But, oddly in the author of *L'Etre et le Néant* who once stressed how different projects can create widely different experiences of a given fact, Sartre fails to explore the historical choice which *makes there be* scarcity in the first place. Marshall Sahlins's study of 'The Original Affluent Society' describes the consequences of what we might call an original decision to adapt to, rather than struggle against, the limitations of the environment. Hunter-gatherers might live amid peace and leisure, amid a plenty based on the systematic minimization of their needs. [16] Certainly if there was an original state of equality and plenty it must have been based on a similar minimal level of need. Seen in such a light, the creation of new needs reaching beyond the capacities for satisfaction afforded by the material environment can be understood as the 'second' historical act — as described by Marx and Plato. An act simultaneous with the creation of classes — permitting the privileged to corner the limited social wealth and live at a much higher level of satisfaction from the many — and the project of labouring to overcome what is now experienced as scarcity. In this hypothesis, so different from Sartre's, scarcity is a human, rather than a natural fact, or rather a natural fact only in so far as it corresponds to a certain level

16. Marshall Sahlins, *Stone Age Economics*, Chicago 1972.

of human development and aspiration. It is a factor at the base of the socio-historical matrix in which, later, facts become what they are.

This consideration underscores the perversity of Sartre's approach. Needs, and their development, are obviously a fundamentally positive fact of human life and history. They indicate an expansion of the human personality, an enrichment of our possibilities. To be sure, Sartre's very use of the notion of scarcity drew him closer to Marxism and material life. But his understanding of *need* and *matter* — as a virtually ineradicable curse lying behind all history — is reminiscent more of the gloom of *La Nausée* than of Marxism's vision of history as a record both of class domination and of human advancement. The student tracing the roots of the *Critique* in *L'Etre et le Néant* will find lack — that privative, negative state of being as such — at the source of *scarcity*.[17] It is this that lends Sartre's account of the human adventure its characteristic ferocity of tone. Moreover, it is striking that Sartre never speaks of needs being *fulfilled*, but dwells everywhere on the overwhelming negative force they exert over us. And similarly, throughout the nearly eight hundred manuscript pages of his unpublished second volume, the dialectic which so systematically entraps humans is never shown to lead to their advancement.

Drawn into the texture of a genuinely social analysis, one which would grant the human adventure its positive as well as its negative side, scarcity could no longer be Sartre's ultimate category. As a dimension of our life, scarcity appears as one decisive factor of a matrix which contains, in the most intimate interconnection, other decisive factors. Co-operative human *praxis* to create our means of subsistence, and the historically variable forms of appropriation of the means of production, are among these. Another is the rising level of productivity and skills, which shows how far a society has advanced in the struggle to create an apparatus for meeting needs and overcoming scarcity.

No single fact 'stands behind' or 'conditions' this matrix in which historical development occurs. Yet, as if to preserve its separateness from lived history, Sartre never once shows scarcity *entering into* the human adventure, in the first volume of the *Critique*. The dialectic of collective *praxis* is traced in independence of scarcity and, indeed, of the struggle for material survival itself. It remains an external,

17. See Jameson, *Marxism and Form*, pp.232-235.

ultimate term. But it is not enough to say that there is 'not enough'. Even famine is a 'decision' of the social apparatus: a certain social organization with its own history and inertia inhibits the development of productive capacities beyond a subsistence level, arresting *praxis,* perpetuating scarcity. In this context calamities of nature become defined as particular human calamities. This context, this matrix — and not any single abstracted and isolated factor such as 'scarcity' — is after all, the 'formal condition of history'. But Sartre lays down a formal condition which, in the manner of *L'Etre et le Néant,* is virtually beyond our grasp and foredooms all efforts to outstrip it. Because of it, the Other will threaten us no matter what. Having paid due respect to Marxism and to the contingency of his 'ultimate' fact, Sartre has fallen back on his old bogeys. In the analyst of scarcity we once again meet the philosopher of 'hell is other people'.

It is, therefore, pertinent to inquire on what order of explanation the first volume of the *Critique* is founded. It is not intended to be a concrete historical account: this is reserved for Volume II. Nor is it supposed to expound a series of dialectical laws which carry us inevitably from the fused group to the institution: Sartre insists that all such changes are reversible and may vault over intermediate forms. Again, he is not trying to account for societies or society as such: these are made up of a shifting constellation of the groupings that he discusses. Rather, his 'theory of practical ensembles' is meant strictly to shape some keys for later research, notably into the different forms of human collectivity and the main features of the passage from one to the other.

This at least is his express intention. Sartre's analysis seeks to grasp the underlying conditions and relations which form the basis for all historical development. But we have seen it willy-nilly become a philosophy of history, elaborating various laws and inevitabilities of human life. Sartre's discussion of scarcity (and, as we shall see, his discussions of the practico-inert and the dialectic of the group) reaches for conclusions which have no place in a study of the 'formal conditions of history'. His error is not that he probes history for its formal conditions, but rather that he uses his findings to explain *too much* about history and, as it were, *too soon.*

Marx also discerned human social activity beneath the finished and frozen products of history: his ontological premiss was that humans create the human world, whose 'laws' and necessities arise from and express the forms of their activity. This starting point left everything still to be investigated. The *German Ideology* in which it was first sketched, was the abandoned preface to a lifetime of study. Sartre, in contrast, wants 'to settle, outside concrete history itself, the incarnations of individual *praxis*, the formal structural conditions of its alienation, and the abstract conditions which encourage the constitution of a common *praxis*.'[18] But analyses conducted 'outside' of history yield timeless problems, problems which cannot be solved within history. The starting point becomes the explanation and 'scarcity' leads (back) to the 'hell' of 'other people'.

The Practico-Inert

Unlike 'scarcity', the second key category of the *practico-inert* does enter and decisively condition Sartre's developing dialectic of social collectivities. This category entails the thesis that, regardless of its intended positive results, our *praxis* is thwarted or confounded. We become dominated by unintended features of our product, or by our tools. This happens sometimes because our activity itself gets out of hand (as in the case of the Chinese peasants who,each clearing the trees from his own land, together caused massive floods over the countryside) and sometimes because the means we develop to ensure our goals themselves make new demands, which carry us away from our original goals or realize them in a deformed manner — thus the fused group inexorably produces the institution and returns its members to seriality, in the name of cohesion. At other times, the practico-inert is the negative power of our tools. The primitive understands that an arrow or a hatchet is to be feared and revered, seeing in them his 'own power become malignant and turned against him'. He senses that 'in the most adequate and satisfactory tool, there is a hidden violence which is the reverse of its docility'.[19] In modern times our tools most notably come to make demands on us and, indeed, to dominate us. The late eighteenth and early nineteenth centuries saw the creation of large-scale machinery for mass production. Unfortunately such machinery is not merely a tool for human purposes: it also shapes the human beings who are to operate it. A 'new being' is created by a type of worked matter which was originally created by humans struggling

18. CRD, p.154; CDR, p.66 (translation changed).
19. CRD, p.249, 250 n; CDR, p.183 and n.

against scarcity. The practico-inert is 'the domination of man by worked matter' in such a way that man becomes 'a product of his product'. [20] A positive fact — the use of coal on a large scale, the development of social wealth through industrialization — has a negative result. It creates a working class which must submit itself to the new means of production in order to survive.

With this fundamental concept, Sartre seeks to render historical materialism intelligible: how is it that we can speak of humans being in some sense determined by the results of their *praxis*, the forces and relations of production in a given society? It must be emphasized that the practico-inert is the 'first dialectical experience of necessity' in the *Critique*. Everything in both volumes points to it as the inevitable outcome of human *praxis*. Is this so because of the effect of scarcity? We have already seen Sartre argue directly against this suggestion in the lengthy passage quoted above. Does it in some sense spring from oppression or class society? No, for Sartre claims that 'every object, in so far as it exists within a given economic, technical and social complex, will in its turn become exigency through the mode and relations of production, and give rise to other exigencies in other objects.'[22] The negative efficacy of the practico-inert is sustained by the fact that all societies rest, finally, on dispersed individuals each transforming nature by himself through his own *praxis*. In other words, the practico-inert finds 'its fundamental intelligibility in the serial action of men'. [23]

As a member of this series, I am dominated not by the direct results of my own *praxis*, but by the entire material field which has been created by the work of all. Isolated, 'men realize unwittingly their own unity in the form of antagonistic alterity through the material field where they are dispersed and through the multiplicity of unifying actions which they perform on this field.'[24] Our 'unity' is imposed by the material system that we have created as separated individuals — and so beyond all individual control from the outset. Its power is not that of *society* over the individual: the practico-inert dominates me as matter which has *escaped* human control. The

20. CRD, p.251; CDR, p.184.
21. CRD, p.282; CDR, p.222.
22. CRD, p.255; CDR, p.189.
23. CRD, p.255; CDR, p.189 (translation changed).
24. CRD, p.280; CDR, pp.220-221.

material field remains external to me because I did not create it, because it emerged from a hundred or a thousand other individual *praxes*. Thus it looms over us, demands specific forms of behaviour, creates us as *its* people. We all bear the same unavailing relationship to it. Alongside each other but separated, we are left facing 'a magical field of quasi-dialectical counter-finality.'[25] It is magical not because I control it through arcane devices, but because it comes to have a life of its own.

Human Society and the Practico-Inert

Sartre's example of Chinese peasants deforesting their land sums up his account and at the same time betrays some of its weaknesses: 'uprooting a tree in a field of sorghum becomes *deforestation* from the point of view of a large plain and of terraces of loess, united by the work of separate men; and *deforestation* as the real meaning of the individual action of uprooting is simply the negative union of all those who are isolated by the material totality which they have produced.'[26] This description is clearly too general and timeless. The Chinese peasants were not the victims of human *praxis* as such, but of a society which they did not rule and whose rulers refused or were unable to exercise social foresight, and of a low level of material and technical development. Their activity escaped them because no one recognized it as social and needing social control: their problem was of a kind which social struggle and historical development can overcome. Sartre, however, presents a 'pure' practico-inert, just as earlier he presented a 'pure' scarcity: facts are abstracted from a complex social-historical matrix and then re-inserted as independent (and awesome) forces.

Moreover, Sartre's account of the practico-inert rests on the assumption of individuals working separately but side by side, as if this is a normal work relation. Why the *series* should be the basic form of collectivity Sartre does not say; nor does he say how people came to be side by side in the first place. He shows no sense of the socio-historical process leading to their separation, although he acknowledges that such a process must have taken place.

But above all, Sartre scarcely entertains the possibility that other

25. CRD, p.283; CDR, p.224.
26. CRD, p.284; CDR, p.225.

social groupings might organize their relations to the material field differently, and so achieve a different relation to their product. Certainly, in some conditions the fruits of human labour become terrifying weapons. But in others they remain useful tools and means of liberation. The pertinent conditions are *social*. The 'worked matter' of which Sartre speaks is never a truly independent or quasi-natural force: it is a social reality from the outset. There is no 'worked matter' as such: there is only *this* apparatus in the life of *this* society, or its counterparts or alternatives in the life of another.

A productive apparatus democratically controlled and operated to meet social needs would weigh on us quite differently from one whose components are controlled separately by a few for their own profit. A socialist factory of the future — one in which the workers truly controlled their productive activity and products as part of a wider social apparatus in which they had decision-making powers — would appear quite different from the capitalist work-places of the present. It might, for example, be designed so that workers could gain maximum familiarity with all its processes, as a necessary concomitant of the regular rotation of functions and of workers' planning. It might be spacious, light, and clean. Even in the ideal situation, of course, workers would have to do a job; they would have to perform these tasks, at this moment. Not even the supersession of assembly lines by work crews would abolish the social and technological necessities whose purpose remains to transform nature in order to meet material needs. But if workers controlled the labour-process itself, if they worked fewer hours and freely exchanged functions, if they were assured of a secure level of subsistence and co-operated in socially meaningful work — then at some point the grim rule of necessity might be brought to an end, and the practico-inert subjected decisively to human control. In these conditions, shot through with human vitality, freedom and power, our very sense of work would change.

Is this prospect a relapse into the 'simplistic Marxism' which Sartre criticizes throughout the *Critique*? In fact, the more simplistic analysis is his own. *Matter*, or the simple fact that it is transformed by humans, does not determine the fact or degree of its dominance over us. We are not dominated by 'every object, in so far as it exists within a given economic, technical and social complex'. The character and degree of its dominance over us is determined by the social-historical matrix in which objects are created and used. Abstracted from their social matrix — and thus voided of their character as products of a process which could conceivably be reoriented — things do in fact appear overwhelming, and our activity, therefore, futile. After all, in an analysis which ignores material progress, which never mentions the satisfaction of our needs or the development of new needs, but which on the contrary sees matter as dominating us to the exact degree that we transform it, there can be little sense that our *praxis* has any positive effect. It is no wonder, then, that Sartre makes direct reference to *L'Etre et le Néant* at the end of his discussion of the practico-inert — and that, seventeen years and supposed worlds of thought later, he now rekindles the vision of the in-itself-for-itself. For after all, it is 'this fundamental relation', the necessity of our creating the practico-inert, 'which explains why, as I have said, man *projects himself* in the milieu of the in-itself-for-itself.'[27] Although Sartre shifts significantly from *L'Etre et le Néant* in affirming now that 'the foundation of necessity is practice', his optic is otherwise unmodified: there is still man, the for-itself, 'revealing itself initially as inert or, at best practico-inert in the milieu of the in-itself.'[28] Whether created by man or simply given, the material world remains for Sartre what it always was — a power over us, a force beyond our control.

If Sartre omits co-operation and progress when discussing scarcity, his analysis of the practico-inert omits all reference to class. He entirely passes over the process whereby small groups appropriate the products of others through their control of the means of production. Is it surprising, in class societies, that our products come to dominate us? But the *Critique* shows no interest in property, or in the basic economic dynamics of class interaction. Focused above all on the way our creations become powers over us, it shows little appreciation of the nature and effects of power in human relations. Our creations may display a certain force, a certain resistance, in any society; but any analysis seeking to explain the formal conditions of human history must carefully distinguish this from the fact that until now they have been appropriated by privileged minorities. The alternative to such an analysis — exemplified in the *Critique* — can only be a gloomy and mystifying ahistorical ontology.

27. CRD, n.1, p.286; CDR, n. 68, p.228.
28. CRD, n.1, p.285; CDR, n.68, p.227.

Separate individuals labour side by side to create an overwhelming world. This vision elevates specific features of advanced capitalist society to the status of universal structures. Conventional discussions about pollution show how a problem stemming from the specific power relations and priorities of a social structure can be mystified, in Sartrean fashion, into a remote and generalized image of human activity run amok. We are told that we should all help to control our waste — government bodies, corporations and private citizens equally. But it is a *political* problem. The worker cannot control his waste any more than he controls any aspect of the productive process without collective action. Furthermore, it is in the very nature of a capitalist enterprise to be concerned with its own profits at whatever social cost, rather than with social well-being; and capitalism is so structured that there is no social control over the economy. Pollution is also a political problem in that capitalism as a system of power develops an ethic and process of functioning in which *no one* is responsible. The 'invisible hand' theoretically coordinates the dispersed activities of millions, and so each capitalist does what he must, and what he wants. The social vision of capitalist society is that there is no society but only individuals labouring separately, coordinated magically. This vision is strangely but aptly reproduced — but not contested — by Sartre's description of the hell of the practico-inert.

The Historical versus the Isolated Individual

Society — and particularly the alienated and contradictory social life of class societies — is the missing term of Sartre's social thought, and the basic problem of the *Critique*. This work of social theory is so constructed as to make the comprehension of social realities impossible. It is built not on any sense of society at all, but on abstract, isolated individuals. How does this come about?

'To consider *an individual* at work is a complete abstraction since in reality labour is as much a relation between men as a relation between man and the material world.'[29] These are Sartre's own words, repeated a half-dozen times in the course of the *Critique*. He even emphasizes that the solitude of the isolated worker can only be produced by a specific historical and social reality.[30] He proclaims his in-

29. CRD, p.174; CDR, p.91.
30. CRD, p.178; CDR, p.95.

tention not to hold the *Critique* at the level of abstract individuality — it would be 'false and idealist' to do so. However, 'since our starting point is individual *praxis,* we must carefully follow up every one of those threads of Ariadne which lead from this *praxis,* to the various forms of human ensembles; and in each case we shall have to determine the structures of these ensembles, their real mode of formation out of their elements, and finally their totalizing action upon the elements which have formed them.'[31] Individual *praxis* and the isolated person who performs it are abstractions which Sartre will use as heuristic devices — the immediate and given starting-points of an inquiry which will penetrate far beneath the individual's apparent isolation. Thus he will 'rediscover through deeper and deeper conditionings, the totality of [the individual's] practical bonds with others and, thereby, the structures of the various practical multiplicities and, through their contradictions and struggles, the absolute concrete: historical man.'[32]

But this process is never completed, either in the portion of the *Critique* Sartre has chosen to publish or in his unfinished second volume. His patently unhistorical, unsocial explanation of historical and social phenomena is at variance with his express commitment to portray the 'absolute concrete historical man'. A look at the construction of the *Critique* will show why.

Following two introductory chapters ('The Dogmatic Dialectic and the Critical Dialectic' and 'Critique of Critical Investigation'), Book I begins: 'From Individual Praxis to the Practico-inert'. In these pages, the argument progresses from the 'abstract' individual *praxis* to the most primary human ensembles: it is here that Sartre locates the basic social relations of the individual, those from which all others spring and to which they return. He first describes individual *praxis.* Then, in no fewer than four separate stages, the isolated individual encounters others. These stages reveal the peculiar unsocial nature of Sartre's social individual.

His first step beyond isolated individual *praxis* is in fact a leap. Beginning with the isolated individual at work on the material field around him, how do we arrive at social groupings? A deeper examination of this individual, which traced the imprint of history and

31. CRD, p.153; CDR, p.65.
32. CRD, p.143; CDR, p.52.

society in all his actions, would open an 'internal' route to sociality. But Sartre simply introduces other individuals. 'From my window I can see a roadmender on the road and a gardener working in a garden. Between them there is a wall with bits of broken glass on top protecting the bourgeois property where the gardener is working. Thus they have no knowledge at all of each other's presence: absorbed as they are in their work, neither of them even bothers to wonder whether there is anybody on the other side. Meanwhile, I can see them without being seen, and my position and this passive view of them at work situates me in relation to them: I am "taking a holiday", in a hotel.'[33] From one individual at work we leap to three individuals at work, separately. But to build social relations simply by multiplying individuals is not to build social relations at all. Three (or a dozen, or a thousand) individuals are not truly social unless links between them appear whose nature and logic is to reveal them in a shared, common activity, as belonging to a reality which is qualitatively different from the sum of its isolated parts. Instead of discovering others in the reality of the lone individual's *praxis,* Sartre simply places them there. We are already familiar enough with this abstract individual's next two social encounters ('Scarcity and Mode of Production' and 'Worked Matter as the Alienated Objectification of Individual and Collective "Praxis" ') to see that they too cast others and the social life that develops with them in this arbitrary, external, asocial role.

Which Comes First, Individual or Social Praxis?

The *Critique* sets out to reach social and historical being from premises that preclude arrival. Its goal, 'historical man', is in contradiction with its basic assumption, the isolated individual. This contradiction explains much of the book's disorder. Side by side with Sartre's repeated references to the abstractness of individual *praxis* and his proclaimed intention to advance to a more socially and historically concrete level, we find a quite different idea. Individual *praxis* is his fundamental principle. It is the source of all dialectic, the only ontological reality. The heuristic device turns out to be the substantive core of the analysis.

Sartre claims that his approach is based on the very nature of the

33. CRD, p.182; CDR, p.100.

dialectic itself. 'The dialectic, if it exists, can only be the totalization of concrete totalizations effected by a multiplicity of totalizing individualities.'[34] No collectivity of individuals can possibly grasp its surrounding material field as a whole, perform an action on it, alter it and so meet human needs — unless *each* individual can do it. 'The *entire historical dialectic rests on individual* praxis *in so far as it is already dialectical.*'[35] Hence it is necessary first of all to study the logic of individual labour. Sartre concedes that separated individuals appear as such only 'in a given society, and given a certain level of technical development'.[36] There is no question, he repeats, but that any relations we study are always specific and historical, so that even between systems of oppression, such as feudalism and capitalism, social relations in the work process differ sharply. However, he continues, 'History determines the content of human relations in its totality, and all these relations, even the briefest and most-private, refer to the whole. But History does not cause there to be human relations in general. The relations which have established themselves between those *initially separate* objects, men, were not products of problems of the organization and division of labour. On the contrary, the very possibility of a group or society being constituted — around a set of technical problems and a given collection of instruments — depends on the permanent actuality of the human relation (whatever its content) at every moment of History, even between two separate individuals belonging to societies with different systems and entirely ignorant of one another.

'This is why the habit of skipping the abstract discussion of the human relation and immediately locating ourselves in the world of productive forces, of the mode and relations of production, so dear to Marxism, is in danger of giving unwitting support to the atomism of liberalism and of analytical rationality. This error has been made by several Marxists: individuals, according to them, are *a priori* neither isolated particles nor directly related activities; it is always up to society to determine which they are through the totality of the movement and the particularity of the conjuncture. But this reply, which is supposed to avoid our "formalism", involves complete formal acceptance of the *liberal* position; the individualistic bourgeoisie requires just one

34. CRD, p.132; CDR, p.37.
35. CRD, p.165; CDR, p.80.
36. CRD, p.178; CDR, p.95.

concession: that individuals passively submit to their relations and that these are conditioned in exteriority by all kinds of other forces; and this leaves them free to apply the principle of inertia and positivistic laws of exteriority to human relations. From this point of view it hardly matters whether the individual really lives in isolation, like a cultivator at certain periods, or whether he lives in highly integrated groups: *absolute separation* consists in the fact that individuals are subject to the historical statute of their relations to others in radical exteriority. In other words — and this amounts to the same thing, though it misleads certain undemanding Marxists — absolute separation is when individuals as products of their own product (and therefore as passive and alienated) *institute* relations among themselves (on the basis of relations established by earlier generations, of their own constitution and of the forces and requirements of the time).'[37]

Sartre's point is that in setting up 'society' as an *a priori* term we institute an overwhelming conditioning force. This abstraction would make our life appear as something suffered, passively undergone, and submitted to. Bourgeois thinkers expressing their class ideology, and 'undemanding Marxists', develop a social image in which we are incapable of transforming the conditions which have created us. Sartre, for his part, continues to try to dissolve this false abstraction and reach a more basic human dimension: 'this brings us back to our problem in the first part of this book: what does it mean to *make* History on the basis of earlier conditions? I then said: if we do not distinguish the project, as transcendence, from circumstances, as conditions, we are left with nothing but inert objects, and History vanishes. Similarly, if human relations are a mere product, they are in essence reified and it becomes impossible to understand what their reification really consists in. My formalism, which is inspired by that of Marx, consists simply in recognizing that men make History to precisely the extent that it makes them. This means that relations between men are always the dialectical consequence of their *activity* to precisely the extent that they arise as a transcendence of dominating and institutionalized human relations. Man exists for man only in given circumstances and social conditions, so every human relation is historical. But historical relations are human in so far as they are

37. CRD, pp.179-180; CDR, p.96-97.

always given as the immediate dialectical consequence of *praxis*, that is to say, of the plurality of *activities* within a single practical field. . . .'[38]

But Sartre is mistaken. In order to understand that human activity is fundamentally dialectical and therefore capable of transforming the conditions in which it takes place, we need not believe that we are talking about individual activity. If *praxis* is individual, it is simultaneously social. Free, transforming, totalizing individual activity which remakes the world is possible only as social activity. Work is not an individual activity that happens, in some circumstances, to be performed alongside other people, but a social activity which members of any society perform, according to their skills, and to arrangements which are always and only social.

Long before there can be any epistemological encounter between the gardener, the road-mender and the vacationing intellectual, there must be a process of co-operation, no matter how antagonistic, in which they share. The intellectual can observe from his window only because there are people to mend the road, tend gardens, plant and grow food, make beds, build hotels, transport food, build trucks, supply fuel, make kitchen utensils, cut vegetables, cook food. The activity of each in this society implies the activity of all others, whatever their 'formal' relations. It is mystified if it is seen as 'purely' individual *praxis*. Individuals perform it, to be sure, but as *social* individuals sharing in a complex and highly organized social *praxis*. My tools, my place of work, the materials I work on, my very patterns of work — all these dimensions of individual *praxis* develop only in and for a society at a certain point in history. This is true even of apparently the most idiosyncratic individual activity. For example, the intellectual on vacation who establishes relations between individuals does so as part of a certain philosophical tradition and his leisure depends on a social division of labour which deems it important that certain groups of people are permitted the time to do such things. Strictly speaking there cannot be individual *praxis* any more than there can be individual reason. Social individuals work with social tools, exercise social skills in a social field, to accomplish a socially defined purpose. The very term, 'the individual', means simultaneously this concrete person and one particular social being — conditioned by and living in history.

38. CRD, p.180; CDR, pp.98-99.

Social Individuals

It might be objected that this conception renders dialectical activity — free activity, *praxis* — unintelligible by refusing to cast the individual as somehow prior to society, and serves bourgeois ideology by making the individual appear determined but not determining. What is this strange entity, society, if it is somehow given simultaneously with individual activity, if it is in some sense prior to and beyond any individual activity? And how is it possible to hope to control or transform it if we do not constantly create it? André Gorz has raised these questions in his vigorous defence of Sartre's standpoint: 'if the individual is explicable through the society, but the society is not intelligible through individuals — that is, if the "forces" that act in history are impermeable and radically heterogeneous to organic *praxis* — then socialism as the socialization of man can never coincide with socialism as the humanization of the social. It cannot come *from* individuals as their reappropriation by collective *praxis* of the resultant of individual *praxis*. It can only come *to* individuals by the evolution of their society according to its inner logic. The positivist (or transcendental materialist) hypothesis is that the historical process is impermeable to dialectical intelligibility. If so, then socialism, born of an external logic, will also remain external to individuals and will not be a submission of society and history to society and its demands on them; not the "full development" but the negation of individuals, not the transparency of the social for individual *praxis*, but the opacity of the individual for himself, insofar as his being and his truth have become completely external to him. Thus the social individual is not the individual recognizing himself and achieving himself — his needs, his interests, his certainties — for the profit of the society experienced as the absolute Other, to the point of regarding it as false to see it as other. We know that this conception of socialism prevailed for a long period, that it still has its adherents, that it profoundly affected Marxist philosophy, and that it must therefore be liquidated on this terrain as well.'[39]

Gorz has modified Sartre's argument slightly but significantly, in that his individuals are *already* social. But the argument remains clear: unless individual *praxis* is seen as the basis of society, society must be

39. 'Sartre and Marx', pp.38-39.

seen as independent of individuals and unchangeable by them. This objection runs into difficulty when we in turn ask what it means to anticipate a society controlled by individuals. What does it mean to speak of 'the humanization of the social' being achieved by 'individuals'? Neither Sartre nor Gorz can possibly have in mind isolated, separated individuals each controlling his or her own sphere of activity. A vision of 'collective *praxis*' can mean only one thing: individuals collectively controlling the society they create. 'Collectively' — that is, acting together in social groups, deriving their authority from the society as a whole, making group decisions about group goals, with the group controlling, in socially understood terms, the product of its labour. No individual can conceivably submit society and history to his demands unless he is a social individual. For socialism to be possible as the collective control of collective activity it is necessary for the individuals involved first to be living a collective life — however alienated. Socialism makes no sense as the 'reappropriation by collective *praxis* of the resultant of . . . individual *praxis*', only as the reappropriation of the resultant of heretofore alienated collective *praxis*. It means bringing under social control the *already* socialized process of production — not somehow transforming individual *into* social production.

Gorz and Sartre are combating the tendency, within socialist as well as bourgeois thought, to make individuals the passive objects of abstract forces beyond their control. However, it is possible to restore the theoretical possibility of humans' making and controlling history without basing their social life on an unintelligible pre-social individual. A necessary part of this restoration is to transcend the interminable debate over 'the individual' and 'society', not to persist in arguing the abstract claims of one or the other. It is true that no theory has decisively resolved this problem, and true too that Sartre has gone further than most in *Question de méthode*; but by and large, the *Critique* falls back on 'the individual'. To correct Sartre therefore, means first of all to insist that there is such an entity as *society*. Individual and society are alike irreparably abstract if separated: we cannot begin to understand either without simultaneously studying the other as its inner meaning. Everything hinges on whether individuals are seen as fundamentally social beings, in their basic activity, in their possibilities for liberation, indeed in their very individuality itself.

The Transition to Volume Two

Having followed the dialectic of collective *praxis* to its hardening in the institution, Sartre caps his discussion with several pages on the cult of personality and Stalin. But the *Critique* has not yet strictly speaking reached the terrain of history. Its concrete discussions function formally as illustrations in an analysis designed to deconstruct history into 'the set of formal contexts, curves, structures and conditionings which constitute the formal *milieu* in which the historical concrete must necessarily occur'.[40] One further structure must be described before the historical concrete is reached, that of class. This in turn can only be understood by means of the categories elucidated so far: scarcity, the practico-inert, *praxis,* the series, the fused group and the institution. And so to conclude the *Critique*'s first volume and lay the basis for the second, Sartre now turns to describe class in terms which considerably alter and deepen the argument developed in *Les Communistes et la paix*: 'class manifests itself not only as an institutionalized apparatus, but also as an ensemble (serial or organized) of direct-action groups, and as a collective which receives its statute from the practico-inert field (through and by productive relations with other classes) and which receives its universal schema of practical unification from the groups which constantly form on its surface.'[41] In a far more complex discussion of class than that in the essays on the Communist Party, Sartre takes in history, the *praxis*-process of exploitation, and the mutual conditioning of the antagonists in struggle. Most notably in his examination of racism and colonization in Algeria, and of the history of the French proletariat, he tries to dissolve 'the ruthless play of economic laws' into human '*praxis* absorbed into a process' which indifferently seems to impose itself on *everyone*. And then, having considered the mutual conditioning of classes by each other, he affirms that class struggle can only be understood dialectically.

Sartre now poses the question which leads to his second volume and to concrete history: can the class struggle be decoded so as to show how opposing classes form an intelligible part of a larger historical process? He has articulated, in a structural but not yet a historical way, the components of an understanding of history. This

40. CRD, p.637; CDR, p.671.
41. CRD, p.649; CDR, p.685.

regressive moment must be followed by a progressive one: 'these structures must be left to live freely, to oppose and to co-operate with one another: and the reflexive investigation of this still formal project will be the object of the next volume.'[42] Impelling the study of the concrete, however, is the 'real problem of history' brought out in Sartre's study of class: how can opposed collectivities, struggling against each other, produce *a single* history? He will now explore how, failing this, the intelligibility of history must vanish into an infinite multiplicity of *praxes*, distorting and splintering each other. History is intelligible only if these divergent *praxes* 'finally appear as partially totalizing and as connected and merged in their very oppositions and diversities by an intelligible totalization from which there is no appeal.'[43] In other words, the problem of history is 'the problem of totalization without a totalizer'.

Volume Two, never finished and never published (except for a brief section extracted and translated by *New Left Review*) begins with this very question: 'if the plurality of epicentres is the real condition *of the* opposed intelligibilities (in so far as there is a comprehensive intelligibility in each system and from each *praxis*), how could there be dialectical intelligibility of the process in course?'[44] Having premissed the first volume on individual *praxis* as the key to intelligibility, Sartre reaffirms his unvarying basic assumption. But he now asks of it the most radical question yet: in examining two *praxes* in conflict he seeks 'to know if *as struggle*, as objective fact of reciprocal and negative totalization', they possess 'the conditions of dialectical intelligibility'.[45] What does it mean to speak of *a* struggle? Sartre consistently refuses to answer this question by giving 'a reality to the verbal unity called *society*', which would indeed lend meaning to individual *praxes*, but by rendering them passive and destroying their intelligibility. He seems now to return to his original starting point to interrogate it afresh. The gardener, the roadmender, the intellectual are replaced here by two boxers: instead of arbitrarily juxtaposing individuals, he is now asking what *unites* them. It is as if he himself were aware of the first volume's limitations, and is now determined once and for all to overcome them by discovering sociality and historicity at the heart of individual *praxis*.

42. CRD, p.755; CDR, p.818.
43. CRD, p.754; CDR, p.817.
44. *Critique de la raison dialectique*, Tome II (unpublished manuscript), p.3. (CRD/II).

Boxers and Sub-groups

Studying two boxers, then (hypothetically) two sub-groups of a larger group, and finally two factions of the CPSU in the late 1920s, Sartre poses questions which, although rarely asked, are crucial in any perspective: how do individuals, groups or classes in conflict produce, in their very conflict, a larger whole which that conflict particularizes? Do they in some sense 'collaborate in fact on a common work'?[46] To call their conflict a contradiction is to appeal to a larger unity: 'but to be able to assimilate a battle to a contradiction and the adversaries to terms of a contradiction in course, it is necessary that they can be considered as the transitory determinations of a more ample and more profound group of which their conflict would actualize a present contradiction; inversely it would be necessary that the group totalize and transcend their ruthless struggle towards a new synthetic reunification of its practical field and an internal reorganization of its structures.'[47] If class struggle is intelligible, we should be able, in totalizing the struggling classes, to 'discover the synthetic unity of a society torn through and through.'[48]

Thus, the second volume of the *Critique* poses what is in one sense the unresolved problem of the first, and, in another, the unresolved problem of Marxism itself. 'Is there a unity of the different classes which supports and produces their irreducible conflicts?'[49] Marxism depends for its truth on an affirmative answer: otherwise 'human history decomposes into a plurality of particular histories.'[50]

Sartre's first analysis introduces a dimension that was earlier lacking: the boxers are understood in terms of their place in 'the world of boxing', an organized hierarchy present in the evening's programme; in terms of the art of boxing incarnated by the two participants, and in terms of their common acceptance of the rules to be observed. He tacitly acknowledges the abstractness of his isolated individuals, attempting to show that 'boxing *as a whole* is present at each moment of battle, as sport and as technique with all the human qualities and all the material conditioning (training, conditions of health, etc.) that

45. CRD/II, p.5.
46. CRD/II, p.14.
47. CRD/II, p.12.
48. CRD/II, p.19.
49. CRD/II, p.20.
50. CRD/II, p.20.

it demands'.[51] He is once again the observer, being entertained by a marginal and casually selected activity. And in studying it, he at first — and very strikingly — ignores the fact that the boxers are fighting *for a living*. Nevertheless, he goes on to relate the match with the whole of social life, as the 'public incarnation of *all* conflict'.[52] More specifically, he discusses the way in which capitalism domesticates the interiorized violence of scarcity into a regulated and profitable unleashing of violence by the oppressed against each other. It pays them to invert violence destined to be returned to their oppressors by releasing it instead against their 'enemy brothers' from the same class and in this way taps and mystifies the violence of those whom it exploits. In boxing, then, the violence of both participants and observers becomes 'the incarnation of their radical impotence, that is, the alienation of their liberating power'.[53] However, the formal purpose of this penetrating but unsystematic discussion is not achieved. Sartre tries to describe the two boxers in the ring as incarnating or singularizing the fundamental violence, based on scarcity, at the heart of society. But he establishes his interpretation more by fiat than by close study, and his discussions never lose their disorderly quality. Sartre labours in vain to clarify the notion of incarnation, distinguishing it from the relationship between a symbol and its symbolized reality, and from that of a general concept to its particular instance; but the meaning of the notion never becomes clear, since it tacitly appeals to a social dimension whose intelligibility still remains theoretically in question.

Sartre soon returns to the problem of the historical unity of a society broken into classes. Before approaching it directly, however, he considers a prior conflict, in which the existence of a larger unity is not an issue: that of sub-groups of a larger group in struggle with each other. His point here, in a discussion wholly lacking in concrete examples, is that competing sub-groups are not merely destructive forces, but rather express the group's larger dialectic at work. Why is an organized group with a common *praxis* split by two sub-groups opposed to each other in the name of the whole? Because in its *praxis* a group creates a practico-inert field which in turn imposes 'the practical realization of an impossible coexistence' between two sub-groups

51. CRD/II, pp.25-26.
52. CRD/II, p.30.
53. CRD/II, p.69.

and their *praxes*. This is the source of conflict, which 'is the sole real form that a contradiction can take at the heart of a group in action — reciprocally, no conflict is even possible in an integrated community if it is not the actualization by men of an objective contradiction.'[54] That is, struggle between two sub-groups develops only in so far as it is based on the actual unfolding of the common *praxis*.

Sartre is of course talking about a moment in the life of a collectivity which, having begun as a fused group, has solidified itself into an organization but is still unified by a common *praxis*. In so far as the survival of the group is at stake, such a post-revolutionary moment can lead to violent splits, liquidation of the vanquished sub-group, and denunciation of its members as traitors. For the split, by breaking its unity, threatens the very life of the group. The intelligibility of a 'victory by liquidation' is thus based on the effort of the victors to reunify 'the split unity by the regrouping of organs and individuals according to new common perspectives and under the interiorized pressure of the urgencies and dangers which characterizes the development of the total *praxis*.'[55]

Socialism in One Country

Sartre selects 'a single, contemporary example: the emergence in the USSR of the ideological monstrosity of "socialism in one country".'[56] With it, he reaches the heart of the second volume, four hundred pages on the Soviet Union, from the conflict within the leadership in the 1920s to Stalin's revival of anti-semitism in the early 1950s. The first part of this long discussion is all designed to make a single point: that the Stalin-Trotsky conflict 'was a totalization, through the protagonists, of a contradiction in the common *praxis* of the Party'.[57] It was in some sense inevitable, not accidental; it issued from and incarnated contradictions in which Bolshevik *praxis* had become enmeshed. Stalin's slogan of 'Socialism in one Country' reunified the party, and then the society, around an impossible and monstrous conception which afterwards became the truth of Soviet development.

---

54. CRD/II, p.81.
55. CRD/II, pp.122-23.
56. CRD/II, p.148; this section appeared in English in *New Left Review*, 100 (November 1976-January 1977), (NLR) p.143.
57. CRD/II, p.212; NLR, p.149.

The contradiction was that, on the one hand, the realization of socialism in the backward and ravaged Soviet Union depended on revolution elsewhere in Europe, while, on the other, the Bolshevik Revolution split the workers' movement everywhere and drove local bourgeoisies into the arms of fascism. 'The contradiction here was due to the fact that the proletarian Revolution in the USSR, instead of being a factor in the liberation and emancipation of the working masses of Europe — as it *should* have been — was accomplished by reducing them to relative impotence.'[58]

The resulting conflict was clear: the revolutionary Soviet government recognized the impossibility of building a genuinely socialist society without the help of more advanced socialist allies. But to act to encourage the creation of those allies under conditions of encirclement, underdevelopment and devastation, and the revolutionary ebb in Europe, was to risk the Bolshevik revolution itself. And yet not to act was to abandon the hope of any but the most hellish socialism. Victorious, the Bolshevik leadership now faced the contradiction engendered by their success, between the torn halves of what had once been a unified revolutionary project: to preserve or to radicalize socialism in Russia. This choice manifested itself in Stalin's Russian particularism and Trotsky's Western universalism, in Stalin's project of turning inwards and Trotsky's espousal of European revolution, in Stalin's caution and Trotsky's ardour, in Stalin's pedantic gearing of Marxist culture to Russian backwardness and Trotsky's brilliance as a Marxist theoretician, in the very reasons why Stalin and Trotsky at different moments advocated similar policies. It was as if the more cultivated, democratic and advanced socialism symbolized by Trotsky was expelled bodily from the Soviet Union and attacked as treason precisely in order that Stalin might adapt the universal concepts of Marxism to the concrete tasks of building *this* socialism.

'Socialism in One Country', Stalin's provocative and distorted answer to Trotsky, 'became the simple signification of the way in which this still-traditionalist country, with its illiterate population, absorbed and assimilated at once the overthrow of its ancient traditions; a traditional withdrawal into itself; and the acquisition of new traditions, through the absorption of an internationalist, universalist ideology which helped the peasants sucked into industry to com-

58. CRD/II, p.214; NLR, p.150.

prehend the transition from rural to factory labour.'[59] In other words, this unintelligible monstrosity became a *praxis*, and as such the deformed truth of the revolution. It succeeded because it united 'theory and practice; the universal and the particular; the traditionalist depths of a still alienated history and the movement of cultural liberation; the negative movement of withdrawal and the positive movement of hope.'[60]

Sartre's analysis augments that of Isaac Deutscher and adds considerably to our understanding of the Stalin-Trotsky conflict. Nevertheless, speaking formally, this is only a secondary goal; he is mainly concerned to demonstrate internal conflict in an already integrated group as 'an incarnation and a historialization' of the group's 'global totalization'.[61] But the significance of the example is limited in as much as the Bolshevik leadership was an *already integrated group*. What happens when we pass to the plane of history and its shifting multitude of collectivities? Do we find a single internally connected history or '*several* totalizations related only by coexistence or some other external relation'?[62] In order to explore this question more closely, Sartre turns to the development of the Soviet working class during the 1930s, in relation to Bolshevik *praxis*.

This is one of the most remarkable passages of the manuscript. Sartre reveals the oppressive features of Soviet development as an intelligible *praxis*-process — not as brutal madness. He illuminates as few others have done the tragic irony of Soviet history: 'in the historical circumstances of Russian industrialization', the revolutionary *praxis* of the leadership entailed 'destroying the workers as free practical organisms and as common individuals, to be able to create man from their destruction.'[63] The discussion proceeds in three stages: first, a study of how revolutionary Bolshevik *praxis* led to the creation of elites within the working class and the bureaucracy; second, of how the demographic upheaval induced by Bolshevik *praxis* created a new working class whose control and integration called for yet greater oppression; and third, an examination of how the Bolshevik struggle against backwardness under threat led to forced collectivization and

59. CRD/II, p.226; NLR, p.155.
60. CRD/II, p.228; NLR, p.156.
61. CRD/II, p.240; NLR, p.161.
62. CRD/II, p.246; NLR, p.163.
63. CRD/II, p.317.

terror, which in turn reduced the Soviet peasantry to a state of impotence and permanent passive resistance.

How — to dwell briefly on the first analysis — did a revolution committed to equality create a society 'of dignitaries where merit is pompously rewarded'?[64] 'The goal of the proletarian revolution', Sartre begins, 'is to permit the construction of a society where the worker will have permanent and integral control over the process of production.'[65] *Human* control, entailing 'liquidation of the practico-inert as field of human alienation'.[66] Moreover, in conditions of scarcity and external threat, the revolutionary leadership is forced to vanquish as quickly as possible 'the resistance of things': the first priority *must be* to develop heavy industry. Soviet voluntarism was a response to the 'absolute necessity' of leaping over stages of development in order to catch up with the menacing West. In such a situation different economic sectors can hardly be left to themselves to determine their own capacities and needs. Centralization combines with voluntarism. 'You should, therefore you can.'[67] However, 'the very development of industry, to the exact degree that it conforms to the plan, meaning common *praxis*, reacts on the directing layers to stratify and multiply the organs of direction.'[68] In calling forth new functions of control and thus sedimenting a practico-inert organizational structure, industrialization engenders this 'skeleton indispensable to all transcendence but which by itself rigorously limits the possibilities of inventing responses to each situation.'[69] This necessary, and necessarily inertial, organizational structure in turn defines the goals and limits of the process, so inducing the 'petrifying repercussion of *praxis* on itself'.[70] We see this most clearly in the establishment of a salary range contradicting Bolshevik egalitarianism. Bolshevik principles could not be conserved *and* the Revolution saved at the same time: it is necessary to choose between the shattering of the Revolution and its *deviation.*'[71]

How was this contradiction lived by the Soviet worker? Originally,

64. CRD/II, p.290.
65. CRD/II, p.265.
66. CRD/II, p.266.
67. CRD/II, p.278.
68. CRD/II, p.278.
69. CRD/II, p.280.
70. CRD/II, p.281.
71. CRD/II, p.281.

his personal need was straightaway a revolutionary social demand. Now, if left free, he would want less work and higher pay, which in the circumstances are strictly personal needs at variance with the compelling social destiny imposed from without: 'his tasks are fixed on him from statistical givens establishing the demands of the productive apparatus, of armament, of consumption, and it is through the vulgarized summaries of these calculated givens that they are communicated to him.'[72] How and why have the most emancipated workers been stripped of their rights of control and direction? — 'not by a deliberate operation of the directing organs, but by the growing disproportion between the necessities of the economic combine and their relative ignorance of these problems';[73] and because free workers would not treat themselves as factors of production whose minimum needs alone must be met, but would make demands endangering the success of the plan itself.

But how, then, could the masses be interested in production? Since no 'interest in production' could be built in as an *objective* condition of labour performed in such circumstances, and could never be generated by simple coercion, the leadership developed Stakhanovism. Lacking the objective conditions for either democratic control or a general rise in living standards, the most productive workers were rewarded by incorporation into a labour elite on the model of the Party and State leadership. The plan engendered the 'man of the plan': a synthesis of 'individualism (ambition, personal interest, pride) and of total devotion to the common cause, meaning socialism'.[74] The leadership was in turn modified by its own creation, needing now to justify its right to distribute such honours by awarding itself the highest honorific distinctions. It was unthinkable, Sartre pungently observes, that the agents of such a society could any longer be 'a group of poor revolutionaries without privileges refusing all titles — as was Lenin'.[75] And so the circle is completed: under conditions of scarcity, the practico-inert field engendered by revolutionary *praxis* reaches back and imposes a contrary *praxis*, shaping its people as it does so. 'Thus *praxis* develops its own counter-finality: by the in-

72. CRD/II, p.283.
73. CRD/II, p.284.
74. CRD/II, p.209.
75. CRD/II, p.291.

termediary of the voluntarists it distinguishes and which it raises above the common lot, it transforms its agents into *dignitaries*. Social stratification becomes both the means imposed to realize economic growth by planning in this underdeveloped country and, as consequence borne by *praxis* but not intended by it, the practico-inert and anti-socialist result of the pursuit of *stimuli* in a situation which does not permit interesting the masses in production.'[76]

In this penetrating example, and in those which follow on the demographic changes and collectivization, Sartre achieves a main goal of the *Critique*: the intelligibility, rooted in *praxis*, of the material structures which dominate human action. He sees more deeply and clearly here than anywhere else in the two volumes. Scarcity is placed at the core of his study, and wholly rooted in the material process of producing the means of subsistence. He shows convincingly how human action can turn back on itself to create results the opposite of those it intends, how a 'given' such as the Soviet hierarchy was created to save a revolution committed to abolishing all hierarchy, and how forced collectivization and its accompanying terror have made it impossible to integrate the Soviet peasantry into society down into to the present. In his next, climactic discussion, Sartre goes on to show how Soviet *praxis* was carried out by the very individual that such a *praxis* demanded.

Stalin

Was there an alternative to Stalin, and to the bloody policies he pursued? The necessitarian tone of the examples discussed so far betrays the most challenging and disturbing theme of the second volume. In what appears to be a total reversal of Sartre's original conception of freedom, it now often seems as if the situation created by a given *praxis inevitably* imposed the whole subsequent course of events, including the subsequent *praxes*.

In *Le Fantôme de Staline* Sartre had already sketched an explanation of the cult of Stalin's personality as the only possible embodiment and form of authority in Soviet society in the oppressive conditions of socialist construction.[77] And in the first volume of the *Critique* he

76. CRD/II, p.290.
77. FS, p.218f; SS, pp.49-62.

sketched a dialectic that leads seemingly inexorably from the fused revolutionary group to the sovereign as organ of integration imposing its unity on a series of impotent individuals. His discussion of the institution observes that unquestionably the initial step in the construction of socialism 'could only be the indissoluble aggregation of bureaucracy, of Terror and of the cult of personality'.[78] But is this 'undeniably' true? Sartre now confronts this issue in a reflection on Stalin's role as sovereign leader of the Soviet state.

He argues in several places that nothing justifies the assertion that Stalin's were the only possible policies. But is this simply a ritual acknowledgement of historical contingency? As the sovereign responds to the new situations created by its *praxis,* Sartre nowhere shows any opening for a course different from the one he himself sketches. The intelligibility of even the anti-semitism of Stalin's last years seems to depend on an argument for broad social necessity (as the 'Iron Curtain' fell against all foreign influences, a native population deeply linked to a western-supported Jewish state became for Stalinist distrust 'the real presence of a core of traitors.'[79])

Many non-Stalinist Marxists accept that industrialization and collectivization required coercion. 'Simply they ask themselves *if it was not possible* to avoid the propaganda lies, purges, police oppression in workers' centres and the terrible repression of the peasant revolts.'[80] Sartre boldly reformulates this question to explore, in the conditions of the singularization of sovereignty called for by the Soviet *praxis*-process, 'a deformation of *praxis* by the sovereign'.[81] Since the purges and the Moscow trials do not seem called for by the mere project of industrial growth in an underdeveloped country, they are often ascribed to the individual personality of Stalin. It might be said, for example, that the same results could have been attained with more flexibility, foresight and respect for human life; and further that Stalin, because of his personal idiosyncrasies,·exaggerated to appalling excess the need to subordinate human need to the construction of machines. To the degree that Stalin bears responsibility for the purges and the trials, they are explained by chance, or by personal factors extrinsic to the revolutionary project.

78. CRD, p.653; CDR, p.662.
79. CRD/II, p.545.
80. CRD/II, p.426.
81. CRD/II, p.426.

In a climactic analysis, Sartre sharply rejects this line of thought as intolerably abstract without, on the other hand, rooting all the specific features of Stalinism in the revolutionary process as such. He now ventures his own solution to the riddle — which dominates historical *praxis*, the individual or the demands of the situation? The circumstances of the Soviet *praxis*-process entailed that its organs of sovereignty could subsist and act only by placing power in the hands of *one* individual. 'But since the regime completely demands a personal sovereign in the name of *maximum integration* and that he be, at the summit of the pyramid, the living suppression of all multiplicity, when the constructive effort of the USSR implies that this society . . . find its unity in the biological indissolubility of one individual, it is not even conceivable that this individual could be in himself and in his *praxis* eliminated as idiosyncrasy on behalf of an abstract objectivity.'[82] But why was singularized sovereignty vested in *this* particular individual, Stalin; and not in someone else capable of unifying the construction of a Russian socialism amid the urgencies of the 1930s — some other dogmatic opportunist sufficiently able to adapt Marxism to the unique Russian situation, some other 'militant known by militants', 'inflexible, without nerves, and without imagination', able to both retain the loyalty of the Party and impose surplus labour on workers and peasants? As we pursue the question, it begins to answer itself. But need the Soviet leader have been precisely 'this former Georgian seminarian'?[83] Stalin's upbringing interiorized the very qualities demanded by the situation. But if 'the situation in 1929 demanded the inflexibility of the sovereign, this demand leaves indeterminate the question of the individual origins of this inflexibility.'[84] Moreover, were there any others available who happened to unite these qualities in themselves? Scarcity, reaching into all sectors of social life, becomes at a time of urgency a *'scarcity of men'*. Stalin, then, becoming the man of the specific situation, 'will adapt himself progressively to *praxis* to the degree that *praxis* adapts itself to his prefabricated idiosyncrasy; from compromise to compromise, equilibrium will realize itself finally by a transformation of the man and a deviation of the enterprise.'[85]

82. CRD/II, p.432.
83. CRD/II, p.445.
84. CRD/II, p.451.
85. CRD/II, p.452.

Stalin is *necessarily* disadapted to his role, because his personal traits, however apt, emerge not from the situation but from elsewhere. Plekhanov was wrong: the situation does not create the man, but rather calls, and not always successfully, for specific individual traits. Thus his inflexibility 'will present itself also and necessarily as *not being exactly the required inflexibility*.'[86] Arising from his childhood, deeply as that may have interiorized fundamental aspects of Russian life, Stalin's inflexibility does not have the building of a new social order as its preordained objective. He can only adapt himself to his tasks *more or less* completely.

There is then, a necessary disjuncture between the individual and his historical tasks. In claiming that the function creates the man who exercises it, Pleaknov ignored the profound fact that history individualizes itself in 'its man' who then changes history according to his idiosyncrasy as he carries out its work. The Soviet situation demanded an individual sovereign who incarnated its vital need to draw exclusively on Russian resources, unflinchingly to drain surplus labour from its own citizens, to present Marxism as a crude dogma to semi-literate peasants who had a need to believe. It was Stalin himself who pressed on to the Great Purges and the Moscow Trials, forms of oppression which, if instigated by *his* eccentricities, soon became absorbed as definitive dimensions of Soviet life. Stalin, not the objective situation, required the 'absurd cultural isolation' into which he led the Soviet Union. The difference in standard of living was so great between Soviet and Western workers as to *propose* the 'Iron Curtain': 'but it did not *demand* endless lies about the condition of the European worker.'[87]

We can imagine a sovereign individual who would have done only and precisely what was necessary rather than, as Stalin did, both more and less — but only *imagine*. Sartre now reaches the crowning point of his entire analysis, showing the way in which 'accident' — Stalin's idiosyncrasies, his excesses — was *necessary* to Soviet history: ' . . . doubtless, if the process of planned growth could be directed by an angel, *praxis* would have the maximum unity joined to the maximum objectivity. The angel would never be blind, nor spiteful, nor brutal: it would be in each case whatever it is necessary to be. But

86. CRD/II, p.452.
87. CRD/II, p.460.

precisely for this reason, angels are not individuals; they are abstract models of virtue and wisdom. In a situation the real individual, ignorant, worried, fallible, flustered by the brusque urgency of perils, will react (according to his history) at first too softly then, at the point of being overwhelmed, too brutally. These jerks, these accelerations, these brakings, these hairpin turns, these violences which characterize Stalinism, were not all required by the objectives and the demands of socialization. However they were inevitable in so far as this socialization demanded, in its first phase, to be directed by one individual.'[88]

The 'Critique' Goes Astray

After a discussion of Stalin's anti-semitism in the 1950s Sartre turns abruptly to new themes, apparently to deepen his foregoing analyses. He begins a series of ruminations on an 'enveloping totalization' — that is, history. He reflects on the diversion of *praxis* — the circularity which returns worked matter back on ourselves. He goes so far as to speculate on an enveloping totalization not overwhelmed or diverted by the practico-inert, and after insisting that the formal structure of circularity would remain unchanged, imagines a *directed* circularity which would make use of the anticipated diversions to control them. But what bearing do such fascinating speculations have on the purpose of the *Critique*? The question is worth asking, for in the course of the last two hundred pages of the second volume it becomes clear that Sartre has gone astray. He suddenly raises the question of the 'real being' of the enveloping totalization and, having declared such concerns part of the ontology of history rather than the critique of dialectical reason, pursues them in any case. He begins to speculate in the ontological style of *L'Etre et le Néant,* and, in an unstructured analysis which drastically loses the clarity and penetration of the first three quarters of the manuscript, meditates anew on the meaning of being-in-itself — now as the in-itself of the enveloping totalization of history. In the midst of these speculations, the manuscript breaks off.

Why does the *Critique* lose its way shortly after Sartre's discussion of the Soviet Union? Moreover, why did it remain unfinished? It is pertinent to recall the purposes of the manuscript, and to ask whether Sartre achieved them. The express objectives of Volume Two were to show dialectical reason at work in the concrete — history itself — and, more substantively, to show how struggling classes created, even in their opposition to each other, a single intelligible history. As certainly as it achieved the first, it did not achieve the second. The *Critique* approached this objective in showing the peasantry in conflict with the Soviet regime in the 1930s, but in an oblique, even evasive manner. We see the intelligibility of oppositions developing with a single unifying *praxis* directed by a sovereign individual, but this discussion tells us nothing about class struggle, especially in societies lacking a sovereign *praxis* of this kind. Again and again we are referred to his analysis of bourgeois society, projected for the second volume, an analysis which we still await as the manuscript breaks off. In some of the most penetrating studies of his entire career, Sartre elicits the intelligibility of certain decisive dimensions of a society organized by a single *praxis*, but he never begins his account of how a *multiplicity* of hostile or unrelated *praxes* cohere. The logic of advanced bourgeois-democratic societies such as his own is left unexplored.

What these observations suggest is that even at their most penetrating, the analyses of the *Critique* remain wholly within the pre-existing limits of Sartre's thought. If Sartre were to explain class struggle, or bourgeois society, he would truly have squared the circle. He can lucidly explain the circularity of a deliberate single practical project, but without a clear sense of a fundamental sociality coexisting alongside and within individuals, he could not hope to explain any but the most coercive forms of social life. Even here, the necessitarian tone of his analysis leaves him morally too neutral in the face of Stalin's brutality. If Stalin seems so necessary, his crimes so little deserving of outrage, is it perhaps also because, according to Sartre's analysis, only some such individual sovereign can sustain the original project of the fused group? Sartre's dialectic of the group, upon which Volume Two is based, ignores any prior social co-operation, any underlying sociality: it is no wonder then that a sovereign individual is needed to preserve the group's purposes — or that Sartre leaves us so little room to ponder alternatives to Stalin's policies, and makes his bloody idiosyncrasies seem so inevitable. However, my primary concern, in these comments, is less to criticize one of Sartre's great unknown achievements than to ask why he never made it available to the public. One reason is its length. To complete the *Critique* on the scale originally planned, Sartre would have had to explore every major sector of world history today, and draw them together in the concrete enveloping totalization. After six hundred pages, however, he had only sketched a few key dimensions of a single history: the project as a whole would have run into many volumes. At the same time Sartre did manage to complete most of a project more than twice the length of the *Critique*, the biography of Flaubert, so the mere prospect of scale is not a sufficient explanation. The more fundamental reason is that because of the limitations of his thought, Sartre lacked the tools for completing the *Critique*. The premises of the second volume were those of the first, and we have already seen their analytic limits. In the second volume, he went as far as he could in explaining social phenomena before the contradiction took effect: not within, but after, his compelling discussion of the Soviet Union, as the time came to turn to explain a capitalist society such as his own, without a sovereign dictator yet based on antagonistic co-operation; to show what unites people acting in apparently complete independence of each other in an atomized, pluralistic society. At this point, the analysis lost focus and wandered into ontology. Sartre would never explain the intelligibility of class struggle. The enveloping totalization — the meaning of history — would remain an unsolved puzzle for his social thought, and so too would the society he lived in.

The Limits of Sartre's Thought

The course of the *Critique* paralleled the trajectory of Sartre's political essays and plays: three great projects, attesting the awesome energies of their author, they all ultimately fell short of their goal. We have examined their strengths and weaknesses now, and can see them as aspects of a single unitary project. The playwright who never created fully concretized individuals in positive action in the historical world was the essayist who never developed a balanced sense of his responsibilities and limits as an intellectual in politics — and this was the individualist social philosopher of the unfinished *Critique*. In what lay the unity of these projects and their common frustration? It is obvious that Sartre's Marxism shared none of the deep optimism of a Marx, Engels, or Lenin. He was at his best when explaining negativity — say, the oppressive weight of the practico-inert. After a brief period of entertaining the most positive hopes — such as his visions of the City of Ends and of a society in permanent revolution — Sartre returned to the negative as his natural focus of attention and the natural tenor of his analysis. We are, it seems, fated to make side by side with one another a world which is forever beyond our control. For Sartre the 'Beginning of History' in Marx's sense would never come: the law of dialectical circularity and much else in the *Critique* are powerful arguments to the contrary. Designed as a philosophical basis for historical materialism, the *Critique* is also a forceful attack on Marxism's hope for humankind.

At the core of Sartre's mature as much as his early thought, we encounter a single dominant mood, his abiding pessimism. Present in his earliest studies, this pessimism was also his major conclusion. The *Critique* displayed a more profound insight into negativity, seeking to explain the social causes of what earlier had seemed a projection of personal idiosyncrasy or cultural mood. In his effort to grasp the source of the negativity he had earlier built into his ontology, Sartre provided a remarkable analysis of the pratico-inert as a human condition. But in the end, his own peculiar intellectual optic cast this new-found sense of materiality in an overwhelmingly bleak light, showing *needs* only in the reified form of scarcity and not as vital springs of human development, and obscuring human progress towards abolishing scarcity and bringing the world under human control or learning to live at peace with it. Pessimism concerning any improvement in our relations with the material world remained at the core of Sartre's thought, even in its Marxist phase. For him, we remain forever this side of taking the universe into human hands, transforming it in our own image or breaking its control over us.

To return the world to its human source was Sartre's abiding project in the *Critique*, but in the end he grasped only the logic which made us, as in *L'Etre et le Néant*, in some way responsible for a world beyond our power. The rare moments of genuine human sovereignty were unstable eruptions doomed to relapse into more stable and alienated forms. In this sense, the *Critique* was an exhaustive demonstration of a logic of human entrapment. It is true, undeniably so, that no revolution yet has ended the reign of necessity over humans, except perhaps during the revolutionary moments themselves, and that today we remain enmeshed in 'pre-history'. But so determined was Sartre to elicit the logic of negativity that his imagination failed at the decisive point. What is 'scarcity' after all, if not a *human* fact, another term for *backwardness*? Our powers are limited, our skills scarce, and so oppression becomes possible, as does class society. A genuine assumption of control by humans over human life depends on *increasing* our powers through a slow and painful course of development and struggle. The revolutionary apocalypse must prove illusory until the day when humans are developed enough to assert power fully and collectively over a world that they have shaped.

What is missing in Sartre is any sense of our historical progress towards a real, an ultimate breakthrough: the historical turning point when a full assumption of control is possible because, finally, our product will have ceased to dominate us, and we will have acquired sufficient collective power to abolish domination by either humans or nature. As Mandel had pointed out, failing to situate itself in history from the outset — in the history of struggle towards this breakthrough — Sartre's approach remained only quasi-dialectical. The major premise of his early thought returned as his main mature conclusion. He failed to go beyond interiority-in-the-world and all it entailed, and one by one his mature projects ran aground on it. In his analyses, momentary breakthrough and inevitable relapse took the place of history, human labour, slow patient progress through struggle on the one hand, and the reality of human backwardness and efforts to perpetuate it, on the other. The non-realization of a breakthrough remained the unresolved issue for Sartre: unable to locate any trends towards it in the real historical world, he pondered it in the form of scattered and momentary insurrectionary flashes. Thus Sartre's Marxism became, in an odd sense, academic. We have already seen how, in his political essays, his penetrating Marxist analyses of the past coexisted with a peremptory emphasis on choice in the present. In the same way, in Volume Two of the *Critique*, he combined his necessitarian analyses of the Soviet past with hopeful comments on the prospects for de-Stalinization in the present. Deeply pessimistic about the long run, Sartre persisted in optimism concerning possible choices in the present. There was thus a striking disjuncture between his sense of action and his sense of understanding.

Marx saw thought as both internally rigorous and wedded indissolubly to political action. This was the basis of the imperative that governed all his theoretical projects: to ground study on the social bases of human activity in order to understand the prospects for social change. While not as centrally concerned to unify theory and practice, Sartre faithfully met his own demand for the intellectual's political engagement in play after play, essay after essay. In *Question de méthode*, however, he proposed a strikingly different objective: to explain the individual. He sought to 'reconquer man within Marxism'. But he conceived this as an intellectual, not a political project: his purpose was to 'see the original dialectical movement in the individual and in his enterprise of producing his life, of objectifying himself'.[1] After breaking off the *Critique* he became absorbed in the longest project of his life: his study of Gustave Flaubert.

On this scholarly level, Sartre was not at all pessimistic. Interviewed in 1971, he said that the 'most important project in the *Flaubert* is to show that fundamentally everything can be communicated, that

---

1. QM, p.101; SM, p.161.

without being God, but simply as a man like any other, one can manage to understand another man perfectly, if one has access to all the necessary elements.'[2] A greater intellectual ambition is scarcely conceivable. This ambition sprang from what was perhaps Sartre's deepest belief: that reality could indeed be understood. Understood, momentarily combated perhaps, but not decisively changed — here was his optimism and here his immoveable pessimism.

Where did this pessimism stem from, finally? What was the source of his abiding sense that the world — even if we shape it — must remain beyond our control. Our basic analysis still holds good: alone, the isolated individual must forever be overwhelmed by his world. Certainly, the individual is split from his or her society virtually everywhere in the world today, and it is perhaps unjust to demand of Sartre that he join in thought what remains sundered in experience. His thought was decisively affected by the objective limitations of the history that he lived through in these years. But if Sartre cannot be taxed with failing to think the unthinkable, or being halted by history's blockages, he nevertheless remained within an unusually constricted individualism — so much so that he was unable to pose the problem explicitly, regarded sociality more as a threat than as a puzzle, and so mystified his own sense of the problem that the *Critique* lost its focus and broke off unfinished. Why did the problematic of his early thought persist, decisively, into his most ambitious work of Marxist theory? Part of the answer at least lay in his conditions of life, where the limits of his personal experience met the limits of social experience in bourgeois society. Living in a world where our social links are lived openly and positively, Sartre might have been impelled by others, by the general climate of experience, to see beyond his personal limitations. As it was, he only reflected the society's own pessimism about humans, its sense of individual isolation and its negativity concerning collective effort. More than this, he reflected its mystifications. Thus, in 1953, he bitterly attacked Claude Lefort's emphasis on the *positive* features of capitalist production and the contemporary division of labour.[3] For Lefort, the positive features of social life under capitalism formed the basis both for social struggle and for a socialist society; for Sartre, in contrast, struggle remained a

2. 'Sur "L'Idiot de la famille" ', *Situations,* X, p.106; 'On *The Idiot of the Family', Life/Situations,* p.121.
3. See 'Réponse a Claude Lefort', *Situations,* VII; 'An Answer to Claude Lefort', CPA.

violent rupture with an overwhelmingly negative daily life.

But Sartre experienced the world of daily life in his own specific ways. After his spectacular rise to fame in post-war France, his personal world of experience was changed dramatically: first, he never had to work in a job again; second, as the *Critique's* glaring weaknesses reveal, his writings would henceforth be published without question or correction. His unique arrangement with Gallimard gave him a fixed monthly stipend, which sheltered him from even the usual professional consciousness of sales figures and royalties. His material conditions of life were henceforth guaranteed: he could work when he wished on whatever he wished, without colleagues, without supervision, without criticism.

Enviable as it may have been, this position left Sartre permanently out of circuit in relation to the daily material pressures suffered not only by the oppressed and exploited, but also by virtually everyone else in the society. Without a wife or children or settled home life, living in residential hotels and eating in cafés, the Sartre who refused the normal trappings of bourgeois life was able now to reject any place in the social division of labour. Furthermore, the irritations of celebrity made him reclusive, led him to shut himself off from all but a few old and close friends. He seldom became absorbed in discussing ideas, and his new situation further restricted his experience and the intellectual currents passing through it. If Sartre was so fundamentally unable to see beyond the categories of bourgeois society, it had to be in part because the peculiar consequences of his celebrity made some of the most negative and mystifying features of capitalist society his own daily reality. Thus Sartre remained free into old age to live out the philosophy of *L'Etre et le Néant*, avoiding encumbrances to the perpetually renewed act of self-definition: 'it is the idea of carrying as many things with me as possible that defines my whole life — everything that represents my daily life at any given moment. The idea, therefore, of being entirely what I am at the present moment and of not depending on anyone, of not needing to ask anyone for anything, of having all my possessions at my immediate disposal....[4]

We have reached the point where biographical and conceptual explanations merge, where the limitations of Sartre's lived experience

4. 'Autoportrait à soixante-dix ans,' *Situations*, X; 'Self-Portrait at Seventy,' *Life/Situations*, p.69.

ratified and reinforced the limitations of his thought. At the moment of his intellectual struggle with the unsituated freedom of a Mathieu, an Orestes or a Hugo, a society of privilege made Sartre one of its elite and conferred on him one of its greatest privileges, a life free of demands. Orestes complained of his unattached freedom, longed for any place, however oppressive, that would be *his*. The anti-social core of Sartre's thought could only have been confirmed in its reasons as he fulfilled his dream of being a writer, and took up a life which never demanded that he experience — as a teacher, for example — a concrete work regime, fixed daily movements, a dependency which, however galling, he would have been obliged to see as the contemporary social norm.

Thus, conceptually, the individual rooted in his interiority but trying to get *to* the world remained enmeshed in the pessimism of his initial isolation. It was for this reason that *commitment* and *responsibility* became key terms for Sartre, and for this reason that his entire theatre project and all of his political essays grappled with the issue of *engagement*. When he spoke of the writer's responsibility, he was speaking from his own position outside and above social conflict, speaking of what he as a free agent *should* do. As Merleau-Ponty saw already in the mid-1950s, Sartre's political essays reflected not a long-term political-intellectual project but a series of *prises de position*. Reading Burnier and de Beauvoir, we are again and again given the impression of his need to *take a stand*. We should contrast this sense of responsibility with the idea of *solidarity*, one of the key terms absent from Sartre's self-conception. Solidarity is engagement *with*, not on behalf of, the oppressed; it entails a sense of connectedness with their struggles, and abolishes distance where 'responsibility' confirms it. Solidarity involves recognizing that one is *already* enmeshed with others, in a way that Sartre never did — or was.

Four

Changing the World, Leaving the World

1

Introducing a Crisis:
'Les Mots'

After abandoning the *Critique,* Sartre entered the self-critical, questioning period announced as early as the 1960 interview in which he confessed to having 'had the experience of a sort of a total impotence from my childhood until now'. This sense achieved its sharpest expression in *Les Mots* and persisted into his new politico-intellectual outlook after May 1968. *Les Mots* introduced the crisis whose outcome was a new definition of the intellectual's political role and the overwhelming biography of Gustave Flaubert.

If Sartre's call for engaged literature was the first watershed in his intellectual career, *Les Mots,* published in late 1963, was certainly the second. *Qu'est-ce que la littérature?* conceptualized the direction already taken by the playwright, novelist, and essayist, pointing ahead to the politico-intellectual project we have just studied. Sixteen years later, *Les Mots* explored Sartre's childhood, searching for the sources of what he had come to regard as his weaknesses: his overvaluing of words and immersion in the imaginary, his need to justify himself through writing and sense of priestly calling as a writer. The energy and optimism of *Qu'est-ce que la littérature?* were cancelled by the valetudinarian fatalism of *Les Mots.* His imposture Sartre concluded, was his very character: 'one gets rid of a neurosis, one doesn't get cured of one's self.'

After thirty years of impassioned, missionary writing in which he sought to reveal one dimension of the human world after another, to guide his audience in thought and action, Sartre took a drastic turn. *Les Mots* was his own account of his apprenticeship to the imaginary as a small boy, of his immersion in an element from which, he now confessed, he had never really escaped. The aggressive, wordly tone of the 1940s and 1950s was absent from these words, as they explored and pondered the past. A strange autobiography for a great writer, *Les Mots* was not concerned to reminisce about its author's brilliant career but to meditate upon the origins of his illusions. It was more of a confession than a celebration, an acknowledgement that something had gone wrong.

(*Les Mots* presents an interesting problem of dating. Sartre himself has said that most of it was written in 1953-54, during what he regarded as his awakening from idealism, at the time of his decision to align himself with the Communists. However, it was not completed and published until 1963. The earlier date sets it in his period of growing political realism, the period of *Le Diable et le bon Dieu*; the later in the time of his personal and political disillusionment. The text itself mentions only one date, 1963, and refers to its author as a 'quinquagenarian'—he was fifty-seven in that year. More important, although Sartre's references to an awakening from idealism suggest an earlier date, his fatalism certainly reflects the later. It is likely that in the early 1960s, under the impact of the kind of spiralling disillusionment we have just studied, he returned to the earlier draft, preserving some of it, but in the three months he spent on it reshaped the work in accordance with his current frame of mind. The earlier insights were absorbed into a new literary unity whose main themes, we shall see, corresponded to the preoccupations of his later work.)

Self-Understanding as Evasion

Kept out of school until after the age of ten, living with an old man and two women, Sartre as a boy related to images and words rather than to other children or things. He lived for play-acting, for movies; books became his religion. This 'imaginary child' without a father, a guest with his girl-mother in his grandparents' home, felt he belonged nowhere and developed a deep-seated sense of his own superfluity. It seemed that writing might change this, might make him necessary to someone, might imbue the events of his life with the importance of an unfolding destiny. But writing was an escape: 'the eagerness to write involves the refusal to live.' Looking back in his late fifties, Sartre accomplished something remarkable. He uncovered the vice, weakness, or neurosis underlying many of the key themes—and problems—that we have identified in his work. *Superfluity*: from the very beginning the child felt he belonged nowhere, had no right to exist. *Negation*: the young Sartre 'was *nothing*: an ineffaceable transparency.'[1] *Isolated individualism*: the child's shaping years were spent in a sequestered, unreal inner world, completely cut off from other children.

An overwhelming world: he never had to encounter the outside, never built up even the most minimal tolerance of and ability to cope with the 'external' world. *Immersion in the* irréel *as a way of living life's problems*: Sartre had been an 'imaginary child', given over to one form of imposture after another. *Art as salvation*: transformed into a writer, into his very books themselves, the boy might finally feel that he belonged. *Adventures, rigour*: he longed to have his life transformed into a destiny by existing for someone else, being important to someone else.

Was all this true only of the little boy, and no longer of the mature writer? Sartre equivocated. Writing pushed him up against reality again and again — the green velvet arm-chair that his grandfather demanded he describe, the real German Kaiser who could not be conquered with his pen while the war went on. But these jolts did not disrupt the project of salvation through writing which, if anything, was more fully consolidated in the ten-year-old's personality structure at book's end. Indeed, this childhood idealism 'took me thirty years to shake off'.[2] But did he ever shake it off? In 1953-54 he may well have thought so. But he also acknowledged, appearing to speak from the early 1960s, the persistent power of his urge to write in order to be forgiven his existence. 'The proof is that I'm still writing fifty years later.'[3]

Sartre's clearest comment on whether or how far he had changed came as *Les Mots* drew to a close: 'I have changed. I shall speak later on about the acids that corroded the distorting transparencies which enveloped me; I shall tell when and how I served my apprenticeship to violence and discovered my ugliness — which for a long time was my negative principle, the quicklime in which the wonderful child was dissolved; I shall also explain the reason why I came to think systematically against myself, to the extent of measuring the obvious truth of an idea by the displeasure it caused me. The retrospective illusion has been smashed to bits; martyrdom, salvation, and immortality are falling to pieces; the edifice is going to rack and ruin; I col-

1. M, p. 73; W, p. 90.
2. M, p. 39; W, p. 51.
3. M, p. 160; W, p. 93.

lared the Holy Ghost in the cellar and threw him out; atheism is a cruel and long-range affair: I think I've carried it through. I see clearly, I've lost my illusions, I know what my real jobs are, I surely deserve a prize for good citizenship. For the last ten years or so I've been a man who's been waking up, cured of a long, bitter-sweet madness, and who can't get over the fact, a man who can't think of his old ways without laughing and who doesn't know what to do with himself. I've again become the traveller without a ticket that I was at the age of seven: the ticket-collector has entered my compartment; he looks at me, less severely than in the past; in fact, all he wants is to go away, to let me finish the trip in peace; he'll be satisfied with a valid excuse, any excuse. Unfortunately, I can't think of any; and besides, I don't even feel like trying to find one. We remain there looking at each other, feeling uncomfortable, until the train gets to Dijon, where I know very well that no one is waiting for me.'[4]

This is an honest and beautiful self-portrayal. The old urge for salvation is gone, and that is good; but Sartre has found no new direction. Disillusioned by the limited power of words but still lost, he 'doesn't know what to do with himself'. 'I've given up the office but not the frock: I still write. What else can I do?'[5] Disillusioned, he would continue to write but without conviction. He had changed, and yet not. The confession continued, slowly coming full circle: 'It's a habit, and besides, it's my profession. For a long time, I took my pen for a sword; I now know we're powerless. No matter. I write and will keep writing books; they're needed; all the same, they do serve some purpose. Culture doesn't save anything or anyone, it doesn't justify. But it's a product of man: he projects himself into it, he recognizes himself in it; that critical mirror alone offers him his image. Moreover, that old, crumbling structure, my imposture, is also my character: one gets rid of a neurosis, one doesn't get cured of one's self. Though they are worn out, blurred, humiliated, thrust aside, ignored, all of the child's traits are still to be found in the quinquagenarian. Most of the time they lie low, they bide their time; at the first moment of inattention, they rise up and emerge, disguised; I claim sincerely to be writing only for my time, but my present notoriety annoys me; it's not glory, since I'm alive, and yet that's enough to belie my old dreams; could it be that I still harbour them secretly? I have, I think,

4. M, pp. 210-11; W, pp. 252-53.
5. M, p. 211; W, p. 253.

adapted them: since I've lost the chance of dying unknown, I sometimes flatter myself that I'm being misunderstood in my lifetime. Griselda's not dead. Pardaillan still inhabits me. So does Strogoff. I'm answerable only to them, who are answerable only to God, and I don't believe in God. So try to figure it out. As for me, I can't and I sometimes wonder whether I'm not playing winner loses and not trying too hard to stamp out my one-time hopes so that everything will be restored to me a hundredfold. In that case, I would be Philoctetes; that magnificent and stinking cripple gave everything away unconditionally, including his bow; but we can be sure that he's secretly waiting for his reward.'[6]

Sartre has suddenly shifted direction. Honesty has given way to evasion. He had changed, he said, by losing the illusion of salvation through writing. Now, without that illusion, he would write on, out of habit. Nevertheless, little as writing accomplished, it still offered people a critical mirror. It was useful. Now came the turn: 'though they are worn out, blurred, humiliated, thrust aside, ignored, all of the child's traits are still to be found in the quinquagenarian'. Perhaps the old dreams were still there — Sartre recalled his childhood heroes Griselda, Pardaillan, Strogoff and Philoctetes. 'So try to figure it out. As for me, I can't . . .' Indeed. The illusions seemed to have dried up on one level but still inhabited him on another. Lost, he would keep on; disillusioned, he would not change. He had understood himself, not so deeply as to affect anything. Self-critical, he resorted nevertheless to what he had once regarded as the ultimate excuse: 'character'. He had confessed, performed a psychoanalytical self-analysis, criticized himself — all without being able to change.

One need not await the book's conclusion to understand this. Beautiful and sensitive as it is, *Les Mots* was bad psychotherapy. It presented self-revelation but reaffirmed what it revealed, in tone and style as much as in its conclusions. Let us consider this famous passage: 'Every man has his natural place; its altitude is determined neither by pride nor by value: childhood decides. Mine is a sixth floor in Paris with a view overlooking the roofs. For a long time I suffocated in the valleys; the plains overwhelmed me: I crawled along the planet Mars, the heaviness crushed me. I had only to climb a molehill for joy to come rushing back: I would return to my symbolic sixth

6. M, pp. 211-12; W, pp. 254-55.

floor; there I would once again breathe the rarefied air of belles lettres; the Universe would rise in tiers at my feet and all things would
humbly beg for a name; to name the thing was both to create and take
it. Without this fundamental illusion I would never have written.

'Today, April 22, 1963, I am correcting this manuscript on the
tenth floor of a new building: through the open window I see a
cemetery, Paris, the blue hills of Saint Cloud. That shows my
obstinacy. Yet everything has changed. Had I wished as a child to
deserve this lofty position, my fondness for pigeon-houses would have
to be regarded as a result of ambition, of vanity, as a compensation
for my shortness. But it's not that; it wasn't a matter of climbing up
my sacred tree: I *was* there, I refused to come down from it. It was not
a matter of setting myself above human beings: I wanted to live in the
ether among the aerial simulacra of Things. Later, far from clinging
to balloons, I made every effort to sink: I had to wear leaden soles.
With luck, I occasionally happened, on naked sands, to brush against
submarine species whose names I had to invent. At other times,
nothing doing: an irresistible lightness kept me on the surface. In the
end, my altimeter went out of order. I am at times a bottle imp, at
others a deep-sea diver, often both together, which is as it should be
in our trade. I live in the air out of habit, and I poke about down below without much hope.'[7]

So, Sartre now lived above the real world, in the 'rarefied air of
belles lettres'. It is easy to be so taken by such unaccustomed glimpses
of the great man's inner thought as not to notice the evasion
perpetrated in this passage. It was evasive first of all in its wordiness.
Sartre presented one metaphor after another: 'valleys-plains', 'Mars',
'molehills', 'pigeon-houses', 'sacred tree', 'naked sands', 'submarine
species', 'a bottle imp', 'a deep-sea diver'. I am unreal, trying to live
above the world, he admitted. But the insight lost most of its effect as
it moved through this profusion of words. Moreover, the style and
tone of the passage converted the insight into something merely
literary. Self-understanding itself became de-realized, transformed
into the imaginary. The revelation that he 'dwells' six floors above
Paris took place not on the solid ground of real feeling, but rather
— six floors above Paris. Sartre's conclusion was not a resolve to
change himself or a moment of self-knowledge, but a precious literary
finis, a self-indulgent device.

7. M, pp. 47-58; W, pp. 60-61 (translation changed).

This was representative of the tone of the entire book. Childhood pain was rendered light and airy, a deep and brutal disconnection from reality presented with enormous charm. Sartre's sense of loss was there, but not his suffering, his sense of unreality but not his alienation.[8] A tortured, contradictory childhood became beautiful, gilded by imagination. *Les Mots* was a search for self which became an escape from self into art, as the source of his writer's neurosis itself became literary. It may be that 'the reader has realized that I loathe my childhood and whatever has survived of it.'[9] But if so, it is only by indications, never by the direct impress of feeling, much less through practical demonstration.

'What Else Can I Do?'

The radical self-criticism implied in *Les Mots* was not adequately articulated or pursued, and was actually cancelled by the text itself. Self-understanding became a means of self-evasion. Yet this work also marked a key reversal of one of Sartre's life-long themes. Why, in 1963, did he still write? Because although 'they are worn out, blurred, humiliated, thrust aside, ignored, all of the child's traits are still to be found in the quinquagenarian'—inscribed in his *character*. Sartre now reinstated what he had so strongly opposed in *La Transcendance de l'ego* and his early theories of the theatre. This was his most radical departure yet from a psychology, a philosophy, and a theory of engaged literature constructed on the assumption that humans were sheer activity, and could change almost at will. His autobiography confirmed, in relation to himself, what he had already suggested in the character of Franz: the whole book explained what had shaped him into the person he could not help but be.

We cannot change at will, and our efforts to change the world produce forces which in turn control us. In the thirties and forties, when he saw the world as an implacable given, Sartre espoused an optimism whose source was his concept of freedom. He had now implicitly abandoned this. His new awareness of the ways in which people became trapped *both* by internal and by external structures was to

8. Adorno has suggested that the entire body of Sartre's committed works likewise failed to arouse the emotions it talked about ('Commitment', *New Left Review*, 87-88, pp. 79, 86).

9. M, p. 137; W, p. 164.

find expression in the immense project that now lay ahead — the biography of Flaubert.

Towards a Breakdown

At the same time, this profound revision foreshadowed a breakdown in Sartre's thought. By the early 1960s his *Critique* lay abandoned, he had stopped writing plays, and had failed to find a satisfactory posture as political essayist. His politico-intellectual project seemed to be running aground. He had now perceived our fundamental unfreedom; and this admission of the depth of our social and psychological conditioning and the force of our character was bound to wreak havoc on a literary practice originally premissed on the translucency of consciousness and a perpetual readiness for change. Sartre had taken his pen for a sword, an instrument that could produce change through the recognitions that it compelled; once the accessibility and translucency of consciousness were supplanted by the more resistant substance of *character,* the power of the pen was no longer evident.

Sartre was unable to resolve this crisis by transforming his thought. Instead, not long after the publication of *Les Mots,* the tensions at the heart of his thought exploded. The dualism of imagination and reality, the separation between sixth floor and ground floor, between individual and society, existentialism and Marxism, became virtually absolute. Persistently questioning the role of radical intellectual, Sartre finally decided, after May 1968, that *as intellectual* he had no political role at all, and high up in his study, engrossed himself in the ultimate apolitical work, a colossal imaginary reconstruction of an 'imaginary man'.

2

Before and After 1968

It would not have been easy, however, to detect any hint of crisis. Contat and Rybalka list even more entries for the eight years after *Les Mots* than for the prolific eight-year period preceding it.[1] Sartre was intensely busy writing essays on politics and on culture, theoretical works, and giving interviews. He also engaged in extended activity, writing on behalf of Arab-Israeli rapprochement, the Vietnamese, and the French near-revolution of May 1968. Above all, he continued his monumental labours on Flaubert.

One peculiarity of this period is worth noting, however: from *Les Mots* to *L'Idiot de la famille* (1971), Sartre published no major work. One minor dramatic project, *Les Troyennes,* a brilliant essay on Patrice Lumumba published at the time of *Les Mots,* and three lengthy lectures on intellectuals given in Japan in 1966, were his most significant works of these years. In the previous eight years, he had written two long plays, *Nekrassov* and *Les Sequestrés d'Altona;* two book-length groups of political essays, on Hungary and Cuba; an extensive manuscript on Merleau-Ponty, most of which remains unpublished; and the massive *Critique,* including *Question de méthode.* Where, then, was Sartre's energy diverted after 1963? For the most part, obviously, it went into the study of Flaubert. But *L'Idiot de la famille* was a significant departure from the main line of Sartre's life's work. In it, he no longer took his pen for a sword. He sought not to move or to change his audience, but only to understand a single human being, Gustave Flaubert.

1. See CRW, 55/265-62/382 (118 entries), and 63/383-70/539 (157 entries), pp.305-569.

The Mid-1960s: Sartre on Lumumba

The writings of the mid-1960s revealed this major shift in the making. Sartre's 1963 essay on Patrice Lumumba — to focus on a single example — was unlike any other of his political writings. Its aim was to describe and to analyse, not to convince its readers or to make them feel or act in a particular way. Unlike the Cuban writings, Sartre's essay on Lumumba did not betray its author at every step. It was free from his faults: the customary Sartrean rhetoric, the extended metaphors, the moralizing and convoluted philosophical digressions, the verbiage and overdramatizations, the personalizing intrusions and frequent false starts. Unlike his prefaces to books by Albert Memmi and Franz Fanon, the essay did not even try to put the reader on the spot. Sartre had a single, carefully controlled purpose in writing it: to lay bare the complex and contradictory situation in which Patrice Lumumba failed, and had to fail, to unify the Congo against its own centrifugal forces as well as its former masters.

Drawn from the countryside and into a religious education, Westernized and then brought into government service, Lumumba was an *evolué,* one of a small number of Congolese who had been allowed to rise to assist the Belgians to govern. An elite among blacks, these *petit-bourgeois* officials knew only too clearly that their rise was limited by the very whites who had made it possible: the highest-ranking native received one-half the salary of a white official. Having no base except among other *evolués,* Lumumba could become a national leader because he took the ideology of his class seriously, rather than using it as a cloak for his own personal interests. He thought and spoke in terms of the rights and needs of *all* Congolese. His class of government officials wanted a strong centralized government which *it* would direct; Lumumba, like Robespierre, became a partisan of centralism because he saw in it the Congo's only hope of controlling the tribal and economic forces that threatened to cripple it. Only the political unity of the Congo would guarantee Congolese control of the national economy. Otherwise, the country would continue to be owned by and governed in the interests of foreign capital.

Sartre showed how, lucid and blind at the same time, Lumumba understood precisely what political structures were needed for Congolese control of the Congo but could not see that the social conditions for such structures were completely absent. A 'revolutionary without

a revolution', he was handed power by the Belgians without having
led a successful struggle against them. In a series of rich analyses,
Sartre compared the Congo's situation with successful anti-colonial
movements elsewhere. In Algeria or Vietnam the struggle had created a powerful national unity in advance of independence; the guerrilla forces developed leadership cadres who were able to step in immediately once the foreigners had been ousted. But the Belgians had
neither educated a native elite for eventual rule, as the British did in
their colonies, nor been displaced by an organized native movement.
Lumumba had no cadres at his disposal; he was merely the leader of
the largest party, having a parliamentary majority and enormous
powers of persuasion. Most of his class saw its power as based on
managing the politically independent Congo for the foreign trusts;
tribal leaders wanted a federation of autonomous regions; the
Belgians encouraged the secesssion of their key economic base,
Katanga.

Receiving political power from the Belgians on July 1, 1960, Lumumba was alone and lost, a hostage in his own capital. Eighty years
of Belgian colonialism had so weakened the country, Sartre argued,
that the Congo's well-being—understood by Lumumba alone—had
no chance of prevailing over the neo-colonialist scheme. Taking over
at 'degree zero' of Congolese history, Lumumba could have succeeded only if his forces had been sufficient to sustain a dictatorship. But
in addition to the centrifugal forces already in play, class divisions appeared the moment independence was granted: Lumumba was
unable even to keep order.

Lumumba's 'Jacobinism', which consisted in asking each group to
sacrifice its interests for the unity of the Congo, was doomed from the
start. Why then did this leader without a mass following, too weak to
realize his vision, have to be killed? In a poignant analysis Sartre concluded that Lumumba alive represented the vigorous rejection of the
neo-colonialist solution. For all of Africa as well as for the Congo, he
represented an uncompromising attachment to black independence.
His assassination removed a possible rallying point in the struggle
ahead, and sealed the alliance between imperialism and the black *petit
bourgeoisie*. 'Dead, Lumumba ceases to be a person to become all of
Africa, with its will to unity, its multiplicity of social and political
regimes, its cleavages, its discords, its strength, and its impotence;
unable to be the hero of pan-Africanism, he will be its martyr. His

story has brought to light, for everyone, the profound link between independence, unity, and the struggle against the trusts.'[2]

'La Pensée politique de Patrice Lumumba' was one of Sartre's best political essays and at the same time, paradoxically, the most scholarly in tone. In it, Sartre seemed to have become comfortable in a new role: not instigating action, but describing reality. Sartre's earlier political writings seemed to strain to change reality in part because their underlying concepts themselves lacked a sure connection with reality. We have seen this thought-in-distance try to seize what it lacked by becoming hyper-activist. Only when, as in this essay, he gave up trying to use words to *change* reality, did he find an adequate way of relating to it. Here he sought only to unveil reality, and, in doing so, accomplished an impressive intellectual feat — he depicted the situation in all its complexity and contradictions, leaving his readers to contemplate the events and their significance and to act as they thought fit. Future readers looking for information about Hungary may not read Sartre; but when they want to learn about Lumumba, neo-colonialism, and the Congo, they will certainly read this essay: for this product of his disillusionment as a political writer was the best of his political writings.

These were the years of the doldrums in France — the years of the Gaullist consolidation of power, the modernization of French industry,[3] and the prostration of the Left. The Communist vote fell from nearly 26% in 1956 to less than 19% in 1958. Even the partial resurgence of 1962 gave the PCF only forty-one out of the 482 seats in the Assembly.

Abroad, meanwhile, between the end of the Algerian War and 1968 the Left experienced an uninterrupted series of setbacks. Already in 1961, Lumumba had been murdered, foreshadowing a worldwide imperialist counter-offensive: the missile crisis of 1962 humiliated both revolutionary Cuba and its Soviet protectors; in 1964 the Algerian Thermidor ousted Ben Bella and turned the revolution

2. 'La Pensée politique de Patrice Lumumba', *Situations*, V, p.252; trans. Helen R. Lane, 'Introduction'. *Lumumba Speaks: The Speeches and Writings of Patrice Lumumba, 1958-1961*, Boston 1972, p.51 (I have used my own translation).

3. Sartre himself acknowledged that in these years the Malthusianism he describes in *Les Communistes et la paix* was replaced by neo-capitalism. See his 1964 note to this essay in *Situations*, VI, p.384 as well as Burnier, *Choice of Action*, n.6, pp.94-95. Sartre's political discouragement in these years is shown in his lack of interest in bringing his analysis up to date.

to the right; Goulart was overthrown in Brazil; 1965 saw the prompt American suppression of the Dominican Revolution, the fall of Nkrumah in Ghana, the bombing of North Vietnam and enormous American escalation of the war in the South, and the counter-revolutionary holocaust in Indonesia. During these years too, the Sino-Soviet dispute exploded into public view, disorienting the Left still further; in 1967, Che Guevara died in an effort to bring a Castro-style movement to Bolivia, and the colonels took power in Greece.

The essay on Lumumba reflected Sartre's continuing involvement in the face of these discouraging trends, as did his perceptive interviews on the French Left and the 1965 elections, his refusal to lecture in the United States in protest at the American escalation in Vietnam, and his expressions of support for the Constitutionalists in the Dominican Republic and condemnation of the violations of human rights in Algeria. The revealing interviews on France expressed his sense of the Left's sickness in 1965, his mistrust of a wholly electoral strategy, especially without a common programme, and his prescient hope for France.[4] They also expressed his new sense of the limitations of intellectuals: 'it is not we who will give birth to a new Popular Front, or a "federation" of the Left, it is not we who will bring about a regroupment of workers' organizations which will restore their political effectiveness. Our work is to expose the real problems of the working class.'[5] His tough-minded pessimism about the immediate future, his sense that the Left needed not to be reorganized but recreated, was tempered by his appreciation of the importance of the joint Socialist-Communist campaign for Mitterrand, and his urgency about 'the enormous work to be done' by the Left.[6]

Sartre's justification of his refusal to go through with his planned lectures at Cornell University showed less percipience and greater pessimism. Echoing his overly negative conclusion that during the Algerian War the Left's 'opposition served no purpose',[7] Sartre expressed the belief that the 'inconspicuous minority of intellectuals' in America who opposed the war were 'totally impotent'.[8] While he res-

---

4. See 'Achever la gauche, ou la guérir?' and 'Le Choc en retour', *Situations*, VIIII, pp.164-65, 171.
5. Ibid., pp.166-67.
6. Ibid., p.174.
7. ' "Il n'y a plus de dialogue possible",' *Situations*, VIII., p.15.
8. Ibid., p.16.

pected the courage of those who struggled in a country 'entirely conditioned by the myths of imperialism and anti-Communism', the American activist seemed to him, unfortunately, the 'wretched of the earth'.

The Russell Tribunal: In the Struggle or Above It?

Political and personal disillusionment, absorption in a writer's
biography and a new sense of his own limitations as writer, and a
grim, exaggerated pessimism about the prospects for change in
France and America—these were the first fruits of *Les Mots* and the
crisis it reflected, and at the same time Sartre's understandable response to the mid-1960s.

Beneath the surface of events, however, a totally contrary historical
direction was being prepared. In France, its first signs were the steps
towards consolidation and resurgence of the Left electorally: Mitterrand's surprisingly close run against de Gaulle in 1965, and the
Left's recovery in the parliamentary elections two years later. Over-
seas, and far more important if more distant, civil-rights agitation in
the American South quickly became a broad national movement in
the early 1960s, catalysing the student movement after 1964 and an
unprecedented wave of protest against the Vietnam War the next
year. The heroic resistance of the Vietnamese against the overwhelming financial and military might of the United States soon became a
worldwide cause and inspiration.

As the war escalated and the anti-war movement grew, Sartre did
not long remain pessimistic or passive. In November 1966, he was
elected executive president of the International Tribunal Against War
Crimes in Vietnam, initiated by Bertrand Russell, which sought to
pass judgment on the United States for its actions in Vietnam.
Although aware that this undertaking could be criticized for its *'petit-
bourgeois* legalism', Sartre justified it precisely as an appeal to the
'ethico-juridical structure of all historical action' and the 'very large
fringe of the middle class' whose eyes might be opened by such
legalism.[9] Sartre involved himself fully in the Tribunal's work in
1967, travelling to Sweden and Denmark for its sessions. As
executive president he was charged with setting out the grounds for
the Tribunal's verdict of genocide in December of that year. The

9. 'The Crime', *Situations*, VIII, p.35.

result was one of his most compelling essays, 'Le Génocide'. Brief, lucid, controlled and direct, the essay traced the roots of genocide in imperialism and the modern bourgeois industrial state, as well as in America's specific neo-colonial policy. Sartre pointed out the two alternatives built into American policy in Vietnam: genocide or withdrawal. 'Le Génocide' was a subdued and carefully reasoned essay. As in his study of Lumumba, Sartre kept himself in the background and rendered an objective analysis, only this time in the service of a direct political goal. to mobilize public opinion against the American presence in Vietnam.

However this first major return to politico-intellectual action since the Algerian War was marked by the shifts that Sartre had been undergoing in the intervening years. His essay, which expressed the Tribunal's official judgment, displayed the same ambiguity as the Tribunal itself. It was, above all, an excellent Marxist analysis, partisan to the core, of indiscriminate mass killing in Vietnam. But this gave its appeals to the Geneva Convention of 1948 a rather lame ring: the radical nature of the argument tended to contradict its appeal to bourgeois legalism.[10] It is striking how closely the posture of the Tribunal resembled the tensions which we have seen throughout Sartre's political career, and which were now becoming explosive. Wholly committed to the Vietnamese struggle against the Americans and their allies, the Tribunal also sought to pass judgment on the Americans from a legal position above the struggle. An activist project, it nevertheless based itself on notions of objectivity and universality more familiar in those who claim to be beyond partisanship. Certainly anti-war activists, no matter how much they might favour the NLF, were right 'to apply its own laws to capitalist imperialism'.[11] But the Tribunal's concluding opinion on genocide was hardly calculated to win over anyone who was not already committed. The first French version of 'Le Génocide' appeared, after all, in *Les Temps Modernes,* the English in *New Left Review,* and in the United States in *Ramparts*: journals of the Left all.

The tension between the Tribunal's partisan origins and intentions and its universalist claims corresponded to a growing divergence be-

---

10. 'Le Génocide', *Situations,* VIII; trans. 'On Genocide', *Against the Crime of Silence: Proceedings of the Russell International War Crimes Tribunal,* ed. John Duffet, New York 1968.

11. 'Le Crime', p.30.

tween Sartre the political acitivist and Sartre the intellectual. *Les Troyennes,* first performed in March 1965, was a vaguely anti-imperialist adaption of Euripides which prompted the audience to condemn all war — something Sartre himself clearly did not do. Given this and also the fact that the play had already been revived in another adaptation during the Algerian war, one is left to wonder at Sartre's purpose in offering a new version. Justifying it, in a discussion which was politically quite thin, he engrossed himself with the stylistic and linguistic problems of making a Greek play 'work' in contemporary France. It is obvious, then, that *Les Troyennes* was scarcely a political project at all, although Sartre felt compelled to justify it. Compared with the rest of his plays, it seemed like an interesting excursion into the 'perennial'.

Sartre's Japanese lectures of fall, 1966 developed the theme of intellectual engagement from a more solidly Marxist perspective than that of his 1947 writings.[12] But he retained his old formal demand based on the *universal* character of intellectual activity (which, he now argued, became diverted towards particular goals in this society) and attempted to demonstrate how the intellectual *should* be engaged. Sartre seemed to be broadly recapitulating and extending his earlier deduction — until he turned to speak specifically about writers. There, in a rather apolitical analysis of literature as the 'singular universal', he abandoned *Qu'est-ce que la littérature?*, discarding its conception of prose as a practical instrument. This conception, which had underlain that of engagement, was now replaced by a new emphasis on the singular universal, which was both profoundly individual and profoundly socio-historical.

By the end of the last lecture, Sartre had traced a new and promising theoretical path, but lost the sense of why this universal being, the writer, might or should become engaged. In fact, he separated the six activist political demands that he had initially proposed to lay before intellectuals from his new fascination with writing as the singular universal. The first two lectures moved in a world totally different from the third. Politics and writing were becoming separate activities for Sartre. Participating in a conference in 1964 entitled 'Que peut la littérature?', he had expressed himself elusively about the writer's political role (returning to the vague idea of mirroring one's

12. 'Plaidoyer pour les intellectuels', *Situations,* VIII; trans. John Matthews, 'A Plea for Intellectuals', *Between Existentialism and Marxism,* London 1974.

times);[13] in an interview on intellectuals and politics given early in 1968, he reiterated the first theme of the Japanese lectures and was quite precise and activist in his responses.[14] Sartre was not changing in these years; he was merely presenting two increasingly separate sides of himself. The activist intellectual on the one hand and, on the other, the writer, creator of the singular universal.

May 1968: A New Left

The separation was not yet complete. By 1972, when his Japanese lectures were published in French, Sartre felt compelled to preface them with a note saying that the intellectual, *qua* intellectual, 'remains objectively an enemy of the people'. He concluded, equally remarkably: 'today I have finally understood that the intellectual cannot remain at the stage of unhappy consciousness (characterized by idealism and inefficacy): he must resolve his own problem — or, if you like, negate his *intellectual moment* in order to try to achieve a new *popular* status.'[15] In other words, the intellectual must subvert his role as intellectual and instead serve the masses. What caused this drastic change of perspective and what did it mean?

The change took place after 1968, one of the most convulsive years of the century and certainly the most turbulent since the world entered the age of electronic communication. In Vietnam, the new year began with the Tet offensive; faced with tremendous opposition, Lyndon Johnson stepped down from the presidency of the United States. Martin Luther King and Robert Kennedy were assassinated; the United States seethed with black rebellion and anti-war demonstrations; and students took over Columbia University in one of the most dramatic actions of the American student movement. In China the Cultural Revolution continued with tidal force; the Prague Spring seemed ready to give birth to 'socialism with a human face'. The Soviet Union invaded Czechoslovakia; and while the whole world watched on television, demonstrators were clubbed down outside the Democratic Convention in Chicago as, inside, Eugene McCarthy was denied the presidential nomination.

13. Yves Buin, *Que peut la littérature?*, Paris 1965, pp.107-127.
14. Interview with J.C. Garot, *Le Point* (Brussels); trans. J.A. Underwood and John Calder, 'Revolution and the Intellectual', *Politics and Literature*, London 1973.
15. Prefatory note to 'Plaidoyer pour les intellectuals', *Situations*, VIII, p.374; 'A Plea for Intellectuals', p.227.

For Sartre, the most spectacular event of all was the near-revolution in France. A new Left exploded into existence at Nanterre and the Sorbonne and catalysed a movement which nearly overthrew de Gaulle: perhaps ten million workers, taking inspiration from the students, spontaneously took over their work-places and declared a general strike. Sartre involved himself wholeheartedly from the first days onwards, doing all he could to encourage the students and win support for them. Now in his sixties, Sartre spent a night at the barricades, spoke before a tumultuous packed house at the Sorbonne, declared his old colleague Raymond Aron unfit to teach because of his attack on the students, and humbly interviewed the student leader, Daniel Cohn-Bendit. Once again, selflessly, and with great courage and commitment, Sartre pitched himself into a major historical movement. The Left that he had been working, writing, and waiting for since the late forties had suddenly materialized. For the first time, he was in the midst of a movement embodying the very things that drew him to socialism. He had observed the Popular Front from a distance, experienced the Resistance as a partisan writer and a lone committed individual, been drawn to the side of the Communists by his outrage at the government's response to the Ridgeway riots, involved himself totally in the struggle to keep de Gaulle from power and to end the Algerian war, and enthusiastically sponsored the Cuban revolution. But now he was in the midst of a movement that demanded everything.

This movement was profoundly revolutionary and democratic, sought to draw all its militants into debate and discussion, and was bound to no pre-established doctrine. It showed enormous energy, optimism and force of imagination. It was thoroughly anti-elitist and demanded power on every level. At the end of his interview with Cohn-Bendit, Sartre warmly welcomed the radical break signalled by the May upsurge: 'What is interesting about your action is that it is putting imagination in power. You have a limited imagination, just like everyone else, but you have a lot more ideas than your elders. We were educated in such a way that we have a precise idea of what is possible and what is not. A professor will say, "Get rid of exams? Never. You can change them, but you can't get rid of them!" Why? Because he has been taking exams for half his life. The working class has often imagined new ways of struggling, but always in relation to the precise situation it found itself in. In 1935 it invented the occupation of the factories because that was the only weapon it had to consolidate and exploit its victory at the polls. You have a much more fertile imagination, as the slogans we are reading on the Sorbonne walls show. Something has come out of you which is confounding, shaking up, rejecting everything which made our society what it is today. It's what I would call an extension of the field of possibilities.'[16]

Sartre, Communism and the New Left

As the movement developed in the months and years that followed, Sartre consolidated his agreement with the main political lines of the new Left. This entailed a definitive break with the worlds of French and Soviet Communism, provoked by the Party's hostility to the students and its cautious behaviour in the face of a near-revolution and confirmed by the Soviet invasion of Czechoslovakia that summer. Able for the first time to view events from the standpoint of a movement to the left of official Communism. Sartre now gave full vent to his disillusionment with the Soviet regime, 'which is not a socialist regime', and to the PCF, which is 'not a revolutionary party'.[17]

Sartre's essay of 1970 denouncing the Soviet invasion of Czechoslovakia was entirely different from his condemnation of the Hungarian intervention. He no longer addressed himself hopefully to the Soviet leaders as comrades caught in an obsolete logic issuing from the original tasks of building socialism: they were now cast as agents of the 'Thing'. 'The machine cannot be repaired; the peoples of Eastern Europe must seize hold of it and destroy it.'[18] He saw Soviet intervention as inevitable, given the nature of the regime 'and the relations of production which generated it and have in turn been reinforced and petrified by it.'[19] But he no longer laboured to derive this inevitability from the exigencies of Soviet history: his concern was to show how this system of imposed socialism had been internalized by

16. 'L'Imagination au pouvoir: Entretien de Jean-Paul Sartre avec Daniel Cohn-Bendit', *Le Nouvel Observateur*, special supplement, May 20, 1968; trans. B.R. Brewster, *The French Student Revolt*, New York 1968. Sartre's conclusion, omitted from the English volume, is translated in CRW, 68/489, pp.526-27.

17. *On a raison de se révolter*, pp.347, 42.

18. 'Le Socialisme qui venait du froid', *Situations*, IX, pp.275-76; 'Czechoslovakia: The Socialism that Came in from the Cold', *Between Existentialism and Marxism*, p.117.

19. Ibid., p.275; p.117.

the Czech and Slovak peoples and how it began to be sloughed off during 1968. With great force and clarity, and making substantive use of the notion of seriality, he described how 'under the reign of fetishized production every real man appears to himself, in his simple daily experience, as an obstacle to the construction of socialism and can evade the crime of living only by suppressing himself altogether.'[20] 'Le Socialisme qui venait du froid' ranked with the study of Lumumba as one of Sartre's best political essays. The contortions of the 1950s essays were replaced by a powerful and passionate political lucidity. Sartre's clear oppositional stance released him from the constricting alternatives of comradely criticism and anti-Communism. He was now able to take an unequivocal position, against 'the old ossified structures of our society' and in favour of a revolution which 'does not give birth to *that sort of socialism*.'[21]

Sartre's alignment with *gauchisme* revitalized his earlier criticism of the French Communists: for their reformism, their authoritarianism, their fear of popular movements outside their control, and the doctrinaire character of their thought. He also rediscovered other old attitudes in his new activist postures: his hostility to elections as confirming the voters' serial passivity, his understanding of conventional authority as based on power alienated from its subjects, his rejection of bourgeois propriety, his acceptance of violence and illegality, and his unending willingness to contest and redirect himself. Violence, morality, spontaneity — these were the characteristics that attracted Sartre, after 1969, to the Maoists, in whom he claimed to recognize 'the only revolutionary force capable of adapting to new forms of the class struggle in a period of organized capitalism'.[22] Coexistent with these terms was the suggestion that political ideas and tactics should not be brought to the masses from the outside, as Lenin's *What Is To Be Done?* had implied, but that revolutionaries should learn from the masses.[23] Sartre rallied to the *gauchistes'* emphasis on democracy, their belief in the creative power of ordinary people, their desire to avoid a hierarchical movement and a hierarchical socialism. 'I am for you', he declared to the Maoists in December,

20. Ibid., p.248; p.98.
21. Ibid., p.276; p.117.
22. 'Les Maos en France', *Situations*, X, p.47; trans. Paul Auster and Lydia Davis, 'The Maoists in France', *Life/Situations*, p.171.
23. See *On a raison de se révolter*, pp.147-60.

1972, 'because at least apparently, you want to prepare a society which will not be founded on the auto-domestication of man, but on his sovereignty.'[24]

Sartre did not wholly adapt to the ultra-left politics of the French Maoists — although he came dangerously close to doing so.[25] One of the most charged moments in the collection of discussions, *On a raison de se révolter*, came when he forcefully defended Israel's right to exist against his young interlocutor's reflexive anti-Zionism.[26] He remained capable of penetrating political insight and argument, as in his attacks on bourgeois law;[27] and *On a raison de se révolter* exhibited such intellectual and political vitality that one writer has seen it as the turning point in Sartre's thought, marking a final break with individualism and a new, though belated, recognition of the centrality of collective processes.[28] Yet Sartre seemed only to make his way back to a more grounded version of his earlier idealism. History was no less callous with human hopes in the 1970s than it had been in the 1950s. And in these years Sartre, encouraged first by May 1968 and then by the workers' takeover of the Lip watch factory in 1973, gave himself more wholeheartedly to hope — and illusion — than to reality.

To counsel, as he did, a boycott of presidential and legislative elections was to opt out of the only arena understood as political by the vast majority of people. And how could it responsibly be argued that a Left electoral victory would bring greater dangers for the far Left than a victory of the Right?[29] Sartre's judgments on such issues were gravely unbalanced. He ended his thirty-year relationship with the Communists by declaring a plague on all established houses. But the PCF was as much a reality of the French Left in the 1970s as in the 1950s.

Sartre was not wrong to attack the PCF from the Left; but his conversations with Victor and Gavi failed to make any realistic assessment of the balance of forces, of the social basis for their new kind of

24. Ibid., p.141.
25. See CRW, 68/488, pp.523/26.
26. See *On a raison de se révolter*, pp.295-298. In 1969 Sartre called for a peace based on Israeli evacuation of the territories occupied in 1967, Arab recognition of Israeli sovereignty, and settlement of the Palestinian refugee problem. See 'Interview', *Situations*, VIII.
27. See 'Justice et l'Etat', *Situations*, X; 'Justice and the State', *Life/Situations*.
28. See the review article by Douglas Kellner, *Telos*, 22 (Winter 1974-75)
29. *On a raison de se révolter*, p.356.

politics, of the weight and effect of the Communists, of the actual chances for creating a new movement after the energy of May had been dissipated. This illuminating series of conversations dealt mostly with specific tactics and actions and with large principles, at the expense of long-range socialist strategy in relation to concrete historical trends. Sartre failed to understand the deep limitations that his choice entailed: his attempt to ascribe his own pessimism to a 'character trait' was symptomatic of political error.

Take to the Streets

Moreover, the reshaping of his politics was overshadowed by the self-willed inversion of his role as a political intellectual. When the long-hoped-for Left emerged, his first impression, 'forgotten afterwards, found again in '69, was that their movement was directed against me.'[30] In 1969 he was invited to a meeting of students and professors to plan action against government repression. He was abruptly made aware that the movement's anti-elitism meant to dismantle the very 'star-system' of which he was a leading member: 'There was a room filled with students and profs and, at the table, next to me, the same mixture. It was a new meeting for me: there were things to decide, and not simply to say — as at the time of the war in Algeria: "Long live the Algerians!" "Down with French government policy!" On the table, in my place, there was a word on a sheet of paper: "Sartre, be brief".'[31] His audience did not listen very attentively, and when he had finished speaking about the problem of youth in general, a few of them booed while some applauded politely. Sartre began to understand that he had nothing to say at this meeting because he was neither professor nor student. He had been brought in, rather clumsily, as a 'star'. Already in 1968, the striking image of Sartre interviewing Cohn-Bendit reflected a growing belief that the day of the classical intellectual was over, or as he later put it, that the time had come for intellectuals to 'contest themselves as intellectuals'.[32] But as he absorbed the experience of May, he decided that the intellectual should first 'suppress himself as intellectual' in order then to put his skills 'directly at the service of the masses'.[33] Did Sartre intend to undo the

30. Ibid., p.82.
31. Ibid., pp.65-66.
32. 'L'Ami du peuple', *Situations*, VIII, p.461.
33. Ibid., pp.467

politico-intellectual synthesis he has been struggling to achieve since the Second World War? This was certainly the implication of his 1972 note to his Japanese lectures of six years before. This new posture was most sharply and provocatively defined in his interview with John Gerassi in 1971.

Sartre here gave the simplest answer yet to his constant question: what should the intellectual do? — he should act. To be a radical intellectual was above all to be committed to put oneself bodily in opposition to the system. In conversation with Gerassi he reviewed his own political history going back to the Occupation and describing his shifting relations with the Communist party thereafter. The Algerian and Vietnamese wars had convinced him of the need to develop a movement to the left of the PCF; and by his own activity, he had helped to bring that new movement into being. 'But I was still a typical intellectual. That is, I did my work at my desk, and occasionally joined a parade in the streets or spoke at some meeting. Then May 1968 happened, and I understood that what the young were putting into question was not just capitalism, imperialism, the system, etc., but those of us who pretended to be against all that, as well. We can say that from 1940 to 1968 I was a left-wing intellectual (*un intellectuel de gauche*) and from 1968 on I became a leftist intellectual (*un intellectuel gauchiste*). The difference is one of action. A leftist intellectual is one who realizes that being an intellectual exempts him from nothing. He forsakes his privileges, or tries to, in actions. It is similar, I think, to what in the US you would call white-skin privileges. A white leftist intellectual, in America, I presume, understands that because he is white he has certain privileges which he must smash through direct action. Not to do so is to be guilty of murder of the blacks — just as much as if he actually pulled the triggers that killed, for example, Bobby Hutton, Fred Hampton, Mark Clark, and all the other Black Panthers murdered by the police, by the system.'[34]

In 1947 Sartre had declared that if words were sick, the writer must cure them. He was now saying that in order to be a radical intellectual, the writer must give up his customary intellectual projects. The role of theoretician to the movement, as he had asserted in an earlier

34. 'Sartre Accuses the Intellectuals of Bad Faith', *The New Times Magazine*, October 17, 1971, p.118.

interview, 'is a completely abandoned position'.[35] 'Today', he said to Gerassi, 'it is sheer bad faith, hence counter-revolutionary, for the intellectual to dwell on his own problems, instead of realizing that he is an intellectual because of the masses and through them: therefore, that he owes his knowledge to them and must be with them and in them: he must be dedicated to work for their problems, not his own.'[36]

One example of such self-sacrificing but exemplary activity was working to create revolutionary newspapers: 'I've lent my name to any revolutionary paper that requested it. Why? Well, of course, at the beginning it's part of the star system, letting my name be used to help launch such papers. Simone de Beauvoir, as you know, has done the same, but the objective is to collectivize these papers, to eliminate names altogether, and eventually to create newspapers written by masses who fight, the role of the editorial collective being only to help, technically, to put these papers together and publish them. Each time there is a seizure of a plant by workers, for example, our job is to make sure that it is the workers themselves who explain why they did it, what they felt and learned from it. Our job is to help them, etc., but never interpreting them, never telling them what they should say. Self-determination is not a ballot-box principle; it's a political act which must lead to power of the people.'[37] Directed at the masses, these newspapers must try to create 'a language that explains the necessary political realities in a way that everyone can understand.'[38] This meant a wholly new style of writing and distributing revolutionary newspapers: 'Say the paper talks about the seizure of a plant in Grenoble, in articles written by workers who participated in the seizure, well then, the militant distributor asks the worker in front of the Renault plant in Billancourt to read it, comment on the article, write about it or talk into a tape recorder, which then becomes an article for the next issue. The militant distributor, who is inevitably an intellectual at first, thus operates merely as a sort of mediator between the workers of Grenoble and Billancourt.'[39]

Prominent American intellectuals should act in the same way. 'It is very easy to denounce the war in Vietnam by signing petitions or

35. 'L'Ami du peuple', p.464.
36. 'Sartre Accuses the Intellectuals of Bad Faith', p.38.
37. Ibid., p.38.
38. Ibid., p.116.
39. Ibid., pp.116-118.

marching in a parade with 20,000 comrades. But it doesn't accomplish one-millionth what could be accomplished if all your big-name intellectuals went into the ghettos, into the Oakland port, to the war factories, and risked being manhandled by the roughs of the maritime union. In my view, the intellectual who does all his fighting from an office is counter-revolutionary today, no matter what he writes.'[40]

'Are you saying,' Gerassi inquired, 'that the responsibility of the intellectual is not intellectual?'

'Yes,' Sartre replied, 'it is in action. It is to put his status at the service of the oppressed directly. Just as the German intellectual who fled Hitler and talked about his anti-Nazism while he earned money writing scripts for Hollywood was as responsible for Hitler as the German who closed his eyes, just as the American intellectual who only denounces the Vietnam war and the fate of your political prisoners but continues to teach in a university that carries out war research and insists on law and order (which is a euphemism for letting the courts and police repress active dissenters) is as responsible for the murders and repression as is the Government and its institutions, so too, here in France, the intellectual who does not put his body as well as his mind on the line against the system is fundamentally supporting the system and should be judged accordingly.'[41]

Intellectual versus Political Activity

This, for all its extravagance, was not merely a provocative utterance of the moment. *On a raison de se révolter*, completed three years later, confirmed the main lines of Sartre's new approach. Part of a Gallimard series on *gauchisme* edited by Sartre, this volume was in the first place an activist project whose royalties were to go to *Libération*, the leftist daily then under Sartre's nominal directorship. The tone of its discussions echoed that of the Gerassi interview. Sartre's young friends treated him as an equal and no more. *They* after all were the activists, and although Sartre no longer seemed swept off his feet by them, their words predominated in the book. Sartre intervened often only at the instigation of Gavi or Victor, who frequently challenged and disagreed with him; his contributions were in many cases reflections on his political biography, his past work or his philosophical principles.

40. Ibid., p.118.
41. Ibid., p.119.

However, the book is far too casual. Interesting as the discussions often are, they are just as often superficial. Too many issues are abandoned, approached but never resolved: why the three are revolutionaries, how the struggle of women and homosexuals is part of the overall revolutionary struggle, how values are formed in the process of production, the character of the Arab-Israeli conflict. *On a raison de se révolter* gave little evidence of the penetration and tenacity with which Sartre normally addressed political issues. The purpose of the book was to present the new Left much as, twenty-five years earlier, a younger Sartre and his colleagues had presented the RDR. But unlike *Entretiens sur la politique,* which had been carefully framed to present a clear political line, *On a raison de se révolter* showed Sartre, Gavi, and Victor in conversation together, little concerned to appeal to their readers.

These discussions revealed certain of Sartre's strengths: his radicalism, his lack of affectation and willingness to become involved. Whatever the weakness of his new posture, it was to Sartre's credit that he retained his openness to historical developments, and listened to the new Left. Moreover, there was a definite consistency in his new approach to the role of the intellectual. It represented yet another attempt to resolve the central issue of his thought and life: what can the writer-intellectual do? In their own ways, this book and the interview with Gerassi restated the question first posed in his discovery of Husserl and studies of the imagination: how should thought be related to, make contact with, reality? Now, Sartre eagerly embraced what his work had always lacked: external demands, the sense of belonging to a collectivity. Until now in perpetual movement *towards* the world, Sartre as *intellectuel gauchiste* found himself already *in* the world. He responded readily to the Maoists in part because they put him in question. He spoke now, in relation to the Maoists and *Libération,* as he had never done in relation to *Les Temps Modernes,* as part of a collective, and professed a belief that could not have been more at variance with his entire life's work: 'I have always thought that to think in a group is better than to think separately.'[42]

After a quarter-century of politically committed writing, Sartre had made a drastic change of course: above all, he now held, intellectuals should act. In his interview with Gerassi he showed no concern for what their writing might or should do; he simply called upon them

42. *On a raison de se révolter,* p.170.

to leave their studies and go into the streets. Anything but concerned about the adequacy of thought in the real world, he appeared to deny that systematic thought was relevant to the real political demands of the time. If the author of the *Critique* had made a gargantuan effort to understand human history, to found and develop socialist theory, the *intellectuel gauchiste* now simply abandoned theory altogether, finding its missing terms *outside* thought, in the spontaneous flow of events. The *gauchiste* effort to reshape the role of the intellectual evoked a strong response in Sartre, but at his most vulnerable point and at a time of disillusionment. If his self-contestation reflected the great verve and originality of the extreme Left and the undiminished radicalism of Sartre himself, its polemical substance was nonetheless tantamount to a kind of nihilism, a sign that something had gone gravely wrong.

The Final Split

May 1968 reanimated Sartre's political hope and gave it a new outlet. But it also undid the politico-intellectual synthesis that he had struggled to develop since the Liberation, and subverted the persona that he now attacked at the *intellectuel de gauche*. May initiated the final phase of Sartre's career, as an anti-intellectual, unquenchably optimistic *gauchiste* emerged as the alter ego of the student of Flaubert. Sartre's failure to transcend his limits, repressed in spontaneist politics, returned in the form of a total separation between the writer and the activist. How did Sartre occupy himself henceforward? As he said to Gavi and Victor: 'I give to your action the greatest part of my time, but not all of it.'[43] As a militant among other militants, he tried to use his fame to gain support and publicity for the actions in which he was involved. He was indicted by the government again and again in the controversies surrounding the various leftist newspapers that he supported.

The point, he would say to other intellectuals, is to act. Our ideas are irrelevant to political action; we must seek to create situations in which the masses can experience *their own* ideas. Intellectuals are useful for their skills — to organize, to communicate, and hopefully, to simplify — and for their status — intellectuals carry more weight with the press and the police than do workers. The anti-intellectual demands that Sartre now laid before intellectuals were most starkly

43. Ibid., p.96.

posed in a conversation between himself and Herbert Marcuse, the text of which appeared in *Libération* in 1974:

SARTRE: The intellectual overtakes little by little another aspect of his existence (that is to say, the revolutionary intellectual) to the precise extent that the society progresses. The two go together: at the present time, for example, there is a certain relative progression, debatable, which consists of young workers, of young students towards that new Left of which we are speaking. The intellectuals are not the first ones who are there. They follow, they accompany.

MARCUSE: They follow whom?

SARTRE: They follow the young workers, the students who themselves envisage the new Left . . .

MARCUSE: The intellectual can always formulate or elaborate or concretize the goal of the progressive movement and the demands of the workers.

SARTRE: Yes! He can do it! But the workers can do it also. And they can do it better for themselves than the intellectuals.

MARCUSE: By themselves?

SARTRE: And for themselves! They can better express what they feel, what they think for themselves than if that was done by an intellectual. The intellectual, not always, but most of the time, is not the best one to formulate. He is the best one to discuss.

MARCUSE But not to formulate?

SARTRE: Not always. The intellectual and the worker were very close for a hundred, a hundred and fifty years. That has changed by virtue of the evolution of the working class and now they are drawing nearer precisely because the intellectual *can polish the worker's thought, but just polish it, not produce it.*

MARCUSE: I am not yet convinced . . . The problems which pose themselves in a revolutionary society, the problem of love, the problem of passion, the problem of all the erotic conflicts, the problem of the demand for the eternity of joy, all that is formulated by the intellectuals of the old type. Do you want to suppress all that?

SARTRE: I want to change all that. Personally I feel myself still an intellectual of the old type.

MARCUSE: I also, I do not contest that.

SARTRE: But me, I contest myself!

MARCUSE: No, I do not have a bad conscience. Excuse me, but I am sincere.

SARTRE: And I do not have a bad conscience. For me, the classical intellectual is an intellectual who ought to disappear. [44]

Yet, while seeming to disdain, or at least to ignore, properly intellectual work, Sartre did not ask intellectuals to abandon it entirely; and his almost casual admission that he himself was 'still an intellectual of the old type' suggested that his own practice had not simply been transformed in accordance with his new-found leftist nostrums. At one point in *On a raison de se révolter*, Victor pressed Sartre strongly to abandon his Flaubert and write a politically useful popular novel. The terms of his refusal — 'it is an intellectual of the classical type who writes the Flaubert'[45] — were an evasion of the issue at stake. If he had not spent a dozen years on Flaubert, and were younger, presumably Sartre would have been able to complete the change into a new intellectual. His Flaubert, he told Gerassi, 'may indeed be a form of *petit-bourgeois* escapism *vis-à-vis* the exigencies of the times, though it is a very political work.'[46] But where political action was concerned, it was simply and radically irrelevant. The imperative was not, as in *Qu'est-ce que la littérature?* and in the twenty years following it, to put our ideas into action, but after a morning of writing, to step out of the study and into the streets.

Sartre's new *gauchiste* argument culminated in an astonishing paradox: it was an avowedly total critique of political intellectuals which yet failed utterly to touch on their daily work, their writing; which, for all its militancy, did not pursue them into their studies and classrooms and demand that they justify and transform what went on *there*. Sartre now demanded the wholesale abandonment of 'all the bourgeois values we have been taught in schools, in the press, at home'.[47] But what could have been more bourgeois than this total separation of writing and scholarship from political action?

Some thirty years earlier, *Qu'est-ce que la littérature?* had visualized overcoming the division between thought and imagination on the one hand, and reality on the other, through an integrative practice of

44. Kellner, pp.195-96 (translation changed).
45. *On a raison de se révolter*, p.105.
46. 'Sartre Accuses the Intellectuals of Bad faith', p.38.
47. Ibid., p.118.

political writing. Now, frustrated in his project, Sartre had elected to be a revolutionary *and* a writer. He plunged into an extravagantly anti-intellectual, anti-theoretical 'serve-the-people' activism, while continuing his sequestered labour on a voluminous and fundamentally apolitical study of an individual writer. The world of intellect and imagination became drained of politics while the world of politics purged itself of intellect. Sartre's abiding problem was finally 'solved' by the mutual alienation of its constituent terms. Biographical habit rather than any kind of synthesizing programme now formed the only connection between a politics scornful of theoretical guidance and an intellectual project heedless of political demands.

All Power to Imagination

It was now, in the midst of the most activist period of his political life, that Sartre published the most wholly contemplative of all his works. In preparation since the mid-1950s, according to Sartre's own testimony, and having monopolized his energies since 1959, Volumes I and II of *L'Idiot de la famille* finally appeared in 1971, Volume III the next year. Even on their own ground they are a shock to most readers. Deceptively presented in volumes the size of the *Critique, Saint Genet and L'Etre et le Néant*, they comprised 2,800 closely-printed pages – a total of one and one quarter million words. These three enormous tomes were equal in length to the entire ten volumes of Sartre's *Situations*, published over thirty years. They made up perhaps a quarter of his collected writings and, more striking still, exceeded the entire bulk of Flaubert's published works and juvenilia.

Close study of the questions left unresolved at the end of the third volume alone suggests that Sartre might have gone on to produce a fourth perhaps equal in size to the first three, had not failing health and eyesight led him to abandon the project in 1975. What was it that drove him to this herculean expenditure of energy – on a project which, moreover, he seemed to regard with deep ambivalence? Discussing it with old or new friends, he was alternately diffident and apologetic, and never accorded it any importance comparable to that of *L'Etre et le Néant* or the *Critique*.

Why, then, did he refuse to abandon it in the face of *gauchiste* demands that he undertake a more political project? He would finish it, he said, because he had by then devoted too much time to it for such a *volte-face* to be conceivable, because 'perhaps one day, independently of its value, this kind of book will be able to serve the masses',[1] and because he was simply too old to change completely from a classical into a leftist intellectual. He summarized his negative feelings towards the Flaubert project in a remarkable lecture given in Brussels in early 1972: 'for the last seventeen years I have been engaged in a work on Flaubert which can be of no interest to the workers, since it is written in a complicated and definitely bourgeois style. Furthermore, the first two volumes of this work were bought and read by bourgeois reformists, professors, students and the like. It was not written by the people or for the people; it was the product of a bourgeois philosopher's reflections over the course of most of his life. Two volumes have appeared, the third is with the printer, and I am preparing the fourth. I am committed to it — meaning that I am sixty-seven years old, I have been working on it since I was fifty, and before that I dreamed about it.

'Now we must say that this work, assuming that it has some value, by its very nature represents the age-old bourgeois swindle of the people. The book ties me to bourgeois readers. Through it, I am still bourgeois and will remain so as long as I continue to work on it. However, another side of myself, which rejects my ideological interests, is fighting against my identity as a classical intellectual. That side of me knows very well that if I have not been co-opted, I have come within a hair of it. And since I am challenging myself, since I refuse to be an elitist writer who takes himself seriously, I find myself among those who are struggling against bourgeois dictatorship. I want to reject my bourgeois situation. There is thus a very special contradiction within me: I am still writing books for the bourgeoisie, yet I feel solidarity with the workers who want to overthrow it. Those workers were the ones who frightened the bourgeoisie in 1968 and who are the victims of greater repression today. As one of them, I should be punished. Yet as the author of *Flaubert*, I am the *enfant terrible* of the bourgeoisie and should be co-opted.'[2]

The gravamen of Sartre's self-criticism was that the Flaubert was for the bourgeoisie, not the workers; it was a work of contemplation, not of agitation or struggle. This rather adventitious act of self-flagellation obscured the fundamental truth of his itinerary even as it

---

1. *Sartre*, p.130.
2. 'Justice et l'Etat', *Situations*, X, pp.61-62; 'Justice and the State', *Life/Situations*, pp.185-86 (translation changed).

expressed it. The Flaubert was, after all, a product of defeat. *L'Idiot de la famille* was erected over the ruin of the *Critique*, the collapse of his political hope, his role as political intellectual and the project of a committed theatre. It was a work of withdrawal, in which Sartre's thought left the world and became absorbed in the life and work of another intellectual recluse. *L'Idiot de la famille* was in fact unique among Sartre's works; and his self-criticism of his past as a 'classical intellectual' was both unduly harsh and misleading. If he was never 'radical' enough to try to give voice to the masses, or to place direct action above literary engagement, he had from the very outset written with a mission. Even *L'Imagination*, we may recall, waged a pitched battle with the theorists of the thing-image on the grounds that they were threatening human freedom. It was only in the sixties and seventies, as the rupture begun in *Les Mots* was made complete, that he ceased to be an activist writer — apparently under the pressure of events, but fundamentally because of the disruption of his project of engagement. His disillusionment, and consequent separation of moral-political action from writing, was a major event in Sartre's career, marking a kind of retirement which gave him the opportunity to write without practical end in view. Not since the descriptive sections of *L'Imaginaire* had Sartre so immersed himself in studies without immediate relevance. He was interested now not in changing his reader or achieving a political effect but in studying Gustave Flaubert so as to discover what can be known about a person. He studied Flaubert for his own sake — not for any lessons that might be learnt from his failures, as in the 1947 study of Baudelaire, and not for any paths to liberation that might be opened by thereby, as in the study of Genet five years later. In so doing, Sartre created a work which was a pioneering effort in human understanding — and returned to the imaginary pole of his earliest work.

What Can We Know About a Man?

In defeat and withdrawal, Sartre created a consummately strange work, a superb study lacking all sense of proportion. It was first of all, a remarkably ambitious biography — 'its subject: what can we know about a man these days. It seemed to me that the only way to answer this question was to study a specific case: what do we know about

Gustave Flaubert, for instance.'[3] We have seen Sartre say of his Flaubert that 'eventually, everything can be communicated and that — without being God, being a man like any other — one can eventually arrive at a perfect understanding of another man as long as one has all the information necessary'. Released from its old commitments, Sartre's intellectual energy was redirected into an exploration of astonishing intensity. To communicate everything, to understand Flaubert completely — this was the goal of *L'Idiot de la famille*.

How do we go about understanding a person? Most biographies, such as Enid Starkie's *Flaubert: The Making of the Master,* employ a range of approaches, never spelling out their goals or methodological assumptions, operating by a kind of intelligent common sense. Thus, while refusing to speculate about Flaubert's deeper motivations or his emotional conflicts, Starkie assumes that the city of Rouen must have affected his character and so devotes more space to it than to his mother. She confirms his homosexuality, assuming it to be important, but refuses to speculate about his hostility to his brother Achille. She does not explore the possible autobiographical meaning of her subject's early writings, but acutely considers and resolves many problems of Flaubert scholarship. Starkie accepts her methods as given, and is above all concerned to use them to depict Flaubert — his actions, the main events of his life, his development as a writer, his friendships and love affairs, his aesthetic doctrine, the structure and meaning of *Madame Bovary*. All this she does, going up to 1857 in only four hundred pages of text, with a second volume given over to the rest of Flaubert's life.[4]

The contrast between this successful conventional work and *L'Idiot de la famille* could not be greater. Sartre's declared objective was to find out what could be known about a man today; and this general question could be answered only by studying a specific case — Gustave Flaubert, 'for example'. Critics have been irritated by the apparently ancillary role allotted to Flaubert himself.[5] But the purpose of Sartre's study was to *develop a method*. The particular interest of Flaubert quite apart, he sought to write a systematic and self-

3. *L'Idiot de la famille*, Paris 1971, vol. I., (F/I), p.1; Introduction trans. in *Le Monde Weekly*, May 20-26, 1971, p.6.

4. Enid Starkie, *Flaubert: The Making of the Master*, New York 1967.

5. See, for example, David Caute, 'The Refusal to be Good', *Modern Occasions,* Spring 1972.

conscious essay in biography which might be applied elsewhere. In contrast with Starkie's relatively unself-conscious, eclectic, and even self-contradictory method, Sartre was concerned to know exactly where he was going at every moment and why. It was not enough, for example, simply to suggest that Gustave's mother did not love him, that he had difficulty in grasping the meaning of language, or that he gave himself over to play-acting. In each case, Sartre set out the general framework within which these facts were analysed: how love was connected with self-valuation and so with an active approach to the world; what language meant as one of the child's first encounters with the world; the meaning of acting. This approach was maintained throughout the book, time and again taking Sartre far away from Gustave to develop the tools necessary for understanding him. In the process, biography became philosophy, then psychological theory, subsumed the biographies of Alfred Le Poittevin and Charles Leconte de Lisle, and the history of Rouen College during the 1830s, digressed to study laughter as a social fact, and to explain how pet dogs relate to the human language, and incorporated a full-length study of the contradictory demands placed on the writer of 1850.

Did Gustave's mother love him? Starkie tells us only that she was 'of a gloomy disposition', adding the few available facts of her life. Her procedure here, as elsewhere, is to stay as close as possible to her data, venturing hypotheses rarely, and even then emphasizing their hypothetical character; her goal is less to explain Gustave than to describe him. Sartre, on the other hand, used the facts as sighting-points in his project of understanding. And as explanations on one level entail yet other levels, so Sartre moved further and further from these primary data in an attempt to elucidate Gustave's character structure. Working from the available evidence he wrote an entire chapter on Caroline Flaubert, explaining how she *must have* felt and what her needs *must have* been. Orphan of a physician, foster-child of another, she became the devoted wife of yet a third. Her obedience, together with Achille-Cleophas's rural *petit-bourgeois* background and domination of the family, made her into an 'incestuous daughter', an 'eternal minor'. Hence, she *must have* wanted to furnish Achille-Cleophas with an heir and so welcomed Achille's birth. She *must have* wanted a daughter in whom she could relive, but with parental care and love, her own childhood. She *could not*, then, have wanted Gustave, and in consequence *must have* cared for him meticulously without loving him. Thus Gustave *must have* been cared for yet deprived, and out of this combination developed his characteristic passivity towards reality.

The exhaustiveness of Sartre's search for the core of Gustave's psychic constitution was only one cause of the extreme length of his study. By page 2,136, Sartre had reached Flaubert's seizure of early 1844, a point which Sarkie reaches by page 120 of her account. Gustave was 22, and would now abandon the law for a semi-invalid state and a writing career. But while for Starkie the major events are yet to come, Sartre held that the decisive steps had already been taken. The brevity of the one and verbosity of the other were due to their very different analytic approaches to their common subject.

Starkie seeks to describe Flaubert as fully and accurately as possible. Certain areas yield no conclusive answers; they will, therefore, be omitted. For the rest, she assembles all the available facts in an interesting and swiftly-paced account. We see Flaubert from the outside, and vividly. Reading Gertrude Collier's memoir, for example, Starkie notes 'the extraordinary beauty and charm of Flaubert at twenty, and the originality and naturalness of his bearing. As we have already seen he was tall, slight and graceful in all his movements, he had the most faultless limbs and the great charm of utter self-consciousness in his own physical and mental beauty.'[6] Nothing could interest Sartre less. *L'Idiot de la famille* sought to *explain* Gustave Flaubert. Sartre assumed that his readers possessed all the relevant information, that they had read Flaubert's major works and were already acquainted with the details of his life, and devoted his analysis to an *interior* biography. To explain Gustave, to understand why he wrote *Madame Bovary* and what he meant by it, he would probe beneath the available information and try to grasp the underlying character structure. Who was Gustave Flaubert? On one level, everything he did and said; but much more fundamentally, he was a particular project, energized by a particular way of experiencing and pursuing his needs in all their contradictoriness and complexity.

Existential Psychoanalysis

We return, at the end of Sartre's career, to the terrain originally sketched in *L'Etre et le Néant* under the heading of existential

6. *Flaubert*, p.79.

psychoanalysis. In fact, although this dimension of Sartre's work has not been emphasized in this study, it was one of his constant preoccupations. In 1943 he announced a programme of existential psychoanalysis as biography; in 1947 he published a moralizing study of Baudelaire's bad faith — 'a very inadequate, an extremely bad one'[7] — and soon after wrote almost five hundred pages on Mallarmé, most of which was later mislaid. In 1952 he published *Saint Genet,* and the next year *Les Mots* was begun. 1954 saw the commencement of what was to become *L'Idiot de la famille,* put aside after almost a thousand pages had been written. In 1957 he published part of a never-completed study of Tintoretto as well as *Question de méthode*, which contained important guidelines for biographical analysis. Then, in 1959, he resumed almost uninterrupted work on Flaubert. As we shall see, Sartre absorbed both Marxism and psychoanalysis into his developing biographical project; and in it, the radicalism of his early thought was preserved and deepened. His original notion of an irreducible freedom here assumed its only viable form: even if in response to impossible demands and in totally oppressive situations, Sartre argued, it is we who make ourselves.

Still, critics of Sartre's Flaubert were most discomfited precisely by his effort to reduce the richness and detail of Flaubert's life and works to a single project, however complex and contradictory.[8] Indeed, Sartre's approach did submerge detail. It allowed for no pluralism or drift, either within or without. Set at a very early age, Gustave's life was his project, unfolding itself across time: the exterior was interiorized, and the interior, in turn, was exteriorized. For Gustave to have had a number of goals, or to have been ambivalent or lackadaisical, would itself have been a project, as would his passive submission to events. These are various ways of choosing to be oneself, of organizing one's needs and purposes and projecting them coherently in a life. This is to say, in Sartre's original terms, that humans are *intentional* — or, as he would have said in 1971, *dialectical.* We act in order to achieve purposes; our life *is* that complex but comprehensible set of actions. To understand someone therefore requires an *interior* study, one which first grasps the essential Gustave and then

7. 'Itinerary of a Thought', p.50.

8. See, for example, Harry Levin, 'A Literary Enormity: Sartre on Flaubert' *The Journal of the History of Ideas,* XXXIII, 4, October-December 1972.

reconstructs the project behind his actions. This *regressive* study tries to reconstruct what might conventionally be called his underlying character structure. Then a complementary *progressive* analysis shows how this structure was created in his particular family situation and how it unfolded as a project in his life.

Gustave's basic project had its source in early childhood. Sartre's angry book on Baudelaire paid no attention to the poet's childhood, but rather assumed a kind of freedom to change in terms of which Baudelaire must be judged an escapist. *Genet* dwelt briefly on the child and discovered there the problem which must be overcome later, but not the project of overcoming which was Genet's liberation. The short study of Tintoretto began when the painter was already a young man of thirty, passionately trying to win a master's reputation. *Les Mots*, on the other hand, did focus on the formative power of early childhood, but not at all with an analytic eye. Sartre located there only a general sense of his schooling in the imaginary as a way of avoiding reality; no problems or contradictions were disclosed. *L'Idiot de la famille* was his first effort to discover the adult wholly in the infant.

Little Gustave was born into a family ruled by a *paterfamilias* who also happened to be a self-made man of science. This bourgeois family, bearing strong traces of the father's rural origins, produced an heir, Achille, destined to succeed his father as Master of the Hôtel-Dieu of Rouen. It also produced a second son, Gustave, destined to be inferior to the first-born, and a girl, longed for by his mother. Before Gustave, other children were born who died at or near birth, so that from the beginning he was handled and cared for as someone bound to die. Destined for inferiority by his bourgeois father, lacking any means of revolt in this quasi-feudal family, cared for meticulously but never loved, Gustave early developed his main character traits: passivity, a sense of destiny, an inability to relate to the real world. [9] He did indeed have a 'Golden Age' at around three or four, when his father loved him and took him around the countryside on his house calls. But lacking the early reciprocity of mother-love, Gustave developed no sense of the reciprocity of language: his father cast him out of grace when, at seven, he could not yet read. So, this child

9. For a good, if ironic, summary of this line of analysis see the *Times Literary Supplement,* September 24, 1971, p.1133.

would become imaginary — actor, then author, then poet, then artist. The artist would write *Madame Bovary*.

Contat and Rybalka provide an admirable summary of Sartre's analysis: 'Excluded from the active, positive, and utilitarian universe of the Flauberts, [Gustave] assumed the familial sentence which condemned him to inertia and, thanks to an intentional and memorable crisis which brought him to his brother's feet one night in January, 1844, at Pont-l'Evêque, avoided the necessity of "taking up a trade" and won the right to devote himself to the passive and quasi-feminine activity which writing will be for him. By means of this writing, he is going to try satanically to make the world unreal by throwing himself and the world headlong into the imaginary, thereby taking the point of view of death on life, of nothingness on being, and adopting a God's-eye view in opposition to science and to his father's triumphant reason. By presenting Flaubert's neurosis as a passive dynamic (*a choice undergone*) engendered dialectically by a strict familial and sociocultural conditioning (his *constitution*) which was in turn assumed by a trapped freedom (*his becoming a person*), Sartre gives an answer in his first two volumes to the question, How does one become a writer? Or more exactly, what kind of man did Flaubert have to be to write *Madame Bovary*?'[10]

Might this be termed a Freudian account? Certainly Sartre had changed enormously since *La Transcendence de l'ego*, holding now that individuals were decisively shaped in their earliest years. He made no use of Freud's conceptual armamentorium — repression, the unconscious, the tripartite personality structure or the stages of sexual development. But he insisted on the absolute primacy of early childhood, of family structure, of the relations between infant and parents. Yet his was a rather unusual determinism: 'there is spontaneity but starting from a prefabricated essence.'[11] That is to say, Gustave did develop his own 'free singular project', but only on the basis of the given internal and external conditions and only along the route made possible and necessary by that network of conditions. Acceptance of these qualifications, of this notion of character, did not lead Sartre to any behaviourist determinism or mechanistic causality. Even from the first day, he insisted, people are fully people and

---

10. CRW, 71/540, p.571
11. F/1, p.351 n.

behave dialectically, creating themselves on the basis of, but by going beyond, the given conditions.

Sartre gave the impression that he had still not read widely in psychological and psychoanalytical theory or pondered it deeply, for he still insisted on combating the notion of the unconscious, even as he deployed his own very similar idea. What after all was *le vécu* (lived experience) but an effort to affirm human intentionality even at the interior of neurosis? 'The conception of "lived experience" marks my change since *L'Etre et le Néant*. My early work was a rationalist philosophy of consciousness. It was all very well for me to dabble in apparently non-rational processes in the individual; the fact remains that *L'Etre et le Néant* is a monument of rationality. But in the end it becomes an irrationalism, because it cannot account rationally for those processes which are "below" consciousness and which are also rational, but lived as irrational. Today, the notion of "lived experience" represents an effort to preserve that presence to itself which seems to me indispensable for the existence of any psychic fact, while at the same time this presence is so opaque and blind before itself that it is also an absence from itself. Lived experience is always simultaneously present to itself and absent from itself. In developing this notion, I have tried to surpass the traditional psychoanalytic ambiguity of psychic facts which are both teleological and mechanical, by showing that every psychic fact involves an intentionality which aims at something, while among them a certain number can only exist if they are comprehended, but neither named nor known. The latter include what I call the "stress" of a neurosis. A neurosis is in the first instance a specific wound, a defective structure which is a certain way of living a childhood. But this is only the initial wound: it is then patched up and bandaged by a system which covers and soothes the wound, and which then, like anti-bodies in certain cases, suddenly does something abominable to the organism. The unity of this system is the neurosis. The work of its "stress" is intentional, but it cannot be seized as such without disappearing. It is precisely for this reason that if it is transferred into the domain of knowledge, by analytic treatment, it can no longer be reproduced in the same manner.'[12] In short, Sartre addressed psychoanalytic theory in the same terms as he had addressed Marxian theory, maintaining that it must be dialectical if it

12. 'Itinerary of a Thought', p.50.

was to explain human experience, that it must see its world of study as turning on intentional human behaviour. Mental illness, as he said elsewhere, was 'the issue that the free organism, in its total unity, invents in order to be able to live in an unliveable situation.'[13] This was the most radical affirmation of *L'Idiot de la famille*: Flaubert made himself.

Return to the Irréel

Did Sartre succeed in showing Gustave's self-creation? Almost. The book was a gamble, the most extreme in a life-time of extreme efforts. Freed from his sense of moral or political mission, Sartre was able to bring the accumulated power of his whole intellectual career to bear on this culminating work. But, freed from the customary tension between reality and the *irréel*, his thought now crossed barriers that previously would have limited and disciplined it, and lost all sense of scale.

It was not only that the book was so often chaotic and contorted, verbose and undisciplined — these traits were shared with *L'Etre et le Néant, Saint Genet,* and the *Critique*. *L'Idiot de la famille* displayed the penchant for artificial construction that its predecessors had also shown while lacking even their often minimal sense of proportion; it preserved their wordiness without their accompanying sense of drama. Free of Sartre's usual moralism, the book was also unmotivated by any need to reach the real world. Much more than the *Critique*, it read like the endless monologue of a patient in psychoanalysis, replete with false starts and blind alleys, self-absorbed and wholly uncontrolled, and unremitting in its demands on its audience. *L'Idiot de la famille* violated the elementary rules of human communication which Sartre had laid down in *Qu'est-ce que la littérature?*. Self-indulgent and tedious, it lacked all respect for its readers.

Moreover, it is a work which the reader is likely to experience as *too long* from the start. No distinction is made between the activity of research and its socially communicable results. The reader must accompany the exploration, wherever it leads and for however long it may take, attempting to elicit what is pertinent and to establish conclusions in a way that Sartre himself was wholly unconcerned to do.

13. Laing and Cooper, *Reason and Violence*, p.7.

For example, analysing Flaubert's juvenilia in order to establish the elements of his attitude towards his father, Sartre takes the reader through the specific meanings of *Passion et Vertu, Quidquid volueris, Rêve d'enfer, Bibliomanie, La Peste à Florence, Un Parfum à sentir,* and the literary journal composed by Gustave at the age of thirteen. One hundred and thirty pages are devoted to roughly an equal number of Flaubert's. Sartre does not analyse all of Flaubert's early writings; he selects the most relevant among them. Yet with too great a sense of leisure, he plunges into them one after another, with a total disregard for proportion, for the reader's stamina, or for the norms of scholarship and argument.

Many reasons might be cited for the monstrous growth of this book, but the most fundamental is that here the themes and preoccupations of the early Sartre returned, now completely untrammelled. If the sense of interiority and attraction to the imaginary were constant aspects of his early work, in his study of Flaubert interiority and the imaginary have become the pure element of his activity. Sartre's thought had finally deserted the world for the *irréel. L'Idiot* is a book nearly devoid of action, a wholly *inward* study. The extended textual analysis of Flaubert's juvenilia, for example, is part of one of two chapters which together take up 468 pages. In these pages Gustave commits not a single physical act. Their entire space is devoted to a study from several angles of the boy's intentional structure. First the basic elements are isolated, using his early writings; then Sartre reconstructs the relationship between each developing layer of Gustave's character structure, showing how one passes into and produces the next; finally these are considered in terms of the way in which Gustave lived them in relation to his parents' ideologies. The second part of the book has Flaubert performing his first plays in the billiards room of the Master of the Hôtel-Dieu, then entering school, clowning with his classmates, reading at night, rebelling and being expelled. But everywhere the main action is internal: Gustave's slow transformation from imaginary child into artist.

In part, of course, the book's inwardness, its air of unreality, is that of its subject. But only in part: Starkie's *Flaubert* remains a lively account, in which events that matter little to Sartre are interestingly described. What Sartre gives, on the other hand, is a detailed analysis of the meaning of events. 250 pages near the end of the second volume are devoted to the implications of Gustave's fainting fit at

Pont L'Evêque, which led to his semi-invalid life — an episode to which Starkie gives three pages. Sartre's interest was not in Gustave's actions but in the ways in which he interiorized his situation and thus created himself. His achievement was to deconstruct the almost infinite complexity of an individual into the intentional unity of a single project. These explanations can have none of the drama of a narrative account, which is why *L'Idiot* cannot help but be a 'bad' story. It is not a 'story' at all, but perhaps a seminal work for specialists, to be studied and mastered over a period of months and even years, one which presumes a thorough acquaintance with Flaubert's life and writings, post-Romantic literature, nineteenth-century French social, economic and political history.

But can this approach give us the real Gustave Flaubert? We may accept, as I do, Sartre's claim that Gustave's intentional structure is decisive, but what he *did* is equally pertinent to any analysis whose purpose is total understanding. However, Sartre did not offer to explore an essential but neglected dimension of Gustave which must later be integrated with others of comparable importance. Rather, he thought of his analysis as rendering the whole person. This claim recalls the constitutional weakness of Sartre's stress on interiority — a weakness which was reproduced again and again in his writings. It fundamentally precluded any sure and confident approach to the real world. Now, as Sartre accepted unprecedented activist demands on his time, his writing surrendered itself unreservedly to a kind of pure interiority. He seemed almost to have a prejudice against seeing Gustave in action, seemed always to prefer moving behind facts to speculate about their meaning.

Moreover, the study was also a work of *imagination*. If Flaubert was an 'imaginary person' it was not only because he became a writer and made himself profoundly unreal in doing so. He was also, now, a character — the *creation* of Jean-Paul Sartre. *L'Idiot de la famille*, Sartre declared, was a 'true novel', because it portrayed Flaubert 'the way I imagine him to have been'.[14] Let us follow a typical lengthy passage, in which Sartre's imagination is at work creating his subject: 'I imagine that Madame Flaubert, a wife by vocation, was a mother from duty. An excellent mother, but not a charming one: punctual,

14. 'Sur "L'Idiot de la famille",' *Situations*, X, p.94; 'On *The Idiot of the Family*', *Life/Situations*, p.112.

assiduous, skilful. Nothing more. The younger son was cautiously handled: his swaddling clothes were changed in an instant; he didn't have to cry, he was always fed in the nick of time. Gustave's aggressiveness did not have the opportunity to develop. But he was frustrated: well before weaning but without crying or rebellion; lack of tenderness is scarcely to the pain of love as undernourishment is to hunger. Later, the *ill-loved* child will consume himself; for the moment he does not really suffer: the need to be loved appeared from birth, before the infant would even be able to recognize the Other, but it does not yet express itself by precise desires. Frustration does *not affect* him — or scarcely does it so — it *makes* him: I mean that this objective negation penetrates him and that it becomes in him an impoverishment of life: an organic poverty and some ingratitude or other at the heart of life-experience. No anguish, he never has occasion to feel himself abandoned. Nor alone. The moment a desire awakens, it is immediately fulfilled; if a pin pricks him and he cries, a quick hand will remove the pain. But these precise operations are also parsimonious: everything is economized at the Flauberts, even time, which is money. Therefore he is washed, fed, cared for without haste but without useless complaisance. Particularly his mother, timid and cold, smiles hardly if at all, and doesn't chatter: why trouble to speak to this child who cannot understand? Gustave has much pain grasping this sparse character of the objective world, of otherness; when he becomes conscious of it, when he recognizes the faces leaning over his cradle, a first chance of love has already escaped him. He does not find himself, on the the occasion of a caress, to be flesh and supreme end. It is now too late, for him to be, in his own eyes, the *destination* of maternal acts: he is their object, that is all. Why? He doesn't know: not a long time will be required for him to feel obscurely that he is a means. For Madame Flaubert, indeed, this child is the means for accomplishing her duties of motherhood; for the doctor-philosopher from whom the young woman is completely alienated, he is first a means for perpetuating the family. These discoveries will come later. For now, he has bypassed valorization: he has never felt his needs as sovereign necessities, the outer world has never been his jewel-box, his larder, the environment reveals itself to him gradually, as to others, but he has only known it first in this cold and dismal consistency that Heidegger has named "*nur-vorbeilagen*". The happy necessity of the loved child compensates and transcends his docility as an object to be manipulated; there is in his desires an intangible imperiousness which can appear as the rudimentary form of the project and, in consequence, of action. . . .'[15]

This characteristic paragraph is constructed from very scant information. Sartre imagines how little Gustave *must have* felt, based on how his mother *must have* acted, feeling as *she* must have done, given a few scanty facts about her: her childhood as an orphan, her apparent devotion to Achille-Cléophas, her sombre bearing, as reported by her niece. From these few facts, Sartre's account spirals upwards, generating its own facts as it goes, according to his understanding of basic structures of childhood, until it sights the passivity and imaginary posture of the mature Flaubert. The paragraph stands out, however, because Sartre follows it with a frank comment on its procedure: 'I confess: this is a fable. Nothing proves that it was like this. And, worse yet, the absence of these proofs — which would necessarily be of singular facts — returns us, even when we create fables, to schematism, to generality: my account fits infants *in general*, not Gustave in particular. No matter, I wanted to carry it to its conclusion for this reason alone: the *real* explanation, I can conjecture without the least resentment, could be exactly the opposite of the one that I invent; *in any event* it would have to pass along the paths that I indicate and would have to refute mine on the ground that I have defined: the body, love. I have spoken of maternal love: this is what gives the objective category of otherness for the newborn, it is this which in the first weeks permits the child to feel as *other* — from the moment he is able to recognize it — the satiny flesh of the breast. It goes without saying that filial love — the oral phase of sexuality — goes from birth to the encounter with the Other — it is the conduct of the mother which fixes its limits and intensity, which determines its internal structure. Gustave is immediately conditioned by his mother's indifference; he desires *alone*; his first sexual and alimentary impulse towards a "flesh-nourishment" is not *reflected* for him by a caress. . . .'[16]

This methodological aside asserts the necessity of constructing general schemata, and this on a firm and defensible basis. *All* children are shaped, from the outset, by the presence or lack of physical

15. F/I, pp.136-37.
16. F/I, pp.139-40.

mother-love, and by its quality — anxious, intense, calm, ambivalent
or whatever it may be. Given this woman, given who Gustave
became, what *must* their initial relation *have been*? The imaginary re-
creation moves through rigorously defined channels, and given Sartre's goals, there is no other way to proceed. To reject the imaginary
quality of Sartre's Flaubert, bizarre as it may seem, is to reject the
entire enterprise. Nevertheless, to accept it is to accept as 'true' an
account which is actually an endless spiral of speculation. The first
two volumes of *L'Idiot* cannot but prompt the reader to ask whether
the real, historical Flaubert has not been left irrecoverably behind.

Marxist Biography

Sartre would reply that the real Flaubert has not yet been reached.
His interior and imaginary study is only the first stage of an analysis
whose goal is to furnish a total understanding of Gustave Flaubert as
a *historical* person, the novelist who wrote the great work of the Second
Empire, *Madame Bovary* — above all, to enable us to understand
Flaubert at work and in the world. So far he has merely been
reconstructing the process whereby Gustave chose to become the man
who later would write *Madame Bovary*.

Sartre's own understanding of existential psychoanalysis had
undergone a deep change since he first formulated it. *Saint Genet*, for
example, remained close to his original definition: 'I have tried to do
the following: to indicate the limit of psychoanalytical interpretation
and Marxist explanation and to demonstrate that freedom alone can
account for a person in his totality; to show this freedom at grips with
destiny, crushed at first by its mischances, than turning upon them
and digesting them little by little; to prove that genius is not a gift but
the way out that one invents in desperate cases; to learn the choice
that a writer makes of himself, or of his life and of the meaning of the
universe, including even the formal characteristics of his style and
composition, even the structure of his images and of the particularity
of his tastes; to review in detail the history of his liberation.'[17] But, as
he later commented, *Genet* was still 'very, very inadequate' at the level
of institutions and of history. He saw Genet as an orphan placed with

17. *Saint Genet: comédien et martyr*, Paris 1952, p.536; trans. Bernard Frechtman, *Saint Genet: Actor and Martyr*, New York 1963.

a peasant family; 'but all the same, this happened in 1925 or so and there was a whole context to this life which is quite absent. The Public Assistance, a foundling, represents a specific social phenomenon, and anyway Genet is a product of the twentieth century; yet none of this is registered in the book.'[18] Sartre resumed work on Flaubert after completing *Les Sequestrés d'Altona*. In the meantime he had written *Question de méthode* and discussed, among other issues, the need for a biography which did justice to both the individual and his social reality. 'The idea of the book on Flaubert was to abandon these theoretical disquisitions, because they were ultimately getting us nowhere, and to try to give a concrete example of how it might be done.'[19] Its aim was 'to try to demonstrate the encounter between the development of the person, as psychoanalysis has shown it to us, and the development of history.'[20] Existentialist psychoanalysis did not now abandon its insistence on the individual creating himself, but it would attempt to show this *praxis*-process as the interiorization of a concrete lived history and its re-exteriorization as the life of this particular individual, who may, on this account, 'fulfil a historical role'.[21]

However, as we know, Sartre took up his Flaubert at a time of disillusionment — and perhaps, in some sense, because of it. How did he now fare as he laboured to understand Flaubert as a social individual? First of all, Sartre directly confronted his earlier weakness and negativity in relation to the social world. *L'Idiot* acknowledged the priority in human development of *a mandate to live* over the feeling of being *de trop*, which *La Nausée* and *L'Etre et le Néant* had made so much of. 'Pure lived life, the simple "being there",'[22] was no longer primary; nor was individual *praxis*, which emerged only in and through a social world. *L'Idiot* differs from every one of Sartre's earlier biographical and autobiographical ventures in defining its subject's development wholly in terms of the socio historical world. Sartre made this plain in his comment on the theme of 'sense and non-sense'. 'In truth sense and non-sense in a human life are human in principle and are transmitted to man in the earliest stages of his life by man himself. Thus we must dismiss those absurd formulas: "life has

18. 'Itinerary of a Thought', p.51.
19. Ibid., p.51.
20. Ibid., p.51.
21. Ibid., p.51.
22. F/I, p.141.

sense"; "it has none"; "it has one that we give to it" — and understand that we discover our goals, the nonsense or the sense of our lives, as realities prior to this coming to consciousness, prior perhaps to our birth and prefabricated in the human universe. The sense of a life comes to the living man through the human society which sustains him and through the parents who engender him: for this reason it is also *always* a non-sense. But inversely the discovery of a life as non-sense (that of children who are supernumeraries, undernourished, consumed by parasites and fever in an underdeveloped society) reveals just as clearly the real sense of this society and, through this reversal, it is life — as organic need — which becomes, in its pure animal necessity, *human sense* and it is the society of men which, by the sentence of unsatisfied need, becomes *pure human non-sense.*'[23] Sartre's new insistence was more than theoretical. He endeavored to show how Flaubert's character structure took shape within his society's primary formative institution, the family. His Marxist and Freudian analysis joined as he argued that adequate love led to self-worth, which alone enabled an individual to relate to the world reciprocally, from a sense of strength. Gustave's early inability to accept words as designating objects showed that he had been cut off from *praxis*, the cardinal social category, by his earliest contact with his mother. 'In this first moment acculturation without love reduces Gustave to the condition of a domestic animal.'[24]

His family — parvenu but patriarchal, resting on individual ability but seeking to found a dynasty — localized socio-historical reality and conveyed it to Gustave. For orientation and self-clarification, for example, the growing child was forced to choose between or somehow combine not an infinite variety of attitudes, but his father's bourgeois atomistic rationalism and his mother's deism. The mature Flaubert's reactionary political attitudes were prefigured in his early relationship of vassalage towards his father, in his rejection of bourgeois values of self-sufficiency and independence, in his desire to live as a rentier. Family structure and parental ideologies did not merely *influence* Gustave: his project of becoming a writer took shape *through* them; he constituted himself in terms of them.

At college in Rouen from 1831 to 1838 he experienced, with the

23. F/I, p.141.
24. F/I, p.147.

other schoolboys, the collapse of the bourgeoisie's universalism, the realization of how narrow were its aspirations to freedom and democracy, and its capitulation to the church. The time for activism and politics was over: together, at night, they retreated into the imaginary, living out their fantasies in Romantic novels, plays and poetry. For some of the schoolboys this was a necessary preparation, for as we shall see, after 1830 the demands on literature were such that the writer had to dwell in the *irréel*. Those most capable of flourishing in this world of withdrawal were those, like Gustave, whose writing was an expression-solution of their neurosis.

Gustave Flaubert, then, was the person produced in and by this singular set of historical conditions. He had no unique instinctual drives, no specific talents, no inherited traits, no pre-given essence of his own which met and was affected by these conditions. Rather, he was that set of conditions as interiorized, lived, totalized, formed into a project, and re-exteriorized. Any male child, we might assume, born into that family on that date would have made himself into the author of *Madame Bovary*.

The Singular Universal

Nothing in this analysis mitigated the fundamental interiority and unreality of the first two volumes. Even at its best, Sartre's representation of socio-historical reality was far more ideological than material: he concerned himself far more with the father's — and later, Gustave's — ideology than with his concrete social relations. In Volume III, however, the study ceased to be an interior reconstruction and moved on to the sphere of action and concrete social reality. Sartre began what is by far the most interesting part of the study by asking its organizing question: how did this young neurotic, whose sickness made him unable to pursue law and gave him the freedom to write, create the signal work of the post-Romantic generation? Flaubert, who believed that 'the earth is the kingdom of Satan' and that 'the worst is always certain', withdrew from life, turned himself into a means to achieve beautiful, permanent works which would dissolve the world in imagination. He so resented change and adaptation to reality, so doggedly held to his morbid sense of the world's meaning, that his friend Maxime du Camp thought his neurosis an obstacle to writing. Sartre asked the opposite question: was not

Gustave's 'nervous illness' in reality 'the means of writing *Madame Bovary*?'[25]

If Gustave did indeed choose the imaginary over the real, if *Madame Bovary* was indeed a neurotic work reflecting Gustave's horror of living, we are left to inquire how 'the return to the subjective had for practical result the production of an object in the social world'.[26] In other words, 'how was the madness of a single person able to become collective madness, and better yet, the *aesthetic reason* of his epoch?'[27] In other periods such morbid, misanthropic works have been passed over in silence: for so neurotic a work to become the acclaimed critical mirror of its epoch it had to strike deep neurotic chords in the 'objective Spirit'. 'To go still further we will say that Gustave's illness will permit him to objectify it in representative works only if it appears as a particularization of what must indeed be called a *neurosis of the objective Spirit.*'[28] It was as if the objective neurosis of this moment of history affirmed itself *through* Flaubert's work. Sartre now turned his analysis around to seek in Gustave the interiorization and re-exteriorization of his the specific, if contradictory social imperatives laid before this new generation's *art-in-the-making* (*art-à-faire*).[29]

How can Gustave's neurosis be both social *and* individual? By what means can an objective process 'direct the internal evolution of his malaise and transform it ineluctably into neurosis because Art, to exist and pass through this disagreeable period, needs neurotic ministers'?[30] In posing these questions, Sartre returned to the unresolved problem of the *Critique*: the nature of the ties between the individual and the collective. He now posited the existence of a practico-inert 'objective Spirit', which imposed demands, by way of the complete body of literature of any period (*littérature-fait*) on those who sought to create the literature of their age (*littérature-à-faire*). His fascinating discussion of this objective Spirit acknowledged the power of social and cultural forces but still refused them any other than a practico-inert status.[31] However, to understand Flaubert's histor-

25. F/III, Paris 1972, p.25.
26. F/III, p.30.
27. F/III, p.32.
28. F/III, p.32.
29. F/III, p.39.
30. F/III, pp.39-40.
31. F/III, pp.41-66.

icity — in the sense that *Madame Bovary* became *the* novel of a certain group of readers at a certain historical moment — was to have explained both how he interiorized *the society* and how he acted upon it and changed it through a great book. Such an explanation, Sartre affirmed, was the prime goal of his study. We must be clear about the significance of this intention for Sartre's work. Without necessarily having to settle the theoretical issues abandoned by the *Critique*, an adequate account of this particular singular universal, Gustave Flaubert, effectively entailed an understanding of the reality that had always eluded Sartre's grasp — an understanding of human sociality.

Sartre began by exploring the situation of the young writer of 1840. Faced with the universalism, concreteness, critical spirit and automony of the great works of the eighteenth century, the writer was also faced with the demand of the now victorious bourgeoisie for eulogies of itself. The revolutionary class of the eighteenth century, which had come to consciousness of itself through its literature, had ceased to represent universal values; it had installed its own particular forms of oppression, adulterated some of its early values such as equality, and established the market-place as the universal social image. No class had yet crystallized to contest the bourgeoisie, and hence, preservation of the autonomy of literature now meant a reversal of its partisan, combative posture of the 1760s. In order to preserve art, the young post-Romantic was to effect an unparalleled historical rupture with his audience: 'a brutal separation between writing and communication'.[32] By placing contradictory demands upon its apprentices, the post-Romantic literature of bourgeois society posed questions that did not permit rational responses. In 'refusing to serve, to integrate itself into a class literature, the work becomes its own end, it poses itself for itself in an inhuman solitude, on the connected abolition of the reader and the author'.[33] Lacking the opportunity to associate their desire for autonomy and contestation with a rising social class, the young writers remained bourgeois but became 'Knights of Nothingness', declassed themselves in an ideal, an unreal fashion and sought 'to deny *everything* in the name of nothing'.[34] Literature 'imposed itself on them, through the objective Spirit, as

32. F/III, p.98.
33. F/III, p.104.
34. F/III, p.140.

having no other domain than the anti-real or pure unreality, posing itself for itself against the perceived world.'[35] The young writer took flight from an impossible situation, choosing unreality over reality. The imaginary quality of writing — which hitherto had served literature's purpose of saying something — became an end in itself. His writing demanded 'a rupture with being'[36] and so he renounced the world, became an exile living in solitude. *Irréalisation* was the cardinal norm of art after 1850, and the main ethical value of whoever aspired to write. Radical negation of self and of the world: 'in other words, Absolute Art insists upon itself as a suicide immediately followed by genocide.'[37]

If Absolute Art dictated a rupture with its audience — the writer would now write to be read by no one, or perhaps by fellow writers, or by a Supreme Reader — it must demand the artist's *failure*. The failure was inherent in the project of making oneself unreal. Divorced from the world but living in it, the petty clerk, teacher or small landowner would look on life as if seeing it from above, assumed the attitude of a tourist having no real links with the country visited. Living modestly, these writers sought to become a nobility of art: 'they have the duty to elevate themselves beyond the bourgeoisie, master of the world, and to make it ashamed of its petty quest for profit in producing this unheard-of luxury that no nobility has been able to create by itself, a masterpiece, free splendour and perfectly useless.'[38] But this was impossible, a failure from the beginning. 'We must note that the neurotic element does not reside in the comedy itself, but in the actor's belief in his character.'

The post-Romantic writer also failed as a *man*, as art now became associated with social ineptitude and suffering.[39] Between 1840 and 1850, these young men had already begun to define literature as feminine, the resort of men without virility who were utterly unable to adapt to society. Incapable of anything else, the writer took pride in his crippled state and gladly let himself become a means to an end: the creation of art. But the work itself must also fail, and this too became an almost religious value for Flaubert's generation. Litera-

35. F/III, p.142.
36. F/III, p.144.
37. F/III, p.144.
38. F/III, p.158.
39. F/III, p.159.

ture was impossible because, although imaginary, it was a real activity of real people. They sought to create Absolute Art, works of pure form, wholly beautiful and saying nothing. But in seeking to create a book or poem of inflexible necessity, the author could never escape the effects of being real, of creating works permeated by the hazards of reality. Thus 'dissatisfaction and the passage to the imaginary are here inseparably linked.'[40]

In another period such men might not have attracted attention, or might have been regarded as cranks. How did writers so systematically and deliberately cut off from their world, so given to failure in their very self-definition, find a vast public which followed them intently? The 'rejected public accepts these negative works because, in some sense, it rejects itself.'[41] By way of elucidation, Sartre described the readers of Flaubert and his generation — the upper layers of the 'middle classes': enlightened, high-level functionaries, educated members of the liberal professions, all those who produced, used, and transmitted knowledge useful to the bourgeoisie; in other words, the social ancillaries of the bourgeoisie, who lived in solidarity with rent and capital yet were excluded from political power both before and after 1848. Unable to question their exclusion from the vote without calling the social system itself into question, these *'demi-nantis'* — nearly rich — agitated in the banquet campaign just prior to the February Revolution and then, after the suppression of the working class in June, were called upon to fashion new ideological supports for the bourgeoisie.

In a brilliant discussion showing the *praxis* of ideology-formation, Sartre sketched the new, deeply pessimistic view of human nature and society engendered by 1848. The bloody massacre of the working class by the middle-class National Guard in June was the turning point: any new outlook would necessarily have hatred of man at its core. The new ideas reflected the bourgeois view of the class struggle after 1848: man became subjected to things, was a being who could affirm himself only by denying himself radically, who treated himself austerely, as a means and not an end. A profoundly pessimistic ethics of effort was elaborated, which valued humans above all for their constant perseverance in failure. In the 'humanism of hatred' created by

40. F/III, p.197.
41. F/III, p.206.

bourgeois scientism, 'progress', the directing principle of bourgeois ideology, became more ethereal than ever: man was sacrificed to unattainable ideals.

The intellectual reflection — and mystification — of French social life produced by the *demi-nantis* under the Second Empire demanded its artistic counterpart. Neurotic Art — writing which spoke to say nothing, which contested itself — appeared and became *their* art. 'When, from 1849, the Knights of Nothingness publish their first works, if the cultivated public adopts them, if it make them *its* poets and *its* novelists, the reason is not that they incite it to a coming to consciousness, nor further that they consolidate its false consciousness in presenting to it its *imago* incarnated in a poem or the hero of a novel. The truth is more complex: the artist imposes himself on both the men of talent and the rich because he differs from them radically, both because they comprehend implicitly his purpose and because they arrange to misunderstand; both because they grasp the homicidal intention which hides itself in its *irréalisation*, enough at least to make it serve their ends, and because a perhaps inevitable misunderstanding defines him in their eyes as a doctrinaire of realism. These strange and twisted links mean that no writer has so much scorned his public and that none has more completely expressed it — not in its historical truth but in the true *pathos* which founds false consciousness and ideological *non-savoir*.'[42]

This, of course, could only be the beginning of Sartre's explanation of this 'strange harmony' based on the fact that writers and readers belonged to the same social layer and reflected the same contradictions — and, above all, on their shared secret hatred of man and insistence on sacrificing man to the 'human thing'. '*Black*, the literature of the 1850s fits the dominant classes exactly because they, in the interim, have been *blackened* by the history they made: what the reader demands of his reading is to permit him to derealize himself by the imaginary satisfaction of his hatred.'[43] However, this thesis must be fully demonstrated before we can see the deep internal affinities between the realistic, scientistic bourgeoisie and the doctrinaires of Absolute Art. *Internal* is the key term here: how, after all, does a work or writer become representative of a historical period? Was the con-

42. F/III, p.302.
43. F/III, p.334.

gruence of *Madame Bovary* and the Second Empire only fortuitous? What would it take to show an internal connection between the book and the period? The congruence would obviously be merely fortuitous unless 'the profound and distant causes of the misanthropy could be considered *also* as those of the movement of February'.[44] And if this were so, then Flaubert's neurosis and its culmination in 1844 would in some sense be prophetic of the class struggles of 1848-51.

Sartre approached this question by citing Lecomte de Lisle's direct involvement and ultimate disillusionment with the movement of 1848. The son of a slaveholder and momentarily a socialist, a minor writer compared with Flaubert, Leconte de Lisle lived the imperatives of Absolute Art far more superficially and formalistically than the latter. His formative historical reality — the Réunion planter aristocracy — matched mid-century France only briefly and as if by misunderstanding. In his work, the nightmare failed: he practised 'Neurotic Art without himself being neurotic'.[45] His pessimism and misanthropy [were] only commodities'.[46] For Neurotic Art to 'succeed', to achieve real historical salience, 'it is necessary to discover in the work a singular quality in the author attesting to the indissoluble unity of the objective neurosis — as interiorization and transcendence of contradictory imperatives, by Failure-Art, of all these contradictions — and of a well-characterized subjective neurosis whose roots plunge into his early childhood.'[47] With this contrastive observation, Sartre returned to his main subject, and attempted to define the profound historicity of Flaubert and *Madame Bovary*. The writer of the 1850s had to reflect a general hatred for human nature while passing in silence over the events of 1848. A book was necessary, Sartre argued, that both expressed the sense of 1848 and hid it beneath a cloak of universality. Thus its author would 'justify in advance political crimes and depoliticization without *ever* recalling them',[48] by means of an atemporal misanthropy rooted in the depths of an individual experience and felt to the marrow, and so 'in condemning *man* without recourse, would exonerate the *men* of '48, even the killers,

44. F/III, p.344.
45. F/III, p.403.
46. F/III, p.398.
47. F/III, p.414.
48. F/III, p.417.

from all particular responsibility.'[49] Granted this sense of human tragedy and universal guilt ordained naturally and from birth, the bourgeois of 1848 could derealize his own guilt. The reader demanded 'that the general themes of Absolute Art be presented to him through an incomparable and true experience which enriched, veiled and diverted them, and above all, in reaching too-evident conclusions, gave them to be *felt* like the very taste of lived experience.'[50] The result was a fascinating object that bound reader and writer in neurotic complicity.

Thus, Sartre proposed, there was a deep parallelism whereby the life of the Flaubert family and that of French literature both expressed, in their different ways, the same development of French society, such that a young neurotic could write a book which, while compensating for and expressing his neurosis, made history. 'Thus the crisis of Pont l'Evêque, with its consequences leading to the death of Achille-Cléophas, would be, in Gustave, *his* February and June days, *his* coup d'etat of December 2 and *his* plebiscite; he would have lived not symbolically but for good and in advance the defeat and the cowardly solace of a class which, to accomplish its destiny and realize its secret primacy, agreed to renounce its visible *praxis* (that is, political action) and to enter into apparent hibernation so as to find its "cover" again — that is, its responsibility as an eternal minor.'[51] Gustave had to go through the *same* development as his epoch — not symbolically, but really — in order to become its author. Both were conditioned by the same factors, followed the *same curve*, were 'oriented towards the same goal, across the same obstacles, by the same intentions'.[52] The microcosm, Gustave, was only a moment of the macrocosm, the historical period. His identity was 'only that of the epoch.'[53] It was the period, then, that produced Gustave's internal determination, and in a profound sense, lay at the root of *Madame Bovary*. Exploring his character, we find an historically and socially defined *programme* of life which determined his internal movement of experience and led him — as it led others, each in his own way — to realize the epoch: the epoch which permeated *Madame Bovary*.

49. F/III, pp.418-419.
50. F/III, p.421-22.
51. F/III, p.430-31.
52. F/III, p.440.
53. F/III, p.440.

This discussion was, of course, only an outline of what was to come in the remainder of *L'Idiot de la famille*. Nevertheless, these pages were the apex of the work. Sartre seemed within sight of understanding Flaubert in his deepest individuality as a historical being, within sight of understanding the profound social reality of *Madame Bovary*. The discussion was far from flawless. Here too Sartre remained almost wholly on the ideological level when talking of society, emphasizing cultural to the neglect of concrete social and material history, and, even within this restricted sphere making little or no reference to specific texts or specific authors. His analysis was to this extent an *interior* history, whose precise contents could not be ascertained. Yet he had seldom thought so boldly, so penetratingly, as here, seldom worked so tenaciously at the frontiers of his field of analytic vision. Here if anywhere he seemed on the verge of a breakthrough to an understanding of sociality.

The breakthrough never came. Sartre never reached his projected analysis of Gustave's historical *programming*. As it transpired, the two hundred pages remaining of Volume III took a puzzling turn reminiscent of the last part of the *Critique*. Sartre now dwelt on Flaubert after the defeat of Napoleon III at Sedan, explaining what the Second Empire had meant to Flaubert, from his own testimony after its downfall. It may well have been useful to understand why the novelist was at this juncture as happy as he was ever to be, and to try to do so at this stage of the biography. But it was clear nevertheless that something had gone wrong. Sartre had deserted the main course of his analysis for a by-way. He never returned: shortly after the discussion of Flaubert's unfinished novel, 'Sous Napoleon III', *L'Idiot de la famille* broke off, unfinished.

The Final Unfinished Work

If the present study has established anything, it is that the promise of *L'Idiot de la famille* was unlikely to be fulfilled. I am thinking not only of the evident and severe flaws of the work: its suffocating interiority, even when discussing the social world; its inability to see even the social world in other than ideological terms; its almost wholly imaginary quality; its sheer interminability. I mean rather that *L'Idiot de la famille* was so obviously a work of withdrawal — into a sea of words, into Flaubert's interiority, into an imaginary realm which the brave works of the 1940s and 1950s had seemed to renounce forever — and also so evidently and deeply ambivalent towards its readers, the social world for which it was supposedly written.

There are wider grounds for the suggestion that the Flaubert was destined to remain unfinished. At their first meeting in Switzerland, André Gorz complained to Sartre about the totally subjective ethics of *L'Etre et le Néant*: all acts seemed equally legitimate if done in good faith.[54] At the time Sartre gave Gorz a rather sophistical answer, but he later laboured long and hard to complete his ontology with an ethics — to devise an objective, worldly norm that would permit discriminations among individual acts. This work was never completed. We have seen the same dynamic at work in the *Critique*: Sartre's social philosophy fell short of its primary objective: sociality itself was left unexplained. In neither case was he able to transcend his original commitment to interiority, to the *cogito*. His last major work was abandoned at the same point. Once again Sartre stopped short of a logic of sociality. It was hardly to be expected that intellectual reclusion would succeed in grasping what had evaded him even in his most missionary and political writings — much less that an understanding of sociality could have guided the construction of a final volume whose predecessors were so permeated by antithetical themes.

Seen in this perspective, *L'Idiot de la famille* was predestined to failure. It was fitting, moreover, that Sartre's ultimate project, to achieve total understanding of one individual, should become a kind of novel — that in order to fathom a real person, Sartre was obliged to absorb himself in the imaginary. Beyond this, the most noteworty feature of the book was its almost wholly negative tone. Flaubert, as seen by Sartre, was a failure, his story is one of defeat. Sartre conveys no sense of Gustave's developing literary powers. The latter dissolves again and again into his neurosis; his generation *is* its neurosis. Reading Sartre we are at a loss to know how this unlikable young neurotic could rise to so commanding a position in the universe of human discourse. In page after countless page, we learn only of his despair, his withdrawal into the imaginary, his 'total literary sterility', of the predestined failure of an entire generation.

54. Gorz, *The Traitor*, p.234.

Exit Laughing

Interiority, individual isolation, an overwhelming world, retreat to the imaginary amid pessimism and gloom — we have traced these themes and moods through Sartre's career. From *Les Mots* onwards, he himself had been trying to discover their sources. His last major work can be seen as an exploration of their historical, social and psychological roots. It is not that Sartre, and not Flaubert, was the true centre of *L'Idiot de la famille*.[55] Rather, he studied Flaubert and his generation in order to understand the literary posture that he himself had inherited, in however attenuated a form. He had questioned — and contested — this posture from the beginning, but it was *his* and remained his to the very end. Unable to transcend the limits of his thought, Sartre returned at last to investigate their historical foundations, as if to master them at least in understanding, on their own terrain of the imaginary.

Is it possible, now that Sartre's life has come to an end, to draw conclusions which weigh strength against weakness, achievement against limitation? Any simple set of conclusions would be as contrary to the spirit of this study as to the spirit of Sartre himself. If Sartre was unable to transcend his starting points, for example, he was able to think — and live — them to their limits, immersing himself in our world and its most powerful cross-currents. Having so much to teach us on so many planes, his adventure and its fruits will repay serious study many times over and for generations to come. When all is said and done, we must perhaps above all recognize that his work represents exactly that, a human adventure lived and thought through as fully as any in its time.

The tension between imagination and reality, between the impulse to individual withdrawal and the commitment to collective political action, was at the core of Sartre's life's work. Unresolved, it condemned his endeavors to what was, strictly speaking, failure; acknowledged and contested, worked on again and again, it was also the condition of a personal-intellectual achievement unparalleled in its own time. Driven by a sense of estrangement from history, of social superfluity, Sartre did more than any other writer of his generation to illuminate the possibilities of individual commitment in history, to dramatize the central issues of life in the twentieth century.

55. See 'Flaubert, c'est moi', *Times Literary Supplement*, September 29. 1972.

The political and theoretical problems so posed were never to be resolved. But, in an appropriately paradoxical late development, Sartre came to believe that, in his own life at least, he had achieved his goal. Three years after the third volume of his Flaubert had appeared, he was interviewed by Michel Contat on the occasion of his seventieth birthday. The result was the remarkable 'Autoportrait à soixante-dix ans'. Contat, personally close to Sartre, probed intimately and deeply, showing Sartre in old age reflecting on his life and on the loss of his powers. His responses were self-deprecating: he argued stubbornly against any suggestion of his own importance or power. Unsentimental, acerbic, nearly blind, Sartre had not lost his old self-confidence, but equally he was without arrogance. He had been crippled by time, but remained very much involved in life, convinced that he had achieved the goal of living simply as 'a man among men'. At seventy, he was 'just a man and nothing else, like everyone else.'

'I have written, I have lived, I have nothing to regret.'[56]

In short, then, Contat asked, 'so far life has been good to you?'

'On the whole, yes. I don't see what I could reproach it with. It has given me what I wanted and at the same time it has shown that this wasn't much. But what can you do?' (The interview ends in wild laughter brought on by the last statement.) 'The laughter must be kept. You should put: "Accompanied by laughter." '[57]

56. 'Autoportrait à soixante-dix ans', *Situations*, X, pp.159,226; 'Self-Portrait at Seventy', *Life/Situations*, pp.28,91.
57. Ibid., p.226; p.92.

Index